SCANDINAVIA

TOP SIGHTS, AUTHENTIC EXPERIENCES

THIS EDITION WRITTEN AND RESEARCHED BY
Anthony Ham, Alexis Averbuck, Carolyn Bain, Oliver Berry,
ristian Bonetto, Belinda Dixon, Peter Dragicevich, Catherine
e Nevez, Virginia Maxwell, Hugh McNaughtan, Becky Ohlsen,
Andy Symington, Donna Wheeler

Welcome to Scandinavia

Effortlessly chic cities meet remote forests, drawing style gurus and wilderness hikers alike. Endless day, perpetual night. Rocking festivals, majestic aurora. Scandinavia: anything but bland.

The great outdoors is rarely greater than in Europe's big north. Epic expanses of wilderness – forests, lakes, volcanoes – and intoxicatingly pure air mean engaging with nature is a viscerally pleasurable experience. National parks cover the region, offering some of Europe's best hiking as well as anything from kayaking to glacier-walking. Spectacular coasts invite exploration from the sea. Wildlife, from whales to wolverines, awaits the fortunate observer.

Stolid Nordic stereotypes dissolve in the region's vibrant capitals. Crest-of-the-wave design can be seen in them all, backed by outstanding modern architecture, excellent museums, imaginative solutions for 21st-century urban living, internationally acclaimed restaurants and a nightlife that fizzes along despite hefty beer prices. Live music is a given: you're bound to come across some inspiring local act, whether your taste is Viking metal or chamber music.

Despite scary subzero temperatures in winter, there's a wealth of things to do: skiing, sledding behind huskies or reindeer, snowmobile safaris to the Arctic Sea, ice fishing, romantic nights in snow hotels, visiting Santa Claus and gazing at the soul-piercing aurora borealis. Summer's long, long days are filled with festivals, beer terraces and wonderful boating, hiking and cycling.

> *Epic expanses of wilderness... Scandinavia is anything but bland.*

Nyhavn canal, Copenhagen, Denmark
ADAM GRIMSHAW/LONELY PLANET ©

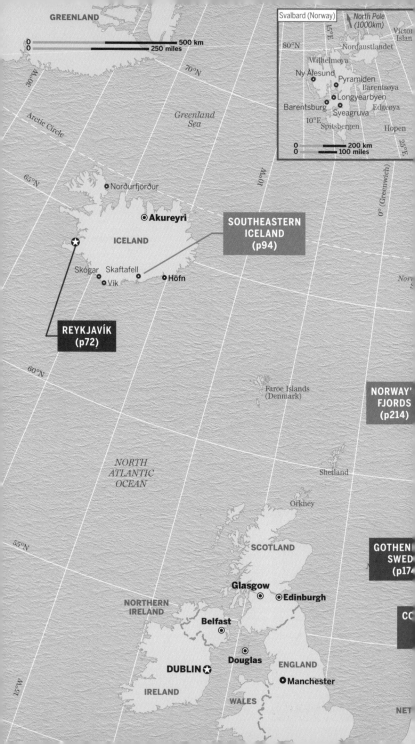

GREENLAND

500 km
250 miles

70°N

Greenland Sea

65°N

Norðurfjörður

Akureyri

ICELAND

SOUTHEASTERN
ICELAND
(p94)

Skógar Skaftafell
Vík **Höfn**

REYKJAVÍK
(p72)

60°N

*Faroe Islands
(Denmark)*

NORWAY'
FJORDS
(p214)

*NORTH
ATLANTIC
OCEAN*

Shetland

Orkney

55°N

SCOTLAND

GOTHEN
SWED
(p17

Glasgow
Edinburgh

NORTHERN
IRELAND

Belfast

CC

Douglas

DUBLIN ✪

ENGLAND

Manchester

IRELAND

WALES

NET

Svalbard (Norway)

*North Pole
(1000km)*

Victor
Islan

80°N

Nordaustlandet

Wilhelmøya

Ny Ålesund

Pyramiden

Barentsøya

Longyearbyen

Barentsburg

Edgeøya

Sveagruva

10°E

Spitsbergen

Hopen

200 km
100 miles

Black sand beach, Jökulsárlón, Iceland
MATT MUNRO/LONELY PLANET ©

Plan Your Trip
Scandinavia's Top 12

SVEN NORDRUM/GETTY IMAGES ©

Norway's Fjords
Landscapes of unrivalled and dramatic beauty

Norway's fjords (p214) cut deep gashes into the interior, adding
texture and depth to the map of northwestern Scandinavia.
Sognefjorden and Hardangerfjord are extensive fjord networks,
but Nærøyfjorden, Lysefjord (pictured above) and Geirangerfjord
(pictured right), with their quiet, precipitous beauty, are possibly
Scandinavia's most beautiful corner.

1

MU YEE TING/SHUTTERSTOCK ©

SIMON'S PASSION 4 TRAVEL/SHUTTERSTOCK ©

Aurora Borealis

Nature's most extraordinary night-sky spectacle

Whether caused by the collision of charged particles in the upper atmosphere, or sparked, as Sami tradition tells, by a giant snow fox swishing its tail in the Arctic tundra, the humbling splendour of the northern lights is unforgettable. The further north you go, such as the Lapland region of Finland (p154), Norway (p214) or Sweden (p236), the better your chances of gazing on nature's light show.

2

Lofoten Islands, Norway

Islands whose peaks reach for the sky

Few forget their first sighting of Lofoten Islands (p167; above: Reine, Lofoten Islands), laid out in summer greens and yellows or drowned in the snows of winter, their razor-sharp peaks dark against the sky. In the pure, exhilarating air, there's a constant tang of salt and a whiff of cod – staple of the seas. A hiker's dream and nowadays linked by bridges, the islands are simple to get to.

3

Design Shopping
Go to the heart of Scandinavian style

Elegant, innovative yet functional takes on everyday items have made the region's creativity world-famous and mean that you won't have to look far before you experience an 'I need that!' moment. There are great design and handicrafts across the region, but Copenhagen and Helsinki (p126), closely followed by Stockholm, are where modern flagship stores, such as Hay House (pictured right), can be found alongside quirky boutiques that present edgier new ideas.

Sami Culture
Draw near to Scandinavia's first people

The indigenous Sami have a near-mystical closeness to the natural environment – the awesome wildernesses of Lapland. Reindeer-herding is still a primary occupation, yet the Sami are a modern people still in touch with their roots. Check out the great museums (p162), the parliament buildings and craft workshops in Inari and Karasjok, and try to coincide with a festival or cultural event, whether reindeerracing (pictured) or *'yoiking'* (traditional singing).

PHOTO: ERIK IRGENS JOHNSEN, UIO ©

Viking History

Learn more about the iconic seafaring Norsemen

Mead-swilling, pillaging hooligans or civilising craftspeople, poets and merchants? A series of memorable burial sites, rune stones, settlements and museums – the Vikingskipshuset in Oslo (pictured; p198) is perhaps the best – across the region brings the fascinating Viking Age to life. Gods and beliefs, their stupendous feats of navigation, customs, trade, longships, intricate jewellery, carvings and the wonderful sagas – it's all here.

Sledding

Explore the icy wastes at a husky's pace

A classic winter experience (p164) is to hitch up a team of reindeer or husky dogs to a sled and swish away under the pale winter sun. Short jaunts are good for getting the hang of steering, stopping and letting the animals know who you think the boss is; once your confidence is high, take off on an overnight trip, sleeping in a hut in the wilderness and thawing those deserving bones with a steaming sauna. Pure magic.

7

National Park Hiking

Hike out into pristine wilderness

If you like dark pine forests populated by foxes and bears, head for northeastern Finland's Karhunkier-ros trail (pictured). Norway's Jotunheimen National Park encompasses hundreds of lofty mountain peaks and crystal-blue lakes. Lying inside the Arctic Circle, Abisko National Park in Sweden is at one end of the epic 440km Kungsleden hiking trail. And walkers will never forget the bleak volcanic slopes, steaming pools and mossy valleys of Iceland's Landmannalaugar to Þórsmörk trek (p104).

KAVALENKAVAVOLHA/GETTY IMAGES ©

Old Town, Tallinn

Medieval architecture and wonderful views

Tallinn's Unesco-protected Old Town (p287) is a 14th- and 15th-century twin-tiered jumble of turrets, spires and winding streets. Most experiences of Estonia's capital begin and end with the cobblestoned, chocolate-box landscape of intertwining alleys and picturesque courtyards. Enjoy the postcard-perfect vistas from one of the observation towers, refuel in one of the cosy vaulted-cellar bars and cafes, or simply stroll, soaking up the medieval magic.

Historic Wooden Towns

Traditional buildings as backdrop to city life

Wooden buildings are a feature of Scandinavia, and towns and cities were once built exclusively from timber. But 'great fires' were common and comparatively few historic districts remain. They are worth seeking out for their quaint, unusual beauty; among others, Bergen (pictured top; p218) and Stavanger in Norway, Rauma (pictured abov in Finland and Gothenburg in Sweden preserve excellent 'timbertowns', perfect for strolling around.

Stockholm, Sweden

Scandinavia's stately belle in a lovely setting

Sweden's capital (p236) is the aristocrat among Scandinavian cities, with an imposing architecture of stately buildings arrayed across a complex, scarcely intelligible geography of islands and waterways. Noble museums, palaces and galleries dignify this former seat of empire with plenty of contemporary innovation to balance it out.

Denmark's Food Scene

The source of New Nordic cuisine

Copenhagen's (p34) culinary prowess is a byword these days. Once known for smørrebrød (open sandwiches) and *frikadeller* (meatballs), Denmark's capital has led the development of New Nordic cuisine, and further innovations are always on the go. The Nordic forage ethos, looking for naturally occurring local ingredients, has had worldwide culinary influence.

Plan Your Trip
Need to Know

When to Go

Warm to mild summers, cold winters
Mild year round
Mild summers, cold to very cold winters
Polar climate

Svalbard
GO Mar–Aug

Iceland
GO Jun–Aug

Lapland
GO Feb–Apr,
Aug–Sep

Fjords
GO Mar–Sep

Helsinki/
Tallinn
GO May–Jul

Copenhagen
GO May–Oct, Dec

High Season (Jun–Aug)

o All attractions and lodgings are open.

o Hotels in many parts are often substantially cheaper.

o Winter sports high season is January to March.

Shoulder (Apr, May, Sep & Oct)

o Expect chilly nights and even snow.

o Not the cheapest time to travel as summer hostels and camping grounds have closed.

o Many rural attractions close or shorten opening hours.

Low Season (Nov–Mar)

o Hotels charge top rates except at weekends.

o January to April is busy for winter sports.

o Short, cool or cold days.

Currency

Denmark: Danish krone
(kr; DKK)
Finland & Tallinn: euro
(€; EUR)
Iceland: Icelandic króna (kr; ISK)
Norway: Norwegian krone (kr; NOK)
Sweden: Swedish krona
(kr; SEK)

Language

Danish, Estonian, Finnish, Icelandic, Norwegian and Swedish
English is widely spoken.

Visas

Generally not required for stays of up to 90 days; some nationalities need a Schengen visa.

Money

ATMs are widespread. Credit/debit cards are accepted everywhere

Mobile Phones

Local SIM cards cheap, widely available. Need an unlocked phone.

Time

Iceland: Western European Time (GMT/UTC plus zero hours)
Denmark, Norway & Sweden: Central Europ & Tallinn: Eastern European Time (GMT/UTC plus two hours)
All but Iceland use summer time from late March to late October.

Daily Costs

Budget: Less than €150

- Dorm bed (HI membership gets you good discounts): €15–40

- Bike hire per day: €10–25

- Lunch specials: €10–18

- National parks: free

Midrange: €150–250

- Standard hotel double room: €80–160

- Week-long car hire per day: €35–60

- Two-course meal for two with wine: €100–150

- Museum entry: €5–15

Top end: More than €250

- Room in boutique hotel: €150–300

- Upmarket degustation menu for two with wine: €200–400

- Taxi across town: €20–40

Useful Websites

Lonely Planet (www.lonelyplanet.com/scandinavia) Destination information, hotel bookings, traveller forum and more.
Go Scandinavia (www.goscandinavia.com) Combined tourist board website for the four mainland Nordic countries.
Direct Ferries (www.directferries.com) Useful booking site for Baltic and Atlantic ferries.

What to Take

- HI membership card, towel and sleep sheet for hostels.

- Tent and sleeping bag for hiking – huts fill fast.

- Powerful insect repellent in summer.

- Eye mask for the never-setting summer sun.

- Swimsuit – there are lots of hot springs, hotel spas and lakes to jump in.

Arriving in Scandinavia

Copenhagen Kastrup Airport The metro and trains run very regularly into the centre (15 minutes). Around 300kr for the 20-minute taxi ride.
Stockholm Arlanda Airport Express trains run all day to Stockholm; airport buses are cheaper but slower. Think 500kr for the 45-minute taxi drive.
Oslo Gardermoen Airport Regular shuttle buses make the 40-minute journey to the centre. Trains run from the airport into the centre of Oslo in 20 minutes. A taxi costs 700kr to 900kr.
Helsinki Vantaa Airport It's a half-hour train ride from the airport to the centre. Local buses and faster Finnair buses do it in 30 to 45 minutes. Plan on €45 to €55 for the half-hour taxi trip.
Keflavík Airport (Reykjavík) Buses run the 45-minute journey into Reykjavík. Taxis charge around kr16,000.

Getting Around

Getting around Scandinavia's populated areas is generally a breeze, with efficient public transport and snappy connections. Remote regions usually have trustworthy but infrequent services.

Bus Comprehensive network throughout region; only choice in many areas.

Train Efficient services in the continental nations, none in Iceland.

Car Drive on the right. Hire is easy but not cheap. Few motorways, so travel times can be long. Compulsory winter tyres.

Ferry Great-value network around the Baltic; spectacular Norwegian coastal ferry, and service to Iceland via the Faroe Islands.

Bike Very bike-friendly cities and many options for longer cycling routes. Most transport carries bikes for little or no charge. Hire widely available.

Planes Decent network of budget flights connecting major centres. Full-fare flights comparatively expensive.

For more on **getting around**, see p305

Plan Your Trip
Hot Spots for...

Beautiful Landscapes

There are few more beautiful corners of Europe, with dramatic landscapes of astonishing variety across the region.

NICK TSIATINIS/GETTY IMAGES ©

Norway's Fjords (p214)
Norway's fjords have to be seen to be believed, with vertiginous rock walls rising above ice-blue waters.

Geirangerfjorden
Norway has many amazing fjords, but none can rival this one (p220).

Southeastern Iceland (p94)
A haunting world of stark volcanoes and black beaches, and vast, empty landscapes of rare, singular beauty.

Jökulsárlón Glacial Lagoon
The gravitas of glaciers is nowhere more accessible than here (p98).

Lakeland, Finland (p134)
There are few more splendid lake landscapes on earth than the Lakeland district.

Seal Lakes
Kolovesi and Linnansaari National Parks are the prettiest (p138).

Activities

Hike the high country in summer or dog-sled across the ice in winter. Scandinavia has numerous opportunities to get active and explore.

V. BELOV/SHUTTERSTOCK ©

Vatnajökull National Park (p102)
All of Iceland's beauty is found within the boundaries of this park, especially epic ice-caps and fiery volcanoes.

Hiking
Fabulous trails that take you beyond the crowds (p102).

Tromsø (p160)
Whatever the season, Tromsø is one of Scandinavia's most appealing places for getting out into the wilds.

Dog-sledding
Let a husky team pull you across a frozen wilderness (p170).

Voss (p230)
Voss is filled with adventure-sport possibilities, and the backdrop is guaranteed to be breathtaking.

Kayaking
Paddle quiet fjord waters beneath soaring rocky cliffs (p231).

Urban Style

Scandinavia's countries have a particular flair for design. The results are ubercool, from shopping possibilities to cutting-edge architecture.

ANDREY SHCHERBUKHIN/SHUTTERSTOCK ©

Helsinki (p114)
Exemplifying Scandinavia's style aesthetic, with its designer boutiques, design districts and daring architecture.

Design District
A museum and neighbourhood devoted to creativity (p120).

Stockholm (p236)
With stunning traditional architecture wedded to contemporary innovation, this is one of the world's most stylish cities.

Skansen
Proof Swedes have been style leaders for centuries (p247).

Tallinn (p258)
A northern European gem of cohesive, uniformly beautiful architecture in a lovely setting by the Baltic Sea.

Old Town
Tallinn's medieval core is like an open-air museum (p266).

Nordic Cuisine

In keeping with Scandinavia's devotion to improving the important things in life, the region's cuisine is both trailblazing and rooted in tradition.

JOANNE MOYES/ALAMY STOCK PHOTO ©

Copenhagen (p34)
If one city epitomises the daring nature of Scandinavia's culinary revolution, it's Copenhagen.

Höst
Affordable New Nordic menus and gorgeous interiors (p49).

Stockholm (p236)
Combining the freshest culinary ingredients of the highest quality with an avant-garde mindset.

Kryp In
Innovation in classy surrounds with no pretensions (p252).

Bergen (p222)
As with most good things in life, Bergen does culinary with freshness and flair.

Torget Fish Market
Finest seafood ready to eat, old-style, right by the water (p227).

Plan Your Trip
Local Life

Activities

Scandinavia is ripe for exploration, and the opportunities to do so in the great outdoors are many and varied. Of the summer activities, hiking is easily the pick, with trails crossing the region within sight of Icelandic volcanoes and glaciers and Norwegian fjords. Boat trips, too, are a fabulous way to see the region's most extraordinary scenery, from glacial lagoons in Iceland to the abundant lakes of Finland's Lakeland district. In winter, dog-sledding is something of a Scandinavian specialty and a marvellous way to experience ice-bound wilderness areas in the high Arctic. And then there's Voss, Scandinavia's adventure-sports capital.

Shopping

Even if you're not normally the shopping kind, Scandinavia may just convince you to make an exception to the habits of lifetime. 'Design' is a much-hyped part of the Scandinavian experience – and with very good reason. From homewares and furnishings (so much more than Ikea) to fashion in all its forms, the region's designers are world leaders, with a particular leaning towards the clean lines and minimalist sensibilities so associated with the Nordic aesthetic. Another must-shop experience is gourmet foods and markets, the perfect complement to the region's restaurant culinary excellence, and as good for buying gifts as for planning a picnic.

Entertainment

Nights in Scandinavia are, at least in urban centres, lively and long-lasting, and much of the nightlife centres around live music. All cities of the region have their particular favourites, from the hard-rock temples of Bergen to the Icelandic pop of Reykjavík, while Copenhagen, Helsinki and Stockholm all have their devotees. Excellent classical music venues and programs, as well as theatre, where you can see works by local

luminaries such as Ibsen, ensure that most tastes are catered for.

Eating

Scandinavian cooking, once viewed as meatballs, herring and little else, has wowed the world in recent years with New Nordic cuisine, a culinary revolution that centred on Copenhagen. While the crest of that wave has now passed, the 'foraging' ethos it championed has made a permanent mark here. It showcases local produce prepared using traditional techniques and contemporary experimentation, and clean, natural flavours.

In the wake of Copenhagen's Noma, which became known as the world's best eatery (but is temporarily closed), numerous upmarket restaurants opened and have flourished across the region's capitals, which are now a foodie's delight. Traditional eateries still abound, however, and are focused on old-school staples.

★ Best for Architecture

Oslo Opera House (p203)

Göteborgs-Utkiken (p181)

Old Town, Tallinn (p287)

Sami Parliament (p162)

Arctic Cathedral (p160)

Drinking & Nightlife

Scandinavians are enthusiastic drinkers, although strong alcohol in Sweden, Norway and Finland can only be bought in state stores. Beer is ubiquitous, and the microbrewery and boutique beer phenomenon has deep roots in the Scandinavian psyche. Each nation also has its own favourite shot to clear the head. Coffee is also an obsession, especially in Norway, and a refined yet casual cafe culture is a deeply ingrained feature for locals and travellers alike.

From left: Ibsen Museet (p202), Oslo; Foraging, Denmark

Plan Your Trip
Month by Month

February

❄ Rørosmartnan, Norway

An old-fashioned and traditional winter fair (http://rorosmartnan.no) livens the streets of the historic Norwegian town of Røros.

◉ Jokkmokk Winter Market, Sweden

The biggest Sami market (www.jokkmokks marknad.se) of the year, with all manner of crafts for sale, preceded by celebrations of all things Sami, featuring reindeer races on the frozen lake.

March

⚘ Sled Safaris & Skiing, Northern Norway, Sweden & Finland

Whizzing across the snow pulled by a team of huskies or reindeer is a pretty spectacular way to see the northern wildernesses. Add snowmobiling or skiing to the mix and it's a top time to be at high latitude.

☆ Reindeer Racing, Finland

Held over the last weekend of March or first of April, the King's Cup (www.siida.fi) is the grand finale of Finnish Lapland's reindeer-racing season and a great spectacle.

April

❄ Sami Easter Festival, Norway

Thousands of Sami participate in reindeer racing, theatre and cultural events in the Finnmark towns of Karasjok and Kautokeino (www.samieasterfestival.com). The highlight is the Sami Grand Prix, a singing and *yoiking* (traditional singing) contest attended by artists from across Lapland.

☆ Jazzkaar, Tallinn

Late April sees jazz greats from all around the world converge on Estonia's picturesque capital for this series of performances (www.jazzkaar.ee).

Above: Roskilde Festival (p24), Denmark

MATT MUNRO/LONELY PLANET ©

May

✵ Aalborg Carnival, Denmark

In late May, Aalborg kicks up its heels hosting the biggest Carnival (www.aalborgkarneval.dk) celebrations in northern Europe, when up to 100,000 participants and spectators shake their maracas and paint the town red.

✵ Bergen International Festival, Norway

One of the biggest events on Norway's cultural calendar, this two-week festival (www.fib.no), beginning in late May, showcases dance, music and folklore presentations – some international, some focusing on traditional local culture.

June

☆ Stockholm Jazz Festival, Sweden

Held on the island of Skeppsholmen in the centre of Stockholm, this well-known jazz fest (www.stockholmjazz.com) brings artists from all over, including big international names.

★ Best Festivals

Midsummer, June

Sled safaris & skiing, March

Roskilde Festival, June & July

Aurora Watching, November

Christmas, December

✵ Midsummer, Denmark, Norway, Sweden & Finland

The year's biggest event in continental Nordic Europe sees fun family feasts, joyous celebrations of the summer, heady bonfires and copious drinking, often at normally peaceful lakeside summer cottages. Held on the weekend between 19 and 26 June.

✵ Frederikssund Vikingespil, Denmark

Held in Frederikssund over a three-week period (late June to early July), this Viking

Above: Midsummer, Sweden

festival (www.vikingespil.dk) includes a costumed open-air drama and a banquet with Viking food and entertainment.

July

☆ Copenhagen Jazz Festival, Denmark

The capital's biggest entertainment event of the year offers 10 days of music at the start of July. The festival (p47) features a range of Danish and international jazz, blues and fusion music, with more than 500 indoor and outdoor concerts.

☆ Roskilde Festival, Denmark

Northern Europe's largest music festival (www.roskilde-festival.dk) rocks Roskilde each summer. It takes place in early July, but advance ticket sales are on offer around October and the festival usually sells out.

☆ Ruisrock, Finland

Finland's oldest and possibly best rock festival (www.ruisrock.fi) has top local and international acts, in early July on an island just outside the southwestern city of Turku.

☆ Wife-Carrying World Championships, Finland

The world's premier wife-carrying event (p153) is held in the village of Sonkajärvi in early July. Winning couples (marriage not required) win the woman's weight in beer as well as significant kudos.

☆ Moldejazz, Norway

Norway has a fine portfolio of jazz festivals, but Molde's version (www.moldejazz.no) in mid-July is the most prestigious. With 100,000 spectators, world-class performers and a reputation for high-quality music it is easily one of Norway's most popular festivals.

August

⚒ Þjóðhátíð, Iceland

Held over the first weekend in August, this festival (www.dalurinn.is) on the Vestman-naeyjar islands is Iceland's biggest knees-up, with three days of music, fireworks and frivolity. It's a big thing for young Iceland-ers; an enormous bonfire is a focal point.

☆ Smukfest, Denmark

This midmonth music marvel (www.smukfest.dk) in Skanderborg bills itself as Denmark's most beautiful festival, and is second only to Roskilde in terms of scale. It takes place in lush parkland in the scenic Lake District and attracts up to 40,000 music fans.

⚒ Copenhagen Cooking & Food Festival, Denmark

Scandinavia's largest food festival (p48) focuses on the gourmet. It's a busy event that lets you see presentations from top chefs, go on food-oriented tours of the city and taste produce.

September

☆ Reykjavík International Film Festival, Iceland

This annual event (www.riff.is) right at the end of September sees blockbusters make way for international art films in cinemas across the city, as well as talks from film directors from home and abroad.

November

☉ Aurora Watching, Iceland, Norway, Sweden & Finland

Whether you are blessed with seeing the aurora borealis is a matter of luck, but the further north you are, the better the chances. Dark, cloudless nights, patience and a viewing spot away from city lights help.

☆ Stockholm International Film Festival, Sweden

Screenings of new international and inde-pendent films, director talks and discussion panels draw cinephiles to this important an-nual festival (www.stockholmfilmfestival.se).

December

⚒ Christmas, Region-wide

Whether visiting Santa and his reindeer in Finnish Lapland, admiring the magic of Copenhagen's Tivoli at night or sampling home-baked delicacies, Christmas, especially if you know a friendly local family, is a heart-warming time to be here.

Plan Your Trip
Get Inspired

Read

Njál's Saga (Anonymous; 13th century) Gloriously entertaining Icelandic story of a bloody family feud.

A Death in the Family (Karl Ove Knausgaard; 2009) First of six searingly honest autobiographical novels.

Kalevala (Elias Lönnrot; 1849) Finland's national epic is a wonderful world of everything from sorcerer-shamans to saunas and home-brewing.

The Emperor's New Clothes (Hans Christian Andersen; 1837) One of Andersen's most famous tales.

The Girl with the Dragon Tattoo (Stieg Larsson; 2005) The first book of the Swedish noir trilogy that captured the world.

Watch

Wild Strawberries (1957) Ingmar Bergman's sensitivity comes to the fore in this masterpiece.

The Man without a Past (2002) Quirky Finnish brilliance from Aki Kaurismäki.

Dancer in the Dark (2000) Provocative director Lars von Trier and Björk combine in this melodramatic but masterful film.

The Bridge (2011) This excellent series takes place between Sweden and Denmark.

Let the Right One In (2008) Superb vampire romance in a northern town.

Sameblod (2016) A stark reminder of historic attitudes to the Sami.

Listen

Máttaráhku Askái (Ulla Pirttijärvi; 2002) Haunting title track from the yoik-inspired Sami artist.

Ghost Love Score (Nightwish; 2004) Epic track from Finland's symphonic metal masters.

Cocoon (Björk; 2001) Among the Icelander's most intimate songs.

In the Hall of the Mountain King (Edvard Grieg; 1875) Brilliant soundtrack to *Peer Gynt's* troll scene.

The Final Countdown (Europe; 1986) You know you love it.

Best of ABBA (ABBA; 1975) It's impossible to pick a favourite.

Barbie Girl (Aqua; 1997) Denmark's all-time No 1.

Above: Sculpture of Hans Christian Andersen in Kongens Have (p45), Copenhagen

Plan Your Trip
Five-Day Itineraries

Nordic Cities

This intense five-day itinerary will allow you to savour the buzz of Scandinavia's stylish and happening cities, even as it will leave you longing for more – this is a taster and a fine first foray into the region.

FROM LEFT: KAVALENKAU/SHUTTERSTOCK ©; ILOZAVR/SHUTTERSTOCK ©

Seal Lakes (p138) Kolovesi and Linnansaari National Parks to showcase the Lakeland region at its best.

Savonlinna (p144) Explore the castle, take a boat trip and seek out the New Valamo Monastery, all in a day. Take a day tour 🚌 or 🚐 1½ hrs to Seal Lakes

Helsinki (p114) Revel for a day in the design-rich environment where art nouveau meets Soviet functionalism. 🚌 4½ hrs to Savonlinna

Tallinn (p258) Estonia's capital is easy to reach from across Europe and the reward is a medieval gem (one day). ✈ 30 mins or 🚢 2 hrs to Helsinki

Echoes of the East

With Russia looming large to the east, Scandinavia's eastern Baltic regions feel like nowhere else. Beyond the cities, you'll leave behind one expanse of water for another, for the lakes that are such a feature of Finland.

Bergen (p222)
Fly into Bergen and spend a day exploring one of the most beautiful small cities on earth.
✈ 1¼ hrs to Copenhagen

①

③

Copenhagen (p34)
Spend a couple of days exploring the Danish capital with an emphasis on taking in its culinary, design and architectural offering.
✈ 1¼ hrs to Stockholm

②

Stockholm (p236) Soak up the style, views and ambient buzz of urban Scandinavia with a couple of days in this elegant city.

②

③

Plan Your Trip
10-Day Itinerary

Nature's Canvas

The formerly Viking lands of Iceland and Norway are intense rivals when it comes to choosing the most beautiful country on earth. Then again, if you've ten days up your sleeve, why not visit both and make up your own mind?

Vatnajökull National Park (p102) A day's hiking here is like a crash course in wild Iceland. 🚗 1 hr 40 min

Jökulsárlón Glacial Lagoon (p98) Spend a day on boats and on foot in one of Iceland's star attractions. 🚗 1¼ hrs to Vatnajökull National Park

Viðey (p74) Echoes of the past dominate the ruins of this uninhabited island. ⛴ 1¼ hrs, then 🚗 6 hrs

Höfn (p106) This Southeast harbour town is a good stopover on the way to see Jökulsárlón. 🚗 1 hr 5 min

Vík (p100) Otherworldly black beaches in a strange and wonderful land. 🚗 2½ hrs, then ✈ 1 hr 10 min to Bergen

Reykjavik (p72) Iceland's capital is a fascinating city and the gateway to all things Icelandic. ⛴ day trip

Aurlandsfjorden (p221) A front-row seat to some of Norway's best fjord views. 🚗 ¼ hrs to Flåm

Bergen (p218) Explore this stunning harbourside town and fjord gateway. 🚗 2 hrs 45 mins to Aurlandsfjorden

Flåm (p221) A good base for accommodation and supplies while visiting the Norway fjords.

Plan Your Trip
Two-Week Itinerary

Scandinavia Grand Tour

Sophisticated cities, wild landscapes, soulful indigenous inhabitants. You'll need to keep on the move, but you can experience all of these in two relentlessly pleasurable weeks, visiting Norway, Finland and Denmark along the way.

Tromsø (p160) Visit the museums, take the cable car and get active hiking or dog-sledding
✈ 1 hr 10 min from Bodø

Karasjok (p162) Immerse yourself in Sami culture through museums, a theme park and architecture (one day). ⊕ 7 hrs from Tromsø

Lofoten Islands (p167) Fly to Bodø, then transfer by ferry to the Lofoten Islands. 🚢 3 hrs
Bodø

Inari (p162) Experience the Finnish side of Sami life with top-notch cultural attractions for a day. ⊕ 1½ hrs from Karasjok

Rovaniemi (p158) Say hi to Santa Claus, visit the museum and explore the hinterland (two days). ⊕ 4 hrs from Inari

Oslo (p194) Norway's capital, and increasingly an icon of Scandi cool, is worth at least a couple of days. ✈ 1½ hrs to Lofoten Islands

Helsinki (p114) Fly to Helsinki and marvel at the spectacular architecture & local design. ✈ 1¼ hrs from Rovaniemi to Helsinki

Copenhagen (p34) Enjoy the urban sophistication of Scandinavia's coolest city. ✈ 1½ hrs from Helsinki

Bornholm (p54) Explore remote Baltic reaches and seek out the curious round churches (two days). ✈ 40 min from Copenhagen

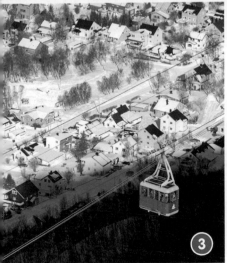

Plan Your Trip
Family Travel

The Low-down

Most of Scandinavia is very child-friendly, with domestic tourism largely dictated by the needs of those travelling as families. Theme parks, amusement parks, zoos and child-friendly beaches and activities are just part of the story, and although there are exceptions, businesses go out of their way to woo families, and children are rarely made to feel unwelcome. Most sights and activities are designed with kids in mind, with free or reduced admission for under-18s and plenty of hands-on exhibits. And what other region of the world can possibly claim such an iconic place to fuel a child's imagination as the home of Santa Claus?

Accommodation

Bigger camping grounds and spa hotels are particularly kid-conscious, with heaps of facilities and activities designed with children in mind. Cots (cribs) are standard in many hotels but numbers may be limited.

Activities

In Denmark, Finland, Norway and Sweden you'll find excellent theme parks, waterparks and holiday activities. Many museums have a dedicated children's section with toys, games and dressing-up clothes.

Iceland is something of an exception: children are liked and have lots of freedom, but they're treated as mini-adults, and there aren't many attractions tailored specifically for kids.

Resources

For all-round information and advice, check out Lonely Planet's *Travel with Children*.

Practicalities

○ Baby food, infant formula, soy and cow's milk, disposable nappies (diapers) etc are widely available in Scandinavian supermarkets.

○ Car-rental firms hire out children's safety seats at a nominal cost, but advance bookings are essential.

TSUGULIEV/SHUTTERSTOCK ©

○ High chairs are standard in many restaurants but numbers may be limited.

○ Restaurants will often have children's menu options, and there are lots of chain eateries aimed specifically at families.

○ Breastfeeding in public is common and often officially encouraged.

○ Many public toilets have baby-changing facilities.

○ Remember that distances in Scandinavia are vast and careful planning is required. Try not to cover too much ground (so as to avoid spending too much time in the car) and consider flying where possible.

When to Go

Easily the best time to travel in Scandinavia with children is the main tourist season that runs from mid-June to mid-August – this is when hotels offer the best deals for families, all sights and attractions are open and the weather is more conducive to a happy family holiday.

★ Best Child-friendly Attractions

Liseberg (p183)

Olavinlinna (p138)

Dog-sledding (p170)

Vikingskipshuset (p198)

Aurora Borealis (p6)

If you've come to Scandinavia for the northern lights or winter activities such as dog-sledding, don't be put off by the bitterly cold weather. It's all about coming prepared with the appropriate clothes (Scandinavian families don't hide in their homes for 10 months of the year!) and winter can be a magical time to be here.

From left: Liseberg (p183), Gothenburg, Sweden; Aurora Borealis, Norway

De Kongelige
Repræsentationslokaler
(p45)

COPENHAGEN

Slotsholms
Kanal

Nørrebro
Copenhagen at its graffiti-scrawled best, jam-packed with indie cafes and rocking retro treasures and buried national legends.

NØRREBRO

Vesterbro
The pinnacle of Copenhagen cool, where post-industrial bars, eateries and galleries mix it with vintage thrift shops and the odd porn peddler.

VESTERBRO

TIVOLI GARDENS

København
Hovedbanegård
(Central Station)

FREDERIKSBERG

KØDBYEI

Slotsholmen
Parliamentary palace, medieval ruins, blue-blooded artefacts and a gob-smacking library: tiny Slotsholmen packs a powerful punch.

Tivoli A
Copen
core, h
cultura
Nation
ageless
Garder

VALBY

0   1 km
0   0.5 miles

Arriving in Copenhagen

Copenhagen Airport (p52) is Scandinavia's busiest hub (in Kastrup, 9km southeast of the city centre) with direct flights to cities in Europe, North America and Asia, plus a handful of Danish cities. It has good eating, retail and information facilities.

Long-distance trains arrive at **Københavns Hovedbanegård**, a 19th-century, wood-beamed hall with currency exchange, a post office, left-luggage facilities and food outlets.

Where to Stay

Copenhagen's accommodation options range from high-end design establishments to excellent budget hotels and hostels, which are mostly on the western side of the Central Station. Reserve well in advance, especially hostels, during the busy summer season.

The **Copenhagen Visitors Centre** (p52) can book rooms in private homes. Depending on availability, it also books unfilled hotel rooms at discounted rates.

Dæmonen roller coaster and Chinese Tower

Tivoli Gardens

The country's top-ranking tourist draw, tasteful Tivoli Gardens has been eliciting gleeful thrills since 1843. Whatever your idea of fun – hair-raising rides, twinkling pavilions, open-air stage shows or alfresco pantomime and beer – this old-timer has you covered.

Great For...

Don't Miss

The city views, taken at 70km/h, from the Star Flyer, one of the world's tallest carousels.

Roller Coasters

The Rutschebanen is the best loved of Tivoli's roller coasters, rollicking its way through and around a faux 'mountain' and reaching speeds of 60km/h. Built in 1914, it claims to be the world's oldest operating wooden roller coaster. If you're after something a little more hardcore, the Dæmonen (Demon) is a 21st-century beast with faster speeds and a trio of hair-raising loops.

The Grounds

Beyond the carousels and side stalls is a Tivoli of landscaped gardens, tranquil nooks and eclectic architecture. Lower the adrenalin under beautiful old chestnut and elm trees, and amble around Tivoli Lake. Formed out of the old city moat, the lake is a top spot to snap pictures of Tivoli's commanding Chinese Tower, built in 1900.

Tivoli Gardens entrance gate

ℹ Need to Know

Tivoli Gardens (📞33 15 10 01; www.tivoli.dk; Vesterbrogade 3; adult/child under 8yr 120kr/free, Fri after 7pm 160kr/free; ⊙11am-11pm Sun-Thu, to midnight Fri & Sat early Apr-late Sep, reduced hours rest of year; ♿; 🚌2A, 5C, 9A, 12, 14, 26, 250S, ⑤København H)

✕ Take a Break

Jolly **Grøften** (www.groeften.dk; ⊙noon-11pm Sun-Thu, to midnight Fri & Sat early Apr-late Sep; 🛜) is a local institution.

★ Top Tip

Rides cost 25kr to 75kr; a multiride ticket is 220kr.

Illuminations & Fireworks

Throughout the summer season, Tivoli Lake wows the crowds with its nightly laser and water spectacular. The Saturday evening fireworks are a summer-season must, repeated again from 26 to 30 December for Tivoli's annual Fireworks Festival.

Live Performances

The indoor **Tivolis Koncertsal** (Concert Hall; www.tivoli.dk; Tietgensgade 30; 🚌1A, 2A, 5C, 9A, 37, 250S, ⑤København H) hosts mainly classical music, with the odd musical and big-name pop or rock act. All tickets are sold at the **Tivoli Billetcenter** (📞33 15 10 01; Vesterbrogade 3; ⊙10am-10.45 Sun-Thu, to 11.45pm Fri & Sat summer, 10am-6pm Mon-Fri rest of year; 🚌2A, 12, 14, 26, 250S, ⑤København H) or through the Tivoli website.

Pantomime Theatre

Each night during the summer this criminally charming theatre presents silent plays in the tradition of Italy's Commedia dell'Arte. Many of the performers also work at the esteemed Royal Ballet.

When to Go

After dusk Tivoli is at its most enchanting when the park's fairy lights and lanterns are switched on.

Friday evenings From early April to mid-September, the open-air Plænen stage hosts free rock concerts from 10pm – go early if it's a big-name act.

Halloween Tivoli opens for around three weeks. See the website for details.

Christmas From mid-November to early January, Tivoli hosts a large market with costumed staff and theatre shows. There are fewer rides, but the *gløgg* (mulled wine) and *æbleskiver* (small doughnuts) are ample compensation.

EWKKA/SHUTTERSTOCK ©

Designmuseum Danmark

Don't know your Egg from your Swan? What about your PH4 from your PH5? For a crash course in Denmark's incredible design heritage, make an elegant beeline for Designmuseum Danmark.

Housed in a converted 18th-century hospital, the museum is a must for fans of the applied arts and industrial design. Its booty includes Danish silver and porcelain, textiles and the iconic design pieces of modern innovators such as Kaare Klint, Poul Henningsen, Arne Jacobsen and Verner Panton.

20th-Century Crafts & Design

The museum's main permanent exhibition explores 20th-century industrial design and crafts in the context of social, economic, technological and theoretical changes. The collection displays celebrated furniture and applied arts from Denmark and abroad.

Great For...

Don't Miss

The iconic 1959 vintage poster 'Wonderful Copenhagen' – a duck and her little ones stopping traffic.

PERNILLE KLEMP/DESIGNMUSEUM DANMARK ©

❶ Need to Know

Designmuseum Danmark (www.designmuseum.dk; Bredgade 68; adult/child 100kr/free; ⊙11am-5pm Tue & Thu-Sun, to 9pm Wed; 🚌1A, Ⓜ Kongens Nytorv) is 250m north of Marmorkirken.

✖ Take a Break

The museum's Klint Cafe, just off the lobby, serves Danish classics and has a fine outdoor courtyard.

★ Top Tip

The museum shop is one of the city's best places to pick up savvy gifts and easy-to-carry souvenirs.

Fashion & Fabric

This permanent exhibition showcases around 350 objects from the museum's rich textile and fashion collections. Spanning four centuries, the collection's treasures include French and Italian silks, ikat and batik weaving, and two extraordinary mid-20th-century tapestries based on cartoons by Henri Matisse. As would you expect, Danish textiles and fashion feature prominently, including Danish *hedebo* embroidery from the 18th to 20th centuries, and Erik Mortensen's collection of haute couture frocks from French fashion houses Balmain and Jean-Louis Scherrer.

The Danish Chair

An ode to the humble chair and an exploration of what goes into making a 'good' one, this permanent exhibition displays more than 100 beautifully designed chairs, including some international guests. Standing room only.

Porcelain

This detailed exhibition celebrates European porcelain and its journey from initial attempts through to the current day.

Danish Design Now

Showcasing contemporary fashion, furniture and products, this captivating exhibition focuses on 21st-century Danish design and innovation.

Central Copenhagen

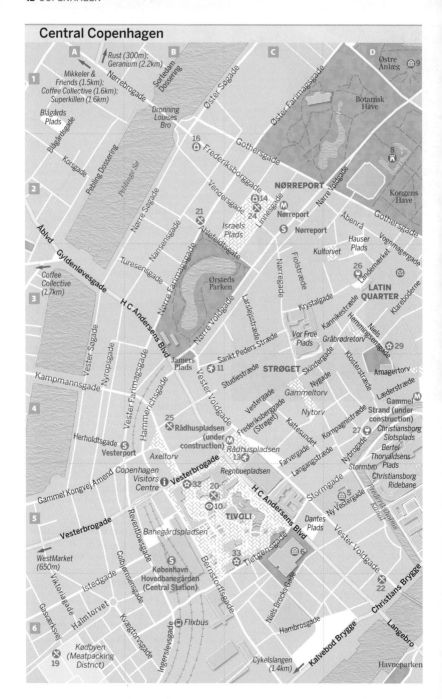

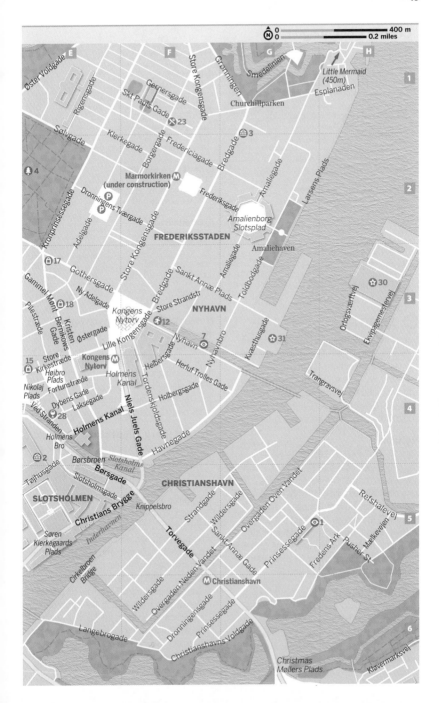

▲ 0 ───── 400 m
Ⓝ 0 ───── 0.2 miles

Øster Voldgade

E

Gernersgade

Skt Pauls Gade

Rørensgade

F

Store Kongensgade

Grønningen

Smedelinien

G

Little Mermaid
(450m)

Esplanaden

H

1

Sølvgade

Klerkegade

Borgergade

Fredericiagade

✕ 23

Churchillparken

🏛 3

Bredgade

2

🟦 4

Kronprinsessegade

Dronningens Tværgade

Adelgade

P

P

Marmorkirken M
(under construction)

Store Kongensgade

Frederiksgade

Amaliegade

Larsens Plads

2

FREDERIKSSTADEN

Amalienborg
Slotsplad

Amaliehaven

🔒 17

Gammel Mønt

Gothersgade

Ny Adelgade

Bredgade

Sankt Annæ Plads

Amaliegade

Toldbodgade

Orlogsværftvej

⭐ 30

Kvintagemestervej

3

🔒 18

Pilestræde

Kristen Bernikows Gade

Østergade

Kongens
Nytorv

Store Strandstr

🔵 12

NYHAVN

Nyhavn

7
◎

Nyhavnsbro

Kvæsthusgade

✪ 31

15
🔒

Store Kirkestræde

Kongens
Nytorv M

Lille Kongensgade

Helsingørsgade

Herluf Trolles Gade

Trangravsvej

4

Nikolaj
Plads

Højbro
Plads

Fortunstræde

Holmens
Kanal

Tordenskjoldsgade

Holbergsgade

Dybens Gade

Laksegade

Holmens Kanal

Ved Stranden

🔵 28

Niels Juels Gade

Havnegade

Holmens
Bro

🏛 2

Børsbroen

Slotsholms
Kanal

CHRISTIANSHAVN

Refshalevej

5

Tøjhusgade

Børsgade

Slotsholmsgade

Strandgade

Wildersgade

Overgaden Oven Vandet

Prinsessegade

🔵 1

SLOTSHOLMEN

Christians Brygge

Knippelsbro

Torvegade

Sankt Annæ Gade

Fredens Ark

Pusher St.

Mælkevejen

Søren
Kierkegaards
Plads

Inderhavnen

Cirkelbroen
Bridge

Wildersgade

Overgaden Neden Vandet

M Christianshavn

Langebrogade

Dronningensgade

Prinsessegade

Christianshavns Voldgade

6

Christmas
Møllers Plads

Kløvermarksvej

Central Copenhagen

◎ SIGHTS

One of the great things about Copenhagen is its size. Virtually all of Copenhagen's major sightseeing attractions are in or close to the medieval city centre. Only the perennially disappointing **Little Mermaid** (Den Lille Havfrue; Langelinie, Østerport; 🚌1A, 🚢Nordre Toldbod) lies outside the city, on the harbourfront.

Nyhavn
Canal

(Nyhavn; 🚌1A, 26, 66, 350S, Ⓜ Kongens Nytorv) There are few nicer places to be on a sunny day than sitting at the outdoor tables of a cafe on the quayside of the Nyhavn canal. The canal was built to connect Kongens Nytorv (Copenhagen's largest square) to the harbour and was long a haunt for sailors and writers, including Hans Christian Andersen, who lived there for most of his life at, variously, No. 20, 18 and 67.

Nationalmuseet
Museum

(National Museum; 🕿33 13 44 11; www.natmus. dk; Ny Vestergade 10; adult/child 75kr/free; ☺10am-5pm Tue-Sun, also open Mon Jul & Aug; 👶; 🚌1A, 2A, 9A, 14, 26, 37, Ⓢ København H) For a crash course in Danish history and culture, spend an afternoon at Denmark's National Museum. It has first claims on virtually every antiquity uncovered on Danish soil, including Stone Age tools, Viking weaponry, rune stones and medieval jewellery. Among the many highlights is a finely crafted 3500-year-old Sun Chariot, as well as bronze *lurs* (horns), some of which date back 3000 years and are still capable of blowing a tune.

Ny Carlsberg Glyptotek
Museum

(🕿33 41 81 41; www.glyptoteket.dk; Dantes Plads 7, HC Andersens Blvd; adult/child 95kr/free, Tue free; ☺11am-6pm Tue-Sun, until 10pm Thu; 🚌1A, 2A, 9A, 37, Ⓢ København H) Fin de siècle architecture dallies with an eclectic mix of art at Ny Carlsberg Glyptotek. The collection is divided into two parts: Northern Europe's largest trove of antiquities, and an elegant collection of 19th-century Danish and French art. The latter includes the largest collection of Rodin sculptures outside France and no less than 47 Gauguin paintings. These are displayed along with works by greats like Cézanne, Van Gogh, Pissarro, Monet and Renoir.

An added treat for visitors is the August/ September Summer Concert Series (admission around 75kr). Classical music is performed in the museum's concert hall, which is evocatively lined by life-size statues of Roman patricians.

De Kongelige Repræsentationslokaler Historic Building

(Royal Reception Rooms at Christiansborg Slot; www.christiansborg.dk; Slotsholmen; adult/child 90kr/free; ☉10am-5pm daily May-Sep, closed Mon Oct-Apr, guided tours in Danish/English 11am/3pm; 🚌1A, 2A, 9A, 26, 37, 66, 🚢Det Kongelige Bibliotek) The grandest part of Christiansborg Slot is De Kongelige Repræsentationslokaler, an ornate Renaissance hall where the queen holds royal banquets and entertains heads of state. Don't miss the beautifully sewn and colourful wall tapestries depicting Danish history from Viking times to today. Created by tapestry designer Bjørn Nørgaard over a decade, the works were completed in 2000. Look for the Adam and Eve–style representation of the queen and her husband (albeit clothed) in a Danish Garden of Eden.

Rosenborg Slot Castle

(📞33 15 32 86; www.kongernessamling.dk/en/rosenborg; Øster Voldgade 4A; adult/child 110kr/free, incl Amalienborg Slot 145kr/free; ☉9am-5pm mid-Jun–mid-Sep, reduced hours rest of year; 🚌6A, 42, 184, 185, 350S, 🅼Nørreport, 🆂Nørreport) A 'once-upon-a-time' combo of turrets, gables and moat, the early-17th-century Rosenborg Slot was built in Dutch Renaissance style between 1606 and 1633 by King Christian IV to serve as his summer home. Today, the castle's 24 upper rooms are chronologically arranged, housing the furnishings and portraits of each monarch from Christian IV to Frederik VII. The pièce de résistance is the basement Treasury, home to the dazzling crown jewels.

Statens Museum for Kunst Museum

(📞33 74 84 94; www.smk.dk; Sølvgade 48-50; adult/child 110kr/free; ☉11am-5pm Tue & Thu-Sun, to 8pm Wed; 🚌6A, 26, 42, 184, 185) **FREE** The National Gallery straddles two contrasting, interconnected buildings: a late-19th-century 'palazzo' and a sharply minimalist extension. The museum houses medieval and Renaissance works and impressive collections of

Dutch and Flemish artists including Rubens, Breugel and Rembrandt. It claims the world's finest collection of 19th-century Danish 'Golden Age' artists, among them Eckersberg and Hammershøi, foreign greats like Matisse and Picasso, and modern Danish heavyweights including Per Kirkeby.

Kongens Have Park

(King's Gardens; http://parkmuseerne.dk/kongens-have; Øster Voldgade; ☉7am-11pm Jul–mid-Aug, to 10pm May–mid-Jun & mid-late Aug, reduced hours rest of year; ⊞; 🚌26, 🅼Nørreport, 🆂Nørreport) **FREE** The oldest park in Copenhagen was laid out in the early 17th century by Christian IV, who used it as his vegetable patch. These days it has a little more to offer, including immaculate flower beds, romantic garden paths and a marionette theatre with free performances during the summer season (2pm and 3pm Tuesday to Sunday).

Superkilen Park

(Nørrebrogade 210, Nørrebro; 🚌5C, 🆂Nørrebro) This fascinating 1km-long park showcases objects sourced from around the globe with the aim of celebrating diversity and uniting the community. Items include a tile fountain from Morocco, bollards from Ghana and swing chairs from Baghdad, as well as neon signs from Russia and China. Even the benches, manhole covers and rubbish bins hail from foreign lands.

🅖 TOURS

You can't visit Copenhagen and not take a canal boat trip. Not only is it a fantastic way to see the city, but you get a perspective that landlubbers never see. Be aware that in most boats you are totally exposed to the elements (even during summer).

Bike Copenhagen with Mike Cycling

(📞26 39 56 88; www.bikecopenhagenwithmike.dk; Sankt Peders Stræde 47; per person 299kr; 🚌2A, 5C, 6A, 14, 250S) If you don't fancy walking, Bike Mike runs three-hour cycling tours of the city, departing Sankt Peders Stræde 47 in the city centre, just east of Ørstedsparken (which is southwest of Nørreport station). Mike is a great character and will really give you the insider's scoop on the city. Book online.

Copenhagen Free Walking Tours
Walking

(www.copenhagenfreewalkingtours.dk; Rådhuspladsen) Departing daily at noon from outside Rådhus (City Hall), these free, three-hour walking tours take in famous landmarks and include interesting anecdotes. Tours are in English and require a minimum of five people. Free 90-minute tours of Christianshavn depart at 4pm Friday to Monday from the base of the Bishop Absalon statue on Højbro Plads. A tip is expected.

Canal Tours Copenhagen
Boating

(⌛32 96 30 00; www.stromma.dk; Nyhavn; adult/child 80/40kr; ⊙9.30am-9pm late Jun–mid-Aug, reduced hours rest of year; 🚼; 🚍1A, 26, 66, 350S, Ⓜ Kongens Nytorv) Canal Tours Copenhagen runs one-hour cruises of the city's canals and harbour, taking in numerous major sights, including Christiansborg Slot, Christianshavn, the Royal Library, Opera House, Amalienborg Palace and the Little Mermaid. Embark at Nyhavn or Ved Stranden. Boats depart up to six times per hour from late June to late August, with reduced frequency the rest of the year.

🛍 SHOPPING

Most of the big retail names and home-grown heavyweights are found on the main pedestrian shopping strip, Strøget. The streets running parallel are dotted with interesting jewellery and antique stores, while the so-called Latin Quarter, to the north, is worth a wander for books and clothing. Arty Nørrebro is home to Elmegade and Jægersborggade, two streets lined with interesting shops.

Bornholmer Butikken
Food & Drinks

(⌛30 72 00 07; www.bornholmerbutikken.dk; Stall F6, Hall 1, Torvehallerne KBH; ⊙10am-7pm Mon-Thu, to 8pm Fri, to 6pm Sat, 11am-5pm Sun; 🛜; 🚍15E, 150S, 185, Ⓜ Nørreport, Ⓢ Nørreport) The 'Bornholm Store' in Torvehallerne Market offers a range of tasty take-home specialties from the Danish island of Bornholm, which is famed for its incredible local products. Tasty treats to bring home include honeys, relishes and jams, Johan Bulow liquorice, salamis, cheeses, herring, liquors and beers.

Operaen

SHC/SHUTTERSTOCK ©

Maduro — Homewares

(☎33 93 28 33; www.maduro.dk; Frederiksborggade 39; ⏱11am-6pm Mon-Fri, 10am-4pm Sat; ☐5C) The motto of Maduro owner Jeppe Maduro Hirsch is that 'good style is more than decor and design.' His small shop is an eclectic mix of lovely products, including ceramics, posters and jewellery. The style ranges from sleek to traditional to quirky, and the selection of children's items is especially charming.

Posterland — Gifts & Souvenirs

(☎33 11 28 21; www.posterland.dk; Gothersgade 45; ⏱9.30am-6pm Mon-Thu, to 7pm Fri, to 5pm Sat; ☐350S, Ⓜ Kongens Nytorv) Posterland is Northern Europe's biggest poster company, and is the perfect place to find something to spruce up your walls. The wide selection includes art, travel and vintage posters, as well as Copenhagen posters of every description including Danish icons Hans Christian Andersen, Tivoli Gardens and the Carlsberg Brewery. You can also pick up souvenirs like postcards, maps, calendars and magnets.

Hay House — Design

(☎42 82 08 20; www.hay.dk; Østergade 61; ⏱10am-6pm Mon-Fri, to 5pm Sat; ☐1A, 2A, 9A, 14, 26, 37, 66, Ⓜ Kongens Nytorv) Rolf Hay's fabulous interior design store sells its own coveted line of furniture, textiles and design objects, as well as those of other fresh, innovative Danish designers. Easy-to-pack gifts include anything from notebooks and ceramic cups to building blocks for style-savvy kids. There's a second branch at Pilestræde 29-31.

Wood Wood — Fashion & Accessories

(☎35 35 62 64; www.woodwood.dk; Grønnegade 1; ⏱10.30am-6pm Mon-Thu, to 7pm Fri, to 5pm Sat, noon-4pm Sun; ☐1A, 26, 350S, Ⓜ Kongens Nytorv) Unisex Wood Wood's flagship store is a veritable who's who of cognoscenti street-chic labels. Top of the heap are Wood Wood's own hipster-chic creations, made with superlative fabrics and attention to detail. The supporting cast includes solid knits from classic Danish brand SNS Herning, wallets from Comme des Garçons, and sunglasses from Kaibosh.

 Changing of the Guard

The Royal Life Guard is charged with protecting the Danish royal family and their city residence, Amalienborg Palace. Every day of the year, these soldiers march from their barracks through the streets of Copenhagen to perform the **Changing of the Guard** (www.kongehuset.dk/en/changing-of-the-guard-at-amalienborg; Amalienborg Slotsplads; ⏱12pm daily; ☐1A) **FREE**. Clad in 19th-century tunics and bearskin helmets, their performance of intricate manoeuvres is an impressive sight. If Queen Margrethe is in residence, the ceremony is even more grandiose, with the addition of a full marching band.

If you miss out on the noon ceremony, a smaller-scale shift change is performed every two hours thereafter.

Guards march near Amalienborg Palace
BIRUTE VIJEIKIENE/SHUTTERSTOCK ©

ENTERTAINMENT

Copenhagen is home to thriving live-music and club scenes that range from intimate jazz and blues clubs to mega rock venues. Blockbuster cultural venues such as **Operaen** (Copenhagen Opera House; ☎box office 33 69 69 69; www.kglteater.dk; Ekvipagemestervej 10; ☐9A, ⛴Operaen) and **Skuespilhuset** (Royal Danish Playhouse; ☎33 69 69 69; https://kglteater.dk; Sankt Anne Plads 36; ☐66, ⛴Nyhavn, Ⓜ Kongens Nytorv) deliver top-tier opera and theatre. The **Copenhagen Jazz Festival** (www.jazz.dk; ⏱Jul), the largest jazz festival in northern Europe, hits the city over 10 days in early July.

 Christiania

Escape the capitalist crunch at Free-town **Christiania** (www.christiania.org; Prinsessegade; 9A, Christianshavn), a free-spirited, eco-oriented commune with various beer gardens, communal eateries and live-music venues. Explore beyond the settlement's infamous 'Pusher St' and you'll stumble upon a semi-bucolic wonderland of whimsical DIY homes, cosy gardens and craft shops, eateries, beer gardens and music venues.

Before its development as an alterna-tive enclave, the site was an aban-doned 41-hectare military camp. When squatters took over in 1971, police tried to clear the area. They failed. Bowing to public pressure, the government allowed the community to continue as a social experiment. Self-governing, ecology-ori-ented and generally tolerant, Christiania residents did, in time, find it necessary to modify their 'anything goes' approach. A new policy was established that outlawed hard drugs, and the heroin and cocaine pushers were expelled.

The main entrance into Christiania is on Prinsessegade, 200m northeast of its intersection with Bådsmandsstræde. From late June to the end of August, 60- to 90-minute guided tours (40kr) of Christiania run daily at 3pm (weekends only September to late June). Tours start just inside Christiania's main entrance on Prinsessegade.

Freetown Christiania
SERG ZASTAVKIN/SHUTTERSTOCK ©

Jazzhouse Jazz

(33 15 47 00; www.jazzhouse.dk; Niels Hemmingsensgade 10; from 7pm Mon-Thu, from 8pm Fri-Sat; 1A, 2A, 9A, 14, 26, 37) Copenhagen's leading jazz joint serves up top Danish and visiting talent, with music styles running the gamut from bebop to fusion jazz. Doors usually open at 7pm, with concerts starting at 8pm. On Friday and Saturday, late-night concerts (from 11pm) are also offered. Check the website for details and consider booking in advance for big-name acts.

EATING

Copenhagen remains one of the hottest culinary destinations in Europe, with more Michelin stars than any other Scandinavian city. **Copenhagen Cooking** (www.copenha-gencooking.dk; Aug), Scandinavia's largest food festival, serves up a gut-rumbling program.

Lillian's Smørrebrød Danish €

(33 14 20 66; www.facebook.com/lillianssmorre brod; Vester Voldgade 108; smørrebrød from 17kr; 6am-2pm Mon-Fri; 1A, 2A, 9A) One of the best, the oldest (dating from 1978) and least costly smørrebrød places in the city, but word is out so you may have to opt for a takeaway as there are just a handful of tables inside and out. The piled-high, open-face sandwich-es are classic and include marinated herring, chicken salad and roast beef with remoulade.

Chicky Grill Danish €

(33 22 66 96; Halmtorvet 21, Vesterbro; mains from 65kr; 11am-8pm Mon-Sat; 10, 14, København H) Blend in with the locals at this perennially popular bar and grill in hip Kødbyen (the 'Meatpacking District'). It has decor that is more diner than 'dining out', but prices are low and portions are huge, with a menu of predominantly grilled meats, fried chicken, burgers and that all-time popular Danish speciality, *flæskesteg* (roast pork).

Torvehallerne KBH Market €

(www.torvehallernekbh.dk; Israels Plads, Nør-report; dishes from around 50kr; 10am-7pm

Mon-Thu, to 8pm Fri, to 6pm Sat, 11am-5pm Sun; 🚌15E, 150S, 185, Ⓜ️Nørreport, ⓈNørreport) Torvehallerne KBH is an essential stop on the Copenhagen foodie trail. A delicious ode to the fresh, the tasty and the artisanal, the market's beautiful stalls peddle everything from seasonal herbs and berries to smoked meats, seafood and cheeses, smørrebrød, fresh pasta and hand-brewed coffee. You could easily spend an hour or more exploring its twin halls.

WestMarket
Market €

(📞70 50 00 05; www.westmarket.dk; Vesterbrogade 97, Vesterbro; meals from 50kr; ⏲️bakeries & coffee shops 8am-7pm, food stalls 10am-10pm; 🛜📶; 🚌6A) Copenhagen's newest foodie hotspot, WestMarket is both a traditional market and a hip street-food emporium. The range of cuisines is impressive: visitors can sample offerings from all over the world, from Danish smør-rebrød at Selma to Ugandan egg wraps at Ugood. Treat yourself to sinfully delicious desserts at Guilty.

Nyboders Køkken
Danish €€

(📞22 88 64 14; www.nyboderskoekken.dk; Borgergade 134; lunch 58-148kr, dinner mains 128-189kr; ⏲️noon-4pm & 5-11.30pm; 🛜; 🚌1A, Ⓜ️Kongens Nytorv) Located in an affluent neighbourhood with a fashionably chic feel, Nyboders Køkken's menu is purposefully deeply traditional; if you are Danish, grandma's kitchen may come to mind. Think apple charlotte, classic wienerschnitzel, prawn cocktail and Danish junket with cream. Among the mains, the roasted slices of pork with parsley sauce has had local food critics swooning.

Höst
New Nordic €€€

(📞89 93 84 09; www.hostvakst.dk; Nørre Farimagsgade 41; 3-/5-course menu 350/450kr; ⏲️5.30pm-midnight, last order 9.30pm; 🚌37, Ⓜ️Nørreport, ⓈNørreport) Höst's phenomenal popularity is a no-brainer: warm, award-winning interiors and New Nordic food that's equally fabulous and filling. The set menu is superb, with three smaller 'surprise dishes' thrown in and evocative creations like beef tenderloin from Grambogaard with onion compote, gherkins, cress and smoked cheese. The 'deluxe' wine menu is significantly

Torvehallerne

Coffee shop in Torvehallerne

better than the standard option. Book ahead, especially later in the week.

Uformel
New Nordic €€€

(☑70 99 91 11; www.uformel.dk; Studiestræde 69; dishes 120kr; ⊙5.30pm-midnight Sun-Thu, to 2am Fri & Sat; ⑤; ☐2A, 10, 12, 250S, ⑤Vesterport) The edgier younger brother of Michelin–starred restaurant Formel B, Uformel ('Informal') offers a more casual take on New Nordic cuisine. The restaurant serves up an ever-changing menu featuring local, seasonal ingredients to create its mouth-watering dishes. Diners can choose several small plates to create their own tasting menu, or opt for the set menu of four courses (775kr).

Geranium
New Nordic €€€

(☑69 96 00 20; www.geranium.dk; Per Henrik Lings Allé 4, Østerbro; lunch/dinner tasting menu 2000kr, wine/juice pairings 1400/700kr; ⊙noon-3.30pm & 6.30pm-midnight Wed-Sat; ⑤☑; ☐14) ✔ Perched on the 8th floor of Parken football stadium, Geranium is the only restaurant in town sporting three Michelin stars. At the helm is Bocuse d'Or prize-winning chef Rasmus Kofoed, who transforms local ingredi-

ents into edible Nordic artworks like venison with smoked lard and beetroot, or king crab with lemon balm and cloudberries.

Kroner-conscious foodies can opt for the slightly cheaper lunch menus, while those not wanting to sample the (swoon-inducing) wines can opt for enlightened juice pairings. Book ahead.

🍷 DRINKING & NIGHTLIFE

Copenhagen is packed with a diverse range of drinking options. Vibrant drinking areas include Kødbyen (the 'Meatpacking District') and Istedgade in Vesterbro, Ravnsborggade, Elmegade and Sankt Hans Torv in Nørrebro, and especially gay-friendly Studiestræde.

Coffee Collective
Coffee

(www.coffeecollective.dk; Jægersborggade 57, Nørrebro; ⊙7am-8pm Mon-Fri, 8am-7pm Sat & Sun; ☐8A) In a city where lacklustre coffee is as common as perfect cheekbones, this micro-roastery peddles the good stuff – we're talking rich, complex cups of caffeinated magic. The baristas are passionate about their beans, and the cafe itself sits on creative Jægersborggade in Nørrebro. There are two other outlets, at food market Torvehallerne KBH (p48) and in **Frederiksberg** (☑60 15 15 25; https://coffeecollective.dk; Godthåbsvej 34b, Frederiksberg; ⊘7.30am-6pm Mon-Fri, from 9am Sat, from 10am Sun).

Ved Stranden 10   Wine Bar

(☑35 42 40 40; www.vedstranden10.dk; Ved Stranden 10; ⊘noon-10pm Mon-Sat; ☎; 🚍1A, 2A, 9A, 26, 37, 66, 350S, Ⓜ Kongens Nytorv) Politicians and well-versed oenophiles make a beeline for this canalside wine bar, its cellar stocked with classic European vintages, biodynamic wines and more obscure drops. Adorned with modernist Danish design and friendly, clued-in staff, its string of rooms lend the place an intimate, civilised air that's perfect for grown-up conversation and vino-friendly nibbles like cheeses and smoked meats.

Ruby   Cocktail Bar

(☑33 93 12 03; www.rby.dk; Nybrogade 10; ⊘4pm-2am Mon-Sat, from 6pm Sun; ☎; 🚍1A, 2A, 14, 26, 37, 66) Cocktail connoisseurs raise their glasses to high-achieving Ruby. Here, hipster-geek mixologists whip up near-flawless libations such as the Green & White (vodka, dill, white chocolate and liquorice root), and a lively crowd spills into a maze of decadent rooms. For a gentlemen's club vibe, head downstairs into a world of Chesterfields, oil paintings and wooden cabinets lined with spirits.

Lo-Jo's Social   Bar

(☑53 88 64 65; www.lojossocial.com; Landemærket 7; ⊘bar 11.30am-midnight Mon-Wed, to 2am Thu-Sat; 🚍350S, Ⓜ Nørreport, Ⓢ Nørreport) It's all in the name: colourful Lo-Jo's is a place to be social, with a range of tasty cocktails available for sharing for up to five people. Wines are largely organic or bio-dynamic, and for something a bit different, there is a bubbly spritz menu and a refreshing apple press menu, using fresh apple juice as a base.

Mikkeller & Friends   Microbrewery

(☑35 83 10 20; www.mikkeller.dk/location/mikkeller-friends; Stefansgade 35, Nørrebro; ⊘2pm-midnight Sun-Wed, to 2am Thu & Fri, noon-2am Sat; ☎; 🚍5C, 8A) This uniquely-designed

    Cykelslangen

Two of the Danes' greatest passions – design and cycling – meet in spectacular fashion with **Cykelslangen**, aka Cycle Snake. Designed by local architects Dissing + Weitling, the 235m-long cycling path evokes a slender orange ribbon, its gently curving form contrasting dramatically against the area's block-like architecture. The elevated path winds its way from Bryggebro (Brygge Bridge) west to Fisketorvet Shopping Centre, weaving its way over the harbour and delivering a whimsical cycling experience. To reach the path on public transport, catch bus 30 to Fisketorvet Shopping Centre. The best way to reach it, however, is on a bike, as Cykelslangen is only accessible to cyclists.

Cykelslangen
GERARD PUIGMAL/GETTY IMAGES ©

beer geek hotspot offers 40 kinds of artisan draft beers from local microbreweries and 200 varieties of bottled beers, ciders and soft drinks. Patrons can snack on gourmet sausages and cheese while enjoying their beer.

Rust   Club

(☑35 24 52 00; www.rust.dk; Guldbergsgade 8, Nørrebro; ⊘hours vary, club usually 8.30pm-5am Fri & Sat; ☎; 🚍3A, 5C, 350S) A smashing place attracting one of the largest, coolest crowds in Copenhagen. Live acts focus on alternative or upcoming indie rock, hip hop or electronica, while the club churns out hip-hop, dancehall and electro on Wednesdays and house, electro and rock on Fridays and Saturdays.

Designer Danes

As wonderful as Danish design-focused shops, museums, hotels and restaurants are, the very best place to see Danish design is in its natural environment: a Danish home. To the Danes, good design is not just for museums and institutions; they live with it and use it every day.

Visit a Danish home and you'll invariably find a Bang & Olufsen stereo and/or TV in the living room, Poul Henningsen lamps hanging from the ceiling, Arne Jacobsen or Hans Wegner chairs in the dining room, and the table set with Royal Copenhagen dinner sets, Georg Jensen cutlery and Bodum glassware.

From 11pm Friday and Saturday, entrance is restricted to over-20s.

INFORMATION

EMERGENCY & IMPORTANT NUMBERS

Dial 112 to contact police, ambulance or fire services; the call can be made free from public phones.

DISCOUNT CARDS

The **Copenhagen Card** (www.copenhagencard.com; adult/child 10-15yr 24hr 389/199kr, 48hr 549/279kr, 72hr 659/329kr, 120hr 889/449kr), available at the Copenhagen Visitors Centre or online, gives you free access to 72 museums and attractions in the city and surrounding area, as well as free travel for all S-train, metro and bus journeys within the seven travel zones.

MONEY

Banks are plentiful, especially in central Copenhagen. Most are open from 10am to 4pm weekdays (to 5.30pm on Thursday). Most have ATMs that are accessible 24 hours per day.

POST

Post Office (☑70 70 70 30; www.postnord.dk; Pilestræde 58; ☺8.30am-7pm Mon-Fri, to 2pm Sat; ☐350S, ⓂKongens Nytorv) A handy post office near Strøget and the Latin Quarter.

There is also a post office in Central Station.

TOURIST INFORMATION

Copenhagen Visitors Centre (☑70 22 24 42; www.visitcopenhagen.com; Vesterbrogade 4A, Vesterbro; ☺9am-8pm Mon-Fri, to 6pm Sat & Sun Jul & Aug, reduced hours rest of year; 🛜; ☐2A, 6A, 12, 14, 26, 250S, ⓢKøbenhavn H) Copenhagen's excellent and informative information centre has a superb cafe and lounge with free wi-fi; it also sells the **Copenhagen Card**.

GETTING THERE & AWAY

AIR

If you're waiting for a flight at **Copenhagen Airport** (☑32 31 32 31; www.cph.dk; Lufthavnsboulevarden, Kastrup; ⓂLufthavnen, ⓢKøbenhavns Lufthavn), note that this is a 'silent' airport and there are no boarding calls, although there are numerous monitor screens throughout the terminal.

BUS

Eurolines (www.flixbus.com; ⓢKøbenhavn H) Operates buses to several European cities. The ticket office is behind Central Station. Long-distance buses leave from opposite the DGI-byen sports complex on Ingerslevsgade, just southwest of København H (Central Station). Destinations include Berlin (329kr, 7.5 hrs) and Paris (699kr, 19 to 22¼ hrs).

TRAIN

DSB Billetsalg (DSB Ticket Office; ☑70 13 14 15; www.dsb.dk; Central Station, Bernstorffsgade 16-22; ☺7am-8pm Mon-Fri, 8am-6pm Sat & Sun; ⓢKøbenhavn H) is best for reservations and for purchasing international train tickets.

Rust (p51)

ℹ️ GETTING AROUND

TO/FROM THE AIRPORT

The 24-hour metro (www.m.dk) runs every four to 20 minutes between the airport arrival terminal (Lufthavnen station) and the eastern side of the city centre. It does not stop at København H (Central Station) but is handy for Christianshavn and Nyhavn (get off at Kongens Nytorv for Nyhavn). Journey time to Kongens Nytorv is 14 minutes (36kr).

By taxi, it's about 20 minutes between the airport and the city centre, depending on traffic. Expect to pay between 250kr and 300kr.

Trains (www.dsb.dk) connect the airport arrival terminal to Copenhagen Central Station (København Hovedbanegården, commonly known as København H) around every 12 minutes. Journey time is 14 minutes (36kr). Check schedules at www.rejseplanen.dk.

BICYCLE

Copenhagen vies with Amsterdam as the world's most bike-friendly city. The superb, city-wide rental system is **Bycyklen** (City Bikes; www.bycyklen.dk; per 1hr 30kr). Visit the Bycyklen website for more information.

CAR & MOTORCYCLE

Except for the weekday rush hour, when traffic can bottleneck, traffic in Copenhagen is generally manageable. Getting around by car is not problematic, except for the usual challenge of finding an empty parking space in the most popular places.

PUBLIC TRANSPORT

Copenhagen has an extensive public transport system consisting of a metro, rail, bus and ferry network. All tickets are valid for travel on the metro, buses and S-tog (S-train or local train), even though they look slightly different, depending on where you buy them. The free Copenhagen city maps that are distributed by the tourist office show bus routes (with numbers) and are very useful for finding your way around the city. Online, click onto the very handy www.rejseplanen.dk for all routes and schedules.

WALKING

The best way to see Copenhagen is on foot. There are few main sights or shopping quarters more than a 20-minute walk from the city centre.

BORNHOLM, DENMARK

Bornholm, Denmark at a Glance...

The sunniest part of Denmark, Bornholm lies way out in the Baltic Sea, 200km east of Copenhagen (and closer to Sweden and Poland than to mainland Denmark). But it's not just (relatively) sunny skies that draw the hordes each year. Mother Nature was in a particularly good mood when creating this Baltic beauty, bestowing on it rocky cliffs, leafy forests, bleach-white beaches and a pure, ethereal light that painters do their best to capture.

Two Days on Bornholm

Divide your first couple of days between **Rønne** (p60), **Dueodde** (p64)and **Gudhjem** (p66). While at Rønne, don't miss the Nylars Rundkirke, and at Gudhjem, leave ample time to explore the Bornholms Kunstmuseum and linger over its contents. If the weather's warm, go for a swim at Dueodde beach.

Four Days on Bornholm

Days three and four on Bornholm – you lucky soul! – will see you exploring the windmills and lovely architecture of **Svaneke** (p65), the mix of architecture and nature at **Sandvig** (p69)and then falling off the map at **Christiansø** (p68). If you've time, return to **Gudhjem** (p66) and take one of the lovely walks in the area.

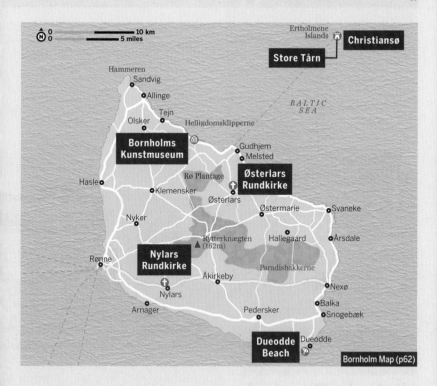

Bornholm Map (p62)

Arriving on Bornholm

The island's airport, Bornholms Lufthavn, is 5km southeast of Rønne. Bus 5 connects the airport with Rønne.

Where to Stay

There's a good mix of camping grounds, hostels and hotels around the island, plus plenty of holiday houses and apartments for rent. Hotels span the spectrum from traditional *badehoteller* (bathing hotels by the seaside) to ultramodern and stylish. The five Danhostels are outlined at www.danhostel-bornholm.dk.

You'd be wise to book well ahead for visits in summer, especially July and August.

Store Tårn

Historic Bornholm

Bornholm's human footprint includes medieval fortresses, thatched fishing villages, iconic rundekirke (round churches) and more. Historic smokehouses, too, are a charming feature.

Great For...

Don't Miss

The round churches that are so distinctive of Bornholm.

Store Tårn

Built in 1684, Christiansø's **Store Tårn** (Great Tower; adult/child 40/20kr; ☺11am-6pm Tue-Thu, to 4pm Fri-Mon mid-Jun–mid-Aug, 11am-4pm Tue-Sun Easter–mid-Jun & mid-Aug–mid-Oct) is an impressive structure measuring a full 25m in diameter, and the tower's 100-year-old lighthouse offers a sweeping 360-degree view of the island. After major restoration work, the tower reopened in June 2017 with new exhibits on local history and birdlife.

Bornholms Kunstmuseum

Occupying a svelte, modern building and overlooking sea, fields and (weather permitting) the distant isle of Christiansø, **Bornholms Kunstmuseum** (☑56 48 43 86;

Nylars Rundkirke

MIŁOSZ MAŚLANKA/SHUTTERSTOCK ©

Christiansø 🏰 **Store Tårn**
Olsker 🛈 **Bornholms Kunstmuseum**
Rundkirke 🏛 ●Gudhjem
🛈
Østerlars
Rønne● **Rundkirke**
🛈 ●Nexø
Nylars
Rundkirke

❶ Need to Know

Bornholm can be reached by plane, ferry or a ferry-bus-train combination via Sweden.

✕ Take a Break

Fru Petersens Café (📞21 78 78 95; www. frupetersenscafe.dk; Almindingensvej 31, Østermarie; cake buffet incl drinks 145kr; ⊙noon-6pm Jun-Aug, to 5pm Wed-Sun Apr, May, Sep, Thu-Sun Oct) is a gorgeous little place with wonderful cakes.

★ Top Tip

Look closely and you'll find a rune stone dating back to the mid-11th century at the Østerlars Rundkirke entrance.

www.bornholms-kunstmuseum.dk; Otto Bruuns Plads 1; adult/child 70kr/free; ⊙10am-5pm Jun-Aug, closed Mon Apr, May, Sep & Oct, shorter hours rest of year) echoes Copenhagen's Louisiana. Among its exhibits, the museum displays paintings by artists from the Bornholm School, including Olaf Rude, Oluf Høst and Edvard Weie, who painted during the first half of the 20th century.

Østerlars Rundkirke

The largest and most impressive of Bornholm's round churches, Østerlars Rundkirke dates to at least 1150, and its seven buttresses and upper-level shooting positions give away its former role as a fortress. The roof was originally constructed with a flat top to serve as a battle platform, but the excessive weight this exerted on the walls saw it eventually replaced with its present conical one. The interior is largely whitewashed, although a swath of medieval frescoes has been uncovered and restored.

Nylars Rundkirke

Built around 1150, **Nylars Rundkirke** (www.nylarskirke.dk; Kirkevej 10K, Nylars; ⊙7am-6pm Apr-Sep, 8am-3.30pm Oct-Mar) is the most well-preserved and easily accessible round church in the Rønne area. Its central pillar is adorned with wonderful 13th-century frescoes, the oldest in Bornholm. The works depict scenes from the creation myth, including Adam and Eve's expulsion from the Garden of Eden. The cylindrical nave has three storeys, the top one a watchman's gallery that served as a defence lookout in medieval times.

Rønne

Rønne is Bornholm's largest settlement and the main harbour for ferries. The town has been the island's commercial centre since the Middle Ages, and while the place has expanded and taken on a more suburban look over the years, a handful of well-preserved quarters still provide pleasant strolling. Especially appealing is the old neighbourhood west of Store Torv with its handsome period buildings and cobblestone streets, among them Laksegade and Storegade.

◉ SIGHTS

Bornholms Museum   Museum

(☑56 95 07 35; www.bornholmsmuseum.dk; Sankt Mortensgade 29; adult/child 70kr/free; ⊙10am-5pm Jul–mid-Aug, closed Sun mid-May–Jun & mid-Aug–late Oct, shorter hours rest of year) Prehistoric finds including weapons, tools and jewellery are on show at Bornholm's museum of cultural history, which has a surprisingly large and varied collection of local exhibits, including some interesting Viking finds. A good maritime section is decked out like the interior of a ship, and there's a hotchpotch of nature displays, antique toys, Roman coins, pottery and paintings.

Erichsens Gård   Museum

(☑56 95 07 35; www.bornholmsmuseum.dk; Laksegade 7; adult/child 50kr/free; ⊙10am-4pm Fri & Sat mid-May–mid-Oct) Pretty in pink, this merchant's house from 1806 is a photogenic half-timbered idyll on a cobbled lane. There are short opening hours, when you can view the rooms and lovely garden.

Mølgaard & Marcussen   Gallery

(☑81 75 48 67; www.mølgaard-marcussen.dk; Raadhusstræde 1A; ⊙10am-4pm Mon-Fri, to 1pm Sat) Bornholm overflows with creative types and has a long tradition of ceramics. The two friendly owners of this studio gallery and store are great proponents of the art, and their pastel-hued creations are truly covetable.

✖ EATING

Hasle Røgeri   Seafood €

(☑56 96 20 02; www.hasleroegeri.dk; Søndre Bæk 20, Hasle; dishes 58-115kr; ⊙10am-9pm

Rønne

CINEMATOGRAPHER/SHUTTERSTOCK ©

Jul-late Aug, to 5pm May, Jun & late Aug-Oct) The closest traditional smokehouse to Rønne is by the water in Hasle, about 11km north of town. This century-old place has the iconic square chimneys, lots of outdoor seating and a super spread of smoked-fish goodness (herring, salmon, mackerel, eel, prawns) in a 149kr lunch buffet.

Torvehal Bornholm Food Hall €
(⌂31 43 72 00; www.torvehalbornholm.dk; Gartnervangen 6; mains from grill 145-190kr; ⊙10am-5pm Wed & Thu, to 8pm Fri-Sun Jun-Aug, shorter hours rest of year) While food elsewhere on the island went gangbusters, Rønne's food scene lagged – but the summer 2017 opening of this food hall in the town's north changed that. In a former slaughterhouse, peruse the output of some of Bornholm's finest producers, nibble on snacks from a food truck, sample beer brewed on site and dine on meat fresh off the grill.

DRINKING & NIGHTLIFE

Take a wander around Store Torv to find drinking spots.

INFORMATION

Tourist Office (Bornholms Velkomstcenter; ⌂56 95 95 00; www.bornholm.info; Nordre Kystvej 3; ⊙9am-5pm Jul-mid-Aug, to 4pm Mon-Fri rest of year, hours vary Sat) is a few minutes' walk from the harbour, this large, friendly office has masses of information on all of Bornholm and Christiansø.

GETTING THERE & AWAY

BOAT

The **ferry terminal** (Findlandsvej) is by the harbour. There is a large car park and a ticket office, plus a bus stop next door.

BUS

There's a bus stop by the ferry terminal, and a busy **bus stop** on Snellemark, close to Store Torv.

 The Round Churches of Bornholm

As the windmills are to Mykonos or the stone heads are to Easter Island, so are the four 12th-century round churches (rundekirke) to Bornholm. The churches are symbols of the island, immediately familiar to every Dane. Each was built with 2m-thick whitewashed walls and a black conical roof at a time when pirating Wends from eastern Germany were ravaging coastal areas throughout the Baltic Sea. They were designed not only as places of worship but also as refuges against enemy attacks – their upper storeys doubled as places to fire arrows from. They were also used as storehouses to protect valuable possessions and trading goods from being carried off by the pirates.

Each church was built about 2km inland, and all four are sited high enough on knolls to offer a lookout to the sea. These striking and utterly distinctive churches have a stern, ponderous appearance, more typical of a fortress than of a place of worship. All four churches are still used for Sunday services. You'll find them at Østerlars (p59), Olsker (p70), Nyker and Nylars (p59).

Østerlars Rundkirke (p59)
 BILDAGENTUR ZOONAR GMBH/SHUTTERSTOCK ©

GETTING AROUND

There are loads of places across the island renting bikes, and many hotels and hostels also offer rental.

Bornholm

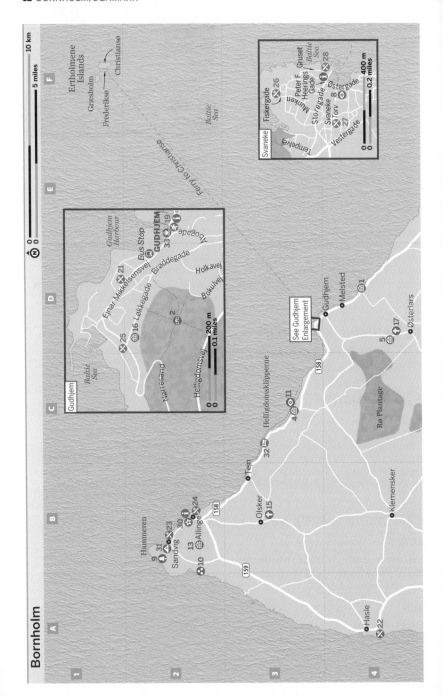

N

0 — 5 miles
0 — 10 km

Ertholmene Islands

Gresholm
Frederikso · Christianso

Baltic Sea

Ferry to Christianso

Gudhjem

Baltic Sea

Gudhjem Harbour

Bus Stop

21

Einar Mikkelsensvej

25

16 Løkkegade

2

Brøddegade

Holkavej

Bøkulvej

GUDHJEM
33 19

Abogade

Nørresand

Helligdomsvej

0 — 200 m
0 — 0.1 miles

Svaneke

Fiskergade
26

Peter F. Gruset,
Heerings
Gade
Munken
Storegade
Svaneke
Torv
8
27
Østergade
28

Baltic Sea

Vestergade

Tempelvej

0 — 400 m
0 — 0.2 miles

Hammeren

9 31
Sandvig
23
30
13
24
Allinge
10

158

Olsker
15

Tejn

Helligdomsklipperne
32
11
4

See Gudhjem Enlargement
Gudhjem
Melsted
1

158

5 17
Østerlars

Ro Plantage

159

Klemensker

Hasle
22

Baltic Sea

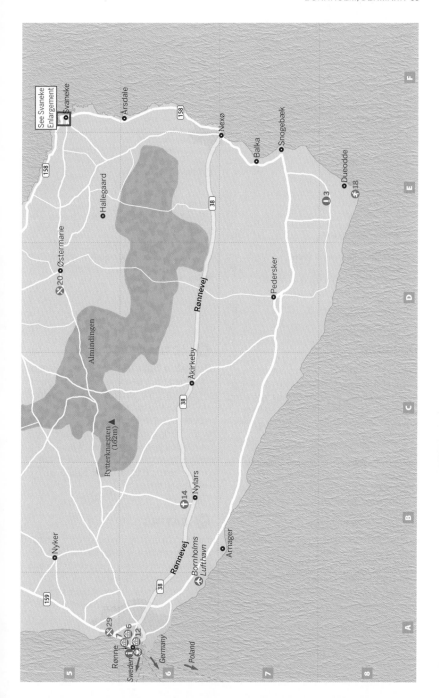

See Svaneke Enlargement

Svaneke

Arsdale

158

Nexø

Balka

Snogebæk

Dueodde

18

3

158

Hallegaard

38

20 Østermarie

Pedersker

Almindingen

Rønnevej

Akirkeby

38

Rytterknægten
(162m)

C

14 Nylars

Nyker

Arnager

Rønnevej

Bornholms
Lufthavn

38

159

29

6

10 12

Rønne

Germany

Sweden

Poland

Bornholm

Dueodde

Dueodde, the southernmost point of Bornholm, is a vast stretch of breathtaking beach backed by deep green pine trees and expansive dunes. Its soft sand is so fine-grained that it was once used in hourglasses and ink blotters.

There's no real village at Dueodde – the bus stops at the end of the road where there's a hotel, a steakhouse restaurant, a couple of food kiosks and a boardwalk across the marsh to the beach. The only beachside 'sight' is a **lighthouse** on the western side of the dunes; you can climb the 197 steps for a view of endless sand and sea. For more views, head 1km back to the main road to visit **Bornholmertårnet** (🖉40 20 52 40; www.bornholmertaarnet.dk; Strandmarksvejen 2; adult/child 75/50kr; ⊙10am-5pm May-Oct).

🔾 ACTIVITIES

Dueodde Beach Beach

(🚼) Dueodde's beach is a fantastic place for children: the water is generally calm and is shallow for about 100m, after which it becomes deep enough for adults to swim. During July and August it can be a crowded trek for a couple of hundred metres to reach the beach. Once there, simply head off to discover your own wide-open spaces.

⊗ EATING

You'll find a cheesy themed steakhouse and a couple of stock-standard kiosks selling ice cream, hot dogs and snacks at the end of the road by the bus stop.

For better food choices (and a supermarket), head to nearby Snogebæk.

GETTING THERE & AWAY

Two access roads head to Dueodde south from Strandmarksvejen. Bus 7 runs here.

Svaneke

Svaneke is a super-cute harbour town of red-tiled 19th-century buildings that has won international recognition for maintaining its historic character. Popular with yachters and landlubbing holidaymakers, its pretty harbourfront is lined with mustard-yellow half-timbered former merchants' houses, some of which have been turned into hotels and restaurants.

Svaneke is also home to plenty of fab island flavours: a renowned smokehouse a notable microbrewery, and beloved makers of gourmet liquorice, caramels and chocolates – all of which are highly recommended.

 SIGHTS

Glastorvet   Square
If you're interested in crafts, there are a number of ceramics and handicraft shops dotted around town, and at Glastorvet in the town centre there's a workshop of renowned local designer Pernille Bülow, where you can watch glass being melted into orange glowing lumps and then blown into clear, elegant glassware. This is a lovely spot to explore local flavours and artisans.

 EATING

Røgeriet i Svaneke   Seafood €
(☑56 49 63 24; www.roegerietsvaneke.dk; Fiskergade 12; snacks & meals 40-120kr; ⊙from 10am Apr-Oct) You'll find a fine selection of excellent smoked fare at the long counter here, including smørrebrød (Danish open

sandwiches), mackerel, trout, salmon, herring, shrimp and *fiskefrikadeller* (fish cakes). Sit inside with a view of the massive, blackened doors of the smoking ovens or at the outdoor picnic tables overlooking the old cannons, with a view of the five iconic chimneys.

Svaneke Chokoladeri   Sweets €
(☑56 49 70 21; www.svanekechokoladeri. dk; Svaneke Torv 5; flødeboller from 20kr; ⊙10.30am-5.30pm Mon-Fri, to 5pm Sat, 11am-5pm Sun; ⏺) Located at the entrance to Bryghuset is one of Bornholm's top chocolatiers. Made on the premises, the seductive concoctions include a very Bornholm *havtorn* (sea buckthorn) dark-choc truffle, and gourmet *flødeboller* (try the raspberry and liquorice combo).

There's also a store on Rønne's Store Torv.

Svanereden   International €
(☑50 50 72 35; www.svanereden.dk; Gruset 4; mains 75-120kr; ⊙10am-9pm mid-May–mid-Sep; ⏺) When the weather gods are smiling, this casual outdoor restaurant positioned above the harbour is a great spot to dine and unwind. The choices are simple and good (from champagne brunch to tapas platters to wok-fried dishes and stews cooked over an open fire). Kids are actively welcomed, and the views and atmosphere are tops.

DRINKING & NIGHTLIFE

Bryghuset   Microbrewery
(☑56 49 73 21; www.bryghuset-svaneke. dk; Svaneke Torv 5; lunch 79-139kr, dinner mains 169-299kr; ⊙11am-midnight, kitchen closes 8.30pm; ⏺) This is one of the most popular year-round dining and drinking hotspots on the island, known through-out Denmark for its excellent beers brewed on the premises. It also serves decent, hearty pub grub that pairs well

with its brews. Danish lunch classics include smørrebrød, *fiskefrikadeller* and a fine burger. Dinner mains are mostly juicy, fleshy affairs.

ℹ INFORMATION

Tourist Office (☎56 95 95 00; Peter F Heerings Gade 7; ⊙10am-4pm Tue-Sat mid-Jun–late Sep) is by the harbour.

ℹ GETTING THERE & AWAY

There are bike-rental places in town. Buses 3, 5, 7 and 8 pass through.

Gudhjem & Melsted

Gudhjem is the best-looking of Bornholm's harbour towns. Its rambling high street is crowned by a squat windmill standing over half-timbered houses and sloping streets that roll down to the picture-perfect harbour. The town is a good base for exploring the rest of Bornholm, with cycling and walking trails, convenient bus connections, plenty of places to eat and stay, and a boat service (p68) to Christiansø.

Melsted blends into Gudhjem just a short walk southeast of the town centre.

◉ SIGHTS

The area around Gudhjem harbours a number of cultural riches, including the island's impressive art museum (p58), it's most striking round church Østerlars Rundkirke (p59), and an intriguing medieval re-creation at Bornholms Middelaldercenter (p67).

Oluf Høst Museet   Museum
(☎56 48 50 38; www.ohmus.dk; Løkkegade 35; adult/child 75kr/free; ⊙11am-5pm Jun-Aug, Wed-Sun Sep & Oct; ⊕) This wonderful museum contains the workshops and paintings of Oluf Høst (1884–1966), one of Bornholm's best-known artists. The museum occupies the home where Høst lived from 1929 until his death. The beautiful back garden is home to a little hut with paper, paints and pencils for kids with a creative itch.

Røgeriet i Svaneke (p65)

MILOSZ MASLANKA/SHUTTERSTOCK ©

Bornholms Middelaldercenter
Museum

(☑56 49 83 19; www.bornholmsmiddelalder-center.dk; Stangevej 1, Østerlars; adult/child 140/70kr; ☉hours vary Easter–Oct; 👪) This 'Medieval Centre' re-creates a medieval fort and village, and gives the Danes another chance to do what they love best: dressing up in period costume and hitting each other with rubber swords. They also operate a smithy, tend fields, grind wheat in a water mill and perform other chores of yore throughout the summer months. In July the activity schedule is beefed up to include archery demonstrations and hands-on activities for children.

Baltic Sea Glass
Gallery

(☑56 48 56 41; www.balticseaglass.com; Melstedvej 47; ☉10am-5pm) Wherever you travel on Bornholm you will come across small independent ceramicists' and glass-blowers' studios. A couple of kilometres south of Gudhjem is one of the best: Baltic Sea Glass. It's a large, modern workshop and showroom with regularly changing exhibitions.

✪ ACTIVITIES

Gudhjem's shoreline is rocky, though sunbathers will find a small sandy **beach** at Melsted, 1km southeast.

A 5km **bike path** leads south from Gudhjem to the thick-walled, stoutly buttressed Østerlars Rundkirke (p59), the most impressive of the island's round churches.

M/S Thor
Boating

(☑56 48 51 65; www.ms-thor.dk; Gudhjem Havn; one-way/return 100/125kr; ☉from Gudhjem 11.30am May-Sep) Take a cruise along the coastline west of Gudhjem to view the rugged rock formations of Helligdomsklipperne. You can stay on the boat and return to Gudhjem, or disembark at the landing place by the cliffs and walk up to visit Bornholms Kunstmuseum (p58).

There are additional sailings in July and August.

 Walks Around the Gudhjem Area

A short five-minute climb up **Bokul,** the heather-covered hill, provides a fine view of Gudhjem town's red-tiled rooftops and out to sea.

From the hill at the southeastern end of Gudhjem harbour you'll be rewarded with a harbour view. You can continue along this path that runs above the shoreline 1.5km southeast to Melsted, where there's a little sandy beach. It's a delightful **nature trail**, with swallows, nightingales and wildflowers.

Heading west for around 6km takes you along the scenic elevated coastline of **Helligdomsklipperne** and to the excellent Bornholms Kunstmuseum (p58). The path *(sti)* heads along the coast from Nørresand.

View of Gudhjem from Bokul
BILDAGENTUR ZOONAR GMBH/SHUTTERSTOCK ©

✪ EATING

Norresan
Cafe €

(☑20 33 52 85; www.facebook.com/norresand; Nørresand 10; cake/sandwich 35/70kr; ☉11am-9pm Jul, shorter hours Apr-Jun & Aug-Oct) In a beautiful old smokehouse by the water (close to Oluf Høst Museet (p66)), this whitewashed cafe wins over visitors with views, home-baked cakes and cookies, tasty ice cream and a sweet ambience. Check its Facebook page for opening hours, and for details of visiting food trucks for sunset-watchers.

Gudhjem Røgeri
Seafood €

(☑56 48 57 08; www.smokedfish.dk; Ejnar Mikkelsensvej 9; dishes 64-115kr, buffet 130-185kr;

 **Christiansø
Wildlife Refuge**

Græsholm, the island to the north-west of Christiansø, is a wildlife refuge and an important breeding ground for guillemots, razorbills and other seabirds.

Together, Christiansø, Frederiksø and Græsholm are known as the Ertholmene Islands, and they serve as spring breeding grounds for up to 2000 eider ducks. The ducks nest near coastal paths and all visitors should take care not to scare mothers away from their nests because predator gulls will quickly swoop and attack the unattended eggs.

The islands also attract a colony of seals.

Guillemots and razorbills on Græsholm island
JOHNNY MADSEN/ALAMY STOCK PHOTO ©

⊗from 10am Apr-Oct) Gudhjem's popular smokehouse serves deli-style fish and salads, including the classic smørrebrød topping known as Sol over Gudhjem (Sun over Gudhjem: smoked herring topped with a raw egg yolk, chives and radish on rye bread). There's indoor and outdoor seating, and live music most nights in July and August.

**Stammershalle
Badehotel** Danish €€€

(Lassens; ☑56 48 42 10; www.stammer shalle-badehotel.dk; Søndre Strandvej 128, Stammershalle; small/large tasting menu 450/595kr; ⊗6-10pm May-Oct, Wed-Sat Mar &

Apr) An ode to relaxed Scandi elegance, the restaurant at **Stammershalle Badehotel** (s/d incl breakfast from 700/900kr; ⊗May-Oct, Wed-Sat Mar, Apr & Nov; P 🛜 🛉) is a local foodie hotspot. Service is knowledgeable and personable, and the sea-and-sunset panorama as inspired as the kitchen's creations. Bookings are essential.

ℹ️ INFORMATION

Tourist Office (☑56 95 95 00; Ejnar Mikkelsens-vej 27; ⊗10am-3.30pm Mon-Fri Jun-Aug) is a small building right by the harbour. It's staffed in summer, and open for self-service (brochures etc) for a few hours in the morning daily from mid-April to mid-October.

ℹ️ GETTING THERE & AWAY

BOAT

Christiansøfarten (☑56 48 51 76; www.chris tiansoefarten.dk; Ejnar Mikkelsensvej 25; Chris-tiansø return adult/child 250/125kr; ⊗hours vary) operates passenger ferries to Christiansø from Gudhjem. From July to late August, ferries depart Gudhjem daily at 10am, 12.30pm and 3pm; return ferries depart Christiansø at 2pm, 4.15pm and 7.30pm. Sailing time is around an hour. Note that there are fewer sailings outside peak summer.

In a gorgeous gesture, 10am sailings in summer are serenaded from Gudhjem's harbour by the local choir.

BUS

The main **bus stop** (Ejnar Mikkelsensvej) in Gudhjem is near the harbour. There are good bus links to other parts of the island.

Christiansø

If you think Bornholm is as remote as Denmark gets, you'd be wrong. Even further east, way out in the Baltic, is tiny Christiansø, an intensely atmospheric 17th-century island fortress about 500m long. It's an hour's sail northeast of

Bornholm (departing from Gudhjem), and makes a lovely and idyllic day-trip destination.

There is something of the Faroe Islands about Christiansø's landscape (on a much less epic scale, of course), with its rugged, moss-covered rocks, historic stone buildings and even hardier people. There is a real sense, too, that you are travelling back in time when you visit here.

◉ SIGHTS

The main sightseeing on Christiansø is provided by the walk along the fortified **stone walls** and cannon-lined batteries that mark the island's perimeter.

There are reefs with nesting seabirds and a couple of secluded swimming coves on Christiansø's eastern side. On the western side, a footbridge links Christiansø with the small neighbouring island of **Frederiksø**. Frederiksø's west coast has a swimming jetty and bird-watching spots.

⊗ EATING

Christiansø Gæstgiveri (☎56 46 20 15; www.christiansoekro.dk; s/d 1150/1250kr; ☉closed late Dec-Jan) serves meals, and there's a snack kiosk next door selling hot dogs and ice cream (open May to September).

ⓘ INFORMATION

Information is online at www.christiansoe.dk.

Dogs or other pets are forbidden on Christiansø.

ⓘ GETTING THERE & AWAY

Christiansøfarten (☎56 48 51 76; www. christiansoefarten.dk; return ticket adult/child 250/125kr; ☉mid-Apr–late Oct) operates passenger ferries to Christiansø from Gudhjem.

Sandvig & Allinge

Sandvig is a genteel seaside hamlet with storybook older homes, many fringed by

Christiansø

Hammershus Slotsruin

rose bushes and flower gardens. It's fronted by a gorgeous sandy bay and borders a network of walking trails throughout the Hammeren area and southwest to Hammershus.

Allinge, the larger and more developed half of the Allinge-Sandvig municipality, is 2km southeast of Sandvig.

◎ SIGHTS

Hammershus Slotsruin   Ruins

(Slotslyngvej) **FREE** The impressive ruins of Hammershus Slot, dramatically perched on top of a cliff 74m above the sea, are the largest in Scandinavia. The castle was thought to have been built in the early 1300s, and a walk through the evocative site, enjoying the views, is a must for Bornholm visitors. The grounds are always open and admission is free. A smart new **visitor centre** is being built, sympathetic to the surrounds (opening 2018; likely with an admission fee for exhibits).

Hammeren   Nature Reserve

Hammeren, the hammerhead-shaped crag of granite at the northern tip of Bornholm, is criss-crossed by **walking trails** leading through hillsides thick with purple heather. Some of the trails are inland, while others run along the coast. The whole area is a delight for people who enjoy nature walks.

Olsker Rundkirke   Church

(Sankt Ols Kirke; Rønnevej 51, Olsker; 10kr; ⊘10am-5pm Mon-Fri May-Oct) Five kilometres south of central Allinge, on the southern outskirts of the small village of Olsker, is the highest (26m) and most slender of the island's four round churches. If you take the inland bus 1 between Rønne and Allinge, you can stop off en route.

ENTERTAINMENT

Gæsten   Live Music

(www.gaestgiveren.dk; Theaterstræde 2,
Allinge; ticket prices vary; ⊙bar from 5pm,
concerts from 8pm Mon-Sat Jul-early Aug) This
summertime institution offers live music
six nights a week in peak summer; see the
program and buy tickets online, or tickets
are generally also available at the door.
There's usually a party atmosphere in the
courtyard, and also a fine vegetarian buffet
from 6pm (160kr; meat and fish dishes
available too).

⊗ **EATING**

Kalas-Kalas   Cafe €

(☑60 19 13 84; www.kalasbornholm.dk;
Strandpromenaden 14, Sandvig; 2/3 ice-cream
scoops 34/44kr, coffee 30-40kr; ⊙11am-10pm
late Jun–mid-Aug, shorter hours rest of year)
The perfect island combination: great
coffee, handmade ice cream the locals
queue for, picture-perfect rocky coastline
out the windows, and beanbags on the
terrace for sunset cocktails. Ice-cream
flavours come courtesy of local gardens
and fields: elderflower, rhubarb, redcur-
rant, various berries. Ask here about boat
trips and snorkelling tours run by the
owners' sons (www.boatingbornholm.
dk). Check the website for hours.

Nordbornholms Røgeri   Seafood €

(☑56 48 07 30; www.nbr.dk; Kæmpestranden
2, Allinge; dishes 60-115kr, buffet 189kr;
⊙11am-10pm; 🐾) Several of Bornholm's
top chefs praise this smokehouse as
the island's best. Not only does it serve
a bumper buffet of locally smoked fish,
salads and soup (ice-cream dessert
included), but its waterside setting makes

 The Windmills of Denmark

The easternmost town in Denmark,
Svaneke is quite breezy and has a number
of windmills. To the northwest of town,
around Møllebakken, you'll find an old
post mill (a type of mill that turns in its
entirety to face the wind) and a **Dutch
mill**, as well as an unusual three-sided
water tower designed in the 1950s by
architect Jørn Utzon (of Sydney's Opera
House fame).

On the main road 3km south of Svaneke
in the hamlet of **Årsdale**, there's a working
windmill where grains are ground and sold.

Årsdale windmill

it the perfect spot to savour Bornholm's
Baltic flavours.

ⓘ **INFORMATION**

Tourist Office (☑56 95 95 00; Sverigesvej 11,
Allinge; ⊙11am-5pm Mon-Fri, 10am-4pm Sat &
Sun Jul & Aug, shorter hours rest of year) is a
helpful spot, by the harbour in Allinge.

ⓘ **GETTING THERE & AWAY**

There are decent bus connections: bus 1 runs
frequently from Rønne, bus 4 from Gudhjem.

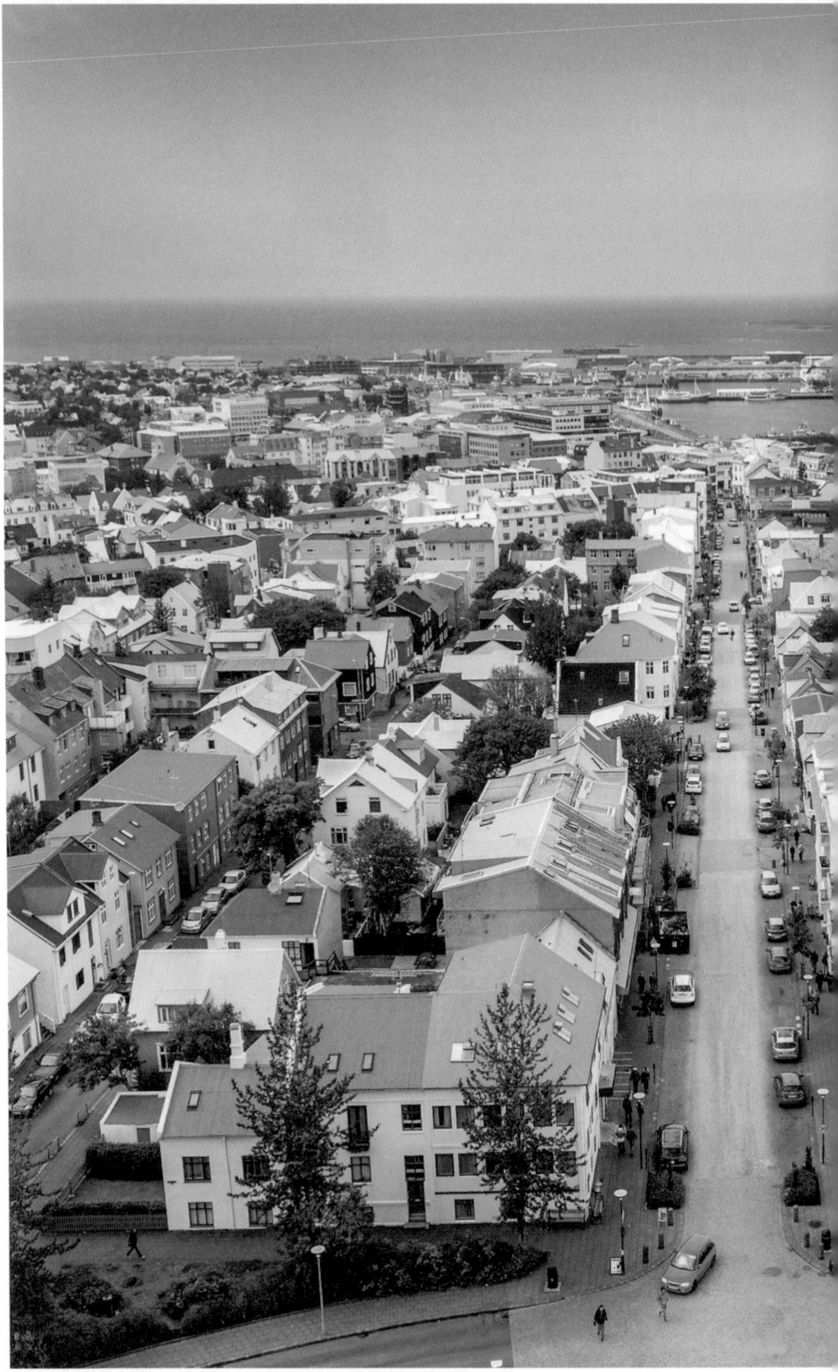

ALEXEY STIOP/SHUTTERSTOCK ©

REYKJAVÍK

In this Chapter

Reykjavík at a Glance...

Reykjavík is loaded with captivating art, rich cuisine and quirky, creative people. The music scene is epic, with excellent festivals, creative DJs and any number of home-grown bands. Even if you come for a short visit, be sure to take a trip to the countryside. Tours and services abound, and understanding Reykjavík and its people is helped by understanding the vast, raw and gorgeous land they anchor. The majority of Icelanders live in the capital, but you can guarantee their spirits also roam free across the land. Absorb what you see, hear, taste, smell – it's all part of Iceland's rich heritage.

Two Days in Reykjavík

Spend the morning exploring historic **Old Reykjavík** (p85) and afternoon shopping and sightseeing along arty **Skólavörðustígur** (p84). Head to **Laugavegur** (p84) for dinner, drinks and late-night dancing.

On day two, catch a **whale-watching cruise** (p85) or explore the **Old Harbour** (p85) and its museums in the morning. While away the afternoon at **Laugardalur** (p87) and your evening at a top Icelandic restaurant (p87).

Four Days in Reykjavík

On day three, rent a bike at the Old Harbour and ferry out to historic **Viðey** (www.videy.com), heading back for last-minute shopping in **Laugavegur** (p84) and **Skólavörðustígur** (p84). Sample the area's seafood then catch a show, an Icelandic movie or some live music.

On day four take a trip to the **Golden Circle** (p80). Visit the **Blue Lagoon** (p78) later in the evening, after the crowds have dwindled.

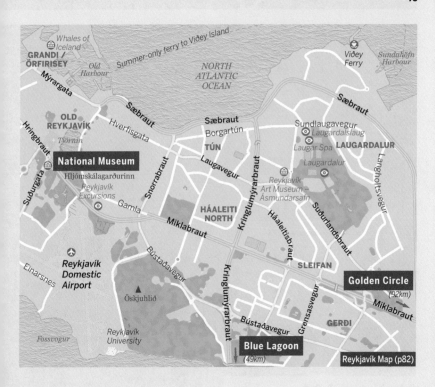

National Museum

Golden Circle (92km)

Blue Lagoon (49km)

Reykjavík Map (p82)

Arriving in Reykjavík

Keflavík International Airport Iceland's primary international airport is 48km west of Reykjavík.

Reykjavík Domestic Airport Only a 2km walk into town.

Smyril Line (www.smyrilline.com) operates a pricey but well-patronised weekly car ferry from Hirtshals (Denmark) through Tórshavn (Faroe Islands) to Seyðisfjörður in East Iceland. It's possible to make a stopover in the Faroes.

Where to Stay

Reykjavík has loads of accommodation choices, with hostels, midrange guesthouses (often with shared bathrooms, kitchen and lounge) and business-class hotels galore, and top-end boutique hotels and apartments seem to be opening daily. Reservations are essential from June through August and prices are high. Plan for hostels, camping or short-term apartment rentals to save money. Most places open year-round and offer discounts online.

VLADIMIR KOROSTYSHEVSKIY/SHUTTERSTOCK ©

National Museum

Iceland's premier museum is packed with artefacts and interesting displays. Exhibits give an excellent overview of the country's history and culture, and the audio guide (kr300) adds loads of detail.

The superb National Museum beautifully displays Icelandic artefacts from settlement to the modern age, providing a meaningful overview of Iceland's history and culture. Brilliantly curated exhibits lead you through the struggle to settle and organise the forbidding island, the radical changes wrought by the advent of Christianity, the lean times of domination by foreign powers and Iceland's eventual independence.

Settlement Era Finds

The premier section of the museum describes the Settlement Era – including how the chieftains ruled and the introduction of Christianity – and features swords, meticulously carved **drinking horns**, and **silver hoards**. A powerful **bronze figure of Thor** is thought to date to about 1000. The priceless

Great For...

Don't Miss

The gaming pieces made from cod ear bones, and the wooden doll that doubled as a kitchen utensil.

❶ Need to Know

National Museum (Þjóðminjasafn Íslands; ☏530 2200; www.nationalmuseum.is; Suðurgata 41; adult/child kr2000/free; ☉10am-5pm May−mid-Sep, closed Mon mid-Sep−Apr; ☐1, 3, 6, 12, 14)

✕ Take a Break

The ground-floor **Museum Café** (National Museum, Suðurgata 41; snacks kr600-1800; ☉10am-5pm May−mid-Sep, 9am-5pm Tue-Fri, 11am-5pm Sat & Sun mid-Sep−Apr; ☎) offers wi-fi and a welcome respite.

★ Top Tip

Free English tours run at 11am on Wednesday, Saturday and Sunday, May to mid-September.

13th-century **Valþjófsstaður church door** is carved with the story of a knight, his faithful lion and a posse of dragons.

Domestic Life

Exhibits explain how the chieftains ruled and how people survived on little, lighting their dark homes and fashioning bog iron. There's everything from the remains of early *skyr* (yoghurt-like dessert) production to intricate pendants and brooches. Look for the Viking−era **hnefatafl game set** (a bit like chess); this artefact's discovery in a grave in Baldursheimur led to the founding of the museum.

Viking Graves

Encased in the floor are Viking−era graves, with their precious burial goods: horse bones, a sword, pins, a ladle and a comb. One of the tombs containing an eight-month-old infant is the only one of its kind ever found.

Ecclesiastical Artefacts

The section of the museum that details the introduction of Christianity is chock-a-block with rare art and artefacts such as the priceless 13th-century **Valþjófsstaður church door**.

The Modern Era

Upstairs, collections span from 1600 to today and give a clear sense of how Iceland struggled under foreign rule, finally gained independence and went on to modernise. Look for the **papers and belongings of Jón Sigurðsson**, the architect of Iceland's independence.

Blue Lagoon

In a magnificent black-lava field, this scenic spa is fed water from the futuristic Svartsengi geothermal plant. With its silver towers, roiling clouds of steam and people daubed in white silica mud, it's an other-worldly place.

Great For...

Don't Miss

A bike or quad-bike tour in the lava fields.

A Good Soak

Before your dip, don't forget to practise standard Iceland pool etiquette: thorough, naked pre-pool showering.

The super-heated spa water (70% sea water, 30% fresh water) is rich in blue-green algae, mineral salts and fine silica mud, which condition and exfoliate the skin – sounds like advertising speak, but you really do come out as soft as a baby's bum. The water is hottest near the vents where it emerges, and the surface is several degrees warmer than the bottom.

Towel or bathing-suit hire is €5.

Explore the Complex

The lagoon has been developed for visitors: there's an enormous, modern complex of changing rooms (with 700 lockers!), restaurants and a gift shop. It is also

❶ Need to Know

Blue Lagoon (Bláa Lónið; ☎420 8800; www.bluelagoon.com; adult/child from kr6990/free; ⏰7am–midnight Jul–mid-Aug, 7am–11pm mid-May–Jun, 8am–10pm Jan–mid-May & mid-Aug–Sep, 8am–9pm Oct-Dec)

✕ Take a Break

Try on-site **Blue Café** (snacks kr1000-2100; ⏰8am-midnight Jun–mid-Aug, reduced hours mid-Aug–May; 🛜) or **LAVA Restaurant** (mains lunch/dinner kr4500/5900; ⏰11.30am-9.30pm Jun-Aug, to 8.30pm Sep-May; 🛜).

★ Top Tip

In summer avoid from 10am to 2pm – go early or after 7pm.

landscaped with hot-pots, steam rooms, a sauna, a silica-mask station, a bar and a piping-hot waterfall that delivers a powerful hydraulic massage. A VIP section has its own interior wading space, lounge and viewing platform.

Massage

For extra relaxation, lie on a floating mattress and have a massage therapist knead your knots (30/60 minutes €75/120). Book spa treatments well in advance; look online for packages and winter rates.

Guided Tours

In addition to the spa opportunities at the Blue Lagoon, you can combine your visit with package tours, or hook up with nearby **ATV Adventures** (☎857 3001; www. atv4x4.is) for quad-bike or cycling tours

(kr9900 from the Blue Lagoon through the lava fields) or bicycle rental. The company can pick you up and drop you off at the lagoon.

Planning Your Visit

Many day trips from Reykjavík tie in a visit to the lagoon, which is 47km southwest of the city. It's also seamless to visit on your journey to/from Keflavík International Airport (there's a luggage check-in in the car park, kr600 per bag, per day).

You should book ahead or risk being turned away. On a tour, always determine whether your ticket for the lagoon is included or if you need to book it separately.

Reykjavík Excursions (Kynnisferðir; ☎580 5400; www.re.is; BSÍ Bus Terminal, Vatnsmýrarvegur 10) and **Bustravel** (☎511 2600; www.bustravel.is) connect the lagoon with Reykjavík and the airport.

Þingvellir National Park

Golden Circle

The Golden Circle is a beloved tourist circuit that takes in three popular attractions all within 100km of the capital: Þingvellir, Geysir and Gullfoss.

Great For...

Don't Miss

The Sigríður memorial near the foot of the stairs from the Gullfoss visitors centre.

The Golden Circle offers the opportunity to see a meeting-point of the continental plates and the site of the ancient Icelandic parliament (Þingvellir), a spouting hot spring (Geysir) and a roaring waterfall (Gullfoss), all in one doable-in-a-day loop.

Visiting under your own steam allows you to visit at off-hours and explore exciting attractions further afield. Almost every tour company in the Reykjavík area offers a Golden Circle excursion, which can often be combined with virtually any activity, from quad-biking to caving and rafting.

If you're planning to spend the night in the relatively small region, **Laugarvatn** is a good base with excellent dining options.

Þingvellir National Park

Þingvellir National Park (www.thingvellir. is), 40km northeast of central Reykjavík,

Strokkur geyser

HEMN PHOTOGRAPHY/GETTY IMAGES ©

❶ Need to Know

Tours generally go from 8.30am to 6pm or from noon to 7pm. In summer there are evening trips from 7pm to midnight.

✕ Take a Break

Eateries, mini-marts and grocery stores dot the route.

★ Top Tip

To go on to West Iceland afterwards, complete the Circle backwards, finishing with Þingvellir.

is Iceland's most important historical site and a place of vivid beauty. The Vikings established the world's first democratic parliament, the **Alþingi**, here in AD 930. The meetings were conducted outdoors and, as with many Saga sites, there are only the stone foundations of ancient **encampments**. The site has a superb natural setting, with rivers and waterfalls in an immense, fissured rift valley, caused by the meeting of the North American and Eurasian **tectonic plates**.

Geysir

One of Iceland's most famous tourist attractions, **Geysir** FREE (gay-zeer; literally 'gusher') is the original hot-water spout after which all other geysers are named. Earthquakes can stimulate activity, though eruptions are rare. Luckily for visitors, the

very reliable **Strokkur** geyser sits alongside. You rarely have to wait more than five to 10 minutes for the hot spring to shoot an impressive 15m to 30m plume before vanishing down its enormous hole. Stand downwind only if you want a shower.

At the time of writing, the geothermal area containing Geysir and Strokkur was free to enter, though there is talk of instituting a fee.

Gullfoss

Iceland's most famous waterfall, **Gullfoss** (Golden Falls; www.gullfoss.is) FREE is a spectacular double cascade. It drops 32m, kicking up tiered walls of spray before thundering away down a narrow ravine. On sunny days the mist creates shimmering rainbows, and it's also magical in winter when the falls glitter with ice.

A tarmac path suitable for wheelchairs leads from the tourist information centre to a lookout over the falls, and stairs continue down to the edge. There is also an access road down to the falls.

Reykjavík

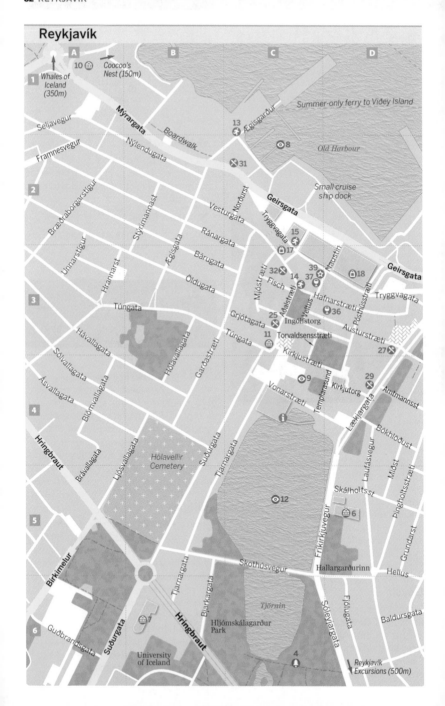

Whales of Iceland (350m)

10

Coocoo's Nest (150m)

Mýrargata

Seljavegur

Framnesvegur

Nýlendugata

Boardwalk

Ægisgarður

13

Summer-only ferry to Viðey Island

8

Old Harbour

31

Small cruise ship dock

Geirsgata

Vesturgata

Norðurst

Tryggvagata

Bræðraborgarstígur

Styrimannst

Ránargata

Bárugata

Öldugata

15

17

Geirsgata

Unnarstígur

Hrannarst

Ægisgata

Mjóstræti

32

Fisch

14

39

37

18

Naustin

Túngata

Hávallagata

Hólavallagata

Garðastræti

Grjótagata

Adalstræti

25

Ingólfstorg

Veltus

Hafnarstræti

36

Pósthússtræti

Tryggvagata

Sólvallagata

Ásvallagata

Björnvallagata

Ljósvallagata

Túngata

11

Torvaldsensstræti

Kirkjustræti

Austurstræti

27

Hringbraut

Brávallagata

Suðurgata

9

Vonarstræti

Templarasund

Kirkjutorg

Kirkjutorg

29

Amtmannsst

Lækjargata

Bókhlöðust

Hólavellir Cemetery

Tjarnargata

12

Skálholtsst

6

Laufásvegur

Mjóst

þingholtsstræti

Grundarst

Birkimelur

Tjarnargata

Blátragata

Hringbraut

Skothúsvegur

Frikirkjuvegur

Hallargarðurinn

Hellus

Guðbrandsgata

Suðurgata

7

Hljómskálagarður Park

Tjörnin

Sóleyjargata

Flólugata

Baldursgata

University of Iceland

4

Reykjavík Excursions (500m)

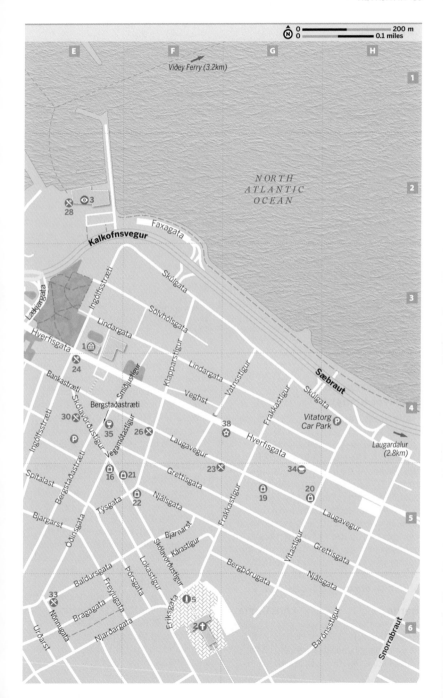

Viðey Ferry (3.2km)

NORTH ATLANTIC OCEAN

Faxagata

Kalkofnsvegur

Laugavegur

Lækjargata

Ingólfsstræti

Skúlagata

Sölvhólsgata

Lindargata

Hverfisgata

1

24

Bankastræti

Skólavörðustígur

Bergstaðastræti

30

35

26

Klapparstígur

Lindargata

Vatnsstígur

Veghst

Frakkastígur

Skúlagata

Sæbraut

Vitatorg
Car Park

38

Hverfisgata

Laugardalur
(2.8km)

Ingólfsstræti

Vegamótastígur

23

34

20

Spítalast

Bergstaðastr

Grettisgata

16

21

Njálsgata

22

Frakkastígur

19

Laugavegur

Bjargarst

Óðinsgata

Týsgata

Vitastígur

Grettisgata

Bjarnarst

Skólavörðustígur

Kárastígur

Bergþórugata

Njálsgata

Baldursgata

Freyjugata

Þórsgata

Lokastígur

33

Nönnugata

Bragagata

Eiríksgata

5

2

Barónsstígur

Urðarst

Njarðargata

Snorrabraut

0   200 m
0   0.1 miles

Reykjavík

Sights

1	Culture House	E3
2	Hallgrímskirkja	F6
3	Harpa	E2
4	Hljómskálagarður Park	C6
5	Leifur Eiríksson Statue	F6
6	National Gallery of Iceland	D5
7	National Museum	B6
8	Old Harbour	C2
9	Old Reykjavík	C4
10	Saga Museum	A1
11	Settlement Exhibition	C3
12	Tjörnin	C5

Activities, Courses & Tours

13	Elding Adventures at Sea	C1
14	Haunted Iceland	C3
15	Literary Reykjavík	C2

Shopping

16	Geysir	E5
17	Kirsuberjatréð	C3
18	Kolaportið Flea Market	D3
19	Kron	G5
20	KronKron	G5
21	Orrifinn	F5
22	Skúmaskot	F5

Eating

23	Bakarí Sandholt	F5
24	Dill	E4
25	Fiskmarkaðurinn	C3
26	Gló	F4
27	Grillmarkaðurinn	D3
28	Kolabrautin	E2
	Matur og Drykkur	(see 10)
29	Messinn	D4
	National Museum Café	(see 7)
30	Ostabúðin	E4
31	Sægreifinn	C2
32	Stofan Kaffihús	C3
33	Þrír Frakkar	E6

Drinking & Nightlife

34	Kaffi Vínyl	G5
35	Kaffibarinn	E4
	Kaldi	(see 26)
36	Loftið	D3
	Micro Bar	(see 14)
	Mikkeller & Friends	(see 24)
37	Paloma	C3

Entertainment

38	Bíó Paradís	G4
39	Húrra	C3

SIGHTS

Laugavegur & Skólavörðustígur

Hallgrímskirkja — Church

(☎510 1000; www.hallgrimskirkja.is; Skólavörðustígur; tower adult/child kr900/100; ⌚9am-9pm Jun-Sep, to 5pm Oct-May) Reykjavík's immense white-concrete church (1945–86), star of a thousand postcards, dominates the skyline, and is visible from up to 20km away. Get an unmissable view of the city by taking an elevator trip up the 74.5m-high **tower**. In contrast to the high drama outside, the Lutheran church's interior is quite plain. The most eye-catching feature is the vast 5275-pipe **organ** installed in 1992.

Harpa — Arts Centre

(☎box office 528 5050; www.harpa.is; Austurbakki 2; ⌚8am-midnight, box office 10am-6pm) With its ever-changing facets glistening on the water's edge, Reykjavík's sparkling Harpa concert hall and cultural centre is a beauty to behold. In addition to a season of top-notch shows (some free), it's worth stopping by to explore the shimmering interior with harbour vistas, or take one of the guided tours and visit areas not open to the general public (see website for daily times and prices).

Culture House — Gallery

(Þjóðmenningarhúsið; ☎530 2210; www.culturehouse.is; Hverfisgata 15; adult/child incl National Museum kr2000/free; ⌚10am-5pm May–mid-Sep, closed Mon mid-Sep–Apr) This superbly curated exhibition covers the artistic and cultural heritage of Iceland from settlement to today. Priceless artefacts are arranged by theme, and highlights include 14th-century manuscripts, contemporary art and items including the skeleton of a great auk (now extinct). The renovated 1908 building is beautiful, with great views of the harbour, and a cafe on the ground floor. Check website for free guided tours.

National Gallery of Iceland
Museum

(Listasafn Íslands; 515 9600; www.listas afn.is; Fríkirkjuvegur 7; adult/child kr1500/ free; 10am-5pm daily mid-May–mid-Sep, 11am-5pm Tue-Sun mid-Sep–mid-May) This pretty stack of marble atriums and spacious galleries overlooking Tjörnin offers ever-changing exhibits drawn from the 10,000-piece collection. The museum can only exhibit a small sample at any time; shows range from 19th- and 20th-century paintings by Iceland's favourite sons and daughters (including Jóhannes Kjarval and Nína Sæmunds- son) to sculptures by Sigurjón Ólafsson and others.

◎ Old Harbour

Saga Museum
Museum

(511 1517; www.sagamuseum.is; Grandagarður 2; adult/child kr2100/800; 10am-6pm; 14) The endearingly blood- thirsty Saga Museum is where Icelandic history is brought to life by eerie silicon models and a multi-language soundtrack with thudding axes and hair-raising screams. Don't be surprised if you see some of the characters wandering around town, as moulds were taken from Rey- kjavík residents (the owner's daughters are the Irish princess and the little slave gnawing a fish!).

There's also a cafe, and a room for pos- ing in Viking dress.

Whales of Iceland
Museum

(571 0077; www.whalesoficeland.is; Fiskislóð 23-25; adult/child kr2900/1500; 10am-5pm; 14) Ever stroll beneath a blue whale? This museum houses full-sized models of the 23 species of whale found off Ice- land's coast. The largest museum of this type in Europe, it also displays models of whale skeletons, and has good audio guides and multimedia screens to explain what you're seeing. It has a cafe and gift shop, online ticket discounts and family tickets (kr5800).

◎ Old Reykjavík

Settlement Exhibition
Museum

(Landnámssýningin; 411 6370; www.reykjavik museum.is; Aðalstræti 16; adult/child kr1600/ free; 9am-6pm) This fascinating archae- ological ruin/museum is based around a 10th-century **Viking longhouse** un- earthed here from 2001 to 2002, and the other Settlement Era finds from central Reykjavík. It imaginatively combines tech- nological wizardry and archaeology to give a glimpse into early Icelandic life.

Tjörnin
Lake

This placid lake at the centre of the city is sometimes locally called the Pond. It ech- oes with the honks and squawks of more than 40 species of visiting birds, including swans, geese and Arctic terns; feeding the ducks is a popular pastime for the un- der-fives. Pretty sculpture-dotted parks like **Hljómskálagarður** line the southern shores, and their paths are much used by cyclists and joggers. In winter hardy souls strap on ice skates and turn the lake into an **outdoor rink**.

✪ ACTIVITIES

Literary Reykjavík
Walking

(www.bokmenntaborgin.is; Tryggvagata 15; 3pm Thu Jun-Aug) FREE Part of the Une- sco City of Literature initiative, free liter- ary walking tours of the city centre start at the main library and include the Dark Deeds tour focusing on crime fiction. There is also a downloadable Culture Walks app with several themes.

Elding Adventures at Sea
Wildlife

(519 5000; www.whalewatching.is; Ægis- garður 5; adult/child kr11,000/5500; har- bour kiosk 8am-9pm; 14) ✔ The city's most established and ecofriendly outfit, with an included whale exhibition and refresh- ments sold on board. Elding also offers angling (adult/child kr13,800/6900) and puffin-watching (adult/child from kr6500/3250) trips and combo tours, and runs the ferry to Viðey. Offers pick-up.

Haunted Iceland
Walking

(www.hauntedwalk.is; adult/child kr2500/free; ⊙8pm Sat-Thu Jun-early Sep) Ninety-minute tour, including folklore and ghost spotting, departing from the Main Tourist Office.

🅰 SHOPPING

Laugavegur and Skólavörðustígur are the central streets of Reykjavík's shopping scene. You'll find them densely lined with everything from stereotypical souvenir shops (derisively called 'Puffin Shops' by Reykjavikers) to design shops and galleries selling beautiful handmade Icelandic arts and crafts, couture clothing lines and cool outdoorwear.

Geysir
Clothing

(⊠519 6000; www.geysir.com; Skólavörðustígur 16; ⊙10am-7pm Mon-Sat, 11am-6pm Sun) For traditional Icelandic clothing and unique modern designs,

Geysir boasts an elegant selection of sweaters, blankets, and men's and women's clothes, shoes and bags.

KronKron
Clothing

(⊠561 9388; www.kronkron.com; Laugavegur 63b; ⊙10am-6pm Mon-Thu, to 6.30pm Fri, to 5pm Sat) This is where Reykjavík goes high fashion, with the likes of Marc Jacobs and Vivienne Westwood. But we really enjoy its Scandinavian designers (including Kron by KronKron) offering silk dresses, knit capes, scarves and even wool underwear. Its handmade shoes are off the charts; the shoes are also sold down the street at **Kron** (⊠551 8388; www.kron. is; Laugavegur 48; ⊙10am-6pm Mon-Fri, to 5pm Sat).

Orrifinn
Jewellery

(⊠789 7616; www.orrifinn.com; Skólavörðustígur 17a; ⊙10am-6pm Mon-Fri, 11am-4pm Sat) Subtle, beautiful jewellery captures the natural wonder of Iceland and its Viking history. Delicate anchors, axes and pen nibs dangle from understated matte chains.

Skúmaskot

Skúmaskot

Arts & Crafts

(📞663 1013; www.facebook.com/skumaskot.art. design; Skólavörðustígur 21a; ⊙10am-6pm Mon-Fri, to 5pm Sat) Ten local designers create these unique handmade porcelain items, women's and kids' clothing, paintings and cards. It's in a recently renovated large gallery beautifully showcasing their creative Icelandic crafts.

Kolaportið Flea Market

Market

(www.kolaportid.is; Tryggvagata 19; ⊙11am-5pm Sat & Sun) Held in a huge industrial building by the harbour, this weekend market is a Reykjavík institution. There's a huge tumble of second-hand clothes and old toys, plus cheap imports. There's also a food section that sells traditional eats like *rúgbrauð* (geothermally baked rye bread), *brauðterta* ('sandwich cake', a layering of bread with mayonnaise-based fillings) and *hákarl* (fermented shark).

Kirsuberjatréð

Arts & Crafts

(Cherry Tree; 📞562 8990; www.kirs.is; Vesturgata 4; ⊙10am-6pm Mon-Fri, to 5pm Sat & Sun) This women's art-and-design collective in an interesting 1882 former bookshop sells weird and wonderful fish-skin handbags, music boxes made from string, and, our favourite, beautiful coloured bowls made from radish slices.

✖ EATING

✖ Laugavegur & Skólavörðustígur

Bakarí Sandholt

Bakery €

(📞551 3524; www.sandholt.is; Laugavegur 36; snacks kr600-1200; ⊙7am-9pm; 📶) Reykjavík's favourite bakery is usually crammed with folks hoovering up the generous assortment of fresh baguettes, croissants, pastries and sandwiches. The soup of the day (kr1540) comes with delicious sourdough bread.

Gló

Organic, Vegetarian €

(📞553 1111; www.glo.is; Laugavegur 20b; mains kr1400-2000; ⊙11am-9pm Mon-Fri, 11.30am-9pm Sat & Sun; 📶🖊) Join the cool cats in this

〰️ Laugardalur: Hot-Springs Valley

On a verdant stretch of land 4km east of the city centre, **Laugardalur** (🚌2, 5, 14, 15, 17) was once the main source of Reykjavík's hot-water supply, and relics from the old wash house remain. It's a favourite with locals for its huge **swimming complex** (📞411 5100; www. reykjavik.is/stadir/laugardalslaug; Sundlaugavegur 30a, Laugardalur; adult/child kr950/150, suit/towel rental kr850/570; ⊙6.30am-10pm Mon-Fri, 8am-10pm Sat & Sun; 🏊), fed by the geothermal spring, alongside a **spa** (📞553 0000; www.laugarspa.com; day pass kr5500; ⊙6am-11pm Mon-Fri, 8am-9.30pm Sat & Sun), a skating rink, botanical gardens, sporting and concert arenas, and a kids' zoo and entertainment park.

Stop by the sun-dappled tables of **Café Flóra** (Flóran; 📞553 8872; www.floran.is; Botanic Gardens; cakes kr10,000, mains kr1500-3100; ⊙10am-10pm May-Sep; 🖊) 🖊 for lovely food made from local ingredients, some from the park's own gardens. Soups come with fantastic sourdough bread, and snacks range from cheese platters with nuts and honey to pulled-pork sandwiches. Weekend brunch, good coffee and homemade cakes round it all out.

Nearby are **Frú Lauga farmers market** (📞534 7165; www.frulauga.is; Laugalækur 6; ⊙11am-6pm Mon-Fri, to 4pm Sat; 🖊) 🖊 and **Reykjavík Art Museum – Ásmundarsafn** (Ásmundur Sveinsson Museum; 📞411 6430; www.artmuseum.is; Sigtún; adult/child kr1600/free; ⊙10am-5pm May-Sep, 1-5pm Oct-Apr; 🚌2, 4, 14, 15, 17, 19).

Café Flóra

Partying in Reykjavík

Reykjavík's renowned *djammið* is the lively surge of drinkers and partyers through central Reykjavík's streets, pubs and dance clubs. Thanks to the high price of alcohol, things generally don't get going until late. Icelanders brave the melee at government alcohol store **Vínbúðin** (www.vinbudin. is; Austurstræti 10a; ⊙11am-6pm Mon-Thu & Sat, to 7pm Fri), then toddle home for a pre-pub party before hitting the streets.

VVOE/SHUTTERSTOCK ©

upstairs, airy restaurant serving fresh, large daily specials loaded with Asian–influenced herbs and spices. Though not exclusively vegetarian, it's a wonderland of raw and organic foods with your choice from a broad bar of elaborate salads, from root veggies to Greek. It also has branches in **Laugard-alur** (✆553 1111; www.glo.is; Engjateigur 19; mains kr1250-2000; ⊙11am-9pm Mon-Fri; 🖥🅟) 🍃 and **Kópavogur** (www.glo.is; Hæðasmári 6; mains kr1300-2300; ⊙11am-9pm Mon-Fri, 11.30am-9pm Sat & Sun; 🖥🅟) 🍃.

Ostabúðin   Deli €€

(Cheese Shop; ✆562 2772; www.ostabudin. is; Skólavörðustígur 8; mains kr3750-5000; ⊙restaurant noon-10pm, deli 10am-6pm Mon-Thu, to 7pm Fri, 11am-4pm Sat) Head to this gourmet cheese shop and deli, with a large dining room, for the friendly owner's cheese and meat platters (from kr1900 to kr4000), or the catch of the day, accompanied by homemade bread.

You can pick up other local goods, like terrines and duck confit, on the way out.

Dill   Icelandic €€€

(✆552 1522; www.dillrestaurant.is; Hverfisga-ta 12; 5-course meals from kr12,000; ⊙6-10pm Wed-Sat) Top New Nordic cuisine is the major drawcard at this elegant yet simple bistro. The focus is very much on the food – locally sourced produce served as a parade of courses. The owners are friends with Copenhagen's famous Noma clan, and take Icelandic cuisine to similarly heady heights. Reservation is a must.

Þrír Frakkar   Icelandic, Seafood €€€

(✆552 3939; www.3frakkar.com; Baldursgata 14; mains kr4000-6000; ⊙11.30am-2.30pm & 6-10pm Mon-Fri, 6-11pm Sat & Sun) Own-er-chef Úlfar Eysteinsson has built up a consistently excellent reputation at this snug little restaurant – apparently a favourite of Jamie Oliver's. Specialities range throughout the aquatic world from salt cod and halibut to *plokkfiskur* (fish stew) with black bread. Non-fish items run towards guillemot, horse, lamb and whale.

Old Harbour

Sægreifinn   Seafood €

(Seabaron; ✆553 1500; www.saegreifinn.is; Geirsgata 8; mains kr1350-1900; ⊙11.30am-11pm mid-May–Aug, to 10pm Sep–mid-May) Sidle into this green harbourside shack for the most famous lobster soup (kr1350) in the capital, or to choose from a fridge full of fresh fish skewers to be grilled on the spot.

Coocoo's Nest   Cafe €€

(✆552 5454; www.coocoosnest.is; Grandagarður 23; mains kr1700-4500; ⊙11am-10pm Tue-Sat, to 4pm Sun; 🖥) Pop into this cool eatery tucked behind the Old Harbour for popular weekend brunches (dishes kr1700 to kr2200; 11am to 4pm Friday to Sunday) paired with decadent cocktails (kr1300). Casual, small and groovy, with mosaic plywood tables;

the menu changes and there are nightly themes, but it's always scrumptious.

Matur og Drykkur   Icelandic €€

(⏩571 8877; www.maturogdrykkur.is; Grandagarður 2; lunch mains kr1900-2700, dinner mains/tasting menus kr3700/10,000; ⏲11.30am-3pm & 6-10pm Mon-Sat, 6-10pm Sun; 🚌14) One of Reykjavík's top high-concept restaurants, Matur Og Drykkur means 'Food and Drink', and you surely will be plied with the best of both. The brainchild of brilliant chef Gísli Matthías Auðunsson, who creates inventive versions of traditional Icelandic fare. Book ahead in high season and for dinner.

Old Reykjavík

Stofan Kaffihús   Cafe €

(⏩546 1842; www.facebook.com/stofan.cafe; Vesturgata 3; dishes kr1500-1700; ⏲9am-11pm Mon-Wed, to midnight Thu-Sat, 10am-10pm Sun; 🛜) This laid-back cafe in a historic brick building has a warm feel, with its worn wooden floors, plump couches and spacious main room. Settle in for coffee, cake or soup, and watch the world go by.

Messinn   Seafood €€

(⏩546 0095; www.messinn.com; Lækjargata 6b; lunch mains kr1850-2100, dinner mains kr2700-4100; ⏲11.30am-3pm & 5-10pm; 🛜) Make a beeline to Messinn for the best seafood that Reykjavík has to offer. The speciality is amazing pan-fries where your pick of fish is served up in a sizzling cast-iron skillet accompanied by buttery potatoes and salad. The mood is upbeat and comfortable, and the staff friendly.

Grillmarkaðurinn   Fusion €€€

(Grill Market; ⏩571 7777; www.grillmarka durinn.is; Lækjargata 2a; mains kr4600-9900; ⏲11.30am-2pm Mon-Fri, 6-10.30pm Sun-Thu, to 11.30pm Fri & Sat) From the moment you enter the glass atrium here, high-class dining is the order of the day. Service is impeccable, and locals and visitors alike rave about the food: locally sourced Icelandic ingredients prepared with culinary imagination by master chefs. The tasting menu (kr10,400) is an extravaganza of its best dishes.

Coocoo's Nest

Mikkeller & Friends

Fiskmarkaðurinn   Seafood €€€

(Fishmarket; ☑578 8877; www.fiskmarkadurinn. is; Aðalstræti 12; mains kr5100-8900; ☺5-11.30pm) This restaurant excels in infusing Icelandic seafood and local produce with unique flavours like lotus root. The tasting menu (kr11,900) is tops, and it is renowned for its excellent sushi bar (kr3600 to kr4600).

🅗 DRINKING & NIGHTLIFE

🅠 Laugavegur & Skólavörðustígur

Laugavegur is the epicentre of Reykjavík's nightlife and you could begin (and end) a night here. Bar-hop until the clubs light up for dancing (late), then wander home under the early-morning sun.

Kaffi Vínyl   Cafe

(☑537 1332; www.facebook.com/vinilrvk; Hverfisgata 76; ☺8am-11pm; 🛜) This new entry on the Reykjavík coffee, restaurant and music scene is popular for its chill vibe, great music, and delicious vegan and vegetarian food.

Mikkeller & Friends   Craft Beer

(☑437 0203; www.mikkeller.dk; Hverfisgata 12; ☺5pm-1am Sun-Thu, 2pm-1am Fri & Sat; 🛜) Climb to the top floor of the building shared by excellent pizzeria Hverfisgata 12 and you'll find this Danish craft-beer pub; its 20 taps rotate through Mikkeller's own offerings and local Icelandic craft beers.

Kaffibarinn   Bar

(☑551 1588; www.kaffibarinn.is; Bergstaðastræti 1; ☺3pm-1am Sun-Thu, to 4.30am Fri & Sat; 🛜) This old house with the London Underground symbol over the door contains one of Reykjavík's coolest bars; it even had a starring role in the cult movie *101 Reykjavík* (2000). At weekends you'll feel like you need a famous face or a battering ram to get in. At other times it's a place for artistic types to chill with their Macs.

Kaldi   Bar

(✆581 2200; www.kaldibar.is; Laugavegur 20b; ⊙noon-1am Sun-Thu, to 3am Fri & Sat) Effortlessly cool, with mismatched seats and teal banquettes, plus a popular smoking courtyard, Kaldi is awesome for its full range of Kaldi microbrews, not available elsewhere. Happy hour (4pm to 7pm) gets you one for kr700. Anyone can play the in-house piano.

Old Reykjavík

Austurstræti is lined with big venues that pull in the drinking crowd. As the night goes on, some of the capital's best dance clubs and late-night hangs can be found around Naustin St.

Micro Bar   Bar

(✆865 8389; www.facebook.com/MicroBar-Iceland; Vesturgata 2; ⊙4pm-12.30am Sun-Thu, to 1.30am Fri & Sat) Boutique brews are the name of the game at this low-key spot in the heart of the action. Bottles of beer represent a slew of brands and countries, but more importantly you'll discover 10 local draughts on tap from the island's top microbreweries – one of the best selections in Reykjavík. Happy hour (5pm to 7pm) offers kr850 beers.

Loftið   Cocktail Bar

(Jacobsen Loftið; ✆551 9400; www.facebook.com/loftidbar; 2nd fl, Austurstræti 9; ⊙4pm-1am Sun-Thu, to 4am Fri & Sat) Loftið is all about high-end cocktails and good living. Dress up to join the fray at this airy upstairs lounge with a zinc bar, retro tailor-shop-inspired decor, vintage tiles and a swanky, older crowd. The basic booze here is the top-shelf liquor elsewhere, and jazzy bands play from time to time.

Paloma   Club

(http://palomaclub.is; Naustin 1-3; ⊙8pm-1am Thu & Sun, to 4.30am Fri & Sat; 🛗) One of Reykjavík's best late-night dance clubs, with DJs upstairs laying down reggae, electronica and pop, and a dark deep-house dance scene in the basement. It's in the same building as the Dubliner.

Icelandic Pop

Iceland's pop music scene is one of its great gifts to the world. Internationally famous Icelandic musicians include (of course) Björk and her former band, the Sugarcubes. Sigur Rós followed Björk to stardom; their concert movie *Heima* (2007) is a must-see. Indie-folk band Of Monsters and Men stormed the US charts in 2011 with *My Head Is an Animal;* their latest album is *Beneath the Skin (2015).* Ásgeir had a breakout hit with *In the Silence* (2014).

Reykjavík's flourishing music landscape is constantly changing – visit www.icelandmusic.is and www.grapevine.is for news and listings. Just a few examples of local groups include Seabear, an indie-folk band, which spawned top acts like Sin Fang (*Flowers;* 2013) and Sóley (*We Sink;* 2012). Árstíðir record minimalist indie-folk, and released Verloren Verleden with Anneke van Giersbergen in 2016.

Other local bands include GusGus, a pop-electronica act, FM Belfast (electronica) and múm (experimental electronica mixed with traditional instruments). Or check out Singapore Sling for straight-up rock and roll. If your visit coincides with one of Iceland's many music festivals, go!

Of Monsters and Men

⭐ ENTERTAINMENT

Bíó Paradís   Cinema
(☎412 7711; www.bioparadis.is; Hverfisgata 54; adult kr1800; 🛜) This totally cool
cinema, decked out in movie posters
and vintage officeware, screens specially
curated Icelandic films with English
subtitles. It has a happy hour from 5pm
to 7.30pm.

Húrra   Live Music
(www.facebook.com/pg/hurra.is; Tryggvagata
22; ⊙6pm-1am Mon-Thu, to 4.30am Fri & Sat, to
11.30pm Sun; 🛜) Dark and raw, this large bar
opens up its back room to make a concert
venue, with live music or DJs most nights,
and is one of the best places in town to close
out the night. It's got a range of beers on tap,
and happy hour runs till 9pm (beer or wine
kr700).

ℹ️ INFORMATION

DISCOUNT CARDS
Reykjavík City Card (www.citycard.is;
24/48/72hr kr3700/4900/5900) offers
admission to Reykjavík's municipal swimming/
thermal pools and to most of the main galleries
and museums, plus discounts on some tours,
shops and entertainment. It also gives free
travel on the city's Strætó buses and on the
ferry to Viðey.

EMERGENCY NUMBERS
Ambulance, fire brigade & police 112

TOURIST INFORMATION
The **Main Tourist Office** (Upplýsingamiðstöð
Ferðamanna; ☎411 6040; www.visitreykjavik.
is; Ráðhús City Hall, Tjarnargata 11; ⊙8am-
8pm) has friendly staff and mountains of free
brochures, plus maps, Reykjavík City Card and
Strætó city bus tickets. It books accommodation, tours and activities.

ℹ️ GETTING THERE & AWAY

Iceland has become very accessible in recent
years, with more flights from more destinations.
Ferry transport makes a good alternative for
people wishing to bring a car or camper from
mainland Europe.

Flights, tours and rail tickets can be booked
online at www.lonelyplanet.com/bookings.

ℹ️ GETTING AROUND

The best way to see compact central Reykjavík
is by foot.

TO/FROM THE AIRPORT
The journey from Keflavík International Airport
to Reykjavík takes about 50 minutes.

Flybus (☎580 5400; www.re.is; 🛜) meets
all international flights. One-way tickets cost
kr2200. Pay kr2800 for hotel pick-up/drop-off,
which must be booked a day ahead. A separate
service runs to the Blue Lagoon (from where you
can continue to the city centre or the airport;
kr3900).

Airport Express (☎540 1313; www.airport
express.is; 🛜) Operated by Gray Line Tours
between Keflavík International Airport and
Lækjartorg Sq in central Reykjavík (kr2100) or
Mjódd bus terminal, or via hotel pick-up/drop-
off (kr2700; book ahead). Has connections to
Borgarnes and points north, including Akureyri.

Airport Direct (☎497 5000; www.reykjavik
sightseeing.is/airport-direct; 🛜) Minibuses
operated by Reykjavík Sightseeing shuttle
between hotels and the airport (kr4500, return
kr8000).

Taxis cost around kr15,000.

BUS
Strætó (www.bus.is) operates regular, easy
buses in the city centre and environs, running
7am until 11pm or midnight daily (from 11am on
Sunday). A limited night-bus service runs until
2am on Friday and Saturday.

Where to Stay

Demand always outstrips supply in Reykjavík. Try to book your accommodation three to six months ahead.

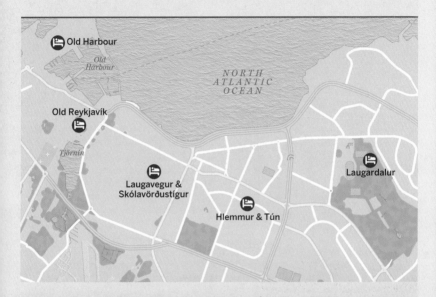

Neighbourhood	Atmosphere
Old Reykjavík	Central, easy with higher-end options. Can be crowded, busier and expensive.
Old Harbour	Less busy once back from the harbour. Guesthouses and hostels are more affordable, but it is slightly less central.
Laugavegur & Skólavörðustígur	Perfect for shopping and partying. Good range of options with certain quiet pockets. It's touristy on the main streets.
Hlemmur & Tún	Loads of high-rise hotels are popping up here. The areas are on the bland side and a bit far from the city centre.
Laugardalur	Near large park and swimming complex. New high-rise hotels. Further from the city centre.

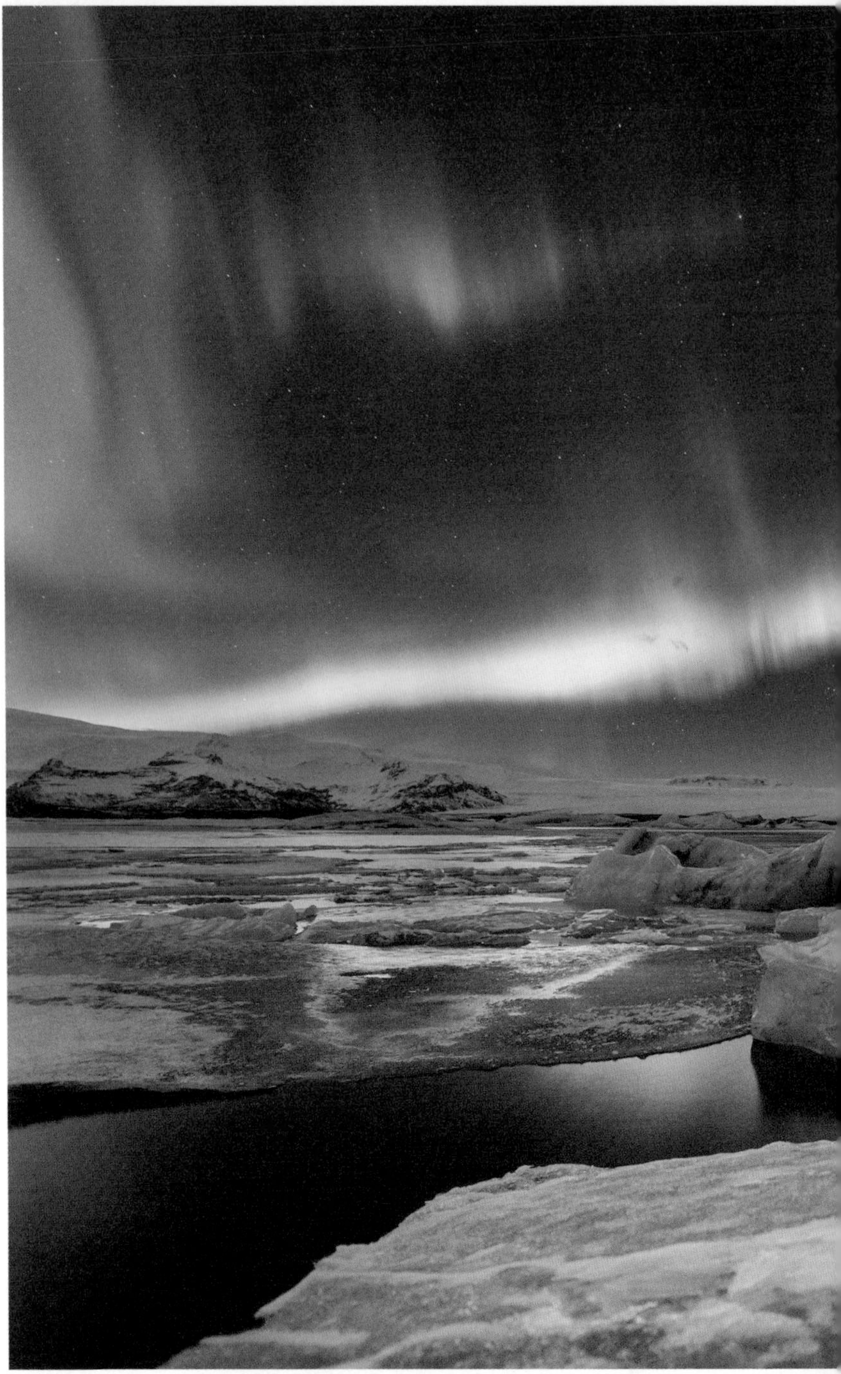

NATAPONG SUPALERTSOPHON/GETTY IMAGES ©

Aurora Borealis over Jökulsárlón Glacial Lagoon

SOUTHEASTERN ICELAND

Southeastern Iceland at a Glance...

The 200km stretch of Ring Road from Kirkjubæjarklaustur to Höfn is truly mind-blowing, transporting you across vast deltas of grey glacial sand, past lost-looking farms, around the toes of craggy mountains, and by glacier tongues and ice-filled lagoons. The only thing you won't pass is a town.

The mighty Vatnajökull dominates the region, its huge rivers of ice pouring down steep-sided valleys towards the sea. Jökulsárlón is a photographer's paradise, a glacial lagoon where wind and water sculpt icebergs into fantastical shapes.

Two Days in the Southeast

Spend a day just driving the ring road, letting the extraordinary scenery and lonely views wash over you. On day two, spend a day in and around the **Jökulsárlón Glacial Lagoon** (p98), including at least one boat trip and one hike. Base yourself in **Höfn** (p106), and get to know a remote southern Icelandic settlement.

Four Days in the Southeast

On day three, spend as much time as you can getting to know the black beaches of **Vík** (p105). On day four, devote all your energies to hiking in **Vatnajökull National Park** (p102), taking in some of Iceland's most iconic vistas. If you've any time left, devote it to exploring **Landmannalaugar** and **Fjallabak Nature Reserve** (p110).

Hågöngulón

Kvíslavatn

Versalir
Kjalvötn

Þórisvatn

Vatnajökull National Park

Stafafell

Bjarnanes
Pveit

Höfn

Stokksnes

Heinabergslón

Fögrufjöll
(1090m)
Grænalón
Vatnajökull
Laki
(818m)
Lómagnúpur
(767m)
Skaftafell
Hali
Jökulsárlón

Jökulsárlón

Önýtavatn
Fjallabak
Nature
Reserve
Landmannalaugar
Jökuldalur
Torfajökull

Laufsalavatn
Kálfafell
Gjátindur

Fjallsárlón
Hvannadalshnúkur
(2110m)
Hof
Öræfi

Kirkjubæjarklaustur
Skeiðarársandur

Myrdalsjökull

Hrífunes
Eldhraun

Katla
(1250m)
Álftaver

Myrdalssandur
Þykkvabæjarklaustur

Vík

Vík
Beaches

Southeastern Iceland (p104)
Höfn Map (p107)

Arriving in the Southeast

Buses drive the Ring Road (Rte 1), connecting Reykjavík and popular towns in Iceland's Southwest with destinations further east along the south coast.

Vík is a popular departure point for Kirkjubæjarklaustur; it's then 200km east to the next town, Höfn – and along the way the primary stops for buses are Skaftafell and Jökulsárlón. Your own wheels allow a more in-depth exploration.

Where to Stay

There are hotels and guesthouses scattered throughout the region, but not nearly enough to satisfy demand. Our advice: book early, and be prepared to pay high rates (some of the country's highest).

The areas around Kirkjubæjarklaustur and Höfn have the most choice; options are very limited around Skaftafell and Jökulsárlón.

MATT MUNRO/LONELY PLANET ©

Jökulsárlón Glacial Lagoon

A host of spectacular, luminous-blue icebergs drift through Jökulsárlón glacial lagoon, right beside the Ring Road between Höfn and Skaftafell. It's one of Iceland's most memorable sights.

Great For...

Don't Miss

When walking along the shore, taste ancient ice by hauling it out of the water.

This is nature at its most dramatic. The icebergs calve from Breiðamerkurjökull, an offshoot of Vatnajökull, crashing down into the water and drifting towards the Atlantic Ocean. They can spend up to five years floating in the 25-sq-km-plus, 260m-deep lagoon, melting, refreezing and occasionally toppling over with a mighty splash, startling the birds. They then move out to sea via Jökulsá, Iceland's shortest river.

Lagoon History

Although it looks as though it's been here since the last Ice Age, the lagoon is only about 80 years old. Until the mid-1930s Breiðamerkurjökull reached the Ring Road; it's now retreating rapidly (up to a staggering 500m per year), and the lagoon is consequently growing.

Lagoon Boat Trips

Take a memorable 40-minute trip in an **amphibious boat,** (☑478 2222; www.icelagoon.is; adult/child kr5500/2000; ⊙9am-7pm Jun-Sep, 10am-5pm May & Oct) which trundles along the shore like a bus before driving into the water. On-board guides regale you with factoids about the lagoon, and you can taste 1000-year-old ice. There is no set schedule; trips run from the eastern car park (by the cafe) regularly – up to 40 a day in summer.

Zodiac Boat Trips

Ice Lagoon (☑860 9996; www.icelagoon.com; adult/child kr9500/6000; ⊙9am-5.30pm mid-May–mid-Sep) deals exclusively with

Zodiac tours (an inflatable boat) of the lagoon. It's a one-hour experience, with a maximum of 20 passengers per boat, and it travels at speed up to the glacier edge (not done by the amphibious boats) before cruising back at a leisurely pace. It pays to book these tours in advance, online; minimum age six years.

Lagoon Hikes

The new **Breiðármörk Trail** has been marked from the western car park at Jökulsárlón, leading to Breiðárlón (10km one way) and Fjallsárlón (15.3km) lagoons. It is classified as challenging. In time, there is a plan to build out this walking route from Skaftafell in the west to Lónsöræfi in the east. The visitor centre at Höfn sells a trail map (kr250).

Puffin on Dyrholaey Peninsula

CHRISTIAN SCHWEIGER/500PX ©

Vík Black Beaches

Images of the black, basalt beaches at Reynisfjara and nearby are among Iceland's most beautiful. Coming here is an opportunity to sample the country's strange, haunting beauty.

Great For...

Don't Miss

Katla Track (p105) runs tours of the area that take in local landmarks and get to the edge of Mýrdalsjökull.

Reynisfjara

On the west side of Reynisfjall, the high ridge above Vík, Rte 215 leads 5km down to black-sand beach **Reynisfjara**. It's backed by an incredible stack of basalt columns that look like a magical church organ, and there are outstanding views west to Dyrhólaey. Surrounding cliffs are pocked with caves formed from twisted basalt, and puffins belly flop into the crashing sea during summer. Immediately offshore are the towering Reynisdrangur sea stacks. At all times watch for rogue waves: people are regularly swept away.

Reynisdrangur

ROEL SLOOTWEG/SHUTTERSTOCK ©

NORTH ATLANTIC OCEAN

❶ Need to Know

Vík is a major stop for all Reykjavík–Höfn bus routes; buses stop at the N1 petrol station.

✕ Take a Break

At Svarta Fjaran (p105), black volcanic cubes house this contemporary cafe-restaurant.

★ Top Tip

The beach can get busy in high season, so try to come early in the day or late in the evening.

Reynisdrangur

Vík's most iconic cluster of sea stacks is known as **Reynisdrangur**, which rise from the ocean like ebony towers at the western end of Vík's black-sand beach. Folklore says they're masts of a ship that trolls were stealing when they got caught in the sun. The nearby cliffs are good for puffin watching. A bracing walk up from Vík's western end takes you to the top of Reynisfjall ridge (340m), offering superb views.

Dyrhólaey

One of the south coast's most recognisable natural formations is the rocky plateau and huge stone sea arch at **Dyrhólaey** (deer-lay), which rises dramatically from the surrounding plain 10km west of Vík, at the end of Rte 218. Visit its crashing black beaches and get awesome views from atop the promontory. The islet is a nature reserve that's rich in bird-life, including puffins; some or all of it can be closed during nesting season (15 May to 25 June). The archway itself is best seen from Reynisfjara.

Skaftafellsjökull glacier

MARCO BOTTIGELLI/GETTY IMAGES ©

Hiking in Vatnajökull National Park

Skaftafell, the jewel in the crown of Vatnajökull National Park, encompasses a breathtaking collection of peaks and glaciers. It's the country's favourite wilderness.

Great For...

Don't Miss

Atlantsflug (☑854 4105; www.flightseeing.is) offers eye-popping scenic flights with six choices of routes.

Thundering waterfalls, twisted birch woods, the tangled web of rivers threading across the sandar, and brilliant blue-white Vatnajökull with its lurching tongues of ice, dripping down mountainsides like icing on a cake.

Svartifoss

Star of a hundred postcards, Svartifoss (Black Falls) is a stunning, moody-looking waterfall flanked by geometric black basalt columns. It's reached by an easy 1.8km trail leading up from the visitor centre via the campsite. To take pressure off the busy trail to Svartifoss, park staff recommend you take an alternative path back to the visitor centre.

Svartifoss waterfall

KAVRAM/SHUTTERSTOCK ©

ⓘ Need to Know

The park produces good maps outlining shorter hiking trails (kr350).

✕ Take a Break

Glacier Goodies (www.facebook.com/glaciergoodies; mains kr2200-2700; ⊘11.30am-7pm mid-May–Sep), close to the visitor centre, does dishes made from local ingredients.

★ Top Tip

To take pressure off the busy trail to Svartifoss, take an alternative path back to the visitor centre.

Skaftafellsjökull

A very popular trail is the easy one-hour return walk (3.7km) to Skaftafellsjökull. The marked trail begins at the visitor centre and leads to the glacier face, where you can witness the bumps and groans of the ice (although the glacier is pretty grey and gritty here). The glacier has receded greatly in recent decades, meaning land along this trail has been gradually reappearing.

Skaftafellsheiði Loop

On a fine day, the five- to six-hour (15.5km) walk around Skaftafellsheiði is a hiker's dream. It begins by climbing from the campsite past Svartifoss and Sjónarsker,

continuing across the moor to 610m-high **Fremrihnaukur**. From there it follows the edge of the plateau to the next rise, **Nyðrihnaukur** (706m), which affords a superb view of Morsárdalur, and Morsárjökull and the iceberg-choked lagoon at its base.

Morsárdalur & Bæjarstaðarskógur

The seven-hour hike (20.6km return) from the campsite to the glacial lake in Morsárdalur is ordinary but enjoyable. Alternatively, cross the Morsá river at the foot of Skaftafellsheiði and make your way across the gravel riverbed to the birch woods at Bæjarstaðarskógur. The return walk to Bæjarstaðarskógur takes about six hours (13km return). This is also the trail to follow if you're exploring on mountain bike (BYO bike).

Southeast Iceland

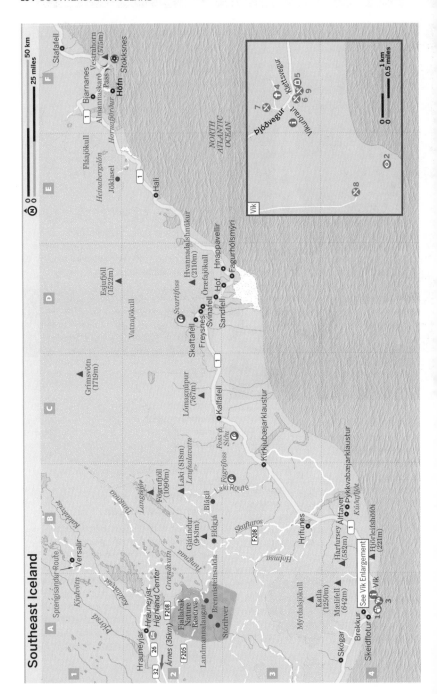

Vík Enlargement

Þjóðvegur

Klettsvegur

Víkurbraut

NORTH ATLANTIC OCEAN

Vík

0   1 km
0   0.5 miles

Stafafell

Bjarnanes
Almannaskarð
Vestrahorn (575m)
Pass
Höfn
Stokksnes

Fláajökull

Hornafjörður

Heinabergslón
Jökulsel
Hali

Vatnajökull

Esjufjöll (1522m)

Grímsvötn (1719m)

Svartifoss

Hvannadalshnúkur (2110m)
Öræfajökull
Hnappavellir
Fagurhólsmýri
Svínafell
Hof
Skaftafell
Freysnes
Sandfell
Oræfi

Lómagnúpur (767m)

Kálfafell

Foss á Síðu

Kirkjubæjarklaustur

Laki (818m)
Laufsárvatn
Fagrifoss
Laki Route

Fögrufjöll (1090m)
Langisjór
Blágil
Gjátindur (943m)
Eldgjá
Skaftáros

Tungnaá

Skaftá

Kúðafljót

F208

Þykkvabæjarklaustur

Hrífunes

Holmsá

Brennisteinsalda
Stórhver

Fjallabak Nature Reserve

Landmannalaugar

Hrauneyjar Highland Center
Versalir
Sprengisandur Route

Kýlingar

Hrauneyjar
Arnes (36km)

32
26
F205
F208

Þjórsá

Kaldakvísl

Kaldakvísl

Myrdalsjökull

Katla (1250m)

Mælifell (642m)

Hafursey (582m)
Hjörleifshöfði (221m)

See Vík Enlargement
Vík

Brekkur
Skeiðflötur
Skógar

N
0   25 miles
0   50 km

Vík

The welcoming little community of Vík (aka Vík í Mýrdal) has become a booming hub for a very beautiful portion of the south coast. Iceland's southernmost town, it's also the rainiest, but that doesn't stop the madhouse atmosphere in summer, when every room within 100km is booked solid. With loads of services, Vík is a convenient base for the beautiful basalt beach Reynisfjara and its puffin cliffs, and the rocky plateau Dyrhólaey (both just to the west) and for the volcanoes running from Skógar to Jökulsárlón glacier lagoon and beyond. Along the coast, white-capped waves wash up on black sands and the cliffs glow green from all that rain. Put simply, it's gorgeous.

SIGHTS

Víkurkirkja   Church

(Hátún) High above town, Vík's 1930s church has stained-glass windows in spiky geometric shapes, but we like it most for its village views.

TOURS

Skógar (33km west of Vík) and Hvolsvöllur are the hubs for activity tours on the south coast. In Vík, you can check with the hostel for tours to Mýrdalsjökull. Many Reykjavík tour companies also make the long haul out here.

Katla Track   Driving

(☑849 4404; www.katlatrack.is) Katla Track runs tours of the area (kr29,900, from Reykjavík kr44,900) that take in local landmarks and get to the edge of Mýrdalsjökull.

SHOPPING

Víkurprjón   Gifts & Souvenirs

(☑487 1250; www.vikwool.is; Austurvegur 20; ⊗8am-7pm) The big Icewear souvenir and knitwear shop next to the N1 station is a coach-tour hit. You can peek inside the factory portion to see woollen wear being made.

Southeast Iceland

✖ EATING

Víkurskáli   International €

(☑487 1230; Austurvegur 18; mains kr1400-3000; ⊗11am-9pm) Grab a booth and a burger at the old-school grill inside the N1 with a view of Reynisdrangur. Daily specials from casserole to lamb stew.

Suður-Vík   Icelandic, Asian €€

(☑487 1515; www.facebook.com/Sudurvik; Suður-víkurvegur 1; mains kr2250-5350; ⊗noon-10pm, shorter hours in winter) The friendly ambience, from hardwood floors and interesting artwork to smiling staff, helps elevate this restaurant beyond the competition. Food is Icelandic hearty, and ranges from heaping steak sandwiches with bacon and Béarnaise sauce to Asian (think Thai satay with rice). In a warmly lit silver building atop town. Book ahead in summer.

Ströndin Bistro   International €€

(☑487 1230; www.strondin.is; Austurvegur 18; mains kr2000-5000; ⊗6-10pm; 🖥) Behind the N1 petrol station is this semi-smart wood-panelled option enjoying sea-stack vistas. Go local with lamb soup or fish stew, or global with pizzas and burgers.

Svarta Fjaran   Cafe €€

(Black Beach Restaurant; ☑571 2718; www.svartafjaran.com; Reynisfjara; snacks kr990, dinner mains kr2500-6000; ⊗11am-10pm; 🖥) Black volcanic cubes, meant to mimic the nearby black beach Reynisfjara with its famous basalt columns, house this contemporary restaurant that serves homemade cakes and snacks during the day and a full dinner menu at night. Plate-glass windows give views to the ocean and Dyrhólaey beyond.

INFORMATION

Tourist Information Centre (487 1395; www.visitvik.is; Víkurbraut 28; ⏱10am-7pm Mon-Fri, 11am-5pm Sat & Sun Jun-Aug; 🛜) Inside Brydebúð.

ℹ GETTING THERE & AWAY

Vík is a major stop for all Reykjavík–Höfn bus routes; buses stop at the N1 petrol station.

Strætó (📞540 2700; www.bus.is) services:

○ Bus 51 Reykjavík–Vík–Höfn (Reykjavík–Vík kr5880, 2¾ hours, two daily) If you take the early bus you can stop in Vík then continue on to Höfn on the later bus; however, from September to May service is reduced and you can't count on that connection.

Sterna (📞551 1166; www.icelandbybus.is) services:

○ Bus 12/12a Reykjavík–Vík–Höfn (Reykjavík–Vík kr5600, 4¼ hours, one daily June to mid-September).

Reykjavík Excursions (📞580 5400; www.re.is) services:

○ Bus 20/20a Reykjavík–Skaftafell (Reykjavík–Vík kr7500, four hours, one daily June to early September).

○ Bus 21/21a Reykjavík–Skógar (Reykjavík–Vík kr7500, 3¾ hours, one daily June to August) One of the two services to Skógar goes as far as Vík each day.

Höfn

Although it's no bigger than many European villages, the Southeast's main town feels like a sprawling metropolis after driving through the emptiness on either side. Its setting is stunning; on a clear day, wander down to the waterside, find a quiet bench and just gaze at Vatnajökull and its guild of glaciers.

Höfn simply means 'harbour', and is pronounced like an unexpected hiccup (just say

'hup' while inhaling). It's an apt name – this modern town still relies heavily on fishing and fish processing, and is famous for its *humar* (often translated as lobster, but technically it's langoustine).

Bus travellers use Höfn as a transit point, and most travellers stop to use the town's services, so pre-book accommodation in summer. On bus timetables and the like, you may see the town referred to as Höfn í Hornafirði (meaning Höfn in Hornafjörður) to differentiate it from all the other *höfn* (harbours) around the country.

SIGHTS

If you're interested, there are various museum-style exhibitions around town, including a rock collection and an old stockfish shed with displays on fishing and seafaring.

Gamlabúð Notable Building, Museum (📞470 8330; www.vjp.is; Heppuvegur 1; ⏱9am-7pm Jun-Aug, to 6pm May & Sep, to 5pm Oct-Apr) **FREE** The 1864 warehouse that once served as the regional folk museum has been moved from the outskirts of town to a prime position on the Höfn harbour front. It's been refurbished to serve as the town's visitor centre, with good exhibits explaining the marvels of the region's flagship national park (including flora and fauna), as well as screening documentaries.

Seamen's Monument Monument (Óslandsvegur) This monument stands on Ósland, the bird-filled promontory south of the harbour. Head here for good walks and views.

ACTIVITIES

Activities that explore Vatnajökull's icy vastness – such as glacier walks, super-4WD tours, lagoon kayaking and snowmobile safaris – are accessed along the Ring Road west of Höfn.

In town, there are a couple of short **waterside paths** where you can amble and gape at the views – one by Hótel Höfn and another on Ósland.

Höfn

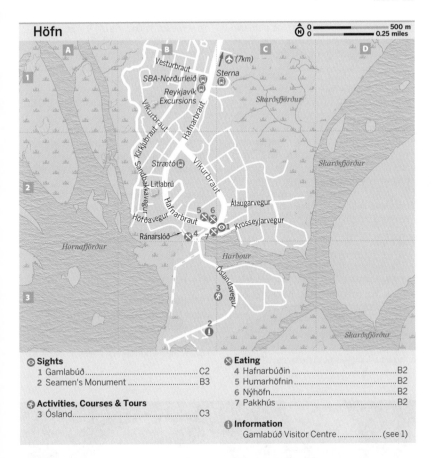

Ósland   Walking

This promontory about 1km beyond the harbour – head for the seamen's monument on the rise – boasts a walking path round its marshes and lagoons. The path is great for watching seabirds, though be wary of dive-bombing Arctic terns.

From the seamen's monument, you can follow a nature trail that has been set up to model the solar system – it's been 'scaled down 2.1 billion fold', and has its sizes and distances in correct proportion.

⊗ EATING

Humar (langoustine) is the speciality on Höfn menus – tails or served whole and grilled with garlic butter is the norm, and prices for main dishes range from kr7000 upwards. You'll find cheaper crustacean-centric options too: bisque, sandwiches or langoustine-studded pizza or pasta.

Look out for the **Heimahumar** food truck, parked out front of Nettó in the summer, for the cheapest lobster wraps and panini in town (around kr1850).

Hafnarbúðin   Fast Food €

(478 1095; Ránarslóð 2; snacks & meals kr400-2800; ⊙9am-10pm Mon-Fri, 10am-10pm Sat & Sun, shorter hours in winter) A fabulous relic, this tiny old-school diner has a cheap-and-cheerful vibe, a menu of fast-food favourites (hot dogs, burgers,

toasted sandwiches) and a fine *humarlo-ka* – langoustine baguette – for kr2000. There's even a drive-up window!

Nýhöfn
Icelandic €€

(📞865 2489; www.nyhofn.is; Hafnarbraut 2; mains kr2900-5900; ⊙noon-10pm mid-May–mid-Sep) This sweet 'Nordic bistro' is in the home that Höfn's first settler built in 1897, and still retains its refined, old-world atmosphere. The menu spotlights local produce, but is an interesting nod to influences near and far, from langoustine bruschetta to Peruvian ceviche by way of organic vegetarian barley burgers. There's a small bar in the cellar, too.

Pakkhús
Icelandic €€€

(📞478 2280; www.pakkhus.is; Krosseyjarvegur 3; mains kr3200-6850; ⊙noon-10pm mid-May–mid-Sep, 5-9pm mid-Sep–mid-May) Hats off to a menu that tells you the name of the boat that delivers its star produce. In a stylish harbourside warehouse, Pakkhús offers a level of kitchen creativity you don't often find in rural Iceland. First-class local langoustine, lamb and duck tempt taste buds, while

clever desserts end the meal in style: who can resist a dish called '*skyr* volcano'?

No reservations taken – you may have to wait for a table, but there is a bar area downstairs.

Humarhöfnin
Icelandic €€€

(📞478 1200; www.humarhofnin.is; Hafnarbraut 4; mains kr2900-8400; ⊙noon-10pm May-Sep, to 9pm Oct-Nov) Humarhöfnin offers 'Gastronomy Langoustine' in a cute, cheerfully Frenchified space with superb attention to detail: herb pots on the windowsills, roses on every table. Mains centred on pincer-waving critters cost upwards of kr7000, but there are also more budget-friendly dishes, including a fine langoustine baguette (kr4300) or pizza (kr2900).

🍷 DRINKING & NIGHTLIFE

Höfn goes to bed early (there are activities to get to early in the morning!), but drinking can be done at most restaurants. Kaffi Hornið has a particularly good beer selection, while Nýhöfn boasts a small cellar bar.

Skyr volcano dessert served at Pakkhús

ℹ️ INFORMATION

Gamlabúð Visitor Centre (470 8330; www.
visitvatnajokull.is; Heppuvegur 1; ⊙9am-7pm
Jun-Aug, to 6pm May & Sep, to 5pm Oct-Apr)
sits inside a harbour-front Gamlabúð house
and has excellent exhibits, plus local tourist
information. Ask about activities and hiking
trails in the area.

ℹ️ GETTING THERE & AWAY

Höfn is about 6km south of the Ring Road on
Rte 99. The nearest towns in either direction
are Kirkjubæjarklaustur, 200km west, and
Djúpivogur, 105km east.

AIR

Höfn's airport is 6.5km northwest of town. Eagle
Air (www.eagleair.is) flies year-round between
Reykjavík and Höfn (one way from kr18,600).

BUS

Bus companies travelling through Höfn have different stops, so make sure you know what operator
you're travelling with and confirm where they pick
up from.

Buses heading from Höfn to Reykjavík stop
at all major towns and landmarks, including
Jökulsárlón, Skaftafell, Kirkjubæjarklaustur,
Vík, Skógar, Hvolsvöllur, Hella and Selfoss. See
websites for up-to-date rates and schedules.

Note that there is no winter bus connection between Egilsstaðir and Höfn (ie bus 62a doesn't run).

SBA-Norðurleið (550 0700; www.sba.is)
services (stop at N1 petrol station):

○ Bus 62a to Egilsstaðir (kr9400, five hours,
one daily June to mid-September; stops at
Djúpivogur, Breiðdalsvík and fjords along Rtes
92 and 96).

○ Bus 62a to Mývatn (kr15,500, 7½ hours, one
daily June to mid-September).

○ Bus 62a to Akureyri (kr19,000, 9¼ hours, one
daily June to mid-September).

Sterna (551 1166; www.icelandbybus.is) services (pick-up/drop-off at campground):

○ Bus 12a to Reykjavík (kr11,600, 10¼ hours,
one daily June to mid-September).

 Smartphone Apps

Useful and practical smartphone apps
include the vital 112 Iceland app for
safe travel, Veður (weather), and apps
for bus companies such as **Strætó**.
Offline maps come in handy.

There are plenty more apps that cover
all sorts of interests, from history and
language to aurora-spotting, or walking
tours of the capital. Reykjavík Grapevine's
apps (Appy Hour, Craving and Appening)
deserve special mention for getting you
to the good stuff in the capital.

VITALII MATOKHA/SHUTTERSTOCK ©

Strætó (540 2700; www.straeto.is) services
(pick-up/drop-off out front of the swimming
pool):

○ Bus 51 to Reykjavík (kr12,180, 7¼ hours, two
daily June to mid-September, one daily Sunday
to Friday the rest of the year).

Reykjavík Excursions (580 5400; www.re.is)
services (stop at N1 petrol station):

○ Bus 19 to Skaftafell (kr5500, 4¼ hours,
one daily June to mid-September). Stops at
Jökulsárlón for 2½ hours. Can be used as a
day tour returning to Höfn (with 5¼ hours at
Skaftafell).

ℹ️ GETTING AROUND

Without your own transport in this area, getting
around can be tricky. **Vatnajökull Travel** (894
1616; www.vatnajokull.is) is a year-round agency
that works with some of the region's tour operators and can shuttle you around.

Icelandic Culture

Iceland blows away concerns such as isolation, never-ending winter nights and its small population with a glowing passion for all things cultural. The country's unique literary heritage begins with high-action medieval sagas and stretches to today's Nordic Noir bestsellers. Every Icelander seems to play in a band, and the country produces a disproportionate number of world-class musicians. The way of life and grand landscapes inspire visual artists who use film, art and design to capture their unique Icelandic perspectives.

Harpa (p84), Reykjavík's art centre
BRIAN MAUDSLEY/SHUTTERSTOCK ©

Stokksnes

About 7km east of the turn-off to Höfn, just before the Ring Road enters a tunnel through the Almannaskarð pass, a signposted road heads south to headland Stokksnes. After 4.5km, there's an opportunity for refreshments; pull in for some coffee or cakes at the Viking Cafe. The farm-owner runs the cafe, and he charges visitors kr800 to explore his incredible property, including a photogenic Viking village **film set** and miles of **black-sand beaches**, where seals laze and the backdrop of Vestrahorn creates superb photos.

Note that the film set (built in 2009 by Icelandic film director Baltasar Kormákur) may finally see action soon, when Baltasar directs *Vikings*, a long-gestating film project he started writing more than a decade ago. The set will hopefully remain in place after its film duties are done.

EATING

Viking Cafe   Cafe €
(www.vikingcafe.is; waffles & cake kr900; ☉9am-7pm May-Oct) In a wild setting under moodily Gothic Vestrahorn mountain, you'll find this cool little outpost, where coffee, waffles and cake are served.

❶ GETTING THERE & AWAY
You'll need your own wheels to get here.

Landmannalaugar & Fjallabak Nature Reserve

Mind-blowing multicoloured mountains, soothing hot springs, rambling lava flows and clear blue lakes make Landmannalaugar one of Iceland's most remarkable destinations, and a must for explorers of the interior. It's a favourite with Icelanders and visitors alike... as long as the weather cooperates.

Part of the Fjallabak Nature Reserve, Landmannalaugar (600m above sea level) includes the largest geothermal field in Iceland outside the Grímsvötn caldera in Vatnajökull. Its multihued peaks are made of rhyolite – a mineral-filled lava that cooled unusually slowly, causing those amazing colours.

The area is the official starting point for the famous Laugavegurinn hike, and there's some excellent day hiking as well. The day-use fee for the facilities at Landmannalaugar is kr500.

❸ ACTIVITIES

There's plenty to do in and around Landmannalaugar, though many hikers skip the area's wonders and set off right away for their Laugavegurinn hike. If you plan to stick around, you'll be happy to know that the crowds dwindle in the evenings and, despite the base's chaotic appearance, you'll find peace in the hills above.

Hiking
If you're day-hiking in the Landmannalaugar area, stop by the information hut to

purchase the useful day-trip map (kr300), which details all of the best hikes in the region. Guided hikes (through operators from Hvolsvöllur to Skógar areas) can also be a great way to explore the area.

The start of the Laugavegurinn hike is behind the Landmannalaugar hut, marked in red.

Frostastaðavatn   Hiking

This blue lake lies behind the rhyolite ridge immediately north of the Landmannalaugar hut. Walk over the ridge and you'll be rewarded with far-ranging views as well as close-ups of the interesting rock formations and moss-covered lava flows flanking the lake. If you walk at least one way on the road and spend some time exploring around the lake, the return trip takes two to three hours.

Brennisteinsalda   Hiking

When the weather is clear, opt for a walk that takes in the region's spectacular views. From Landmannalaugar climb to the summit of rainbow-streaked Brennisteinsalda – covered in steaming vents and sulphur

deposits – for a good view across the rugged and variegated landscape (it's a 6.5km round trip from Landmannalaugar). From Brennisteinsalda it's another 90 minutes along the Þórsmörk route to the impressive **Stórihver** geothermal field.

Hot Springs

Follow the wooden boardwalk just 200m from the Landmannalaugar hut, to find a steaming river filled with bathers. Both hot and cold water flow out from beneath Laugahraun and combine in a natural pool to form an ideal hot bath. Landmannalaugar could be translated as the People's Pools...and here they are.

Horse Riding

Landmannalaugar has on-site **horse-riding tours** (⌂868 5577; www.hnakkur. is; 1/2hr tour kr9000/12,500) from July to mid-August. The horse farms on the plains around Hella also offer riding (usually longer trips) in and around the Landmannalaugar area.

Stokksnes

Landmannalaugar

Shopping

**Mountain
Mall**   Food & Drinks, Clothing
(www.landmannalaugar.info) The Mountain
Mall on the Landmannalaugar grounds
is set up inside two buses, selling basic
supplies from hats, long johns, hot tea and
maps to beer (kr1000), soup (kr1000) and
fresh fish from the nearby lakes. It also sells
fishing licences.

🍽 EATING

There are no restaurants at Landmannalaugar; bring all of your own food. The
Mountain Mall shop sells some basic food
supplies at a premium, and the huts have
cooking facilities for guests.

ℹ INFORMATION

The Landmannalaugar hut wardens can answer
questions and provide directions and advice on
hiking routes. They also sell a map of day hikes
(kr300) and the Laugavegurinn hike (kr1700), as
well as a booklet in English and Icelandic on the

hike (kr3000). Note that wardens do not know
if it will rain (yes, this is the most frequently
asked question here). At the time of writing there
was no wi-fi, but there was some mobile-phone
reception.

ℹ GETTING THERE & AWAY

BUS

Landmannalaugar can be reached by rugged,
semi-amphibious buses from three different
directions. They run when the roads are open to
Landmannalaugar (check www.road.is).

From Reykjavík Buses travel along the western
part of the Fjallabak Rte, which first follows Rte
26 east of the Þjorsá to F225.

From Skaftafell Buses follow the Fjallabak Rte
(F208).

From Mývatn Buses cut across the highlands via
Nýidalur on the Sprengisandur Rte (F26).

It's possible to travel from the capital and be
in Landmannalaugar for two to 10 hours before
returning to Reykjavík, or three to five hours before going on to Skaftafell. That's about enough
time to take a dip in the springs and/or a short

walk. Schedules change, but morning buses usually reach Landmannalaugar by midday. Alternatively, stay overnight and catch a bus out when you're done exploring.

Reykjavík Excursions (p106) services:

○ Bus 10/10a Skaftafell–Landmannalaugar (kr9000, five hours, one daily late June to early September).

○ Bus 11/11a Reykjavík–Landmannalaugar (kr8000, 4¼ hours, three to four daily mid-June to mid-September).

○ Bus 14/14a Mývatn–Landmannalaugar (kr16,500, 10 hours, one daily late June to early September).

Sterna (p106) services:

○ Bus 13/13a Reykjavík–Landmannalaugar (kr8000, four hours, one daily late June to early September).

Trex (🖱587 6000; www.trex.is) services:

○ Bus T21 Reykjavík–Landmannalaugar (kr7900, 4¼ hours, two daily mid-June to early September).

CAR

Roads to Landmannalaugar are open in summer only (approximately late June to September) depending on weather and road conditions (check www.safetravel.is and www.road.is). There are three routes to Landmannalaugar from the Ring Road, all requiring a minimum of a 4WD. Driving from Mývatn to Landmannalaugar takes all day along the Sprengisandur Rte route (4WD only). If you have a small 4WD, you will have to leave your vehicle about 1km before Landmannalaugar, as the river crossing here is too perilous for little cars, and cross by footbridge. Two-wheel-drive rentals are not allowed to drive on F roads to Landmannalaugar.

There's no petrol at Landmannalaugar. The nearest petrol pumps are 40km north at **Hrauneyjar** (Hotel Highland; 🖱487 7782; www. hrauneyjar.is; Hrauneyjar; guesthouse s/d incl breakfast from kr19,900/22,500, hotel s/d incl breakfast kr32,050/36,250; 🅿🛜), close to the beginning of the F208 and also in the Fjallabak Reserve; and 90km southeast at Kirkjubæjarklaustur, but to be on the safe side you should fill

 Ring Road from Skógar to Vík

As the Ring Road arcs east from Skógar to Vík, the haunches of the foothills rise to the glaciers, mountain tops and volcanoes inland, while rivers descend from mysterious gorges and course across the broad sweep of pastures to black-sand beaches and the crashing ocean. This rural area may be dotted with farmhouses (many of which have guesthouses), but considering the volume of summertime visitors, it still feels alternately dramatic and pastoral.

Ring Road, Iceland
ADRENALINERUSHDIARIES/SHUTTERSTOCK ©

up along the Ring Road if approaching from the west or the north.

F208 Northwest You can follow the west side of the Þjorsá (Rte 32), passing Árnes, then take Rte F208 down into Landmannalaugar from the north. This is the easiest path to follow for small 4WDs. After passing the power plant, the road from Hrauneyjar becomes horribly bumpy and swerves between power lines all the way to Ljótipollur ('Ugly Puddle').

F225 On the east side of the Þjorsá, follow Rte 26 inland through the low plains behind Hella, loop around Hekla, then take Rte F225 west until you reach the base. This route is harder to tackle (rougher roads).

F208 Southeast The hardest route comes from the Ring Road between Vík and Kirkjubæjarklaustur. This is the Skaftafell–Landmannalaugar bus route.

You can also take a super-4WD tour with local tour operators, which will take you out to Landmannalaugar from Reykjavík, or from anywhere in the south.

HELSINKI, FINLAND

Helsinki, Finland at a Glance...

Spectacularly entwined with the Baltic's bays, inlets and islands, Helsinki's boulevards and backstreets are awash with magnificent architecture, intriguing drinking and dining venues and ground-breaking design – its design scene is one of the most electrifying in the world today. Fresh Finnish flavours can be found all over Helsinki, from the historic kauppahalli (covered market) to venerable restaurants, creative bistros and Michelin–starred gastronomy labs. Helsinki is surrounded by a sublime natural environment that's easily reached from all across the city.

Two Days in Helsinki

Nearby Helsinki's iconic art-nouveau **train station** (p132) are outstanding galleries **Kiasma** (p124) and **Ateneum** (p124). Shop-stroll **Esplanadin Puisto** (p130) and Kaisaniemi, then catch a show at **Musiikkitalo** (p128).

On day two, visit **Tuomiokirkko** (p124) and **Uspenskin Katedraali** (p125), then explore **Suomenlinna** (p119), before a meal at **Suomenlinnan Panimo** (p129)

Four Days in Helsinki

Start day three at **Seurasaaren Ulko-museo** (p125). After a picnic lunch, make for **Temppeliaukion Kirkko** (p125), wander through **Kansallismuseo** (p125) then explore **Helsinki Art Museum (HAM)** (p125). Dine at **Saaga** (p129) before trying Finnish craft beer at **Birri**.

Day four begins at **Vanha Kauppahalli** (p128) followed by the **Design Museum** (p125) and the **Museum of Finnish Architecture** (p125). Explore the Design District shops, then dine at the **Savoy** (p129).

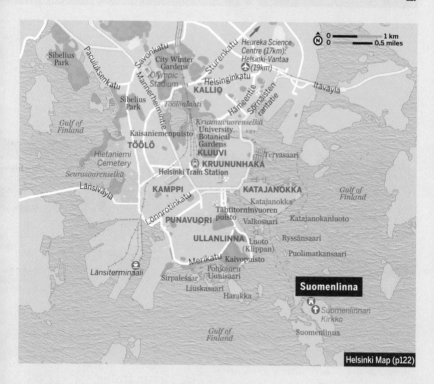

Helsinki Map (p122)

Arriving in Helsinki

Helsinki-Vantaa Airport The airport-city rail link (www.hsl.f; €5, 30 minutes, 5.05am to 12.05am) serves Helsinki's train station. The airport is also linked to central Helsinki by fast Finnair buses (€6.30, 30 minutes, every 20 minutes, 5am to midnight). A Taksi Helsinki cab costs around €45 to €50.

Helsinki Train Station Helsinki's central train station, serving international and domestic trains, is linked to the metro (Rautatientori stop).

Where to Stay

Helsinki is dominated by chain hotels, particularly Sokos and Scandic, but there are some boutique and designer gems, too. Budget accommodation is in short supply. Apartment rentals range from one-room studios to multiroom properties ideal for families. Often you'll get use of a sauna, parking area and other facilities.

From mid-May to mid-August book well ahead, though July is quieter for business and high-end hotels.

Suomenlinna castle

Suomenlinna

Suomenlinna, the 'fortress of Finland', straddles a cluster of car-free islands connected by bridges, and is a marvellous place to spend an afternoon or morning.

This Unesco World Heritage site was originally built by the Swedes as Sveaborg in the mid-18th century. Several museums, former bunkers and fortress walls, as well as Finland's only remaining WWII submarine, are fascinating to explore; its tourist office (p126) has info.

Jetty Barracks

At Suomenlinna's main quay, the pink Rantakasarmi (Jetty Barracks) building is one of the best preserved of the Russian era. It holds a small exhibition and a helpful, multilingual tourist office, with downloadable content for your smartphone. Guided tours (p126) of Suomenlinna depart from here.

Great For...

Don't Miss

The most atmospheric part of Suomenlinna, Kustaanmiekka, is at the end of the blue trail.

Suomenlinna fortress walls

❶ Need to Know

Suomenlinna (Sveaborg; www.suomen
linna.fi)

✗ Take a Break

Suomenlinnan Panimo (p129), by the
main quay, brews excellent beers and
offers good food to accompany them.

★ Top Tip

At around 5.15pm it's worth finding a spot
to watch the enormous Baltic ferries pass
through the narrow gap between islands.

Russian Orthodox Church

Near the tourist office you'll find Suomenlinna's distinctive **church** (www.helsing
inkirkot.fi; Suomenlinna; ⊙noon-4pm Wed-Sun,
plus Tue Jun-Aug). Built by the Russians in
1854, it served as a Russian Orthodox place
of worship until the 1920s when it became
Lutheran. It doubles as a lighthouse.

Suomenlinna-Museo

Suomenlinna-Museo (adult/child incl Vesikko
€7/4; ⊙10am-6pm May-Sep, 10.30am-4.30pm
Oct-Apr) is a two-level museum covering the history of the fortress. Displays
include maps and scale models. A helpful
25-minute audiovisual display plays every
30 minutes.

Bunkers & Beyond

Exploring the old bunkers, crumbling
fortress walls and cannons will give you
an insight into this fortress, and there
are plenty of grassy picnic spots. Monu-
mental King's Gate was built in 1753–54
as a two-storey fortress wall, which had a
double drawbridge and a stairway added.
In summer you can get a waterbus back
to Helsinki from here, saving you the walk
back to the main quay.

Getting There

Ferries (www.hsl.fi; single/return €3.20/5,
15 minutes, four hourly, fewer in winter) depart from the passenger quay at Helsinki's
kauppatori.

From May to September, **JT-Line** (www.
jt-line.fi; return €7) runs a waterbus from
the kauppatori, making three stops on
Suomenlinna (20 minutes).

Art & Design Walking Tour

Helsinki is renowned for its architecture, and this walk takes in many exemplars of the city's dramatically varying styles. It reveals the city's evolution from market town to the cutting-edge capital it is today.

Start Vanha Kauppahalli
Distance 3.2km
Duration 3 hours

7 Continue walking northwest then west through leafy backstreets to the **Temppeliaukion Kirkko** (p125), an extraordinary rock-hewn church.

6 National Romantic splendour reaches its peak at Helsinki's spectacular **train station** (p132), topped by a copper-caped clock tower.

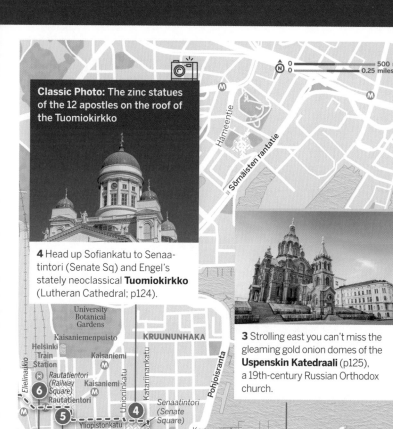

Classic Photo: The zinc statues of the 12 apostles on the roof of the Tuomiokirkko

4 Head up Sofiankatu to Senaa-tintori (Senate Sq) and Engel's stately neoclassical **Tuomiokirkko** (Lutheran Cathedral; p124).

3 Strolling east you can't miss the gleaming gold onion domes of the **Uspenskin Katedraali** (p125), a 19th-century Russian Orthodox church.

University Botanical Gardens

Kaisaniemenpuisto

KRUUNUNHAKA

Helsinki Train Station

Kaisaniemi

Rautatientori (Railway Square)

Rautatientori

Yliopistonkatu

Senaatintori (Senate Square)

Kanavaranta

Sofiankatu — Aleksanterinkatu

Pohjoisesplanadi
Eteläesplanadi

START

2 The bustling **kauppatori** (p119) (market square) is flanked by stately 19th-century buildings.

Take a Break...
Fuel up first with coffee and a pastry at the **Vanha Kauppahalli** (p128).

5 Walk west to the country's finest art museum, the **Ateneum** (p124), in a palatial 1887 neo–Renaissance building.

1 Helsinki's traditional market hall, **Vanha Kauppahalli** (p128), was built in 1888 and remains a traditional Finnish market

Helsinki

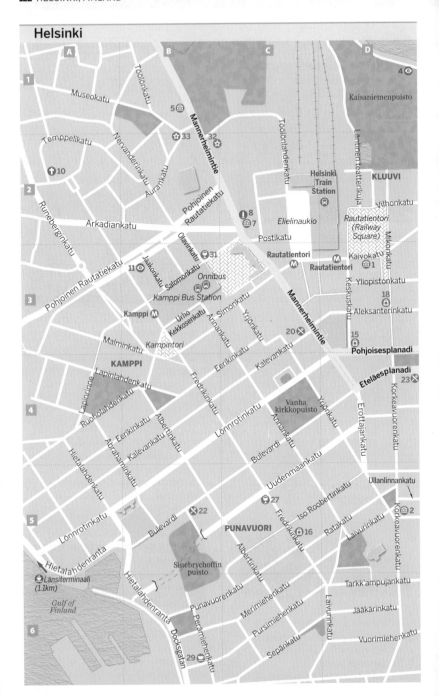

A **B** **C** **D**

1

Museokatu

Töölönkatu

Kaisaniemenpuisto

4

5

Mannerheimintie

33 32

Temppelikatu

Nervanderinkatu

Töölönlahdenkatu

KLUUVI

Helsinki
Train
Station

10

Aurankatu

Pohjoinen
Rautatiekatu

8

7

Elielinaukio

Vilhonkatu

Rautatientori
(Railway
Square)

2

Runeberginkatu

Arkadiankatu

Postikatu

Lähdenteatterikuja

Kaivokatu

Mikonkatu

Olavinkatu

31

Rautatientori

1

Jaakonkatu

11

Rautatientori

Yliopistonkatu

Pohjoinen Rautatiekatu

Salomonkatu

Onnibus

Kamppi Bus Station

Keskuskatu

18

3

Kamppi

Uriho
Kekkosenkatu

Simonkatu

Aleksanterinkatu

Annankatu

Yrjönkatu

20

15

Malminkatu

Kampintori

Pohjoisesplanadi

KAMPPI

Lapinlahdenkatu

Eerikinkatu

Kalevankatu

Mannerheimintie

Etelaesplanadi

23

Lapinrinne

Ruoholahdenkatu

Fredrikinkatu

Vanha
kirkkopuisto

Yrjönkatu

Korkeavuorenkatu

4

Eerikinkatu

Albertinkatu

Lönnrotinkatu

Annankatu

Erottajankatu

Abrahaminkatu

Kalevankatu

Hietalahdenkatu

Bulevardi

Uudenmaankatu

Ullanlinnankatu

Lönnrotinkatu

Bulevardi

27

Iso Roobertinkatu

Ratakatu

Laivurinkatu

Korkeavuorenkatu

2

5

22

PUNAVUORI

Fredrikinkatu

16

Hietalahdenranta

Sinebrychoffin
puisto

Albertinkatu

Merimiehenkatu

Tarkk'ampujankatu

Länsiterminaali
(1.1km)

Punavuorenkatu

Laivurinkatu

Jääkärinkatu

*Gulf of
Finland*

Hietalahdenranta

Perämiehenkatu

Pursimiehenkatu

Sepänkatu

Vuorimiehenkatu

6

Docksgatan

29

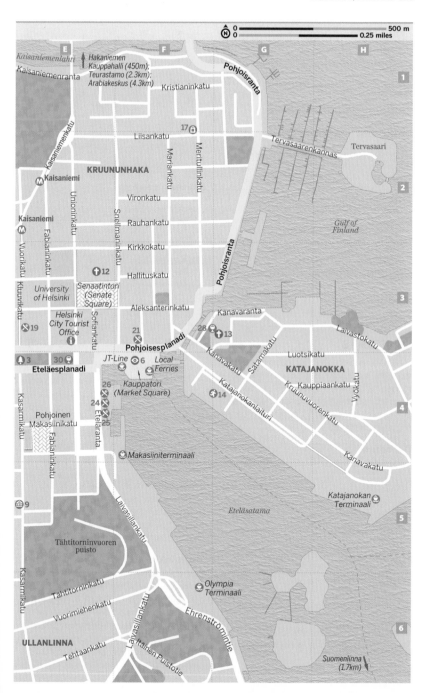

E

F

G

H

0   500 m

Ⓝ 0   0.25 miles

Kaisaniemenlahti

Kaisaniemenranta

↑ Hakaniemen
Kauppahalli (450m);
Teurastamo (2.3km);
Arabiakeskus (4.3km)

Pohjoisranta

1

Kristianinkatu

Kaisaniemenkatu

Tervasaarenkannas

Tervasaari

17 🔒

Liisankatu

KRUUNUNHAKA

Mariankatu

Meritullinkatu

Ⓜ Kaisaniemi

2

Unioninkatu

Vironkatu

Snellmaninkatu

Kaisaniemi

Ⓜ

Fabianinkatu

Rauhankatu

*Gulf of
Finland*

Vuorikatu

Kluuvikatu

Kirkkokatu

🔵 12

Hallituskatu

Pohjoisranta

University
of Helsinki

*Senaatintori
(Senate
Square)*

3

Aleksanterinkatu

Sofiankatu

Kanavaranta

🔵 19

*Helsinki
City Tourist
Office*
ℹ️

21
❌

28 ❌🔵 13

Laivastokatu

Pohjoisesplanadi

3 🔵 30 🔵

Eteläesplanadi

JT-Line ⊙ 6

*Local
Ferries*

Kanavakatu

Satamakatu

Luotsikatu

KATAJANOKKA

Kasarminkatu

26
❌

*Kauppatori
(Market Square)*

Kauppiaankatu

Vyökatu

24 ❌

🔵 14

Katajanokanlaituri

Kruunuvuorenkatu

Fabianinkatu

Eteläranta

25

Pohjoinen
Makasiinikatu

4

🔵 Makasiiniterminaali

Kanavakatu

🏛️ 9

Laivasillankatu

Eteläsatama

Katajanokan
Terminaali 🔄

5

*Tähtitorninvuoren
puisto*

Kasarminkatu

Tähtitorninkatu

🔄 *Olympia
Terminaali*

Laivalaituri

Vuorimiehenkatu

Laivastokatu

Ehrenströmintie

6

ULLANLINNA

Tehtaankatu

Eteläinen Puistotie

*Suomenlinna
(1.7km)* ↘

Helsinki

◎ SIGHTS

Helsinki has more than 50 museums and galleries, including many special-interest museums that will appeal to enthusiasts. For a full list, check the tourist office website (www.visithelsinki.fi), or pick up its free *Museums* booklet.

Ateneum   Gallery
(www.ateneum.fi; Kaivokatu 2; adult/child €15/free; ⊙10am-6pm Tue & Fri, to 8pm Wed & Thu, to 5pm Sat & Sun) Occupying a palatial 1887 neo–Renaissance building, Finland's premier art gallery offers a crash course in the nation's art. It houses Finnish paintings and sculptures from the 'golden age' of the late 19th century through to the 1950s, including works by Albert Edelfelt, Hugo Simberg, Helene Schjerfbeck, the von Wright brothers and Pekka Halonen. Pride of place goes to the prolific Akseli Gallen-Kallela's triptych from the Finnish national epic, the *Kalevala*, depicting Väinämöinen's pursuit of the maiden Aino.

Kiasma   Gallery
(www.kiasma.fi; Mannerheiminaukio 2; adult/child €14/free, 1st Sun of month free; ⊙10am-5pm Tue & Sun, to 8.30pm Wed-Fri, to 6pm Sat) Now one of a series of elegant contemporary buildings in this part of town, curvaceous and quirky metallic Kiasma, designed by Steven Holl and finished in 1998, is a symbol of the city's modernisation. It exhibits an eclectic collection of Finnish and international contemporary art, including digital art, and has excellent facilities for kids. Its outstanding success is that it's been embraced by the people of Helsinki, with a theatre and a hugely popular glass-sided cafe and terrace.

Tuomiokirkko   Church
(Lutheran Cathedral; www.helsinginseurakunnat.fi; Unioninkatu 29; ⊙9am-midnight Jun-Aug, to 6pm Sep-May) FREE One of CL Engel's finest creations, the chalk-white neoclassical Lutheran cathedral presides over Senaatintori. Created to serve as a reminder of God's supremacy, its high flight of stairs is now a popular meeting place. Zinc statues

of the 12 apostles guard the city from the roof of the church. The spartan, almost mausoleum-like interior has little ornamentation under the lofty dome apart from an altar painting and three stern statues of Reformation heroes Luther, Melanchthon and Mikael Agricola.

Uspenskin Katedraali   Church

(Uspenski Cathedral; www.hos.fi/uspenskin-kat edraali; Kanavakatu 1; ⊙9.30am-4pm Tue-Fri, 10am-3pm Sat, noon-3pm Sun) **FREE** The eye-catching red-brick Uspenski Cathedral towers above Katajanokka island. Built as a Russian Orthodox church in 1868, it features classic golden onion-topped domes and now serves the Finnish Orthodox congregation. The high, square interior has a lavish iconostasis, with the Evangelists flanking panels depicting the Last Supper and the Ascension.

Kansallismuseo   Museum

(National Museum of Finland; www.kansallis museo.fi; Mannerheimintie 34; adult/child €10/ free, 4-6pm Fri free; ⊙11am-6pm Tue-Sun) Built in National Romantic art nouveau style and opened in 1916, Finland's premier historical museum looks a bit like a Gothic church, with its heavy stonework and tall square tower. A major overhaul is under way until 2019, but the museum will remain open throughout. Already-completed sections include an exceptional prehistory exhibition and the Realm, covering the 13th to the 19th century. Also here is a fantastic hands-on area for kids, Workshop Vintti.

Temppeliaukion Kirkko   Church

(☑09-2340-6320; www.helsinginseurakunnat. fi; Lutherinkatu 3; adult/child €3/free; ⊙9.30am-5.30pm Mon-Thu & Sat, to 8pm Fri, noon-5pm Sun Jun-Aug, shorter hours Sep-May) Hewn into solid stone, the Temppeliaukio church, designed by Timo and Tuomo Suomalainen in 1969, feels close to a Finnish ideal of spirituality in nature – you could be in a rocky glade were it not for the stunning 24m-diameter roof covered in 22km of copper stripping. Its acoustics are exceptional; regular concerts

take place here. Opening times vary depending on events, so phone or search for its Facebook page updates. There are fewer groups midweek.

Helsinki Art Museum   Museum

(HAM; www.hamhelsinki.fi; Eteläinen Rautatiekatu 8; adult/child €10/free; ⊙11am-7pm Tue-Sun) Inside the **Tennispalatsi** (Tennis Palace;), Helsinki's contemporary-art museum oversees 9000 works, including 3500 city-wide public artworks. The overwhelming majority of its 20th- and 21st-century works are by Finnish artists; it also presents rotating exhibitions by emerging artists. Exhibits change every seven weeks. There's always at least one free exhibition that doesn't require a ticket to the museum's main section.

Design Museum   Museum

(www.designmuseum.fi; Korkeavuorenkatu 23; combination ticket with Museum of Finnish Architecture adult/child €10/free; ⊙11am-6pm Jun-Aug, 11am-8pm Tue, to 6pm Wed-Sun Sep-May) An unmissable stop for Finnish design aficionados, Helsinki's Design Museum has a permanent collection that looks at the roots of Finnish design in the nation's traditions and nature. Changing exhibitions focus on contemporary design – everything from clothing to household furniture. From June to August, 30-minute tours in English take place at 2pm on Saturday and are included in admission. Combination tickets with the nearby **Museum of Finnish Architecture** (Arkkitehtuurimuseo; ☑045-7731-0474; www.mfa.fi; Kasarmikatu 24; adult/child €10/free, combination ticket with Design Museum €12/free; ⊙11am-6pm Tue & Thu-Sun, to 8pm Wed) are a great-value way to see the two museums.

Seurasaaren Ulkomuseo   Museum

(Seurasaari Open-Air Museum; www.kansal lismuseo.fi/en/seurasaari-openairmuseum; Seurasaari; adult/child €9/3; ⊙11am-5pm Jun-Aug, 9am-3pm Mon-Fri, 11am-5pm Sat & Sun mid-late May & early–mid-Sep) Situated 5.5km northwest of the city centre, this excellent island-set museum has a collection of 87 historic wooden buildings transferred here from around Finland. There's everything from haylofts to a mansion, parsonage and church, as well as the beautiful giant rowboats used to transport church-going communities. Prices and hours refer to entering the museum's buildings, where guides in traditional costume demonstrate folk dancing and crafts. Otherwise, you're free to roam the picturesque wooded island, where there are several cafes.

🌀 TOURS

Happy Guide Helsinki
Walking, Cycling

(📱044-502-0066; www.happyguidehelsinki. com; walking/bike tours from €20/55) Happy Guide Helsinki runs a range of original, light-hearted but informative cycling and walking tours around the city. Just some of its bike-tour options include berry-picking or a sunset sauna tour; walking tours range from an old-town tour to food tours and craft-beer tours. Meeting points are confirmed when you book.

Suomenlinna Guided Tours
Walking

(📱029-533-8420; www.suomenlinna.fi; Rantakasarmi, Suomenlinna; adult/child €11/4; ☺up to 3 times daily Jun-Aug, 1.30pm Sat & Sun Sep-May) Guided tours of Suomenlinna (p119) lasting one hour depart from the **Rantakasarmi Information Centre** (📱029-533-8420; www.suomenlinna.fi; Suomenlinna; ☺10am-6pm May-Sep, to 4pm Oct-Apr). Tours cover the fortress' main sights, with informative explanations in English.

🔒 SHOPPING

Helsinki is a design epicentre, from fashion to furniture and homewares. Its hub is the Design District Helsinki (https://designdis trict.fi), spread out between chic Esplanadi to the east, retro-hipster Punavuori to the south and Kamppi to the west. Hundreds of shops, studios and galleries are mapped on its website; you can also pick up a map at the tourist office.

Artek

Artek Design

(www.artek.fi; Keskuskatu 1B; ⊙10am-7pm Mon-Fri, to 6pm Sat) Originally founded by architect and designers Alvar Aalto and his wife Aino in 1935, this iconic Finnish company maintains the simple design principle of its founders. Textiles, lighting and furniture are among its homewares. Many items are only available at this 700-sq-metre, two-storey space.

Tre Design

(www.worldoftre.com; Mikonkatu 6; ⊙11am-7pm Mon-Fri, to 6pm Sat) If you only have time to visit one design store in Helsinki, this 2016-opened emporium is a brilliant bet. Showcasing the works of Finnish designers in fashion, jewellery and accessories, including umbrellas, furniture, ceramics, textiles, stationery and art, it also stocks a superb range of architectural and design books to fuel inspiration.

Lasikammari Antiques

(www.lasikammari.fi; Liisankatu 9; ⊙noon-5pm Tue, Wed & Thu, to 2pm Mon, Fri & Sat) Vintage Finnish glassware from renowned brands such as Iittala, Nuutajärvi and Riihimäki, and individual designers such as Alvar Aalto and Tapio Wirkkala, make this tiny shop a diamond find for collectors. Along with glasses, you'll find vases, jugs, plates, bowls, light fittings and artistic sculptures. Prices are exceptionally reasonable; international shipping can be arranged on request.

Awake Design

(www.awake-collective.com; Fredrikinkatu 25; ⊙12.30-6.30pm Tue-Fri, 11am-4pm Sat) 🖋 At this super-minimalist art gallery–concept store, changing displays of handmade, Finnish–only designs range from men's and women's fashion and accessories, including watches, jewellery, bags and shoes, to birch plywood furniture and homewares such as rugs, carpets, sheets and blankets. Everything is ecologically and sustainably produced. Regular evening art and fashion shows are accompanied by champagne – check the website for announcements.

 Brunssi

Finns like a lie-in on the weekend, after the excesses of Friday and Saturday nights, so *brunssi* (brunch) was sure to catch on. Usually offered as a fixed-price buffet with everything from fruit and pastries to canapes, salads and pasta, it's so popular that you'll often have to book or wait. It's typically served from around 10.30am to 3.30pm, weekends only.

MAISICON/SHUTTERSTOCK ©

Arabiakeskus Design

(www.arabia.fi; Hämeentie 135, Toukola; ⊙noon-6pm Tue, Thu & Fri, to 8pm Wed, 10am-4pm Sat & Sun) Arabia refers to a whole district where the legendary Finnish ceramics company has manufactured its products since 1873. The complex, 5km north of Helsinki, includes a design mall, with a large Arabia/Iittala outlet. Run by Helsinki's Design Museum (p125), the free **Iittala & Arabia Design Centre museum** tells of the brand's history. Take tram 6 or 8 to the Arabiankatu stop.

⊗ ENTERTAINMENT

Catching live music – from metal to opera – is a highlight of visiting Helsinki. The latest events are publicised in the free *Helsinki This Week* (http://helsinkithisweek.com). Tickets for big events can be purchased from Ticketmaster (www.ticketmaster.fi), Lippupiste (www.lippu.fi), LiveNation (www.livenation.fi)

The Call of Kallio

For Helsinki's cheapest beer (around €3 to €4 a pint), hit working-class Kallio (near Sörnäinen metro station), north of the centre. Here, there's a string of dive bars along Helsinginkatu, but it, the parallel Vaasankatu and cross-street Fleminginkatu are also home to several more characterful bohemian places: go for a wander and you'll soon find one you like.

ALINA ZAMOGILNYKH/SHUTTERSTOCK ©

and Tiketti (www.tiketti.fi), which also has a booking office in Kamppi.

Musiikkitalo   Concert Venue

(Helsinki Music Centre; 020-707-0400; www. musiikkitalo.fi; Mannerheimintie 13; tickets free-€30) Home to the Helsinki Philharmonic Orchestra, Finnish Radio Symphony Orchestra and Sibelius Academy, the glass-and copper-fronted Helsinki Music Centre, opened in 2011, hosts a diverse program of classical, jazz, folk, pop and rock. The 1704-capacity main auditorium, visible from the foyer, has stunning acoustics. Five smaller halls seat 140 to 400. Buy tickets at the door or from www.ticketmaster.fi.

Storyville   Jazz

(050-363-2664; www.storyville.fi; Museokatu 8; jazz club 7pm-3am Thu, to 4am Fri & Sat, bar 7pm-2am Tue, to 3am Wed & Thu, to 4am Fri & Sat) Helsinki's number-one jazz club attracts a refined older crowd swinging to boogie woogie, trad jazz, Dixieland and New Orleans most nights. As well as the

performance space, there's a stylish bar that has a cool outside summer terrace, restaurant and outdoor charcoal grill in the park opposite, where some summer concerts also take place.

✖ EATING

Vegan and vegetarian cafes are especially well represented in this hip city, along with art-filled hangouts and some great independent restaurants and bistros serving gastropub-style fare. The former slaughterhouse complex **Teurastamo** (https:// teurastamo.com; Työpajankatu 2; 9am-9pm Mon & Tue, to 10pm Wed-Sat, to 8pm Sun) has a fantastic smokehouse, Asian food and much more. Look out for Finnish staples and snacks at the traditional market hall **Hakaniemen Kauppahalli** (www.hakaniemenkauppahalli.fi; Hämeentie 1; 8am-6pm Mon-Fri, to 4pm Sat;) .

Vanha Kauppahalli   Market €

(www.vanhakauppahalli.fi; Eteläranta 1; 8am-6pm Mon-Sat, plus 10am-5pm Sun Jun-Aug;) Alongside the harbour, this is Helsinki's iconic market hall. Built in 1888 it's still a traditional Finnish market, with wooden stalls selling local flavours such as liquorice, Finnish cheeses, smoked salmon and herring, berries, forest mushrooms and herbs. Its centrepiece is its superb cafe, **Story** (www.restaurantstory.fi; Vanha Kauppahalli, Eteläranta; snacks €3.20-10, mains €12.80-17; kitchen 8am-3pm Mon-Fri, to 5pm Sat, bar to 6pm Mon-Sat;) . Look out too for soups from **Soppakeittiö** (www.katijafille. fi/soppakeittio/; Vanha Kauppahalli; soups €9-10; 11am-5pm Mon-Sat;).

Karl Fazer Café   Cafe €

(www.fazer.fi; Kluuvikatu 3; dishes €4-12; 7.30am-10pm Mon-Fri, 9am-10pm Sat, 10am-6pm Sun;) Founded in 1891 and fronted by a striking art deco facade, this cavernous cafe is the flagship for Fazer's chocolate empire. The glass cupola reflects sound, so locals say it's a bad place to gossip. It's ideal, however, for buying dazzling confectionery, fresh bread, salmon or shrimp sandwiches, or digging into towering sundaes or spectacular cakes. Gluten-free dishes are available.

Suomenlinnan Panimo   Finnish €€

(☏020-742-5307; www.panimoravintola.fi; Suomenlinna C1; mains €15-30; ☉noon-10pm Mon-Sat, to 6pm Sun Jun-Aug, shorter hours Sep-May) By the main quay, this microbrewery is the best place to drink or dine on Suomenlinna. It brews three ciders and seven different beers, including a hefty porter, plus several seasonal varieties, and offers good food to accompany it, such as pike-perch with mustard tar sauce, or a game platter, smoked reindeer and wild pheasant rillettes.

Saaga   Finnish €€

(☏09-7425-5544; www.ravintolasaaga.fi; Bulevardi 34; mains €22-27, 3-course menus €49-65; ☉6-11pm Mon-Fri late May-Aug, 6-11pm Mon-Sat Sep & Oct) Chandeliers made from reindeer antlers and split-log benches lined with reindeer furs adorn this rustic timber-lined Lappish restaurant. Specialities from Finland's far north include chargrilled whitefish with sour milk sauce, and roast elk with juniper berry sauce, followed by desserts such as Lappish squeaky cheese with sea buckthorn cream or liquorice cake with birch ice cream and cloudberries.

Olo   Finnish €€€

(☏010-320-6250; www.olo-ravintola.fi; Pohjoisesplanadi 5; 4-course lunch menu €53, dinner tasting menus short/long from €79/109, with paired wines €173/255; ☉6-11pm Tue-Sat Jun–mid-Aug, 11.30am-3pm & 6-11pm Tue-Fri, 6-11pm Sat mid-Aug–May) At the forefront of new Suomi cuisine, Michelin–starred Olo occupies a handsome 19th-century harbourside mansion. Its memorable degustation menus incorporate both the forage ethos and molecular gastronomy, and feature culinary jewels such as fennel-smoked salmon, herring with fermented cucumber, Åland lamb with blackcurrant leaves, juniper-marinated reindeer carpaccio, and Arctic crab with root celery. Book a few weeks ahead.

Savoy   Finnish €€€

(☏09-6128-5300; www.ravintolasavoy.fi; Eteläesplanadi 14; mains €37-44, 3-course lunch

Musiikkitalo

Karl Fazer Café (p128)

menu €63; ☉11.30am-3pm & 6pm-midnight Mon-Fri, 6pm-midnight Sat) Designed by Alvar and Aino Aalto in 1937, this is one of Helsinki's grandest dining rooms, with birch walls and ceilings and some of the city's finest views. The food is a modern Nordic tour de force, with the 'forage' ethos strewing flowers and berries across plates that bear the finest Finnish game, fish and meat.

🍷 DRINKING & NIGHTLIFE

Diverse drinking and nightlife in Helsinki ranges from cosy bars to specialist craft-beer and cocktail venues, and clubs with live music and DJs. In summer early-opening beer terraces sprout all over town. Some club nights have a minimum age of 20 or older; check event details on websites before you arrive.

Kappeli   Bar
(www.kappeli.fi; Eteläesplanadi 1; ☉10am-midnight; 🛜) Dating from 1867, this grand bar-cafe opens to an outdoor terrace seating 350 people and has regular jazz, blues and folk music in the nearby bandstand in

Esplanadin Puisto (Esplanadi Park) from May to August. Locals and visitors alike flock here on a sunny day.

Steam Hellsinki   Cocktail Bar
(www.steamhellsinki.fi; Olavinkatu 1; ☉4pm-4am Mon-Sat; 🛜) A wonderland of steampunk design, with futuris-tic-meets-19th-century industrial steam-powered machinery decor, includ-ing a giant Zeppelin floating above the gondola-shaped bar, mechanical cogs and pulleys, globes, lanterns, radios, cande-labras, Chesterfield sofas and a Zoltar fortune-telling machine, this extraordinary bar has dozens of varieties of gin, and DJs spinning electro-swing. Ask about gin-ap-preciation and cocktail-making courses in English.

Kaffa Roastery   Coffee
(www.kaffaroastery.fi; Pursimiehenkatu 29A; ☉7.45am-6pm Mon-Fri, 10am-5pm Sat; 🛜) Pro-cessing up to 4000kg of beans every week, this vast coffee roastery supplies cafes throughout Helsinki, Finland and beyond. You can watch the roasting in progress

through the glass viewing windows while sipping Aeropress, syphon or V60 brews in its polished concrete surrounds. It also stocks a range of coffee grinders, espresso machines and gadgets.

Birri   Microbrewery

(Il Birrificio; http://ilbirri.fi; Fredrikinkatu 22; ⏱11am-11pm Mon-Thu, to 1am Fri & Sat, to 4pm Sun) Birri brews three of its own beers on-site at any one time, stocks a fantastic range of Finnish–only craft beers and also hand-crafts its own seasonally changing sausages. The space is strikingly done out with Arctic–white metro tiles, brown-and-white chequerboard floor tiles, exposed timber beams and gleaming silver kegs.

Holiday   Bar

(http://holiday-bar.fi; Kanavaranta 7; ⏱4-11pm Tue-Thu, to 2am Fri, noon-2am Sat; 🛜) Even on the greyest Helsinki day, this colourful waterfront bar transports you to more tropical climes with vibrant rainforest wallpapers and plants such as palms, tropical-themed cocktails like frozen margaritas and mojitos (plus two dozen different gins) and a seafood menu that includes softshell crab. A small market often sets up out front in summer, along with ping-pong tables.

ℹ INFORMATION

DISCOUNT CARDS

The **Helsinki Card** (www.helsinkicard.com; one/two/three day pass €46/56/66) gives you free public transport around the city and local ferries (Kauppatori) to Suomenlinna, entry to 28 attractions in and around Helsinki and a 24-hour hop-on, hop-off bus tour.

The **Helsinki & Region Card** (one/two/three day pass €50/62/72) offers the same benefits and adds in free transport to/from the airport.

Both cards are cheaper online; otherwise, get them at tourist offices, hotels or transport terminals.

TOURIST INFORMATION

Helsinki City Tourist Office (☎09-3101-3300; www.visithelsinki.fi; Pohjoisesplanadi 19; ⏱9am-

 Finnish Music

Finland's music scene is one of the world's richest, and the output of quality musicians per capita is amazingly high, whether a polished symphony orchestra violinist or a headbanging bassist for the next big death-metal band. Summer in Helsinki and across the country is all about music festivals of all conceivable types.

Finland has one of the most storming metal scenes around, and Helsinki is ground zero. The city's biggest exports are HIM with their 'love metal' and darkly atmospheric Nightwish. Catchy light-metal rockers the Rasmus continue to be successful. All genres of metal, as well as a few made-up ones, are represented, including Finntroll's folk metal (blending metal and humppa), the 69 Eyes' Gothic metal, Apocalyptica's classical metal, Children of Bodom's melodic death metal and Stratovarius' power metal.

Local hip-hop, known as Suomirap, also has a dedicated following, thanks to artists such as Elastinen, Heikki Kuula and Pyhimys, and there's always some new underground project.

Jazz is also very big in Helsinki, with dedicated clubs and a huge festival at Espoo each April.

Finnish band Apocalyptica
DOMINIONART/SHUTTERSTOCK ©

6pm Mon-Sat, to 4pm Sun mid-May–mid-Sep, 9am-6pm Mon-Fri, 10am-4pm Sat & Sun mid-Sep–mid-May) Busy multilingual office with a great quantity of information on the city. Also has an office at the **airport** (www.visithelsinki.fi; Terminal 2, Helsinki-Vantaa Airport; ☺10am-8pm May-Sep, 10am-6pm Mon-Sat, noon-6pm Sun Oct-Apr).

Strömma (www.stromma.fi; Pohjoisesplanadi 19; ☺9am-6pm Mon-Sat, to 4pm Sun mid-May–mid-Sep, 9am-6pm Mon-Fri, 10am-4pm Sat & Sun mid-Sep–mid-May) In the city tourist office; sells various tours and local cruises, as well as package tours to Stockholm, Tallinn and St Petersburg. Also sells the Helsinki Card and Helsinki & Region Card.

🛈 GETTING THERE & AWAY

AIR

Helsinki-Vantaa Airport (www.helsinki-vantaa.fi), 19km north of the city, is Finland's main air terminus. Direct flights serve many major European cities and several intercontinental destinations.

Finnair (☎09-818-0800; www.finnair.fi) covers 18 Finnish cities, usually at least once per day.

BOAT

International ferries sail to Stockholm, Tallinn, St Petersburg and German destinations.

Ferry companies have detailed timetables and fares on their websites. Purchase tickets online, at the terminal, or at ferry company offices. Book well in advance during high season (late June to mid-August) and on weekends.

There are five main terminals: **Katajanokan Terminaali** (Katajanokan), **Makasiiniterminaali** (Eteläranta 7), **Olympia Terminaali** (Olympi-aranta 1), **Länsiterminaali** (West Terminal; Tyynenmerenkatu 8) (West Terminal) and **Hansaterminaali** (Provianttikatu 5, Vuosaari).

BUS

Kamppi bus station (www.matkahuolto.fi; Salomonkatu) has a terminal for local buses to Espoo in one wing, while longer-distance buses also depart from here to destinations throughout Finland. From Kamppi bus station, **Onnibus** (www.onnibus.com) runs budget routes to several Finnish cities.

Destinations with several daily departures include the following:

Jyväskylä €30, 4½ hours, up to three hourly

Kuopio €34, six hours, hourly

Lappeenranta €30, 3½ hours, up to three hourly

Oulu €55, 9½ hours, up to 13 per day

Savonlinna €30, 5½ hours, nine daily

Tampere €25, 2½ hours, up to four hourly

Turku €28, 2½ hours, up to four hourly

TRAIN

Helsinki's central **train station** (Rautatieasema; www.vr.fi; Kaivokatu 1) is linked to the metro (Rautatientori stop) and situated 500m east of Kamppi bus station.

The train is the fastest and cheapest way to get from Helsinki to major centres.

Destinations include the following:

Joensuu €44, 4½ hours, three daily

Kuopio €45, 4¼ hours, four daily

Lappeenranta €28, two hours, six daily

Oulu €56, six hours, four daily

Rovaniemi €80, eight hours, four daily

Tampere €21, 1½ hours, two hourly

Turku €20, two hours, hourly

There are also daily trains (buy tickets from the international counter) to the Russian cities of Vyborg, St Petersburg and Moscow; you'll need a Russian visa.

🛈 GETTING AROUND

○ **Walking** Central Helsinki is compact and easily covered on foot.

○ **Bicycle** Helsinki's shared-bike scheme City Bikes (www.hsl.fi/citybikes) has some 1500 bikes at 150 stations citywide.

○ **Tram** Ten main routes cover the city. Three of these, trams 2, 4 and 6, can double as budget sightseeing tours.

○ **Bus** Buses serve the northern suburbs, Espoo and Vantaa; most visitors won't need to use them.

○ **Metro** Helsinki's single, forked metro line has 17 stations. Most are beyond the centre; the most useful for visitors are in the centre and Kallio.

○ **Ferry** Local ferries serve island destinations, including Suomenlinna.

Where to Stay

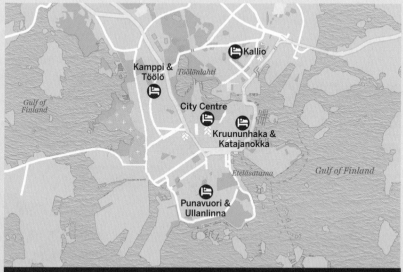

Neighbourhood	For	Against
City Centre	As central as it gets, with excellent shopping, major museums and parks.	Drinking and dining options are limited in this small area. Quiet at weekends.
Kamppi & Töölö	Kamppi has plenty of food and drink options and is home to the main bus station. Töölö is leafier and quieter.	Kamppi can be busy and may be noisy. Residential Töölö has very few options.
Kruununhaka & Katajanokka	Katajanokka is handy for the ferry terminal, and accessible to the centre. Mainly residential, Kruununhaka has some standout eateries.	Options are limited on Katajanokka and virtually nonexistent in Kruununhaka.
Punavuori & Ullanlinna	Great cafes, restaurants, bars and shops in Design District hub Punavuori. Peaceful Ullanlinna has parks and open spaces.	Parts of Punavuori close to the centre can be busy and/or noisy. Few options in Ullanlinna.
Kallio	Gentrifying area with hip, creative businesses, vintage shops and cheap bars. Good metro access.	Some areas can be edgy. There are some chain hotels and the usual home-sharing services.

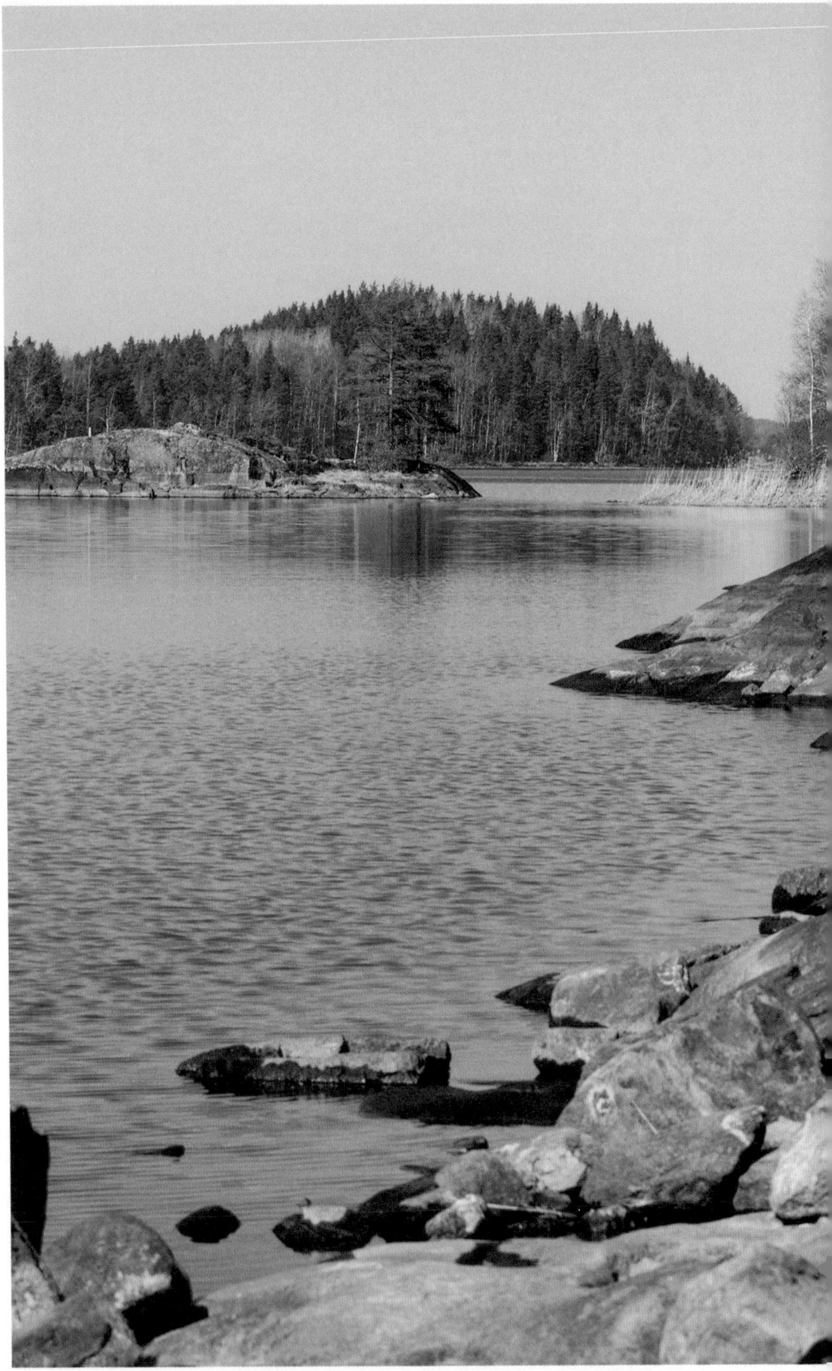

MMARTIN/SHUTTERSTOCK ©

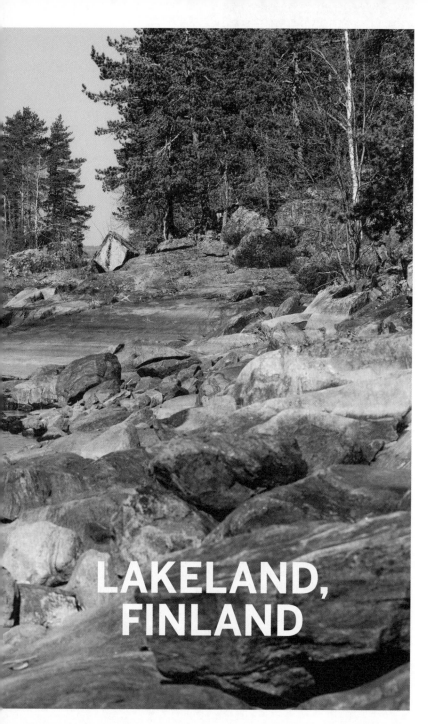

LAKELAND, FINLAND

Lakeland, Finland

Most of Finland could be dubbed 'lakeland', but around here it seems there's more aqua than terra firma. Reflecting the sky and forests as clearly as a mirror, the sparkling, clean water leaves an indelible impression. When exploring the region, it's almost obligatory to get waterborne. On land, there's just as much to do. Architecture buffs from around the globe make the pilgrimage here to visit Alvar Aalto's buildings, opera aficionados arrive en masse to attend the world-famous Savonlinna Opera Festival, and outdoor enthusiasts shoulder their packs. And at day's end, there are always saunas to relax in.

Two Days in Lakeland

Begin in **Savonlinna** (p138)and spend an entire day soaking up its charms; a boat trip, a tour of **Olavinlinna** (p138), and if you're really lucky, you'll be in town for the opera festival. Allow time also for a trip to the Seal Lakes, perhaps on day two, with time also for an exploration of the **New Valamo Monastery** (Valamon Luostari; p140).

Four Days in Lakeland

On day three, explore **Lakeland's churches** (p142) and widely spread museums, do some shopping in **Savonlinna** (p138), and perhaps overnight in **Joensuu** (p147).

Day four is all about **Jyväskylä** (p150), which is one of Scandinavia's most important architectural centres, with the work of Alvar Aalto front and centre. Walking and boat cruises are also recommended.

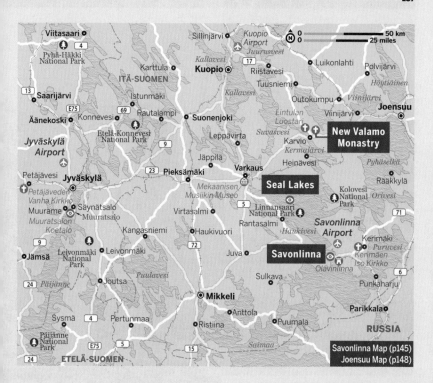

Savonlinna Map (p145)
Joensuu Map (p148)

Arriving in Lakeland

Buses and, to a lesser degree, trains link most cities and towns in the region. Some services are reduced or cancelled on weekends.

Saimaan Laivamatkat Oy (p139) runs cruises between Savonlinna and Kuopio, stopping at Oravi in the **Seal Lakes** (p138) en route. It also sails between Kuopio and **New Valamo** (p140).

Where to Stay

There are sleeping options for every budget in Jyväskylä and Savonlinna, including outstanding boutique choices. Outside these towns, the range of options is limited and less impressive.

Olavinlinna

NIKIFOROV ALEXANDER/SHUTTERSTOCK ©

Savonlinna & the Seal Lakes

The historic frontier settlement of Savonlinna is one of Finland's prettiest towns and most compelling tourist destinations. Nearby, seal-inhabited lakes are a real draw.

Great For...

Don't Miss

The stories told by castle guides – the soldiers, for instance, were partly paid in beer!

Olavinlinna

Built directly on rock in the middle of the lake (now accessed via bridges), this heavily restored 15th-century **fortification** (St Olaf's Castle; ☎029-533-6941; www.kansallismuseo.fi; Olavinlinna; adult/child €9/4.50; ⏱11am-5.15pm Jun–mid-Aug, 10am-3.15pm mid-Aug–May, closed mid-Dec–early Jan) was constructed as a military base on the Swedes' restless eastern border. The currents in the surrounding water ensure that it remains unfrozen in winter, which prevented enemy attacks over ice. To visit the castle's upper levels, including the towers and chapel, you must join a one-hour guided tour. Guides bring the castle to life with vivid accounts of its history.

🛈 Need to Know

You can reach Savonlinna by air, boat, bus or train.

✕ Take a Break

Savonlinna's very own microbrewery, Huvila (p146) is a lovely spot for a Golden Ale.

★ Top Tip

For a list of festivals and events staged in Savonlinna, go to http://visitsavonlin na.fi/en/events-in-savonlinna-region.

Savonlinna Opera Festival

The **Savonlinna Opera Festival** (Savonlinnan Oopperajuhlat; 📞015-476-750; www.operafestival.fi; Olavinkatu 27; ⊘early Jul-early Aug) enjoys an enviably dramatic setting: the covered courtyard of Olavinlinna Castle. Inaugurated in 1912, it stages four weeks of top-class opera performances between early July and early August each year. The atmosphere in town during the festival is reason enough to come: it's buzzing, with restaurants serving post-show midnight feasts, and animated discussions and impromptu arias on all sides.

Seal Lakes

Easily reached from Savonlinna, the watery **Linnansaari** (www.outdoors.fi) and **Kolovesi**

(www.outdoors.fi) National Parks are great to explore by canoe and are the habitat of a rare inland seal. See www.nationalparks.fi for information on the parks, and http://visitsavonlinna.fi/en and www.oravivillage.com for transport, accommodation, activities and equipment-hire services in the area.

Take a Cruise

Saimaan Laivamatkat Oy (📞015-250-250; www.mspuijo.fi; Satamapuistonkatu; one-way €95, return by same-day car €130, return with/ without overnight cabin €180/150; ⊘mid-Jun–mid-Aug) runs cruises on century-old M/S *Puijo* from Savonlinna to Kuopio on Monday, Wednesday and Friday at 9am (10½ hours), returning on Tuesday, Thursday and Saturday. The boat passes through scenic waterways, canals and locks. On-board meals are available.

New Valamo Monastery

At once rich in history, studded with treasures and filled with a strange spiritual power, the New Valamo Monastery (Valamon Luostari) is deservedly one of Finland's premier attractions.

Great For...

Don't Miss

Take in at least one worship service, whether prayer service, liturgy, matins or vespers.

The Church

Finland's only Orthodox monastery is idyllically located on an island in Juojävi. Visitors are free to roam the site and enter the churches. The first church was made by connecting two sheds; the rustic architecture contrasts curiously with its gilded icons. The modern church has an onion-shaped dome and an incense-saturated interior featuring an elaborate iconostasis. Visitors can follow a 4.5km marked walking trail to a pilgrim's wooden cross located on the lake's edge.

❶ Need to Know

Valamon Luostari (New Valamo, New Valaam; ☏017-570-111; www.valamo.fi; Valamontie 42, Heinävesi; ⊗9am-9pm)

✗ Take a Break

Order a coffee or tea with a sandwich or bun at **Trapesa** (www.valamo.fi; Valamon Luostari; buffet lunch adult/child €14/7; ⊗7.30am-6pm Mon-Thu, to 9pm Fri & Sat) and enjoy it on the front terrace.

★ Top Tip

The most pleasant way to arrive in summer is on the **M/S Puijo** (☏015-250-250; www.mspuijo.fi) from Kuopio.

New Valamo History

The date when the Valamo community was initially established is disputed, but most historians cite the late 14th century. Originally located on Lake Ladoga, it survived the Russian Revolution's aftermath because the original monastery (now in Russian Karelia) fell just within newly independent Finland. This changed during the 1939-40 Winter War, when the region fell to the Soviets. Fortunately, Ladoga froze (a rare occurrence), allowing a hurried evacuation of 190 monks, icons and treasures. The evacuated monks set up a new community here in Heinävesi in 1940, and the original monastery became a Russian military base; it was only in 1989 that a monastic community was re-established there.

Services & Guided Tours

There's a prayer service at noon on Saturday and liturgy at 9am on Sunday. Matins are held at 6am Monday to Saturday and vespers or a vigil at 6pm daily. Guided tours (adult/child €6/3, 75 minutes) of the monastery are offered between 10am and 5pm on Sundays and on other days in high summer.

Sleep Overnight

Valamo (☏017-570-1810; www.valamo.fi; s/d without bathroom €45/66, hotel s/d €80/130; P 🛜 🛉) is especially peaceful once the day-trippers depart and evening descends. Guesthouses in picturesque wooden buildings provide comfortable, no-frills sleeping with shared bathrooms; there are also hotel rooms with private bathrooms.

Petäjävesi Vanha Kirkko

PECOLD/SHUTTERSTOCK ©

Lakeland Churches

Churches are such a feature of Finland's Lakeland, and seeking them out will appeal to both architecture buffs and those eager for the soaring complements to all those watery expanses.

Great For...

Don't Miss

A souvenir shop near Lintulan Luostari's entrance sells hand-made candles, supplied to all Finland's Orthodox churches.

Kerimäen Iso Kirkko

Kerimäki may be small (population 5000), but **Kerimäen Iso Kirkko** (Kerimäki Church; www.kerimaenseurakunta.fi; ☉10am-6pm late Jun & early Aug, to 7pm Jul, to 4pm early Jun & late Aug) **FREE**, its Lutheran church, certainly isn't. Built in 1847, the building was designed to accommodate 5000 and is commonly described as the world's largest wooden church. The building's scale is immense and the grand, light-drenched interior features stained-glass lamps and unusual wood panels painted to resemble marble.

Lintulan Luostari

Finland's only Orthodox convent, **Lintulan Luostari** (Lintula Convent; ☎040-485-7603; www.lintulanluostari.fi; Honkasalontie 3, Palokki; ☉10am-6pm Jun-Aug) is particularly

Kerimäen Iso Kirkko

Jyväskylä Airport · Keitele · Lintulan Luostari · Viinijärvi · Karvio · Mekaanisen Musiikin Museo · Petäjävesi · Varkaus · Orivesi · Haukivesi · Petäjäveden Vanha Kirkko · Savonlinna Airport · Kerimäki · Päijänne · Puulavesi · Kerimäen Iso Kirkko

❶ Need to Know

Buses and, to a lesser degree, trains link most cities and towns in the region.

✕ Take a Break

There are cafes in the grounds of Lintulan Luostari and Kerimäen Iso Kirkko.

★ Top Tip

Come in August for decent weather but without the July crowds.

lovely in early summer, when the many flowers in its beautifully tended gardens bloom. The order was founded in Karelia in 1895 and its nuns relocated to this location near New Valamo after WWII. When here, be sure to follow the walking trail from the car park past the small cemetery and down through the forest to the shed-like Chapel of St Paraskeva on the shore of Koskijärvi.

Mekaanisen Musiikin Museo

This extraordinary collection of mechanical **musical instruments** (Mechanical Music Museum; ☎050-590-9297; www. mekaanisenmusiikinmuseo.fi; Pelimanninkatu 8, Varkaus; adult/child €16/8; ☺11am-6pm Tue-Sat, to 5pm Sun Mar–mid-Dec, to 6pm daily Jul) in Varkaus ranges from a ghostly keyboard-tinkling Steinway to a robotic violinist to a full-scale orchestra emanating from a large cabinet. Entry is by multilanguage guided tour that lasts around 75 minutes.

Petäjävesi Vanha Kirkko

Petäjäveden Vanha Kirkko (Petäjävesi Old Church; ☎040-582-2461; www.petajavesi.fi/ kirkko; Vanhankirkontie, Petäjävesi; adult/child €6/4; ☺10am-6pm Jun-Aug, reduced hours Sep, other times by appointment), a wonderfully gnarled Unesco–listed wooden church, is located in Petäjävesi, 35km west of Jyväskylä. Finished in 1765, it's a marvellous example of 18th-century rustic Finnish architecture, with crooked wooden pews, a pulpit held up by a rosy-cheeked St Christopher, and a fairy-tale shingle roof.

Savonlinna

Scattered across a garland of small islands strung between Haukivesi and Pihlajavesi lakes, Savonlinna's major attraction is the visually dramatic Olavinlinna Castle (p138), constructed in the 15th century and now the spectacular venue of July's world-famous Savonlinna Opera Festival. In summer, when the lakes shimmer in the sun and operatic arias waft through the forest-scented air, the place is quite magical. In winter, it's blanketed in fairytale-like snow, and its friendly locals can be relied upon to offer visitors a warm welcome.

◉ SIGHTS

Riihisaari Museum

(Lake Saimaa Nature & Culture Centre; ☑044-417-4466; www.savonlinna.fi/museo; adult/child €7/3, incl Olavinlinna €10/4.50; ☺ 9am-5pm Mon-Fri & 10am-5pm Sat & Sun May, 10am-5pm daily Jun-Aug, 10am-5pm Tue-Sun Sep-Apr) On an island that was once a naval Lakelandport, this museum housed in a handsome 16th-century granary recounts local history and the importance of water transport. It also has a number of exhibits about the history, flora and fauna of Lake Saimaa, including a 12-minute video about the underwater world of Torsti, an endangered ringed seal pup living in the lake. Exhibits on the ground floor are more interesting than those upstairs.

⊕ ACTIVITIES

Savonlinna's surrounding area has quiet country lanes and gently sloping hills, and so is terrific for **bicycle touring**. Bikes can be carried on board lakeboats for a small fee.

See http://visitsavonlinna.fi/en for information about canoe and kayak hire in and around the city.

SS Mikko Cruise

(☑044-417-4466; adult/child €15/10; ☺Jul) Part of the watercraft collection of the Riihisaari, this 1914 wooden steam barge offers 90-minute cruises on the lake during July.

VIP Cruise Cruise

(☑050-025-0075; www.vipcruise.info/en; Satamapuistonkatu; ☺Jun-Aug) Operates three historic steamships – S/S *Paul Wahl*, S/S *Punkaharju* and S/S *Savonlinna* – offering 90-minute sightseeing cruises on Lake Saimmaa (adult/child €20/10).

⊕ SHOPPING

Runo Design Design

(☑050-3059-715; www.runodesign.fi; Satamakatu 11; ☺10am-3pm Mon, to 4pm Tue-Fri) Everything in this gorgeous atelier has been handmade in Savonlinna. Textile designer Mervi Pesonen uses natural materials such as flax, wool, park skirt and cotton marshmallow to make stylish bags, cushions, throws and tea towels.

Studio Marja Putus Clothing

(☑040-526-5129; www.marjaputus.fi; Linnankatu 10; ☺9am-5pm Mon-Fri, daily during Opera Festival) Artist and fashion designer Maria Putus makes and sells stylish outfits (many made using Marimekko fabric) at her atelier in a timber house in Savonlinna's historic precinct.

⊗ EATING

Head for the lakeside kauppatori (market square) for cheap and tasty snacks such as the local speciality, *lörtsy* (turnovers). These come with meat (*lihalörtsy*), apple (*omenalörtsy*) or cloudberry (*lakkalörtsy*) fillings and cost between €2.50 and €3.50. Savonlinna is also famous for fried *muikku* (vendace, or whitefish, a small lake fish). Restaurants open later during the opera festival; many have reduced hours from September to May and some close altogether.

Kahvila Saima Cafe €

(☑015-515-340; www.kahvilasaima.net; Linnankatu 11; dishes €7-17; ☺9.30am-5pm Jun-Aug, 10.30am-4.30pm Wed-Sun Sep-May) Set inside a wooden villa with stained-glass windows, and opening to a wide

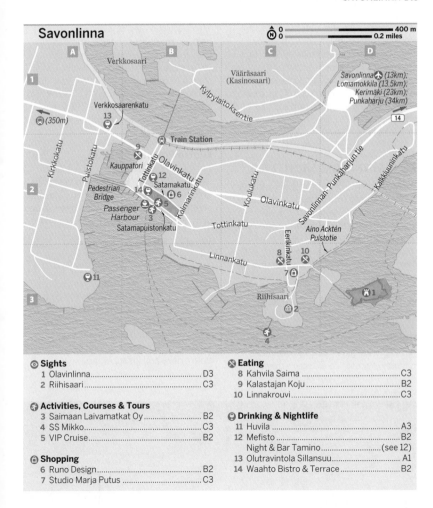

Savonlinna

(N) 0 — 400 m
0 — 0.2 miles

Sights
| 1 Olavinlinna | D3 |
| 2 Riihisaari | C3 |

Activities, Courses & Tours
3 Saimaan Laivamatkat Oy	B2
4 SS Mikko	C3
5 VIP Cruise	B2

Shopping
| 6 Runo Design | B2 |
| 7 Studio Marja Putus | C3 |

Eating
8 Kahvila Saima	C3
9 Kalastajan Koju	B2
10 Linnakrouvi	C3

Drinking & Nightlife
11 Huvila	A3
12 Mefisto	B2
Night & Bar Tamino	(see 12)
13 Olutravintola Sillansuu	A1
14 Waahto Bistro & Terrace	B2

terrace out the back, this charmingly
old-fashioned cafe is adorned with
striped wallpaper and serves home-style
Finnish food, including good cakes and
baked items. It stays open till 11.30pm on
opera days.

Kalastajan Koju   Seafood €
(www.kalastajankoju.com; Kauppatori; fried
muikku €9.50, with dip, mayonnaise or
remoulade €10.50, with potato & salad €16.90;
⊙11am-10pm Mon-Thu, to midnight Fri & Sat,
to 9pm Sun) Owned by a fisherman who

heads out on the lake each morning to
catch the *muikku* (vendace, or whitefish, a
common lake fish) that this place specialises in, Kalastajan Koju is conveniently located on the water by the kauppatori and
is particularly busy in summer. The menu
also includes fish and chips, bratwurst
and fried salmon.

Linnakrouvi   Finnish €€
(☑015-576-9124; www.linnakrouvi.fi; Linnankatu
7; mains €18-33; ⊙noon-10pm or later Mon-Sat,
3-10pm or later Sun late Jun–mid-Aug) Overlooking

Olavinlinna Castle, this summer restaurant employs chefs from Helsinki and serves Savonlinna's most sophisticated food. Unsurprisingly, it's hugely popular during the opera season. There's tiered outdoor seating, an attractive interior and a range of fare running from burgers to freshly caught and beautifully prepared fish from Lake Saimaa. There's a limited but impressive wine list.

🍷 DRINKING & NIGHTLIFE

There are plenty of summer bars and cafes on the lakefront (most opposite the castle), but all of these close outside the summer months. Bars in the town centre open year-round. **Mefisto** (☎029-123-9600; http://kattaasavon.fi; Kauppatori 4-6; cover varies; ⊙10pm-3am Fri & Sat) and **Night & Bar Tamino** (☎015-20-202; http://kattaasavon.fi; Kauppatori 4-6; cover price varies; ⊙11pm-4am Fri & Sat) in the Original Sokos Hotel Seurahuone complex are the only clubbing options.

Huvila   Microbrewery
(☎015-555-0555; www.panimoravintolahuvila.fi; Puistokatu 4; mains €24-35, 3-course menu €45-50; ⊙noon-10pm Jun-Aug; 🛜) Sitting across the harbour, Huvila is operated by the Waahto brewery and is a delightful destination in warm weather, when its lakeside deck is full of patrons relaxing over a pint or two of the house brew (try the Golden Ale). There's also an attractive dining area in the old timber house. Sadly, the menu promises more than it delivers.

Olutravintola Sillansuu   Pub
(Verkkosaarenkatu 1; ⊙2pm-2am Tue-Sat, to midnight Sun & Mon) Savonlinna's best pub is compact and cosy, offering an excellent variety of international bottled beers, a decent whisky selection and friendly service.

Waahto Bistro & Terrace   Bar
(☎015-510-677; www.waahto.fi; Satamapuistonkatu 5; mains €19-34; ⊙noon-10pm Mon-Thu, to 11pm Fri & Sat, to 8pm Sun Jun-Aug, 4-10pm Tue-Sat Sep-May) By the kauppatori and harbour, this pub is owned by the local brewery and has a great summer terrace that's perfect for a sundowner. Come here for a drink rather than to eat, as the food is both pricey and disappointing.

Savonlinna harbour

INFORMATION

Savonlinna has no official tourist office, but the ticket desk in the **Riihisaari** (p144) stocks maps and brochures about the city and region. Other information can be accessed via www.savonlinna.fi.

GETTING THERE & AWAY

AIR

Savonlinna Airport (SVL; ✆020-708-8101; www.finavia.fi; Lentoasemantie 50) is situated 14km north of town, and is predominantly used by charter flights. Finnair flies here during the opera season.

BOAT

Boats connect Savonlinna's **passenger harbour** (Satamapuistonkatu) with many lakeside towns; check www.oravivillage.com for seasonal schedules.

BUS

Savonlinna is not on major bus routes, but buses link the **bus station** (Tulliportinkatu 1) with Helsinki (€30, 5½ hours, up to nine daily), Mikkeli (€20, 1½ hours, up to 14 daily) and Jyväskylä (€30, 3½ hours, up to eight daily).

TRAIN

Punkaharju (€3, 30 minutes, at least four daily) is one of the few destinations that can be accessed via a direct service from Savonlinna. To get to Helsinki (€48, 4¼ hours, up to four daily) and Joensuu (€25, 2¼ hours, up to four daily), you'll need to change in Parikkala. The train station is in the town centre near the kauppatori. Buy your ticket at the machines – there's no ticket office.

GETTING AROUND

Savonlinna airport is 14km northeast; shared **taxis** (✆0500-250-099; www.jsturvataksit.fi) meet flights.

There are car-hire agencies at the airport, and a **Hertz** (✆020-555-2750; www.hertz.fi; Rantakatu 2; ⊙7.30am-9pm Mon-Fri, 9am-9pm Sat & Sun) office in town. Book well ahead.

Several places hire bikes in summer, including **InterSport** (Olavinkatu 52; per day/week €20/70; ⊙9.30am-6pm Mon-Fri, to 5pm Sat, 11am-3pm Sun).

Alvar Aalto–Designed Buildings

Jyväskylä's (p150) portfolio of Aalto–designed works include the main **university campus** (1953–70); **Alvar Aalto Museo** (✆040-135-6210; www.alvaraalto.fi; Alvar Aallonkatu 7; adult/child €6/free; ⊙ 10am-6pm Tue-Fri Jul-Aug, 11am-6pm Tue-Sun Sep-Jun), built 1971–73; **Keski-Suomen Museo** (Museum of Central Finland; www.jyvaskyla.fi/keskisuomenmuseo; Alvar Aallonkatu 7; adult/child €6/free; ⊙11am-6pm Tue-Sun), built 1957–62; the three buildings (1964–82) forming the town's **Administrative and Cultural Centre**; the **Workers' Club Building** (Kauppakatu 30), built 1924–25; the 1962 **Vitatorni Apartment Tower** (Viitaniementie 16) and a scattering of houses in the residential parts of town. For a handy map showing notable architectural works in the town, including all of Aalto's buildings, go to http://visitjyvaskyla.fi/filebank/1913-arkkitehtuurikartta_2014.pdf. Notable works outside town include the **Säynätsalon Kunnantalo** (Säynätsalo Town Hall; ✆040-197-1091; www.aaltoinfo.com; Parviaisentie 9, Säynätsalo; tours €8; ⊙tours noon-6pm Mon-Fri, 2-6pm Sat & Sun Jun-Sep) **FREE**, built 1949–52, and **Muuratsalon Koetalo** (p153), built 1952–53.

Säynätsalon Kunnantalo
CLAUDIO DIVIZIA/SHUTTERSTOCK ©

Joensuu

At the egress of the Pielisjoki (Joensuu means 'river mouth' in Finnish), North Karelia's capital is a spirited university town, with students making up almost a third of the population. Joensuu was founded by Tsar Nikolai I and

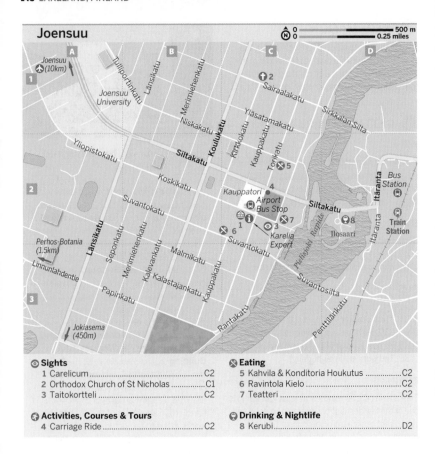

Joensuu

◉ Sights
1 Carelicum	C2
2 Orthodox Church of St Nicholas	C1
3 Taitokortteli	C2

◉ Activities, Courses & Tours
4 Carriage Ride	C2

◉ Eating
5 Kahvila & Konditoria Houkutus	C2
6 Ravintola Kielo	C2
7 Teatteri	C2

◉ Drinking & Nightlife
8 Kerubi	D2

became an important trading port following the 1850s completion of the Saimaa Canal. During the Winter and Continuation Wars, 23 bombing raids flattened many of its older buildings, and today most of its architecture is modern. It's a lively place to spend some time before heading into the Karelian wilderness.

◉ SIGHTS

Carelicum
Museum

(www.joensuu.fi; Koskikatu 5; adult/child €5/3; ⊙10am-4.30pm Mon-Fri, to 3pm Sat & Sun) Themed displays – on the region's prehistory, its war-torn past, the Karelian

evacuation, the importance of the sauna etc – cover both sides of Karelia's present-day border at this excellent museum. Highlights include a Junkers bomber engine, and local hunting and fishing equipment including a two-century-old crossbow.

Taitokortteli
Arts Centre

(013-220-140; www.taitokortteli.fi; Koskikatu 1; ⊙10am-5pm Mon-Fri, 10am-3pm Sat year-round, plus noon-4pm Sun Jul) Dating back over a century, these charming wooden buildings are some of the few remaining in Joensuu; some have been relocated here from other parts of town. They now comprise an arts and crafts centre where you can see weavers at work, browse contemporary art and purchase clothing, toys and homewares by local designers. There's a gallery space as well as cafes and bars.

Orthodox Church
of St Nicholas
Church

(Pyhän Nikolaoksen Kirkko; ☏020-610-0590; www. joensuunortodoksit.fi; Kirkkokatu 32; ⊙10am-4pm Mon-Fri mid-Jun–mid-Aug or by appointment) Joensuu's most intriguing church is the wooden Orthodox church, built in 1887 with icons painted in St Petersburg during the late 1880s. Services are held at 6pm Saturday and 10am Sunday; visitors are welcome.

TOURS

Carriage Ride
Tours

(Koskikatu 5; tours from €20) From the park by the kauppatori you can take a carriage tour in a 19th-century Victorian buggy from June to mid-August. In winter, the operator switches to sled tours.

EATING

As a student hub, Joensuu has plenty of good, inexpensive places to dine, as well as some higher-end restaurants. At the busy kauppatori food stalls, look for Karelian specialities such as the classic *karjalanpiirakka* (rice-filled savoury pastry) and *kotiruoka* (homemade) soups.

Kahvila & Konditoria
Houkutus
Cafe, Bakery €

(www.houkutus.fi; Torikatu 24; small dishes €1.50-5.50, mains €8-17; ⊙7.30am-7pm Mon-Fri, 8.30am-5pm Sat) Houkutus does great coffee and even better cakes (the mint blackcurrant cake is a treat), along with savoury pastries such as quiches, meal-sized salads and filled bread rolls.

Teatteri
Karelian €€

(☏010-231-4250; www.teatteriravintola.fi; Rantakatu 20; lunch buffet €8.60-10.50, mains €18-32, menus €46-65; ⊙11am-10pm Mon & Tue, 11am-11pm Wed & Thu, 11am-midnight Fri, 11.30am-midnight Sat) ✔ Locally sourced ingredients prepared

in innovative ways are served in the town hall's art deco surrounds and on its beautiful summer terrace. Dishes span nettle ricotta with wild herb salad to liquorice-glazed goose with kale pesto; desserts like fennel and apple sorbet with blackberry panna cotta are the icing on the cake. Menus can be accompanied by wine or craft beer pairings.

Ravintola Kielo
Karelian €€€

(☏013-227-874; www.ravintolakielo.fi; Suvantokatu 12; mains €20-29, tasting menu €46, with wine €75; ⊙4-10pm Mon-Sat) At the high end of Karelian cuisine, Kielo's artfully presented miniature starters such as whitefish escabeche with mussel mayo or sugar- and salt-cured Arctic char with smoked sour cream and fennel consommé set the stage for mains like pan-fried pike perch with sautéed forest mushrooms or braised pork belly with caramelised beetroot and roast Lapland potatoes. Wine pairings are superb.

🍸 DRINKING & NIGHTLIFE

The pedestrianised area of Kauppakatu has several late-night bars that get busy on weekends. On the river, boat bars are popular in the summer months; the lakeside Jokiasema is another summer favourite.

Kerubi
Bar, Club

(☏013-129-377; www.kerubi.fi; Siltakatu 1; ⊙bar 11am-2pm Mon, 11am-11pm Tue-Thu, 11am-4am Fri, noon-4am Sat, 2pm-7pm Sun, club 10pm-4am Fri & Sat) Joensuu's best bar/club occupies its own island in the Pielisjoki, linked to the city centre by a bridge. DJs spin techno, trance and electronica on Friday and Saturday; live bands and stand-up comedy take place in the adjacent hall Tuesday to Saturday. Fantastic burgers, salads and steaks are served at its restaurant, which opens to a terrace overlooking the island's beach.

Jokiasema
Bar

(www.jokiasema.fi; Hasanniementie 3; ⊙8am-midnight Jun-Aug; 🛜) Sunsets are spectacular from this bar perched on the Pyhäselkä lake's edge, with a resident peg-leg pirate statue and seating on the terrace

 Savonlinna
Opera Festival

The **Savonlinna Opera Festival** (p139)
is a key reason to visit Savonlinna in the
summertime. The festival's website
details the program: there are rotating
performances of four or five operas by
the Savonlinna company, as well as at
least one opera by an international guest
company and a few concert performances. The muscular castle walls are
a magnificent backdrop to the set and
add great atmosphere. There are tickets
in various price bands. The top grades
(€139 and up) are fine, but the penulti-
mate grades (€85 to €112) put you in
untiered seats, so it helps to be tall. The
few cheap seats (€55) have a severely
restricted view. Buy tickets up to a year in
advance online.

DPRM/SHUTTERSTOCK ©

and pier, as well as a sauna in a rustic red
timber building.

INFORMATION

Karelia Expert (☑040-023-9549; www.visitkarelia.
fi; Koskikatu 5; ☺10am-5pm Mon-Fri; 🛜) In the
Carelicum, enthusiastic staff handle tourism information and bookings for the region.

GETTING THERE & AWAY

AIR

The **airport** (JOE; www.finavia.fi; Lentoasemantie
30) is 11km northwest of central Joensuu. An airport
bus service (one way €5) meets all incoming flights,

and departs from the **bus station** (65 minutes
before flight departures) and from the **corner of**
Koskikatu and Kauppakatu (one hour before departures). A **taxi** (☑060-110-100; www.taksiitasuomi.
fi) costs €25.

Finnair operates several flights a day between
Helsinki and Joensuu.

BUS

The bus station is on the eastern side of the river.

Major **Matkahuolto** (www.matkahuolto.fi)
services include:

Helsinki (€30, 6½ hours, five express services
daily)

Jyväskylä (€30, four hours, five daily)

Kuopio (€29.90, 2¼ hours, three express services
daily)

Lappeenranta (€30, 4½ hours, two daily)

Nurmes (€20, two hours, three daily)

Oulu (€40, 6½ hours, two daily)

Onnibus (www.onnibus.com) has cheaper but less
frequent services to destinations including Helsinki
(€15, 6¼ hours, two daily), Imatra (€5, 2½ hours,
one daily) and Lappeenranta (€7, 3¼ hours, one
daily).

TRAIN

The **train station** (Itäranta) is east of the river,
next to the bus station.

Services include the following:

Helsinki (€44, 4½ hours, four daily)

Lieksa (€14, 1¼ hours, two daily)

Nurmes (€21, two hours, one daily)

Savonlinna (€25, 2¼ hours, four daily); change at
Parikkala

Jyväskylä

Vivacious and modern, western
Lakeland's main town has a wonderful
waterside location, an optimistic feel and
an impeccable architectural pedigree.
Thanks to the work of Alvar Aalto (p147),
who started his career here, Jyväskylä
(yoo-vah-skoo-lah) is of global architectural interest. At the other end of the
cultural spectrum, petrolheads the world

round know it as a legendary World Rally Championships venue. The large student population and lively arts scene give the town plenty of energy and nightlife.

⊙ SIGHTS

For architecture buffs the best visiting days are Tuesday to Friday, as many buildings are closed on weekends and the Alvar Aalto Museum is closed on Monday.

Jyväskylä's museums are all free on Fridays between September and May.

✪ ACTIVITIES

An enjoyable 12km circuit can be walked or cycled around the lake, and can be cut in half using the road bridge. There are numerous boating options – check http://visitjyvaskyla.fi for information, or wander along the pleasant harbour area, where you'll also find boat bars, jet-ski hire, houseboats (www.houseboat.fi) and floating saunas for rent.

Water craft can be hired from www.tavinsulka.com.

Päijänne Risteilyt Hilden   Cruise
(☎010-320-8820; www.paijanne-risteilythilden.fi; ⊙early Jun–mid-Aug) This cruise operator offers full-day or half-day cruises on the Keitele canal departing daily from the **passenger harbour** (Satamakatu 8) and costing between €40 and €60 for adults, half-price for kids. There's also a weekly Alvar Aalto architectural cruise in July and August, which visits the architect's Säynätasalo Town Hall and returns to Jyväskylä by bus (per person €33, 4½ hours).

✖ EATING

Jyväskylä is a university town, so it's not surprising that there are hipster-style cafes, bars selling pub grub, and vegan and vegetarian eateries here. For fine dining, head to Pöllöwaari (p152), one of the region's most impressive restaurants.

Alvar Aalto Museo (p147)

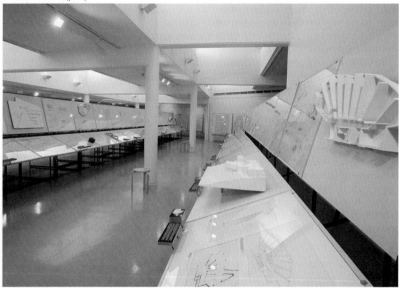

MARIA GOLOVIANKO/SHUTTERSTOCK ©

Jyväskylä (p150)

Beans & More Vegan €

(☑050-351-7731; www.beansandmore.fi; Asemakatu 11; dishes €10-15; ☺10am-6pm Mon-Fri, 9am-5pm Sat; 🗷🌱) Artek furniture, a vaulted ceiling and artfully dangling light-fittings provide a stylish setting at this on-trend vegan cafe. The friendly staff serve up burgers, salads piled with kale and other goodies, sandwiches on gluten-free bread and vegetarian snack plates featuring seasonal produce. Coffee is made with oat, almond or soy milk, and there's a range of teas to choose from.

Ristorante Rosso Italian €

(☑010-767-5441; Kauppakatu 19; pizzas €13-16, pastas €12-16; ☺11am-9pm Mon & Tue, to 10pm Wed & Thu, to 11pm Fri & Sat, noon-9pm Sun) Billing itself as 'the familiar Italian', this branch of a popular Finnish chain serves up decent pizza and pasta in pleasant surroundings (we love the fresh herbs planted in the tomato-paste cans). It's located opposite the Kirkkopuisto and is a good choice for a cheap and *gustoso* (tasty) meal.

Figaro Winebistro Tapas €€

(☑020-766-9811; www.figaro.fi; Asemakatu 2; lunch mains €15-18, tapas €3-9, dinner mains €16-28; ☺11am-11pm Mon-Fri, 1-11pm Sat, 2-10pm Sun; 🗟) The three-course lunch menu (€25) at this this welcoming wine bar is an excellent deal, but most regulars head here after work or on weekends to graze on tapas and order drinks from the large and top-quality wine and beer list. It's so pleasant that many choose to stay on for a steak or burger dinner.

Pöllöwaari Finnish €€€

(☑014-333-900; www.ravintolapollowaari.fi; Yliopistonkatu 23; mains €22-29; ☺11am-10.30pm Mon-Fri, 1-10.30pm Sat; 🗟) We're of the view that Hotel Yöpuu's fine-dining restaurant is the best in the region. Its menu places a laudable emphasis on seasonality, and the kitchen's execution is exemplary. Choose one of the set menus (€56 to €79, or €84 to €127 with wine matches) or order à la carte – the main courses are exceptionally well priced considering their quality. Excellent wine list, too.

🍷 DRINKING & NIGHTLIFE

Head to the eastern end of Kauppakatu to find the main bar strip, or to the harbour for relaxed decktop drinking on a boat bar.

Papu Cafe

(☑050-368-0340; www.paahtimopapu.fi; Yliopistonkatu 26D; ⊘10am-6pm Mon & Tue, to 9pm Wed-Fri, noon-6pm Sat) It would be easy to describe Papu as a hipster haunt, but this laid-back cafe doesn't lend itself to easy categorisation. Yes, its baristas have tattooed sleeves and a preference for pour-over coffee, but the loyal customer base is multi-aged and eclectic. The coffee is made with house-roasted organic beans, and there's also espresso tonic and iced chocolate on offer.

Sohwi Pub

(☑014-615-564; www.sohwi.fi; Vaasankatu 21; ⊘2pm-midnight Tue-Thu, to 2am Fri, noon-2am Sat, 2-10pm Sun & Mon; 🛜) A short walk from the city centre is this excellent bar with a spacious wooden terrace and plenty of lively student and academic discussion lubricated by a range of good bottled and draught beers. It also has a good menu of snacks and soak-it-all-up bar meals (pizza €15, burgers €12.50 to €17), including vegan options. Great stuff.

ℹ️ INFORMATION

Tourist Office (☑014-266-0113; www.visitjyvaskyla.fi; Asemakatu 7; ⊘10am-5pm Mon-Fri, to 3pm Sat Jun-Aug, 10am-4pm Mon-Fri Sep-May) Helpful office where you can source plenty of information. Staff can arrange visits to the **Muuratsalon Koetalo** (Muuratsalo Experimental House; ☑014-266-7113; www.alvaraalto.fi; Melalammentie, Muuratsalo; adult/student €18/9; ⊘1.30pm Mon, Wed & Fri Jun, Jul & 1st half Sep, 1.30pm Mon-Fri Aug).

ℹ️ GETTING THERE & AWAY

AIR

The airport is at Tikkakoski, 23km northwest of the city centre. Finnair flies to/from Helsinki.

 Summer Detour

What began as a heathenish medieval habit of pillaging neighbouring villages in search of nubile women has become one of Finland's oddest – and most publicised – events. Get to Sonkajärvi, in the northern Lakeland, for the **Wife-Carrying World Championships** (Eukonkanto; www.eukonkanto.fi) in early July.

It's a race over a 253.5m obstacle course, where competitors must carry their 'wives' through water traps and over hurdles to achieve the fastest time. The winner gets the wife's weight in beer and the prestigious title of World Wife-Carrying Champion. To enter, men need only €50 and a consenting female. There's also a 40-plus and team competition, all accompanied by a weekend of drinking, dancing and typical Finnish frivolity.

Wife-Carrying World Championships in Sonkajärvi
TIMO HARTIKAINEN/AFP/GETTY IMAGES ©

BUS

The bus and train stations share the **Matkakeskus** (Jyväskylä Travel Centre; ⊘6am-10pm Mon-Sat, from 8am Sun). Daily express buses connect Jyväskylä to southern Finnish towns, including frequent departures to Tampere (€20, 2¼ hours) and Helsinki (€25 to €30, 3½ to 4½ hours).

TRAIN

The train station is in the **Matkakeskus**. There are regular trains to/from Helsinki (from €32, 3½ hours), many of which travel via Tampere and Hämeenlinna.

THE FAR NORTH
& ARCTIC CIRCLE

The Far North & Arctic Circle at a Glance...

Scandinavia's Arctic realms rank among the region's most evocative corners, one of few places where reality lives up to the legends that swirl around the destination. This is the land of the Sami and of Santa Claus. Up here, you can get around by dog-sled or snowmobile in winter while the aurora borealis (northern lights) dances across the sky. It is also home to one of northern Europe's most memorable small cities (Tromsø) and landscapes that seem as if they were sculpted by the gods (Lofoten Islands).

Two Days in the Far North

With two days, concentrate on Santa–themed fun and the museums of **Rovaniemi** (p158), before high-tailing it north to divide your time on day two between **Inari** and **Karasjok**. The latter two enable you to immerse yourself in Sami culture in the heart of this ancient people's homeland.

Four Days in the Far North

Tromsø (p160) is worth at least a day of your life (make it day three). The combination of museums and scenery means that you could very easily spend two days diving in. With little time left, fly or drive to the **Lofoten Islands** (p167) for some of the Arctic's most astonishing scenery, and the starting point of a whole new adventure.

Arriving in the Far North

To access this region, you've a long drive north. Alternatively, it is possible to fly from southern Scandinavian capitals into **Rovaniemi** (p158), **Tromsø** (p160) and Bodø (for the Lofoten Islands). Each of these is compact and easy to get around, with taxis and airport buses whisking you into town centres.

Where to Stay

There are excellent places to stay across the region, although as ever in Scandinavia choices are dominated by chain hotels with more comfort than character. Out in the hinterlands of these towns, choices tend to be more intimate, with B&Bs and more personal, family-run hotels.

ROMAN BABAKIN/SHUTTERSTOCK ©

Rovaniemi (Santa Claus Village)

Situated right by the Arctic Circle, the 'official' terrestrial residence of Santa Claus is the capital of Finnish Lapland and a tourism boom town.

Great For...

Don't Miss

Arktikum (p164), one of Finland's finest museums.

Where Arctic Finland begins (or ends), atop the Arctic Circle, the 'official' Santa Claus Village is a complex of shops, activities and accommodation.

Santa Claus Grotto

Santa sees visitors year-round in this impressive **grotto** (www.santaclausvillage.info; Sodankyläntie, Napapiiri; visit free, photographs from €20; ⊗9am-6pm Jun-Aug, 10am-5pm mid-Jan–May, Sep & Nov, 9am-7pm Dec–mid-Jan) **FREE**, with a huge clock mechanism (it slows the earth's rotation so that Santa can visit the whole world's children on Christmas Eve). The portly saint is quite a linguist, and an old hand at chatting with kids and adults alike.

Need to Know

Santa Claus Village (www.santaclaus village.info; Tarvantie 2, Napapiiri; ⊙9am-6pm Jun-Aug, 10am-5pm mid-Jan–May, Sep & Nov, 9am-7pm Dec–mid-Jan) `FREE`

✕ Take a Break

Escape Santa Claus Village and head for Aitta Deli & Dine (p167) for excellent local food.

★ Top Tip

A private chat with Santa is free, but no photos; official photos of your visit start at €20.

Santa Claus Post Office

Within the Santa Claus Village, this **post office** (Sodankyläntie, ⊙9am-6pm Jun-Aug, 10am-5pm mid-Jan–May, Sep & Nov, 9am-7pm Dec-Jan) `FREE` receives more than half a million letters each year from children worldwide. You can browse a selection, which range from rather mercenary requests for thousands of euros' worth of electronic goods to heart-rending pleas for parents to recover from cancer. Postcards sent from here bear an official Santa stamp; you can arrange to have one deliv-ered at Christmas time. For €7.95 Santa will send you a Christmas card.

Santapark

Built inside a cavern in the mountain, this Christmas–themed **amusement park** (https://santaparkarcticworld.com/santapark; Tarvantie 1; adult/child winter €33/27.50, summer €17.50/15; ⊙10am-6pm late Nov–mid-Jan, to 5pm Mon-Sat mid-Jun–mid-Aug) features an army of elves baking gingerbread, a magic sleigh ride, a carousel, an ice bar, a theatre, a restaurant and, of course, Santa himself. The most in-triguing section is the gallery of ice sculpture.

Arctic Cathedral

VICHIE81/SHUTTERSTOCK ©

Cultural Tromsø

Located 400km north of the Arctic Circle, Tromsø bills itself as Norway's gateway to the Arctic. Surrounded by chilly fjords and craggy peaks, it has some fabulous museums and architecture.

Great For...

Don't Miss

The summit of Fjellheisen, a cable car that takes you to extraordinary views.

Arctic Cathedral

The 11 triangles of the 1965 **Arctic Cathedral** (Ishavskatedralen; ☏476 80 668; Hans Nilsens veg 41; adult/child 50kr/free, organ recitals 70-170kr; ⏱9am-7pm Mon-Sat, 1-7pm Sun Jun–mid-Aug, 3-6pm mid-Aug–mid-May, opens at 2pm Feb), aka Tromsdalen Church, suggest glacial crevasses and auroral curtains. The glowing stained-glass window that occupies the east end depicts Christ descending to earth. The west end is filled by a futuristic organ and icicle-like lamps of Czech crystal.

Polar Museum

Fittingly for a town that was the launchpad for many pioneering expeditions to the Pole, Tromsø's fascinating **Polar Museum** (Polarmuseet; ☏77 62 33 60; www.uit.no/tmu/polarmuseet; Søndre Tollbodgate 11; adult/

Polar Museum

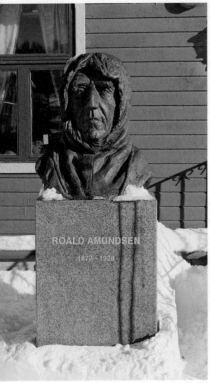

ROALD AMUNDSEN
1872 - 1928

ℹ Need to Know

Tromsø's **tourist office** (☑77 61 00 00; www.visittromso.no; Kirkegata 2; ⊗9am-5pm Mon-Fri, 10am-5pm Sat & Sun Jan-Mar & mid-May–Aug, shorter hours rest of year; 🛜) books accommodation and activities, and has free wi-fi, and publishes the *Tromsø Guide*.

✖ Take a Break

Ølhallen (p172) is the brewpub for the famous Mack Brewery. There are 67 ales to try...

★ Top Tip

Tromsø has some of Scandinavia's best nightlife, whatever the weather.

child 60/30kr; ⊗9am-6pm mid-Jun–mid-Aug, 11am-5pm rest of the year) is a rollicking romp through life in the Arctic, taking in everything from the history of trapping to the groundbreaking expeditions of Nansen and Amundsen. There are some fascinating artefacts and black-and-white archive photos; the stuffed remains of various formerly fuzzy, once-blubbery polar creatures are rather less fun. It's in a harbourside building that served as Tromsø's customs house from 1833 to 1970.

Tromsø University Museum

Near the southern end of Tromsøya, this **museum** (☑77 64 50 00; www.uit.no/tmu; Lars Thøringsveg 10; adult/child 60/30kr; ⊗9am-6pm Jun-Aug, 10am-4.30pm Mon-Fri, noon-3pm Sat, 11am-4pm Sun Sep-May) has well-presented and documented displays

on traditional and modern Sami life, ecclesiastical art and accoutrements, and a small section on the Vikings. Downstairs, learn about rocks of the north and ponder a number of thought-provoking themes (such as the role of fire, the consequences of global warming and loss of wilderness).

Mack Brewery

This venerable **institution** (Mack Ølbryggeri; ☑77 62 45 80; www.mack.no; Storgata 5) merits a pilgrimage. Established in 1877, it produces 18 kinds of beer, including the very quaffable Macks Pilsner, Isbjørn, Haakon and several dark beers. At 3.30pm Monday to Friday year-round (plus 2pm, June to August) tours (170kr, including two tastings) leave from the brewery's own Ølhallen Pub (p172). It's wise to reserve in advance.

Sami parliament

HILDAWEGES PHOTOGRAPHY/SHUTTERSTOCK ©

Sami Culture

When it comes to drawing near to the Sami, two heartlands stand out: Karasjok in Norway and Inari in Finland. Although separated by an international border, they're easy to combine.

Great For...

Don't Miss

Karasjok's Sami Parliament is a glorious building, encased in mellow Siberian wood and shaped like a Sami tent.

Siida

One of Finland's most absorbing museums, state-of-the-art **Siida** (www.siida.fi; Inarintie 46; adult/child €10/5; ☺9am-7pm Jun-Aug, to 6pm Sep, 10am-5pm Wed-Mon Oct-May) offers a comprehensive overview of the Sami and their environment. The main exhibition hall consists of a fabulous nature exhibition around the edge, detailing northern Lapland's ecology by season, with wonderful photos and information panels.

Sajos

The spectacular wood-and-glass Sami **cultural centre** (www.samediggi.fi; Siljotie 4; ☺9am-5pm Mon-Fri) **FREE** stands proud in the middle of town. It holds the **Sami parliament** (Sámediggi; ☎78 47 40 00; www.samediggi.no; Kautokeinoveien 50;

Sami woman in traditional dress, Inari

❶ Need to Know

Karasjok and Inari are 117km apart by road. There are no border formalities.

✕ Take a Break

In Karasjok **Biepmu Kafeà** (Biepmu Cafe; ☑78 46 61 51; Finlandsveien; mains 140-240kr; ⊙1-8pm), **Aanaar** (☑016-511-7100; www.hotelkultahovi.fi; Saarikoskentie 2; mains €13.50-31.50, 3-/5-course menu €43.50/62, with paired wines €62/85; ⊙11am-2.30pm & 5-10.30pm) ✿ in Inari.

★ Top Tip

Take a tour of Karasjok's Sami Parliament and library (with more than 35,000 volumes) to learn about Sami history.

⊙hourly tours 8.30am-2.30pm Mon-Fri except 11.30am late Jun–mid-Aug, 1pm Mon-Fri rest of year) **FREE** as well as a library and music archive, a restaurant, exhibitions and a craft shop.

Sami National Musuem

Exhibits at the **Sami National Museum** (Sámiid Vuorká Dávvirat, De Samiske Samlinger; ☑78 46 99 50; www.rdm.no; Museumsgata 17; adult/concession/child 90/60kr/free; ⊙9am-6pm mid-Jun–mid-Aug, shorter hours rest of year), also called the Sami Collection, include displays of colourful, traditional Sami clothing, tools and artefacts, and works by contemporary Sami artists. Outdoors, you can roam among a cluster of traditional Sami constructions and follow a short trail, signed in English, that leads past and explains ancient Sami reindeer-trapping pits and hunting techniques.

Sápmi Park

Sami culture is big business here, and this impressive **theme park** (☑78 46 88 00; www.visitsapmi.no; Leavnnjageaidnu 1, off Porsangerveien; adult/child/family 160/80/400kr; ⊙9am-7pm mid-Jun–mid-Aug, 9am-4pm late Aug, 9am-4pm Mon-Fri, 11am-3pm Sat Sep–mid-Dec, 10am-2pm Mon-Fri Jan–May) includes a wistful, hi-tech multimedia introduction to the Sami in the 'Magic Theatre', plus Sami winter and summer camps and other dwellings to explore on the grounds. Reindeers are also often around.

Rovaniemi

Right on the Arctic Circle, Rovaniemi is more than just Santa Claus' home town (p158). There are also excellent museums and it's a fantastic base from which to organise activities.

◎ SIGHTS

Thoroughly destroyed by the retreating Wehrmacht in 1944, the town was rebuilt to a plan by Alvar Aalto, with the major streets in the shape of a reindeer's head and antlers (the stadium near the bus station is the eye). Rovaniemi's concert hall, **Lappia-talo** (☑040-028-2484; www. rovaniementeatteri.fi; Hallituskatu 11; ☺box office 1-5pm Tue-Fri, 11am-1pm Sat & 1hr prior to performances), is one of several buildings in Rovaniemi designed by Alvar Aalto; others include the adjacent library and town hall. Its utilitarian buildings are compensated for by its marvellous riverside location.

Arktikum   Museum
(www.arktikum.fi; Pohjoisranta 4; adult/child €12/5; ☺9am-6pm Jun-Aug, 10am-6pm Tue-Sun mid-Jan–May & Sep-Nov, 10am-6pm Dec–mid-Jan) With its beautifully designed glass tunnel stretching out to the Ounasjoki, this is one of Finland's finest museums. One half deals with Lapland, with information on Sami culture and the history of Rovaniemi; the other offers a wide-ranging display on the Arctic, with superb static and interactive displays focusing on flora and fau na, as well as on the peoples of Arctic Europe, Asia and North America. Downstairs, an audiovisual – basically a pretty slide show – plays on a constant loop.

Pilke Tiedekeskus   Museum
(www.tiedekeskus-pilke.fi; Ounasjoentie 6; adult/child €7/5; ☺9am-6pm Mon-Fri, 10am-4pm Sat & Sun mid-Jun–Aug, shorter hours rest of year) Downstairs in the Metsähallitus (Finnish Forest and Park Service) building next to the Arktikum, this is a highly entertaining exhibition on Finnish forestry with a sustainable focus. It has dozens of interactive displays that are great for kids of all ages, who can clamber up into a bird house, build a timber-framed dwelling, get behind the wheel of a forest harvester or play games about forest management. Multilingual touch-screens provide interesting background information.

◐ ACTIVITIES

Rovaniemi is a great launching pad for winter and summer activities, offering frequent departures with multilingual guides. You need a driving licence to operate a snowmobile; there's a 50% supplement if you want one to yourself.

Rovaniemi's ski area, **Ounasvaara** (☑044-764-2830; https://ounasvaara.fi; Taunontie 14; winter lift ticket per day €38, ski hire per day €38; ☺winter activities early Nov-late Mar, summer activities late Jun–mid-Aug), is just east of the river.

Bear Hill Husky   Dog Sledding
(☑040-760-0020; www.bearhillhusky.com; Sinettäjärventie 22; kennel tours incl sled ride adult/child €59/29, expeditions from €119/59; ☺Jul-Mar) Wintertime husky-pulled sled expeditions start at two hours' duration (prices include transport to/from Rovaniemi). Overnight tours run on Saturdays from late January to March, with accommodation in a traditional wilderness cabin with smoke sauna. If you just want a taster, kennel tours, where you meet the Alaskan huskies, include a 1km ride with their mushers (sled drivers).

Safartica   Outdoors
(☑016-311-485; www.safartica.com; Koskikatu 9; ☺3hr reindeer sled tour €148, 4hr mountain-bike tour €121) In addition to reindeer-pulled sled tours and mountain-bike tours, this superb outfit runs river activities such as summer berry-picking trips (three hours €75), midnight-sun lake floating in special flotation suits (three hours €92), ice fishing (2½ hours €89), snowshoe hiking (two hours €69) and a six-hour snowmobile adventure (€192).

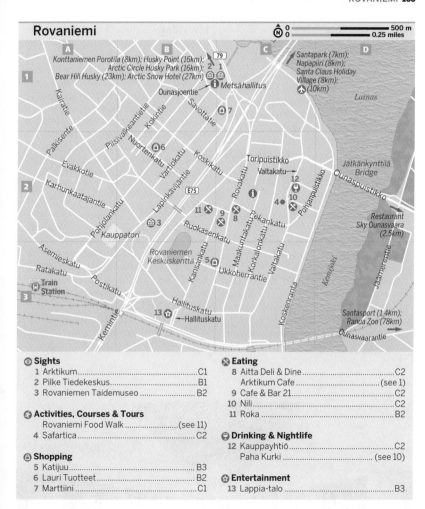

Rovaniemi

Konttaniemen Porotila (8km); Husky Point (16km);
Arctic Circle Husky Park (16km);
Bear Hill Husky (23km); Arctic Snow Hotel (27km)

Santapark (7km);
Napapiiri (8km);
Santa Claus Holiday
Village (8km);
(10km)

✪ TOURS

Rovaniemi Food Walk   Food

(☏040-488-7173; www.aittadeli.com; €50,
with drinks €75; ⊙by reservation) Offering a taster of Lapland cuisine, these
three-hour tours are literally a moveable
feast, starting at street-food restaurant
Roka (☏050-311-6411; www.ravintolaroka.fi;
Ainonkatu 3;

lunch buffet €9.90, street-food dishes €8.50-
12, mains €15.50-23; ⊙10.30am-9pm Mon-
Thu, to 11pm Fri, noon-11pm Sat, noon-9pm
Sun), followed by a contemporary Finnish
main course (such as slow-cooked reindeer or whitefish with pickled cucumber)
at Aitta Deli & Dine (p167), and finishing with dessert and a cocktail at Cafe &
Bar 21 (p166).

🅐 SHOPPING

Lauri Tuotteet   Arts & Crafts

(www.lauri-tuotteet.fi; Pohjolankatu 25; ⊘10am-5pm Mon-Fri) Established in 1924, this former knife factory in a charming log cabin at the northwestern edge of town still makes knives today, along with jewellery, buttons, felt boots and traditional Sami items like engraved spoons and sewing-needle cases. Everything is handmade from local materials, including reindeer antlers, curly birch and goats willow timbers, and Finnish steel.

Katijuu   Fashion & Accessories

(http://katijuu.fi; Rovakatu 11; ⊘10am-4pm Mon-Fri) Reindeer and moose leather, lambskin, and red fox, mink and marten fur are used by Lapland designer Kati Juujärvi to create hats, gloves and mittens, belts and fur collars, as well as clothing for men, women and children such as vests, jackets, dresses and trousers. Seasonal collections are named for places along the Kemijoki river.

Marttiini   Arts & Crafts

(www.marttiini.fi; Vartiokatu 32; ⊘10am-6pm Mon-Fri, to 4pm Sat Sep-May, plus noon-3pm Sun Jun-Aug) This former factory of Finland's famous knife manufacturer Marttiini is now a shop open to visitors with a small knife exhibition, and cheaper prices than you can get elsewhere. It's near the Arktikum (p164); there are branches at Santa Claus Village (p159) and at the Rinteenkulma shopping centre in the town centre, as well as one in Helsinki.

🅧 EATING

Cafe & Bar 21   Cafe €

(www.cafebar21.fi; Rovakatu 21; dishes €10-14; ⊘11am-8.30pm Mon & Tue, to 9.30pm Wed & Thu, to 11pm Fri, noon-11pm Sat, noon-8.30pm Sun; 🛜) A reindeer-pelt collage on the grey-concrete wall is the only concession to place at this artfully modern designer cafe-bar. Black-and-white decor makes it a stylish haunt for salads, superb soups, tapas and its house-speciality waffles

Arktikum (p164)

ALE_RIZZO/SHUTTERSTOCK ©

(both savoury and sweet), along with creative cocktails. The bar stays open late.

Aitta Deli & Dine   Finnish, Deli €€

(☑040-488-7173; www.aittadeli.com; Rovakatu 26; lunch buffet €10, platters €10-30, 4-course dinner menu €44, with paired wine or beer €69; ☺restaurant 11am-4pm Mon & Tue, to 10pm Wed-Sat, to 3pm Sun, deli 11am-6pm Mon-Fri, to 3pm Sat) ✦ Locally sourced, organic food at Aitta includes sharing platters piled high with reindeer heart and tongue, lingonberry and moose stew, bear and nettle sausages, and rye and barley breads. Two- and three-course menus are available at lunch and dinner, but the pick of the dinner offerings is the four-course Taste of Lapland menu paired with natural wines or craft beers.

Nili   Finnish €€

(☑040-036-9669; www.nili.fi; Valtakatu 20; mains €19-35, 4-course menu €56, with paired wines €100; ☺5-11pm Mon-Sat) A timber-lined interior with framed black-and-white photos of Lapland, kerosene lamps, traditional fishing nets, taxidermied bear and reindeer heads, and antler chandeliers gives this hunting-lodge-style spot a cosy, rustic charm. Local ingredients are used in dishes such as Zandar lake fish with tar-and-mustard foam and reindeer with pickled cucumber and lingonberry jam, accompanied by Finnish beers, ciders and berry liqueurs.

Restaurant Sky Ounasvaara   Finnish €€€

(☑016-323-400; www.laplandhotels.com; Juhannuskalliontie; mains €24-36, 5-course menu €69, with wine €127; ☺6-9.30pm Mon-Sat, to 9pm Sun Jun-Apr) For a truly memorable meal, head to the 1st floor of the **Sky Ounasvaara** (d/tr/f/apt from €101/126/135/143; ☺Jun-Apr; **P**☺) hotel, where wraparound floor-to-ceiling glass windows onto the forest outside create the impression of dining in a tree house. Specialities include Lappish potato

⛰🚣 Exploring the Lofoten Islands

Every traveller in Arctic Scandinavia should consider a detour to the Lofoten Islands, which spread their tall, craggy physique against the sky like some spiky sea dragon. The beauty of this place is simply staggering.

The main islands, Austvågøy, Vestvågøy, Flakstadøy and Moskenesøy, are separated from the mainland by Vestfjorden, but connected by road bridges and tunnels. Each has sheltered bays, sheep pastures and picturesque villages. The vistas, and special quality of the Arctic light, have long attracted artists, represented in galleries throughout the islands.

Sights (unless you count the extraordinary scenery) are few, although there is an excellent **Viking museum** (☑76 15 40 00; www.lofotr.no; adult/child incl guided tour mid-Jun–mid-Aug 200/150kr, rest of year 140/100kr; ☺10am-7pm Jun–mid-Aug, shorter hours rest of year; 👶), an extraordinary glass-blowing gallery called **Glasshytta** (☑76 09 44 42; www.glasshyttavikten.no; Vikten; ☺10am-7pm May-Aug) and some of the Arctic's prettiest villages. Among the latter are Henningsvær, Nusfjord, Reine and Å.

Svolvær is the gateway to Lofoten, and has the largest selection of accommodation and restaurants. You'll need your own wheels and at least three days to see the best that Lofoten has to offer.

Reine, Lofoten Islands
KENNETH SCHOTH/500PX ©

dumplings with local mushrooms, reindeer tartar with spruce-smoked mayo, Arctic char with sour-milk sauce, and sea-buckthorn meringue with reindeer yoghurt.

DRINKING & NIGHTLIFE

Paha Kurki   Bar
(www.pahakurki.com; Koskikatu 5; ⊙4pm-3am; 🛜) Dark yet clean and modern, this rock bar has a fine variety of bottled beers, memorabilia on the walls and a good sound system. A Finnish rock bar is what other places might call a metal bar: expect more Pantera than Pixies.

Kauppayhtiö   Bar
(www.kauppayhtio.fi; Valtakatu 24; ⊙11am-9pm Tue-Thu & Sun, to 3.30am Fri, 1pm-3.30am Sat; 🛜) Almost everything at this oddball gasoline-themed bar-cafe is for sale, including colourful plastic tables and chairs, and retro and vintage toys, as well as new streetwear and Nordic clothing at the attached boutique. DJs play most evenings and there are often bands at weekends – when it's rocking, crowds spill onto the pavement terrace. Its burgers are renowned. Bonus: pinball machines.

❶ INFORMATION

DISCOUNT CARDS

A Culture Pass combination ticket (adult/child €20/10) offering unlimited access to the three major sights, the **Arktikum** (p164), **Pilke Tiedekeskus** (p164) and **Rovaniemen Taidemuseo** (Korundi; www.korundi.fi; Lapinkävijäntie 4; adult/child €8/4; ⊙11am-6pm Tue-Sun), is valid for a week. Pick it up from the museums or the tourist office.

TOURIST INFORMATION

Metsähallitus (☑020-564-7820; www.metsa.fi; Pilke Tiedekeskus, Ounasjoentie 6; ⊙9am-6pm Mon-Fri, 10am-4pm Sat & Sun mid-Jun–Aug, shorter hours rest of year) Information centre for the national parks; sells maps and fishing permits.

Tourist Information (☑016-346-270; www.visitrovaniemi.fi; Maakuntakatu 29; ⊙9am-5pm Mon-Fri mid-Aug–mid-Jun, plus 10am-3pm Sat mid-Jun–mid-Aug; 🛜)) is in the square in the middle of town.

❶ GETTING THERE & AWAY

AIR

Rovaniemi's **airport** (RVN; ☑020-708-6506; www.finavia.fi; Lentokentäntie), 8km northeast of the city, is the 'official airport of Santa Claus' (he must hangar his sleigh here) and a major winter destination for charter flights. Finnair and Norwegian have several flights daily to/from Helsinki.

Airport minibuses (☑016-362-222; http://airportbus.fi) meet arriving flights, dropping off at hotels in the town centre (€7, 15 minutes).

A taxi to the city centre costs €20 to €30 depending on the time of day and number of passengers.

BUS

Daily connections serve just about everywhere in Lapland. Some buses continue north into Norway.

TRAIN

One direct train per day runs from Rovaniemi to Helsinki (€80, eight hours), with two more requiring a change in Oulu (€14, 2¼ hours).

Tromsø

Beautifully sited by the water's edge and in the shadow of mountains, as rich in cultural signposts as great places to eat and drink, Tromsø is one of the Arctic's most desirable urban experiences.

SIGHTS

Around town you'll find a number of interesting churches. **Domkirke** (www.kirken.tromso.no; Storgata; ⊙1-3pm Mon-Fri Jun & Jul, 1-4pm Mon-Fri Aug, 1-5pm Mon-Fri rest of the year) **FREE** is one of Norway's largest wooden churches. Up the hill is the

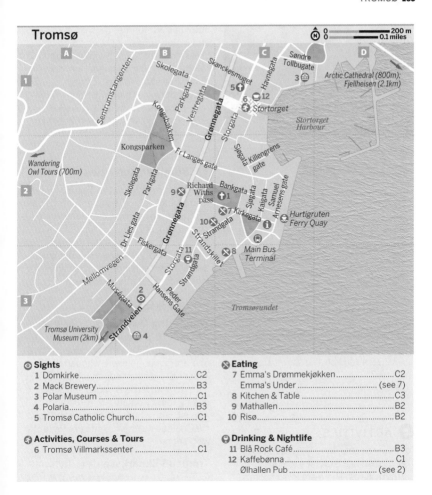

Tromsø

200 m
0.1 miles

town's **Tromsø Catholic Church** (Storgata 94; ⊕9am-7.30pm) **FREE**. Both were built in 1861 and each lays claim to be 'the world's northernmost bishopric' of its sect.

You'll find more early-19th-century timber buildings around the town centre, including a stretch of 1830s shops and merchants' homes along Sjøgata.

Polaria   Museum, Aquarium
(⌨77 75 01 11; www.polaria.no; Hjalmar Johansens gate 12; adult/child 130/65kr; ⊕10am-7pm mid-May–Aug, 10am-5pm Sep–mid-May) This

Arctic–themed attraction provides a multimedia introduction to northern Norway and *Svalbard*. Kick things off by watching the two films *In the Land of the Northern Lights* and *Spitsbergen – Arctic Wilderness*, then follow the Arctic walkway past exhibits on shrinking sea ice, the aurora borealis, aquariums of cold-water fish and – the big draw – some yapping, playful bearded seals (feeding time is at 12.30pm year-round, plus 3pm in summer or 3.30pm in winter).

Festival Fun

In summer at the Arctic Cathedral, there are Midnight Sun Concerts (adult/child 170/50kr; 11pm June to mid-August) and organ recitals (70kr; 2pm June and July). Experiencing the swelling organ and the light of the midnight sun streaming through the huge west window could be one of the great sensory moments of your trip.

The **Domkirke** (www.kirken.tromso.no; ☺1-3pm Mon-Fri Jun & Jul, 1-4pm Mon-Fri Aug, 1-5pm Mon-Fri rest of the year) holds half-hour organ recitals (70kr; 5pm June, 3pm July) of classical music and folk tunes.

Domkirke, Tromsø
MAYLAT/SHUTTERSTOCK ©

🌀 ACTIVITIES

For many people, the main reason to visit Tromsø is the chance to hunt for the northern lights. There are lots of companies around town offering aurora-spotting safaris. Go with a small, independent operator, otherwise you might end up with a coach party from one of the city's big hotels.

The tourist office's *Summer Activities in Tromsø* and its winter equivalent provide comprehensive checklists of tours and activities.

🌀 Winter Activities

In and around Tromsø (operators will normally collect you from your hotel), winter activities outnumber those in summer, and include chasing the northern lights, cross-country skiing, Sami encounters, reindeer herding, reindeer- and dog-sledding, snowshoe safaris, ice fishing and snowmobiling. Whale-watching in a variety of boats (including kayaks!) is also an exciting possibility, with the season running from late October to mid-January or into February.

🌀 Summer Activities

Summer activities in the Tromsø hinterland include hiking, fishing, visits to Sami camps, food-centric excursions, boat sightseeing and sea-kayaking. Trips to scenic locations to see the midnight sun and general sightseeing trips are widely available. Wildlife enthusiasts can also go looking for seabirds and seals.

🌀 Operators

Wandering Owl Tours   Adventure
(📱484 60 081; www.wanderingowl.com; Sommerlystvegen 7a) One of the more creative operators around town, Wandering Owl Tours has excellent summer guided hikes, a trip to a wilderness sauna and scenic driving tours from mid-May to mid-August, with a host of winter activities that include northern lights photography workshops.

Tromsø Villmarkssenter   Outdoors
(📱77 69 60 02; www.villmarkssenter.no; Stortorget 1, Kystens Hus) Tromsø Villmarkssenter offers dog-sled excursions ranging from a one-day spin to a four-day trek with overnight camping. This booking office is in town; the centre, 24km south of Tromsø on Kvaløya, also offers a range of summer activities such as trekking, glacier hiking and sea-kayaking, as well as seal and seabird safaris.

Tromsø Friluftsenter   Adventure Sports
(📱907 51 583; www.tromso-friluftsenter.no; Kvaløyvågvegen 669) Tromsø Friluftsenter runs summer sightseeing, boat trips and

a full range of winter activities (including trips to Sami camps). One intriguing possibility is their five-hour humpback whale and orca safari from late November to mid-January. Book online or at Tromsø's tourist office (p161).

🗡 EATING

Risø Cafe €

(📞416 64 516; www.risoe-mk.no; Strandgata 32; mains 95-179kr; ⏲7.30am-5pm Mon-Fri, 9am-5pm Sat) You'll find this popular coffee and lunch bar packed throughout most of the day: young trendies come in for their hand-brewed Chemex coffee, while local workers pop in for the daily specials, open-faced sandwiches and delicious cakes. It's small, and the tables are packed in tight, so you might have to queue.

Emma's Under Norwegian €€

(📞77 63 77 30; www.emmasdrommekjokken. no; Kirkegata; lunch mains 165-335kr; ⏲11am-10pm Mon-Fri, noon-10pm Sat) Homely and down-to-earth Norwegian cuisine is the order of the day here. You'll find hearty

dishes like fish gratin, king crab and baked *clipfish* (salt cod) on the lunch menu, served in a cosy space designed to echo a traditional kitchen à la grandma. Upstairs is the more formal Emma's Drømmekjøkken, which shares its menu with Emma's Under after 5.30pm.

Emma's Drømmekjøkken Norwegian €€€

(📞77 63 77 30; www.emmasdrommekjokken. no; Kirkegata; mains 285-365kr, 3-/5-course menu 390/630kr; ⏲6pm-midnight Mon-Sat) Upstairs from Emma's Under, this stylish and highly regarded place pulls in discriminating diners with its imaginative cuisine, providing traditional Norwegian dishes married with top-quality local ingredients such as *lutefisk* (stockfish), blueberry-marinated halibut, ox tenderloin and gratinated king crab. Advance booking is essential.

Kitchen & Table Norwegian, International €€€

(📞77 66 84 84; www.kitchenandtable.no/ tromso; Kaigata 6; mains 235-375kr; ⏲5-10pm

Whale-watching, Tromsø

KJELL-OLE LEIKNES/EYEEM/GETTY IMAGES ©

Reindeer sledding, Tromsø

Mon-Sat, to 9pm Sun) Combining a touch of Manhattan style with Arctic ingredients, chef Marcus Samuelsson serves up some of the freshest and most original tastes in Tromsø – there's reindeer fillet with mango chutney, reindeer ratatouille, burgers with quinoa or kimchi, and even slow-cooked Moroccan lamb.

Mathallen   Bistro €€€

(☑77 68 01 00; www.mathallentromso.no; Grønnegata 60; lunch mains 100-210kr, dinner mains from 310kr, 4-course tasting menu 685kr; ⊗bistro 11am-11pm Tue-Sat, deli 10am-6pm Mon-Fri, 10am-4pm Sat) With its industrial styling, exposed pipes and open-fronted kitchen, this elegant place wouldn't look out of place in Oslo or Stockholm. It serves some of the best modern Norwegian food in town, majoring in fish and local meats; the lunchtime special is a steal at 100kr. There's a deli next door selling tapenades, cheeses, smoked salmon and *lutefisk* (stockfish).

🍷 DRINKING & NIGHTLIFE

Ølhallen Pub   Pub

(☑77 62 45 80; www.olhallen.no; Storgata 4; ⊗10am-7.30pm Mon-Wed, 10am-12.30am Thu-Sat) Reputedly the oldest pub in town, and once the hangout for salty fishermen and Arctic sailors, this is now the brewpub for the excellent Mack Brewery (p161). There are 67 ales to try, including eight on tap – so it might take you a while (and a few livers) to work your way through them all.

Blå Rock Café   Bar

(☑77 61 00 20; www.facebook.com/Blaarock; Strandgata 14/16; ⊗11.30am-2am Mon-Thu, 11.30am-3am Fri & Sat, 1pm-2am Sun) The loudest, most raving place in town has theme evenings, almost 50 brands of beer, occasional live bands and weekend DJs. The music is rock, naturally. Every Monday hour is a happy hour.

Kaffebønna Cafe

(☎77 63 94 00; www.kaffebonna.no; Stortorget 3;
⏰8am-6pm Mon-Fri, 9am-6pm Sat, 10am-6pm Sun)
One of our favourite Tromsø cafes, this cool little spot right in the town centre does the city's
best coffee, accompanied by tasty pastries.

ℹ️ INFORMATION

The **Tourist Office** (p161) is in a wooden building by the harbour, Tromsø's busy tourist office
books accommodation and activities, and has
free wi-fi. It also publishes the comprehensive
Tromsø Guide.

ℹ️ GETTING THERE & AWAY

AIR

Tromsø Airport (☎77 64 84 00; www.avinor.no/fly
plass/tromso) is about 5km from the town centre,
on the western side of Tromsøya and is the main
airport for the far north. Destinations with direct
Scandinavian Airlines flights to/from the airport
include Oslo, Harstad/ Narvik, Bodø, Trondheim,
Alta, Hammerfest, Kirkenes and Longyearbyen.

Norwegian (www.norwegian.no) flies to and from
most major cities in Norway, plus UK destinations
including London Gatwick, Edinburgh and Dublin.

Widerøe (www.wideroe.no) has several flights
a day to Svolvær and Leknes in the Lofoten
Islands. All flights are via Bodø.

BOAT

Tromsø is a major stop on the Hurtigruten coast-
al-ferry route. All ferries on the route will stop at
the **Hurtigruten ferry quay** (Samuel Arnesens
gate), until the opening of the new terminal (at
the time of research scheduled for autumn 2018).

BUS

The **main bus terminal** (Samuel Arnesens
gate) (also known as Prostneset) is on Kaigata,

🚗 Worth A Trip: Sommarøy

From Tromsø, this half-day trip is more
for the drive than the destination.
It's an extraordinarily pretty, lightly
trafficked run across Kvaløya, much of
it down at wet-your-feet shore level as
far as the small island of Sommarøy.
If you decide to stay the night, there's
the **Sommarøy Kurs & Feriesenter**
(☎77 66 40 00; www.sommaroy.no; Skip-
sholmsveien 22, Sommarøy; r 1090-1490kr,
apt from 2300kr, sea house from 3400kr;
P@🛜).

If you're arriving from Senja by the
Botnhamn–Brensholmen ferry (www.
tromskortet.no), the vistas as you cross
Kvaløya, heading westwards for Tromsø,
are equally stunning.

Sommarøy
TRAMONT_ANA/GETTY IMAGES ©

beside the Hurtigruten ferry quay. There are
up to three daily express buses to/from Narvik
(280kr, 4¼ hours) and one to/from Bodø
(410kr, 6½ hours).

Tromskortet (www.tromskortet.no) has a daily bus on weekdays to Narvik, where there's
a connecting bus to Svolvær (eight hours) in
the Lofoten Islands.

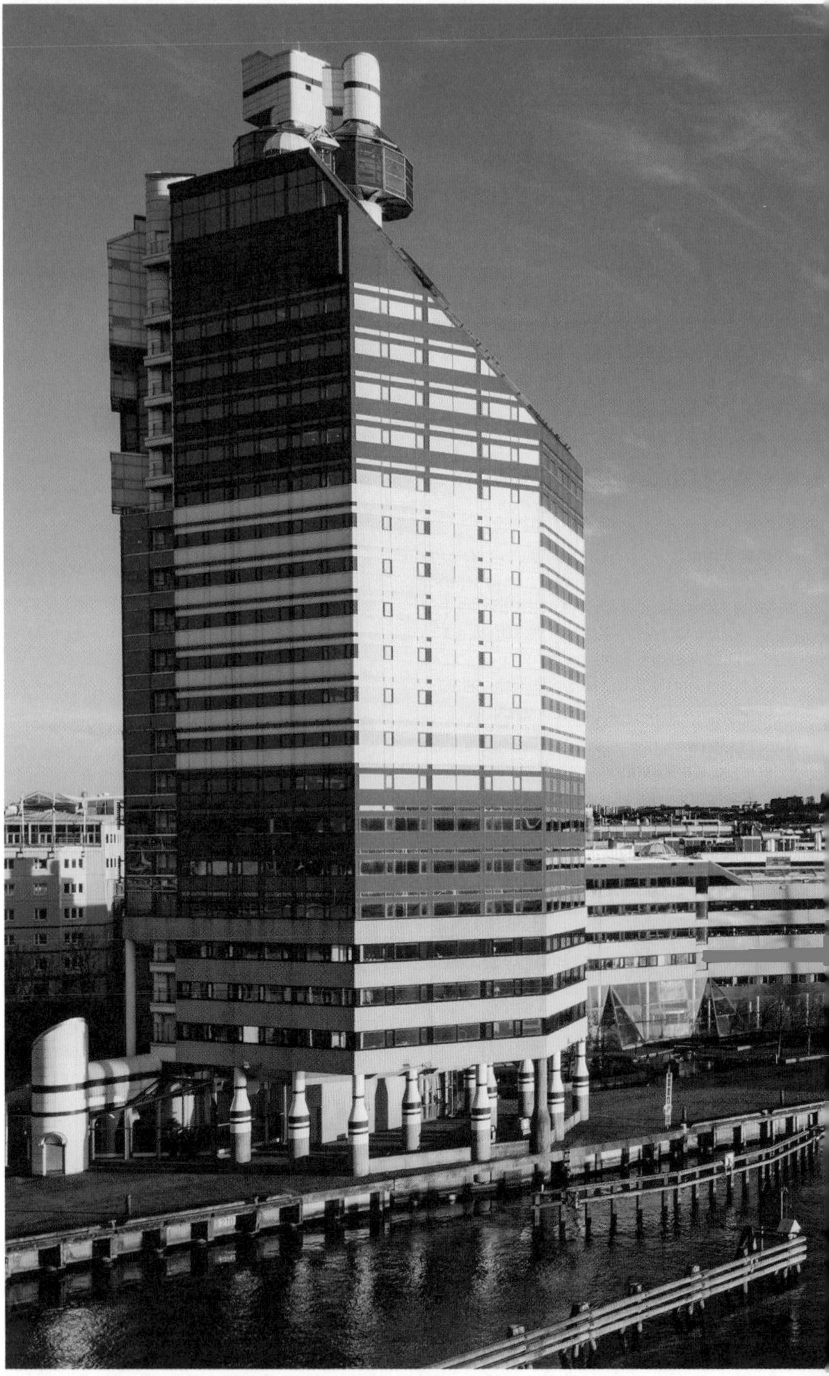

JOHNER IMAGES/GETTY IMAGES ©

GOTHENBURG, SWEDEN

Gothenburg, Sweden at a Glance...

Gregarious, chilled-out Gothenburg (Göteborg) has great appeal. Neoclassical architecture lines its tram-rattled streets, locals sun themselves beside canals, and there's always an interesting cultural or social event going on. It's also very walkable. From Centralstationen, shop-lined Östra Hamngatan leads southeast across one of the city's 17th-century canals, through verdant Kungsparken (King's Park) to the boutique- and upscale-bar-lined 'Avenyn' boulevard. The waterfront abounds with all things nautical (ships, aquariums, museums, the freshest fish). To the west, the Vasastan, Haga and Linné districts buzz with creativity and an appreciation of well-preserved history.

Two Days in Gothenburg

Spend a day at **Liseberg** (p183) amusement park, staying for a healthy lunch or dinner. Afterwards, stop for Scandinavian beer at **NOBA Nordic Bar** (p179).

Next day, visit excellent **Konstmuseum** (p182), then visit some independent galleries, like **Galleri Nils Åberg** (p181). Head to **Röda Sten Konsthall** (p182). Continue the art theme with a meal at **Thörnströms Kök** (p188).

Four Days in Gothenburg

On day three, shop in the **Haga district** (p183), stopping for lunch at **En Deli i Haga** (p187). Stroll through Linné district then grab a drink at **Notting Hill** (p190) or any of the comfy pubs in the area.

Next day, take the train to **Mölndals Museum** (p183) for its Swedish cultural artefacts. Grab a tasty shrimp sandwich at **Feskekörka** (p187), or opt for a fancy hot dog at **Gourmet Korv** (p187).

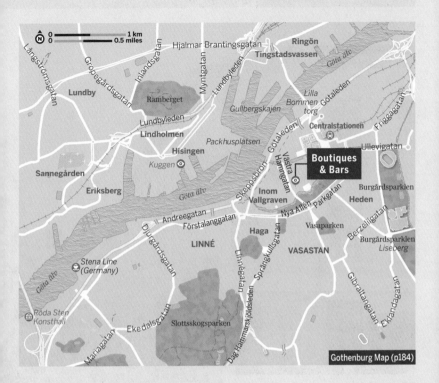

Gothenburg Map (p184)

Arriving in Gothenburg

Göteborg Landvetter Airport (p191) is located 25km east of the city.

Flygbuss (www.flygbussarna.se) runs to Landvetter Airport from Nils Ericson Terminalen every 15 to 20 minutes from 4.20am to 9pm and from the airport to the city between 5am and 11.30pm. Discounts are available for online bookings.

The fixed taxi rate with **Taxi Göteborg** (p193) from the city to the airport is 453kr.

Where to Stay

Gothenburg has a solid range of accommodation in all categories. The majority of hotels offer decent discounts at weekends and during the summer. Check www.goteborg.com for deals. Most hostels are clustered southwest of the centre; all are open year-round.

Haga District

Boutiques & Bars

Designer boutiques are a Gothenburg speciality, with everything from handmade jewellery to organic honey. Breezy bars, too, are a highlight: seek out a sun-soaked terrace and watch the world go by.

Great For...

Don't Miss

The idiosyncratic small shops in the Haga district.

DesignTorget

This **place** (www.designtorget.se; Vallgatan 14; ⊙10am-7pm Mon-Fri, to 5pm Sat, noon-4pm Sun; ⬛1, 2, 5, 6, 9 Domkyrkan) has cool, brightly coloured, affordable designer kitchenware, jewellery and more from both established and up-and-coming Scandi talent.

J. Lindeberg

This established Stockholm **designer** (www.jlindeberg.com; Korsgatan 17; ⊙11am-6pm Mon-Fri, to 5pm Sat; ⬛1, 6, 9, 11 Domkyrkan) offers slick knitwear, casual shirts and those perfect autumn/winter coats for the discerning gent.

❶ Need to Know

Shops rarely open before 10am, and some don't get going until noon.

✕ Take a Break

Any bar is good for a mid-shop break.

★ Top Tip

Use the tram (not car) to get around, especially if you're having a few drinks.

Champagne Baren

What's not to like? This **champagne bar** (www.forssenoberg.com; Kyrkogatan; ⏲5-11pm Tue-Thu, 4pm-midnight Fri & Sat; ☎; ▥1 Domkyrkan) has an idyllic setting on an inner courtyard with uneven cobbles, picturesque buildings and plenty of greenery. Along with glasses of bubbly, there are platters of cheese, oysters and cold cuts. Very popular with the boho-chic set. You can expect some cool background beats, as well as occasional live jazz.

NOBA Nordic Bar

With ye olde maps of Scandinavia on the walls and a glassed-over beer patio with birch tree stumps for stools, this **bar** (www.noba.nu; Viktoriagatan 1A; ⏲4pm-1am Mon-Thu, to 3am Fri & Sat, 5pm-1am Sun; ▥1, 2, 3, 7, 10 Viktoriagatan) takes its Nordic beers very seriously. From Iceland's Freyja to Denmark's Kärlek, you name it, they've got it. The free-flowing whiskies liven up the scene on weekends.

Ölhallen 7:an

This well-worn Swedish **beer hall** (Kungstorget 7; ⏲11am-midnight Sun-Tue, to 1am Wed-Sat; ▥3, 4, 5, 7, 10 Kungsportsplatsen), the last remaining from its era, hasn't changed much in more than 100 years. It attracts an interesting mix of bikers and regular folk with its homey atmosphere and friendly service. The illustrations lining the walls are Liss Sidén's portraits of regulars in the old days.

Art & Architecture Walking Tour

Gothenburg has imagination and creativity to spare. Independent galleries brim with up-and-coming talent, and architectural flights of fancy spring up like mushrooms after the rain.

Start Kuggen
Distance 7.5km
Duration 3 hours

Myntgatan

Lundbyleden

Göta älv

START ①

Göta älv

Oscarsleden

Djurgårdsgatan

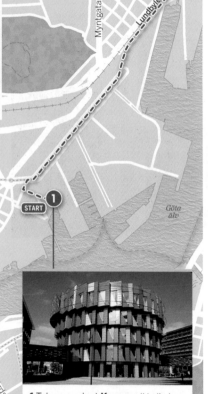

1 Take a peek at **Kuggen** (Lindholmsplatsen) for a taste of what 'green' engineering can mean.

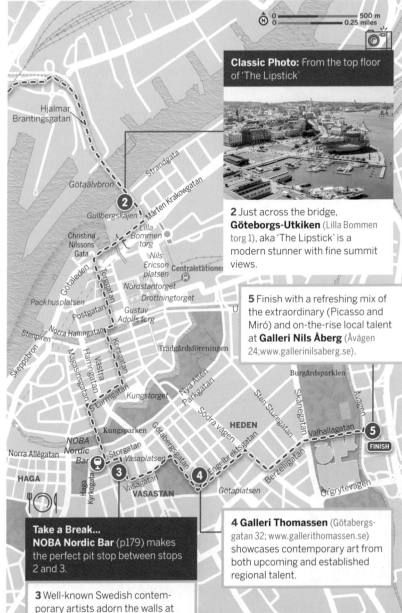

Classic Photo: From the top floor of 'The Lipstick'

2 Just across the bridge, **Göteborgs-Utkiken** (Lilla Bommen torg 1), aka 'The Lipstick' is a modern stunner with fine summit views.

5 Finish with a refreshing mix of the extraordinary (Picasso and Miró) and on-the-rise local talent at **Galleri Nils Åberg** (Åvägen 24; www.gallerinilsaberg.se).

FINISH

Take a Break...
NOBA Nordic Bar (p179) makes the perfect pit stop between stops 2 and 3.

4 Galleri Thomassen (Götabergs-gatan 32; www.gallerithomassen.se) showcases contemporary art from both upcoming and established regional talent.

3 Well-known Swedish contemporary artists adorn the walls at **Galleri Ferm** (Karl Gustavsgatan 13; www.galleriferm.se), along with some class international acts.

1 SEBASTIAAN KROES/GETTY IMAGES © // TRANSURFER/SHUTTERSTOCK ©

◉ SIGHTS

Most of the city's sights are located within walking distance of the centre and, after Liseberg, museums are Gothenburg's strongest asset: admission to most is covered by the Göteborg City Card (p191). All the museums have good cafes attached and several have specialist shops.

Konstmuseum
Gallery

(www.konstmuseum.goteborg.se; Götaplatsen; adult/child 40kr/free; ⊙11am-6pm Tue & Thu, to 8pm Wed, to 5pm Fri-Sun; ♿; 🚋4 Berzeliigatan) Home to Gothenburg's premier art collection, Konstmuseet displays works by the French Impressionists, Rubens, Van Gogh, Rembrandt and Picasso; Scandinavian masters such as Bruno Liljefors, Edvard Munch, Anders Zorn and Carl Larsson have pride of place in the **Fürstenburg Galleries**.

Other highlights include a superb sculpture hall, the **Hasselblad Center** with its annual *New Nordic Photography* exhibition, and temporary displays of next-gen Nordic art.

Röda Sten Konsthall
Gallery

(www.rodastenkonsthall.se; Röda Sten 1; adult/child 40kr/free; ⊙noon-5pm Tue, Thu & Fri, to 8pm Wed, to 6pm Sat & Sun; 🚋3 Vagnhallen Majorna) Occupying a defunct power station beside the giant Älvsborgsbron, Röda Sten's four floors are home to such temporary exhibitions as edgy Swedish photography and cross-dressing rap videos by Danish–Filipino artist Lilibeth Cuenca Rasmussen that challenge sexuality stereotypes in Afghan society. The indie-style cafe hosts weekly live music and club nights, and offbeat one-offs like punk bike races, boxing matches and stand-up comedy. To get here, walk towards the Klippan precinct, continue under Älvsborgsbron and look for the brown-brick building.

Universeum
Museum

(www.universeum.se; Södra Vägen 50; adult/child 250/195kr; ⊙10am-6pm, to 8pm Jul & Aug; P♿; 🚋2 Korsvägen) In what is arguably the best museum for kids in Sweden, you find yourself in the midst of a humid rainforest, complete with trickling water, tropical birds and butterflies flitting through the

Konstmuseum

greenery, and tiny marmosets. On a level above, roaring dinosaurs maul each other, while next door, denizens of the deep float through the shark tunnel and venomous beauties lie coiled in the serpent tanks. In the 'technology inspired by nature' section, stick your children to the Velcro wall.

Haga District   Area

(www.hagashopping.se; 🚋25 Hagakyrkan, 🚋2 Handelshögskolan) The Haga district is Gothenburg's oldest suburb, dating back to 1648. A hardcore hippie hang-out in the 1960s and '70s, its cobbled streets and vintage buildings are now host to a cool blend of cafes, trendy shops and boutiques. During some summer weekends and at Christmas, store owners set up stalls along Haga Nygata, turning the neighbourhood into one big market. Check out the charming three-storey timber houses, built as housing for workers in the 19th century.

Trädgårdsföreningen   Park

(www.tradgardsforeningen.se; Nya Allén; ⊘7am-8pm; 🚋3, 4, 5, 7, 10 Kungsportsplatsen) Laid out in 1842, the lush Trädgårdsföreningen is a large protected area off Nya Allén. Full of flowers and tiny cafes, it's popular for lunchtime escapes and is home to Europe's largest **rosarium**, with around 2500 varieties. The gracious 19th-century **Palmhuset** (open 10am to 8pm) is a bite-size version of the Crystal Palace in London, with five differently heated halls: look out for the impressive camellia collection and the 2m-wide tropical lily pads.

Liseberg   Amusement Park

(www.liseberg.se; Södra Vägen; 1-day pass 455kr; ⊘11am-11pm Jun–mid-Aug, hours vary rest of year; 🅿🚻; 🚋2 Korsvägen) The attractions of Liseberg, Scandinavia's largest amusement park, are many and varied. Adrenalin blasts include the venerable wooden roller coaster Balder; its 'explosive' colleague Kanonen, where you're blasted from 0km/h to 75km/h in under two seconds; AtmosFear, Europe's tallest (116m) free-fall tower; and the park's biggest new attraction, Loke, a

Creative Outskirts

The tiny, creative hub of Kvarnbyn, a district of Mölndals 8km south of Gothenburg, has long attracted architects, designers and artists looking to escape the high rents and pressures of the city. Here, a brooding landscape of roaring rapids gripped by grain mills and historic factories (Mölndal means 'valley of the mills') has been transformed into a dynamic yet low-key cultural centre.

The district's nexus is the smart, interactive **Mölndals Museum** (📞031-431 34; www.museum.molndal.se; Kvarnbygatan 12; ⊘noon-4pm Tue-Sun; 🅿🚻; 🚋752, 756, 🚉Mölndal) FREE. Located in an old police station, the museum is like a vast warehouse, with a 10,000-strong collection of local nostalgia that includes a 17th-century clog, kitchen kitsch and a re-created 1930s worker's cottage.

The district also hosts some noteworthy cultural events. On a Saturday in mid- to late April, **Kvarnbydagen** (Kvarnbyn Day; www.kvarnbydagen.se) sees local artists and designers open their studios to the public. In September **Kulturnatt** (http://kulturnatta.goteborg. se/) is a starlit spectacle of open studios and art installations, as well as dance and music performances.

To reach Kvarnbyn from Gothenburg, catch a Kungsbacka–bound train to Mölndal station, then bus 756 or 752 to Mölndals Museum.

fast-paced spinning 'wheel' that soars 42 metres into the air. Softer options include carousels, fairy-tale castles, an outdoor dance floor, adventure playgrounds, and shows and concerts.

 SHOPPING

Gothenburg is right up with Stockholm when it comes to shopping. The Haga

Göteborg (Gothenburg)

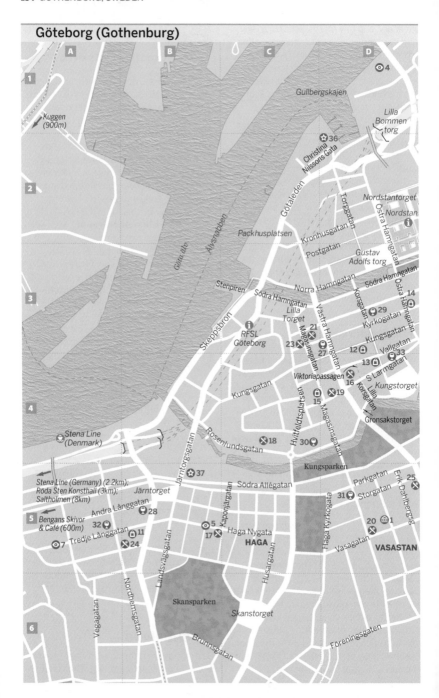

Kuggen (900m)

Gullbergskajen

Lilla Bommen torg

Christina Nilssons Gata

Nordstantorget

Östra Nordstan

Packhusplatsen

Kronhusgatan

Postgatan

Gustav Adolfs torg

Stenpiren

Norra Hamngatan

Södra Hamngatan

Södra Hamngatan
Lilla Torget

Östra Hamngatan

Kyrkogatan

Kungsgatan

Vallgatan

S Larmgatan

Kungstorget

Viktoriapassagen

Gronsakstorget

Stena Line (Denmark)

Kungsgatan

Rosenlundsgatan

Kungsparken

Parkgatan

Erik Dahlbergsg.

Stena Line (Germany) (2.2km);
Röda Sten Konsthall (3km);
Saltholmen (8km)

Järntorget

Södra Allégatan

Storgatan

Bengans Skivor & Café (600m)

Andra Långgatan

Tredje Långgatan

Haga Nygata

HAGA

Vasagatan

VASASTAN

Skansparken

Skanstorget

Brunnsgatan

Föreningsgatan

Vegagatan

Nordhemsgatan

Landsvägsgatan

Kaponjärgatan

Husargatan

Haga Kyrkogata

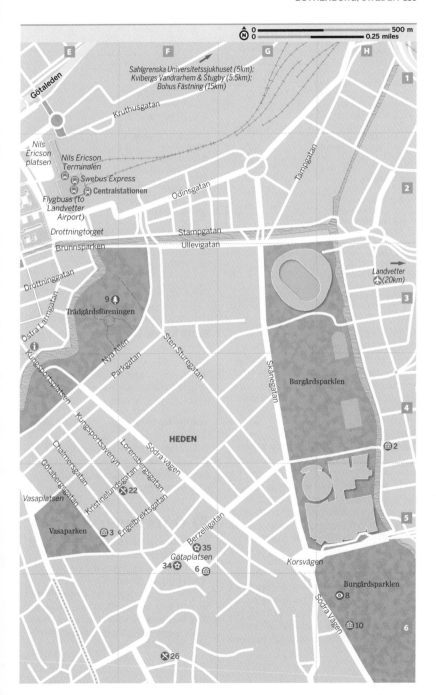

N
0 — 500 m
0 — 0.25 miles

E

F

G

H

Götaleden

1

Sahlgrenska Universitetssjukhuset (5km);
Kvibergs Vandrarhem & Stugby (5.5km);
Bohus Fästning (15km)

Kruthusgatan

Nils
Ericson
platsen

Nils Ericson
Terminalen

Swebus Express

Centralstationen

Flygbuss (to
Landvetter
Airport)

Odinsgatan

Tampgatan

2

Drottningtorget

Stampgatan

Brunnsparken

Ullevigatan

Landvetter
✈(20km)

Drottninggatan

Östra Larmgatan

9 🛈
Trädgårdsföreningen

Nya Allén

Sten Sturegatan

3

Kungsportsplatsen

Parkgatan

Skånegatan

Burgårdsparklen

4

Kungsportsavenyn

Lorensbergsgatan

Södra vägen

HEDEN

🍴2

Chalmersgatan

Götabergsgatan

Kristinelundsgatan

🍴22

Engelbrektsgatan

Vasaplatsen

Berzeligatan

5

Vasaparken

🍴3

🎭35
Götaplatsen

34🎭 6🍴

Korsvägen

Burgårdsparklen

◉8

Södra Vägen

🍴10

6

🍴26

Göteborg (Gothenburg)

district is good for quirky, small boutiques. At the other end of the scale are designer boutiques and national chains on 'the Avenyn' boulevard. For one-stop shopping head to central Nordiska Kompaniet, a hub of Swedish and international brands.

Nordiska Kompaniet   Department Store

(www.nk.se; Östra Hamngatan 42; ⊙10am-8pm, to 6pm Sat, 11am-5pm Sun; 🚊3,4, 5, 7, 10 Kungsportsplatsen) A local institution since 1971, the four floors of this venerable department store host the likes of Tiger, RedGreen, NK Boutique and Mayla amid its a mix of Swedish and international designers.

Bengans Skivor & Café   Music

(☏031-14 33 00; www.bengans.se; Stigbergstorget 1; ⊙10am-6.30pm Mon-Fri, 10am-4pm Sat, noon-4pm Sun; 🚊3, 9,11 Stigbergstorget) Gothenburg's mightiest music store is set in an old cinema, complete with retro signage and an indie-cool cafe.

Butik Kubik   Clothing

(www.butikkubik.se; Tredje Långgatan 8; ⊙noon-8pm Tue-Fri, to 6pm Sat; 🚊1, 6 Prinsgatan) Run by two young designers, this basement shop is a great place to check out local, bright, flowery threads.

Velour by Nostalgi   Clothing

(www.velour.se; Magasinsgatan 19; ⊙11am-6.30pm Mon-Fri, to 5pm Sat, noon-4pm Sun; 🚊1, 6, 9, 11 Domkyrkan) Revamped flagship store of local label. Stocks slick, stylish streetwear for guys and gals.

❂ ENTERTAINMENT

Widely recognised as Sweden's premier music city, Gothenburg has a lively music scene, as well as one of the country's top opera houses. Check out www.goteborg. com to find out what's on. There are also several annual music festivals, including **Way Out West** (www.wayoutwest.se), which takes place in August and draws fans from all over Europe.

Pustervik — Live Music, Theatre

(www.pusterviksbaren.se; Järntorgsgatan 12; 🚊1, 3, 5, 9, 11 Järntorget) Culture vultures and party people pack this hybrid venue, with its heaving downstairs bar and upstairs club and stage. Gigs range from independent theatre and live music (anything from emerging singer-songwriters to Neneh Cherry) to regular club nights spanning hip-hop, soul and rock.

Göteborgs Konserthuset — Classical Music

(Concert Hall; 🕿031-726 53 10; www.gso. se; Götaplatsen; tickets 100-360kr; ⊗closed summer) Home to the local symphony orchestra, with top international guests and some sterling performances.

GöteborgsOperan — Opera

(🕿031-13 13 00; www.opera.se; Christina Nilssons Gata; tickets 100-850kr; 🚊5, 10 Lilla Bommen) Designed by architect Jan Izikowitz, the opera house is a striking contemporary glass building with a sloped roof overlooking Lilla Bommen harbour. Performances include classics such as *Phantom of the Opera* as well as contemporary dance by up-and-coming artists.

Göteborgs Stadsteatern — Theatre

(🕿031-708 71 00; www.stadsteatern.goteborg.se; Götaplatsen; tickets from 110kr) Stages theatre productions in Swedish.

⊗ EATING

Gothenburg's chefs are at the cutting edge of Sweden's Slow Food movement, and the city boasts top-notch restaurants. Happily, there are also more casual options for trying old-fashioned *husmanskost* (home cooking) and a good range of vegan and vegetarian options. Cool cafes, cheap ethnic gems and foodie favourites abound in Vasastan, Haga and Linné districts.

Saluhall Briggen — Market €

(www.saluhallbriggen.se; Nordhemsgatan 28; ⊗9am-6pm Mon-Fri, to 3pm Sat; 🚊1 Prinsgatan) This covered market will have you drooling over its bounty of fresh bread, cheeses, quiches, seafood and ethnic treats. It's particularly handy for the hostel district.

En Deli i Haga — Deli €

(Haga Nygata 15; combo plate weekday/weekend 105/135kr; ⊗8am-7pm Mon-Fri, 10am-5pm Sat & Sun; 🖋; 🚊1, 3, 5, 6, 9 Järntorget) En Deli dishes out great Mediterranean–style salads and meze, as well as good soup and sandwiches. Can't decide? Try some of everything, with the deli plate. An extra perk is the local beer and organic wine to accompany your meal.

Feskekörka — Market €

(www.feskekörka.se; Rosenlundsgatan; salads from 75kr; ⊗9am-5pm Tue-Thu, to 6pm Fri, 10am-3pm Sat; 🚊3, 5, 9, 11 Hagakyrkan) A market devoted to all things that come from the sea, the 'Fish Church' is heaven for those who appreciate slabs of gravadlax, heaped shrimp sandwiches and seafood-heavy salads. The outdoor picnic tables are the ideal place to munch on them.

Da Matteo — Cafe €

(www.damatteo.se; Vallgatan 5; sandwiches & salads 65-95kr; ⊗7.30am-6pm Mon-Fri, 8am-6pm Sat, 10am-5pm Sun; 🚊1, 3, 5, 6, 9 Domkyrkan) The perfect downtown lunch pit stop and a magnet for coffee lovers, this cafe serves wickedly fine espresso, mini *sfogliatelle* (Neapolitan pastries), sandwiches, pizza and great salads. There's a sun-soaked courtyard and a second branch on Viktoriapassagen.

Gourmet Korv — Hot Dogs €

(www.gourmetkorv.se; Södra Larmgatan; dogs 30-40kr, meals 67-95kr; ⊗10am-6pm Mon-Fri, to 4pm Sat, to 3pm Sun; 🚊2, 5, 6, 11 Grönsakstorget) A festival of sausages to sate the hungriest of the carnivorously inclined. Choose from the likes of currywurst, bierwurst and

 Fortress Defence

Gamla Älvsborg fortress, standing guard over the river 3km downstream of the centre, is Gothenburg's oldest significant structure and was a key strategic point in the 17th-century territorial wars. The Swedes founded Gothenburg in 1621 to be free of the extortionate taxation rates imposed on their ships by the Danes.

Fearful of Danish attack, the Swedes employed Dutch experts to construct a defensive canal system in the centre. The workers lived in what is now the revitalised Haga area: around a fifth of the original buildings are still standing. Most of Gothenburg's oldest wooden buildings went up in smoke long ago – the city was devastated by no fewer than nine major fires between 1669 and 1804.

Once Sweden had annexed Skåne in 1658, Gothenburg expanded as a trading centre. Boom time came in the 18th century, when merchants such as the Swedish East India Company made huge amounts of wealth from trade with the Far East, their profits responsible for numerous grand houses that are still standing.

Gothenburg was sustained largely by the shipbuilding industry until it went belly up in the 1980s. These days, the lifeblood of Scandinavia's busiest port is heavy industry (Volvo manufacturing in particular) and commerce.

Gamla Älvsborg fortress
GVICTORIA/SHUTTERSTOCK ©

the immensely satisfying, cheese-squirting *käsekrainer* and have it in a bun or with a full spread of salad and mash.

Moon Thai Kitchen Thai €€
(www.moonthai.se; Kristinelundsgatan 9; mains 139-189kr; ⊘11am-11pm Mon-Fri, noon-11pm Sat & Sun; 🚋4, 5, 7, 10 Göteborg Valand) The owners have opted for a 'Thailand' theme and decided to run with it a few miles, hence the kaleidoscopic whirl of tuktuks, flowers and bamboo everything. Luckily, the dishes are authentic, the whimsical menu features such favourites as *som tum* (spicy papaya salad) and the fiery prawn red curry will make you weep with pleasure and gratitude.

Restaurant 2112 Burgers €€
(☏031-787 58 12; Magasinsgatan; burgers 189kr; ⊘4pm-1am, from 2pm Sat; 🚋1, 3, 5, 6, 9 Domkyrkan) Appealing to refined rockers and metalheads, this upmarket joint serves only burgers and beer. But what burgers! These masterpieces range from the superlative Smoke on the Water with its signature Jack Daniels glaze to the fiery Hell Awaits Burger, featuring habanero dressing. The hungriest of diners will meet their match in the 666g monster Number of the Beast.

Thörnströms Kök Scandinavian €€€
(☏031-16 20 66; www.thornstromskok.com; Teknologgatan 3; mains 325-355kr, 4-course menu 675kr; ⊘6pm-1am Mon-Sat; 🛜; 🚋7 Kapellplatsen) Specialising in modern Scandinavian cuisine, owner-chef Håkan shows you how he earned that Michelin star through creative use of local, seasonal ingredients and flawless presentation. Feast on the likes of rabbit with pistachios, pickled carrots and seaweed; don't miss the milk-chocolate pudding with goat's-cheese ice cream. A la carte dishes are available if multicourses overwhelm you.

Smaka Swedish €€€
(☏031-13 22 47; www.smaka.se; Vasaplatsen 3; mains 175-285kr; ⊘5-11pm; 🛜; 🚋1 Vasaplatsen) For top-notch Swedish *husmanskost*,

like the speciality meatballs with mashed potato and lingonberries, it's hard to do better than this smart yet down-to-earth restaurant-bar. Mod–Swedish options might include hake with suckling pig cheek or salmon tartar with pickled pear.

Magnus & Magnus
Modern European €€€

(☑031-13 30 00; www.magnusmagnus.se; Magasinsgatan 8; 4-/6-course menu 495/745kr; ☺from 6pm Mon-Sat; 🚋1, 2, 5, 6, 9 Domkyrkan) Ever-fashionable Magnus & Magnus serves inspired and beautifully presented modern European dishes in an appropriately chic setting. It's an unpretentious place in spite of its popularity, with pleasantly down-to-earth staff. The menu tantalises with its lists of ingredients (pork belly, king crab, melon, feta cheese), and the courtyard draws Gothenburg's hipsters in summer.

Koka
Swedish €€€

(☑031-701 79 79; www.restaurangkoka. se; Viktoriagatan 12C; 3-/5-/7-course meals 480/680/880kr; ☺from 6pm Wed-Sat; 🚋1,

2, 3, 7, 10 Vasaplatsen) Stylish Koka is distinguished by its smart, contemporary decor – blond wood, clean lines, mood lighting – and a dedication to conjuring up inspired dishes from the seasonal ingredients of Sweden's west coast. Brace yourself for the likes of mackerel with gooseberries, pork with blackcurrant and chervil ice cream.

🍷 DRINKING & NIGHTLIFE

While Kungsportsavenyn brims with beer-downing tourists and after-work locals, there are some savvier options – in summer, seek out a perch on a sun-soaked terrace and watch the street life go by.

Clubs have minimum-age limits ranging from 18 to 25, and many have a cover charge on popular nights.

Barn
Bar

(www.thebarn.se; Kyrkogatan 11; ☺5pm-late Mon-Sat, from 2pm Sun; 🚃; 🚋1 Domkyrkan) As the name suggests, this bar is all roughly hewn wood and copper taps, and the beer/wine selection is guaranteed to get

Trädgårdsföreningen (p183)

Cafe Santo Domingo

you merry. Excellent cocktails – vouched for by local bartenders. The burgers make fantastic stomach-liners, too.

Notting Hill   Pub
(www.nottinghill.se; Nordhemsgatan 19A; ⊘4pm-midnight Mon-Thu, to 2am Fri & Sat; 🚋1, 3, 5, 6, 9 Järntorget) This friendly and pretty local pub between the Haga and Linné districts – on a corner crammed with appealing drinking establishments – looks like it could've dropped in from the Cotswolds. There's a respectable selection of tipples, British and Swedish pub fare (meatballs, fish and chips) and football on the big screen.

Greta's   Gay
(☏031-13 69 49; Drottninggatan 35; ⊘9pm-3am Fri & Sat; 🚋1, 3, 4, 5, 6, 9 Brunnsparken) Decked out with Greta Garbo memorabilia, Greta's is Gothenburg's dedicated gay club, featuring flamboyant Tiki parties, DJs and other kitsch-a-licious fun on Friday and Saturday nights.

Nefertiti   Club
(www.nefertiti.se; Hvitfeldtsplatsen 6; admission 120-220kr; ⊘Hours vary; 🚋1, 5, 6, 9, 11 Grönsakstorget) Named rather incongruously after an Egyptian goddess, this Gothenburg institution is famous for its smooth live jazz and blues, as well as club nights spanning everything from techno and deep house to hip-hop and funk and a weekly soul night.

Cafe Santo Domingo   Bar
(www.cafesantodomingo.se; Andra Långgatan 4; ⊘9am-late; 🚋1, 3, 5, 6, 9 Järntorget) Cafe–record shop serving mean espressos by day turns into a bar with a great array of beers and rowdy live-music sets by night.

ⓘ INFORMATION

TOURIST INFORMATION

Cityguide Gothenburg (www.goteborg.com/apps) Info on the city's attractions, events and more, available as an Android and iPhone app. City map available offline.

Tourist Office (www.goteborg.com; Nils Eriksongatan; ⊙10am-8pm Mon-Fri, to 6pm Sat, noon-5pm Sun) Branch office inside the Nordstan shopping complex.

Tourist Office (⊘031-368 42 00; www.goteborg. com; Kungsportsplatsen 2; ⊙9.30am-8pm late Jun–mid-Aug, shorter hours rest of year) Central and busy; has a good selection of free brochures and maps.

RFSL Göteborg (⊘031-788 25 10; www.rfsl.se/ goteborg; Stora Badhusgatan 6; ⊙6-9pm Wed) Comprehensive information on the city's gay scene, events and more.

❶ GETTING THERE & AWAY

AIR

Göteborg Landvetter Airport (www.swedavia. se/landvetter; ⊟Flygbuss) has daily flights to/from Stockholm Arlanda and Stockholm Bromma airports, as well as weekday services to Umeå and several weekly services to Borlänge, Falun, Visby and Sundsvall.

Direct European routes include Amsterdam (KLM), Brussels (SAS), Copenhagen (SAS and Norwegian), Frankfurt (Lufthansa), Berlin (Air Berlin), Helsinki (Norwegian and SAS), London (British Airways and Ryanair), Munich (Lufthansa), Oslo (Norwegian) and Paris (Air France and SAS).

BOAT

Gothenburg is a major ferry terminal, with several services to Denmark and Germany.

Stena Line (Denmark) (www.stenaline.se; Danmarksterminalen, Masthuggskajen; foot-passenger one-way from 200kr; 🚊3 Masthuggstorget)

Stena Line (Germany) (www.stenaline.se; Elof Lindälusgatan 11; foot passenger one-way/return from 500kr; 🚊3 Jaegerdorffsplatsen)

For a special view of the region, jump on a boat for an unforgettable journey along the **Göta Canal** (www.gotakanal.se/en/). Starting in Gothenburg, you'll pass through Sweden's oldest lock at Lilla Edet, opened in 1607. From there the trip crosses the great lakes Vänern and Vättern through the rolling country of Östergötland and on to Stockholm.

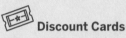 **Discount Cards**

The brilliant **Göteborg City Card** (www. goteborg.com/citycard; 24-/48-/72hr card adult 395/545/695kr, child 265/365/455kr) is particularly worthwhile if you're into intensive sightseeing: it gives you free access to most museums and Liseberg amusement park, discounted and free city tours, unlimited travel on public transport and free parking in a city with infamously dedicated traffic wardens. The card is available at tourist offices, hotels, Pressbyrån newsstands and online.

The **Göteborgspaketet** (http://butik. goteborg.com/en/package; adult from 635kr) is an accommodation-and-entertainment package offered at various hotels, with prices starting at 635kr per person per night in a double room. It includes the Göteborg City Card for the number of nights you stay; book online in advance.

BUS

Västtrafik (⊘0771-41 43 00; www.vasttrafik. se) and **Hallandstrafiken** (⊘0771-33 10 30; www.hlt.se) provide regional transport links. If you're planning to spend some time exploring the southwest counties, a monthly pass or a *sommarkort* offers cheaper travel in the peak summer period (from late June to mid-August).

The bus station, **Nils Ericson Terminalen**, is next to the train station and has excellent facilities including luggage lockers (medium/large up to 24 hours 70/90kr). There's a Västtrafik information booth here, providing information and selling tickets for all city and regional public transport within the Gothenburg, Bohuslän and Västergötland area.

Swebus (⊘0771-21 82 18; www.swebusex press.com) operates frequent buses to most major towns and cities; non-refundable advance tickets work out considerably cheaper than on-the-spot purchases. Swebus services include:

Day Trip to Marstrand

A quick and rewarding day trip from Gothenburg, Marstrand is a well-known summer retreat, and has been since King Oscar II and co started taking the waters here in the 1880s. Before that, the island enjoyed fame as the herring capital of Europe, and (though the herring come and go) its seafood is still a major draw.

Solitude-seekers beware: dozens of visitors shuffle off and on the ferry linking the mainland to Marstrand island every 15 minutes. But it's easy to ditch the crowds if you follow signs to the nature trail (*'naturstig'*), which leads around the rocky edges to the far side of the island for epic views and secluded sunbathing nooks.

Carlstens Fästning (www.carlsten.se; adult/child 95/50kr; ⊘11am-3pm Apr-May, 11am-5pm Jun & Aug, 10.30am-6.30pm Jul, 11am-3pm Sat & Sun Sep-Oct; 🚗; 🚢Marstrand) fortress was built in the 1660s after the Swedish takeover of Marstrand and Bohuslän and appears to loom over the town. Marstrand's ice-free port was key to trade, so King Karl X Gustav built the fortress to defend it. The port continued to be fought over for decades. Carlstens has also been a prison, known for especially brutal conditions. Admission includes a guided tour. It's worth walking up even if you don't go in: the views of the archipelago are stunning.

Carlstens Fästning
SOPHIE MCAULAY/SHUTTERSTOCK ©

- Stockholm (from 159kr, 6½ to seven hours, four to five daily)
- Halmstad (from 109kr, 1¾ hours, five to seven daily)
- Helsingborg (from 139kr, 2¾ hours, five to eight daily)
- Copenhagen (from 239kr, 4¾ hours, four daily)
- Malmö (from 119kr, 3½ to four hours, seven to nine daily)
- Oslo (from 229kr, 3½ hours, five to 10 daily)

CAR & MOTORCYCLE

The E6 motorway runs north–south from Oslo to Malmö just east of the city centre. There's also a complex junction where the E20 motorway diverges east for Stockholm.

International car-hire companies have desks at Göteborg Landvetter Airport and near the central train/bus stations.

Avis (www.avisworld.com)

Europcar (www.europcar.com)

Hertz (www.hertz-europe.com)

TRAIN

All trains arrive at and depart from Centralstationen, Sweden's oldest railway station and a heritage-listed building. The main railway lines in the west connect Gothenburg to Karlstad, Stockholm, Malmö and Oslo. In the east, the main line runs from Stockholm via Norrköping and Linköping to Malmö. Book tickets online via **Sveriges Järnväg** (SJ; www.sj.se) or purchase from ticket booths at the station.

Left Luggage Luggage lockers (medium/large up to 24 hours 70/90kr) are available at Centralstationen.

ⓘ GETTING AROUND

BICYCLE

Cyclists should ask at the tourist office for the free map *Cykelkarta Göteborg*, covering the best routes.

Styr & Ställ (www.goteborgbikes.se; per season 75kr) is Gothenburg's handy city-bike system. It involves buying a 'season pass' which then gives

Liseberg (p183)

you unlimited access to bicycles stationed across the city. With the pass, all journeys under half an hour are free, making this ideal for quick trips. (There's a small fee for longer journeys.) You can also download directly onto your smartphone the app allbikesnow.com, which has a city map showing all the bike locales, plus how many bikes are free at any given time.

Cykelkungen (☎031-18 43 00; www.cykelkungen.se; Chalmersgatan 19; per day/wk 200/700kr; ☺10am-6pm Mon-Fri) Reliable spot for longer-term bike hire.

PUBLIC TRANSPORT

Buses, trams and ferries run by Västtrafik (p191) make up the city's public-transport system; there are Västtrafik information booths selling tickets and giving out timetables inside Nils Ericson Terminalen, in front of the train station on Drottningtorget and at Brunnsparken.

The most convenient way to travel around Gothenburg is by tram. Colour-coded lines, numbered 1 to 13, converge near Brunnsparken (a block from the train station). Trams run every few minutes between 5am and midnight; some lines run a reduced service after midnight on Friday and Saturday.

A city **transport ticket** costs 29/22kr per adult/child. One- and three-day **travel cards** (90/180kr, from Västtrafik information booths, 7-Eleven minimarkets or Pressbyrån newsagencies) can work out much cheaper. Holders of the **Göteborg City Card** travel free.

Västtrafik also has a handy app, Västtrafik To Go, which allows you to buy tickets on your phone.

TAXI

Taxi Göteborg (☎031-65 00 00; www.taxigoteborg.se) One of the larger taxi companies.

Taxis can be picked up outside Centralstationen, at Kungsportsplatsen and on Kungsportsavenyn.

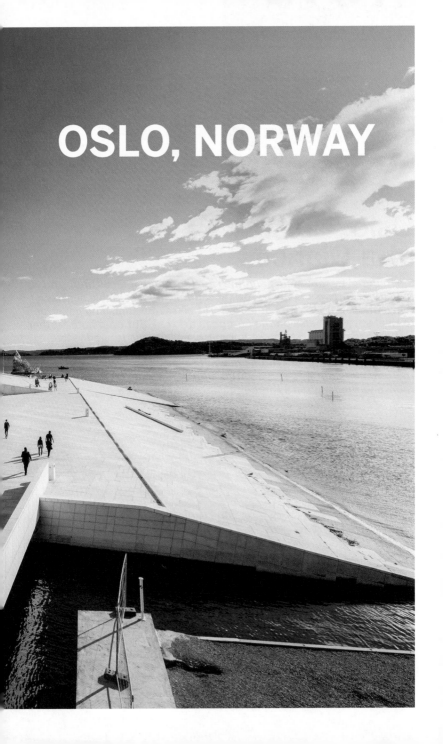

OSLO, NORWAY

In this Chapter

Oslo, Norway at a Glance...

Surrounded by mountains and the sea, this compact, cultured, and fun city is Europe's fastest-growing capital with a palpable sense of reinvention. Oslo is also home to world-class museums and galleries to rival anywhere else on the European art trail. But even here Mother Nature has managed to make her mark, and Oslo is fringed with forests, hills and lakes awash with opportunities for hiking, cycling, skiing and boating. Add to this mix a thriving cafe and bar culture, top-notch restaurants and nightlife options ranging from opera to indie rock, and the result is a thoroughly intoxicating place.

Two Days in Oslo

Begin at the **Nasjonalgalleriet** (p202), explore **Akershus Fortress** (p202), then the museums of **Bygdøy (p198)**. Finish your evening in Aker Brygge. On day two, poke around the **Ibsen Museet** (p202), wander **Slottsparken** (p203), take a **Royal Palace tour** (p203) and take in the **Astrup Fearnley Museet** (p203) and the **Tjuvholmen Sculpture Park** (p203). Have dinner and cocktails at Tjuvholmen's **Vingen** (p209).

Four Days in Oslo

Walk the roof of **Oslo Opera House** (p203), then head inside for a tour. A quick tram ride from Central Station will take you to **Frogner** (p206) where you can explore **Frognerparken** (p206) and **Vigelandsanlegget** (p206). Finish your day with Neo Nordic cuisine at **Sentralen Restaurant** (p208).

On your fourth day, climb the **Holmenkollen Ski Jump** (p206) and enjoy the panoramic views. Then head back to hip Grünerløkka for potato bread hot dogs at **Syverkiosken** (p209) followed by a short 10-minute walk to **Torggata Botaniske** (p211) for cocktails.

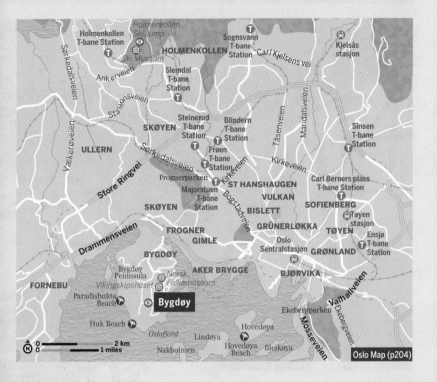

Oslo Map (p204)

Arriving in Oslo

Oslo Gardermoen International Airport The city's main airport, 50km north of the city, is serviced by the high-speed train service **Flytoget** (www.flytoget.no) as well as standard NSB intercity and local trains. The bus service **Flybussen** (www.flybussen.no) also runs directly to the city.

Oslo Sentral All trains from Sweden arrive and depart from here and it's serviced by T-bane, trams, buses and taxis.

Where to Stay

Aker Brygge, the city centre, Opera House, Bjørvika and Bygdøy are the most popular choices – they're close to everything with plenty of attractions, restaurants, cafes etc. Frogner and Western Oslo are serene and close to the Slottsparken and city, while Grünerløkka and Vulkan are fantastic choices for experiencing local life.

Polarship Fram Museum

ALENA.KRAVCHENKO/SHUTTERSTOCK ©

History on Bygdøy

Best accessed by ferry, pretty, residential and rural-feeling Bygdøy is home to the city's most fascinating, quintessentially Norwegian museums, featuring Vikings, traditional architecture and modern-day explorers.

Great For...

Don't Miss

The most impressive and ostentatious of the three Viking ships is the *Oseberg*.

Vikingskipshuset

Around 1100 years ago, Vikings dragged two **longships** (Viking Ship Museum; ☎22 13 52 80; www.khm.uio.no; Huk Aveny 35; adult/child 80kr/free; ◷9am-6pm May-Sep, 10am-4pm Oct-Apr; ☺91) from the shoreline and used them as the centrepiece for grand ceremonial burials, most likely for important chieftains or nobles. Along with the ships, they buried many items for the afterlife: food, drink, jewellery, furniture, carriages, weapons and even a few dogs and servants for companionship. Discovered in Oslofjord in the late 19th century, the ships have been beautifully restored and offer an evocative, emotive insight into the Viking world.

Polarship Fram Museum

A **museum** (Frammuseet; ☎23 28 29 50; www.frammuseum.no; Bygdøynesveien 36; adult/child

Norsk Folkemuseum

TRAGANTOG/SHUTTERSTOCK ©

❶ Need to Know

Ferry 91 makes the 15-minute run to Bygdøy from Rådhusbrygge 3.

✕ Take a Break

Before catching the ferry to Bygdøy, stop by Pipervika (p209) for a fresh-shrimp baguette.

★ Top Tip

Pre-buy your ferry ticket – and buying a return ticket is far cheaper.

100/40kr, with Oslo Pass free; ⊙9am-6pm Jun-Aug, 10am-5pm May & Sep, to 4pm Oct-May; ☷91) dedicated to one of the most enduring symbols of early polar exploration, the 39m schooner Fram (meaning 'Forward'). You can wander the decks, peek inside the cramped bunk rooms and imagine life at sea and among the polar ice. There are detailed exhibits complete with maps, pictures and artefacts of various expeditions, from Nansen's attempt to ski across the North Pole to Amundsen's discovery of the Northwest Passage.

Kon-Tiki Museum

A favourite among children, this worthwhile **museum** (☑23 08 67 67; www.kon-tiki.no; Bygdøynesveien 36; adult/child 100/40kr, with Oslo Pass free; ⊙9.30am-6pm Jun-Aug, 10am-5pm Mar-May, Sep & Oct, 10am-4pm Nov-Feb; ☷91) is dedicated to the balsa raft Kon-Tiki, which Norwegian explorer Thor Heyerdahl sailed from Peru to Polynesia in 1947. The museum also displays the totora-reed boat Ra II, built by Aymara people on the Bolivian island of Suriqui in Lake Titicaca. Heyerdahl used it to cross the Atlantic in 1970.

Norsk Folkemuseum

Norway's largest open-air **museum** (Norwegian Folk Museum; ☑22 12 37 00; www. norskfolkemuseum.no; Museumsveien 10; adult/child 130/40kr, with Oslo Pass free; ⊙10am-6pm mid-May–mid-Sep, 11am-3pm Mon-Fri, 11am-4pm Sat & Sun mid-Sep–mid-May; ☷91) and one of Oslo's most popular attractions is this folk museum. The museum includes more than 140 buildings, mostly from the 17th and 18th centuries, gathered from around the country, rebuilt and organised according to region of origin. Paths wind past old barns, elevated *stabbur* (raised storehouses) and rough-timbered farmhouses with sod roofs sprouting wildflowers. Little people will be entertained by the numerous farm animals, horse and cart rides, and other activities.

Oslo Walking Tour

Once a heavily industrialised port area, Oslo's waterfront has been totally transformed over the last 20 years and is still in the process of rapid change. It makes for a heady mix of the new and the historic, and the industrial and the natural.

Start Ekebergparken
Distance 4.5km
Duration 2.5 hours

5 At charming **Pipervika** (p209) you can eat this morning's catch straight from the boats.

4 Akerhusstranda makes for a nice waterfront stroll, with the fortress looming above.

6 The city's most-visited stretch of waterfront gives way to the serene sails of Renzo Piano's **Astrup Fearnley Museet** (p203).

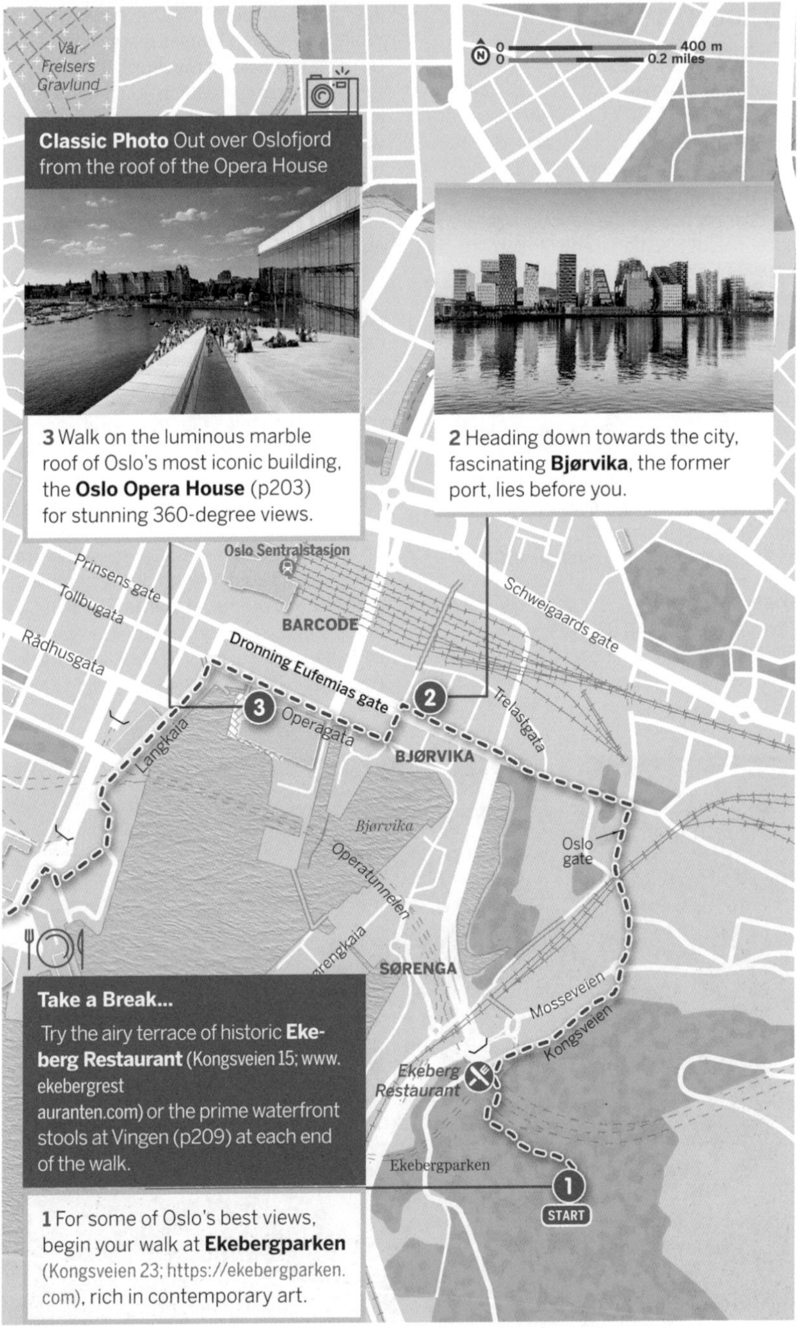

Vår
Frelsers
Gravlund

Classic Photo Out over Oslofjord from the roof of the Opera House

3 Walk on the luminous marble roof of Oslo's most iconic building, the **Oslo Opera House** (p203) for stunning 360-degree views.

2 Heading down towards the city, fascinating **Bjørvika**, the former port, lies before you.

Oslo Sentralstasjon

Prinsens gate
Tollbugata
Rådhusgata
BARCODE
Dronning Eufemias gate
Schweigaards gate
Operagata
BJØRVIKA
Langkaia
Bjørvika
Operatunnelen
Trelastgata
Oslo gate
Sørengkaia
SØRENGA
Mosseveien
Kongsveien

Take a Break...
Try the airy terrace of historic **Ekeberg Restaurant** (Kongsveien 15; www.ekebergrestauranten.com) or the prime waterfront stools at Vingen (p209) at each end of the walk.

Ekeberg Restaurant

Ekebergparken

START

1 For some of Oslo's best views, begin your walk at **Ekebergparken** (Kongsveien 23; https://ekebergparken.com), rich in contemporary art.

◎ SIGHTS

◎ City Centre

Nasjonalgalleriet   Gallery

(National Gallery; ☎21 98 20 00; www.nasjonal museet.no; Universitetsgata 13; adult/child 100kr/ free, Thu free; ⊘10am-6pm Tue, Wed & Fri, to 7pm Thu, 11am-5pm Sat & Sun; ⊡Tullinløkka)
The Gallery houses the nation's largest collection of traditional and Modern art, and many of Edvard Munch's best-known creations are on permanent display, including his most famous work, *The Scream*.

There's also an impressive collection of European art, with works by Gauguin, Claudel, Picasso and El Greco, plus Impressionists such as Manet, Degas, Renoir, Matisse, Cézanne and Monet. Nineteenth-century Norwegian artists have a strong showing, too, including key figures such as JC Dahl and Christian Krohg.

The gallery is set to relocate in 2020.

Ibsen Museet   Museum

(Ibsen Museum; ☎40 02 36 30; www. ibsenmuseet.no; Henrik Ibsens Gate 26; adult/ child 115/30kr; ⊘11am-6pm May-Sep, to 4pm Oct-Apr, guided tours hourly; ⊡Slottsparken)
While downstairs houses a small and rather idiosyncratic museum, it's Ibsen's former apartment, which you'll need to join a tour to see, that is unmissable. This was the playwright's last residence and his study remains exactly as he left it, as does the bedroom where he uttered his famously enigmatic last words 'Tvert imot!' ('To the contrary!'), before dying on 23 May 1906.

Akershus Festning   Fortress

(Akershus Fortress; ⊘6am-9pm; ⊡Christiania Square) **FREE** When Oslo was named capital of Norway in 1299, King Håkon V ordered the construction of Akershus, strategically located on the eastern side of the harbour, to protect the city from external threats. It has, over the centuries, been extended and modified, and had its defences beefed up a number of times. Still dominating the Oslo harbourfront, the sprawling complex consists of a **medieval castle** (Akershus Castle; ☎22 41 25 21; www.nasjonalefestningsverk. no; Kongens gate; adult/child 60/30kr, with Oslo Pass free; ⊘11am-4pm Mon-Sat, noon-5pm Sun;

Akershus Festning

PAULO MIGUEL COSTA/SHUTTERSTOCK ©

Christiania Square), fortress and assorted other buildings, including still-active military installations.

Royal Palace   Palace

(Det Kongelige Slott; ☏81 53 31 33; www.royal court.no; Slottsparken 1; palace tours adult/child 135/105kr, with Queen Sonja Art Stable 200kr; ☺guided tours in English noon, 2pm, 2.20pm & 4pm Jun–mid-Aug; 🚊Slottsparken) The Norwegian royal family's seat of residence emerges from the wood-like **Slottsparken** (☺24hr; 🚊Slottsparken) **FREE**, a relatively modest, pale buttercup neoclassical pile. Built for the Swedish (in fact, French) king Karl Johan, the palace was never continuously occupied before King Haakon VII and Queen Maud were installed in 1905.

◎ Opera House & Bjørvika

Oslo Opera House   Architecture

(Den Norske Opera & Ballett; ☏21 42 21 21; www. operaen.no; Kirsten Flagstads plass 1; foyer free; ☺foyer 10am-9pm Mon-Fri, 11am-9pm Sat, noon-9pm Sun; Ⓣ Sentralstasjonen) The centrepiece of the city's rapidly developing waterfront is the magnificent Opera House, considered one of the most iconic modern buildings of Scandinavia. Designed by Oslo–based architectural firm Snøhetta and costing around €500 million to build, the Opera House opened in 2008, and resembles a glacier floating in the waters of the Oslofjord. Its design is a thoughtful meditation on the notion of monumentality, the dignity of cultural production, Norway's unique place in the world and the conversation between public life and personal experience.

◎ Aker Brygge & Bygdøy

Astrup Fearnley Museet   Gallery

(Astrup Fearnley Museum; ☏22 93 60 60; www. afmuseet.no; Strandpromenaden 2; adult/ child 120kr/free; ☺noon-5pm Tue, Wed & Fri, to 7pm Thu, 11am-5pm Sat & Sun; 🚊Aker Brygge) Designed by Renzo Piano, this private contemporary art museum is housed in a wonderful building of silvered wood, with a sail-like glass roof that feels both maritime

Oslo Pass

Oslo Pass (www.visitoslo.com/en/activities-and-attractions/oslo-pass; 1/2/3 days adult 395/595/745kr, child 210/295/370kr), sold at the tourist office, is a good way of cutting transport and ticket costs around the city. The majority of the city's museums are free with the pass, as is public transport within the city limits (barring late-night buses). Other perks include restaurant and tour discounts.

If you're planning to visit just the city-centre museums and galleries, it's worth checking which on your list are free before buying a pass.

RAILELECTROPOWER/GETTY IMAGES ©

and at one with the Oslofjord landscape. While the museum's original collecting brief was conceptual American work from the '80s (with artists such as Jeff Koons, Tom Sachs, Cindy Sherman and Richard Prince well represented), it has in recent times broadened beyond that, with, for example, a room dedicated to Sigmar Polke and Anselm Keifer.

Tjuvholmen
Sculpture Park   Sculpture

(http://afmuseet.no/en/om-museet/skulpturparken; Tjuvholmen; ☺24hr; 🚊Aker Brygge) **FREE** Like the Astrup Fearnley Museet that it surrounds, this sculpture park was designed by Renzo Piano and is also dedicated to international contemporary art. Don't miss Louise Bourgeois' magnificent and rather cheeky *Eyes* (1997),

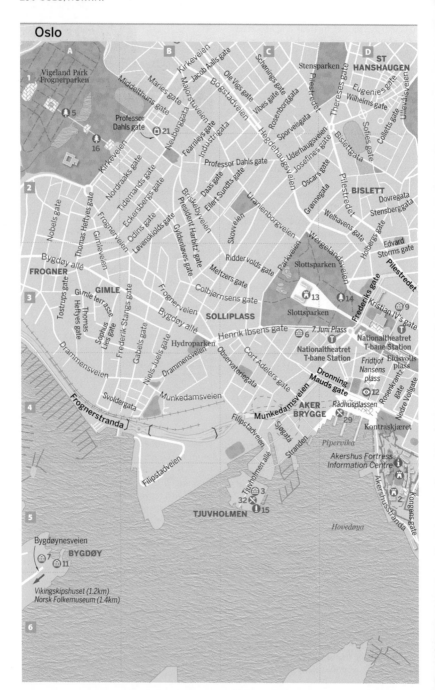

Oslo

Ugo Rondinone's totemic and enchanting *Moonrise. east. november* (2006) and Franz West's bright and tactile *Spalt* (2003). There are also works by Antony Gormley, Anish Kapoor, Ellsworth Kelly, and Peter Fischli and David Weiss. Along with the artwork there are canals and a small child-pleasing pebble beach.

◎ Frogner & Western Oslo

Vigelandsanlegget　　　　　Park

(Vigeland Sculpture Park; www.vigeland. museum.no/no/vigelandsparken; Nobels gate 32; ⊙Tue-Sun noon-4pm; ⊤Borgen) The centrepiece of Frognerparken is an extraordinary open-air showcase of work by Norway's best-loved sculptor, Gustav Vigeland. Statistically one of the top tourist attractions in Norway, Vigeland Park is brimming with 212 granite and bronze Vigeland works. His highly charged oeuvre includes entwined lovers, tranquil elderly couples, bawling babies and contempt-ridden beggars. Speaking of

bawling babies, his most famous work here, *Sinnataggen* (*Angry Boy*), portrays a child in a mood of particular ill humour.

Frognerparken　　　　　Park

(⊤Borgen) Frognerparken attracts westside locals with its broad lawns, ponds, stream and rows of shady trees for picnics, strolling or lounging on the grass. It also contains Vigelandsanlegget, a sprawling sculpture-park-within-a-park. To get here, take tram 12 to Vigelandsparken from the city centre.

◎ Greater Oslo

Holmenkollen Ski Jump　Mountain

(☑916 71 947; www.holmenkollen.com; adult/ child 130/65kr, with Oslo Pass free; ⊙9am-8pm Jun-Aug, 10am-5pm May & Sep, 10am-4pm rest of year; ⊤Holmen) The Holmenkollen Ski Jump, perched on a hilltop overlooking Oslo, offers a panoramic view of the city and doubles as a concert venue. During Oslo's annual ski festival, held in March, it draws the world's best ski jumpers. Even if you're not a daredevil ski jumper, the complex is well worth a visit thanks to its **ski museum** (Kongeveien 5; incl Holmenkollen Ski Jump adult/child 130/65kr, with Oslo Pass free; ☺9am-8pm Jun-Aug, 10am-5pm May & Sep, 10am-4pm rest of year; ⓣHolmen) and a couple of other attractions.

🟢 ACTIVITIES

Avid skiers, hikers and sailors, Oslo residents will do just about anything to get outside. That's not too hard given that there are over 240 sq km of woodland, 40 islands and 343 lakes within the city limits. And you can jump on a train with your skis and be on the slopes in less than 30 minutes.

The **DNT office** (DNT, Norwegian Mountain Touring Club; www.turistforeningen.no; Storget 3, Oslo; ☺10am-5pm Mon-Wed & Fri, to 6pm Thu, to 3pm Sat; 🚃Jernbanetorget), which maintains several mountain huts in the Nordmarka region, can provide information and maps covering longer-distance hiking routes throughout Norway.

🔒 SHOPPING

Oslo's centre and its inner neighbourhoods have a great selection of small shops if you're not into the malls. The city centre's Kirkegaten, Nedre Slottsgate and Prinsens gate are home to a well-considered collection of Scandinavian and international fashion and homewares shops, with Frogner and St Hanshaugen also having some good upmarket choices. Grünerløkka is great for vintage and Scandinavian fashion too.

Norwegian
Rain   Fashion & Accessories
(📞996 03 411; http://norwegianrain.com; Kirkegata 20; ☺10am-6pm Mon-Fri, to 5pm Sat; 🚃Nationaltheatret) Bergen comes to Oslo! This west coast design superstar creates

what might be the world's most covetable raincoats. This Oslo outpost stocks the complete range as well as creative director T-Michael's woollen suits, detachable collar shirts, leather shoes and bags, not to mention limited editions of Kings of Convenience LPs.

FWSS   Fashion & Accessories
(Fall Winter Spring Summer; http://fallwinterspringsummer.com; Prinsens gate 22; ☺10am-7pm Mon-Fri, to 6pm Sat; 🚃Øvre Slottsgate) New flagship of this fast-growing Norwegian label, known for its easy basics as well as seasonal collections that combine Scandinavian simplicity with a pretty, playful edge.

Vestkanttorget
Flea Market   Market
(Amaldus Nilsens plass; ☺10am-4pm Sat; ⓣMajorstuen) If you're happy sifting through heaps of, well, junk in search of an elusive vintage band T-shirt or mid-century ceramic coffee pot, take a chance here. It's at the plaza that intersects Professor Dahls gate, a block east of Vigeland Park, and it's a more than pleasant way to pass a Saturday morning.

Gutta På Haugen   Food & Drinks
(📝22 60 85 12; http://gutta.no/; Ullevålsveien 45; ☺8am-7pm; 🚃37) For picnic or self-catering supplies, head to this well-stocked St Hanshaugen institution. There's a huge cheese selection with both Norwegian and European produce, a lovely array of local sausage and boxes of the must-try Norwegian flatbread. Its fresh produce is the best of the season and you can grab an excellent soft serve to go at its ice-cream van across the road.

⭐ ENTERTAINMENT

Oslo has a thriving live-music scene – it's said that the city hosts more than 5000 gigs a year. Its venues are spread across the city but are concentrated on Møllergata, in Vulkan, Grünerløkka and Grønland. World-class opera or ballet performances are held at the Oslo Opera

B&B in the City

Oslo has plenty of accommodation, including a growing number of small B&Bs and private rentals that offer more character than the chain hotels. Hotels are usually well run and comfortable, but tend towards the bland, and – yes, you guessed it – you'll pay a lot more for what you get compared with other countries. Most hotels have wi-fi access.

B&B Norway (www.bbnorway.com) Lists many of Norway's better-established B&Bs.

House (p203) Book ahead or try for the last-minute 100kr standing seats.

Blå   Live Music, Dance
(www.blaaoslo.no; Brenneriveien 9c; ⊙1pm-4am; 🚋54) Blå is all things to everyone, with DJs (it happens to be the city's best spot for hip hop), live gigs and jazz. On Sundays there is a live big band that's been playing every afternoon for years. Or just come early for a drink at one of the pretty riverside tables.

⊗ EATING

Oslo's food scene has come into its own in recent years, attracting curious culinary-minded travellers who've eaten their way round Copenhagen or Stockholm and are looking for new sensations. Dining out here can involve a Michelin-starred place, a hot-dog stand, peel-and-eat shrimp, a place doing innovative Neo Nordic small plates or a convincingly authentic Japanese, Italian, French, Indian or Mexican dish.

⊗ City Centre

Sentralen
Restaurant   New Nordic €€
(☏22 33 33 22; www.sentralen.no; Øvre Slottsgate 3; small plates 85-195kr; ⊙11am-10pm Mon-Sat; 🚋Øvre Slottsgate) One of Oslo's best dining experiences is also its most relaxed. A large dining room with a bustling open kitchen, filled with old social club chairs and painted in tones of deep, earthy green, draws city workers, visitors and natural-wine-obsessed locals in equal measure. Small-plate dining makes it easy to sample across the appealing Neo Nordic menu.

Grand Café   Norwegian €€
(☏23 21 20 18; www.grand.no; Karl Johans gate 31; mains 145-295kr; ⊙11am-11pm Mon-Fri, from noon Sat, noon-9pm Sun; 🚋Stortinget) At 11am sharp, Henrik Ibsen would leave his apartment and walk to Grand Café for a lunch of herring, beer and one shot of aquavit (alcoholic drink made from potatoes and caraway liquor). His table is still here. Don't worry, though, today you can take your pick from perfectly plated, elegantly sauced cod and mussels, spelt risotto with mushrooms, or cured lamb and potato.

⊗ Opera House & Bjørvika

Maaemo   New Nordic €€€
(☏22 17 99 69; https://maaemo.no; Schwei-gaards gate 15; menu 2600kr; ⊙6pm-midnight Wed & Thu, from noon Sat & Sun; 🚋Busster-minalen Grønland) This is not a meal to be taken lightly: firstly, you'll need to book many months in advance, and secondly, there will, for most of us, be the indenting of funds. But go if you can, not for the three Michelin–star accolades, but for Esben Holmboe Bang's 20 or so courses that are one of the world's most potent

culinary experiences and a sensual articulation of what it means to be Norwegian.

😵 Aker Brygge & Bygdøy

Vingen New Nordic €€

(📞901 51 595; http://vingenbar.no; Strandpromenaden 2; mains 145-240kr; ⊙10am-9pm Sun-Wed, to midnight Thu-Sat; 🚋Aker Brygge) While honouring its role as Astrup Fearnley's (p203) cafe and a super-scenic pit stop, Vingen is so much more. Do drop in for excellent coffee, but also come for lunch or dinner with small, interesting menus subtly themed in homage to the museum's current temporary show. Nightfall brings cocktails, and sometimes DJs and dancing in the museum lobby and, in summer, on the waterfront terrace.

Pipervika Seafood €€

(www.pipervika.no; Rådhusbrygge 4; mains 175-250kr, shrimp per kg 130kr; ⊙7am-11pm; 🚋Aker brygge) If the weather is nice, nothing beats a shrimp lunch, with fresh shrimp on a baguette with mayonnaise and a spritz of lemon eaten dockside. The revamped fisherman's coop still does takeaway peel-and-eat shrimp by the kilo, but you can now also relax with a sushi plate, oysters or a full seafood menu including fish burger on brioche or killer fish and chips.

Everything is prepared with daily bounty from the Oslofjord.

😵 Grünerløkka & Vulkan

Syverkiosken Hot Dogs €

(📞967 08 699; Maridalsveien 45; hot dogs from 20kr; ⊙9am-11.30pm Mon-Fri, from 11am Sat & Sun; 🚌34) It might look like a hipster replica but this hole-in-the-wall *pølser* (hot dogs) place is absolutely authentic and one of the last of its kind in Oslo. Dogs can be had in a potato bread wrap in lieu of the usual roll, or with both, and there's a large range of old-school accompaniments beyond sauce and mustard.

Bass New Nordic €€

(📞482 41 489; http://bassoslo.no; Thorvald Meyers gate 26; dishes 70-175kr; ⊙5pm-1am Tue-Sat, 3-8pm Sun; 🚋Birkelunden) In what

Holmenkollen Ski Jump (p206)

NANISIMOVA/SHUTTERSTOCK ©

Vestkanttorget Flea Market (p207)

could be yet another Grunerløkka corner cafe, you'll find one of the city's best small-plate dining options, served beneath vintage seascapes on classic Norwegian ceramics by jovial Løkka locals. Most dishes are what might be called contemporary Norwegian–meets-international – from fried chicken and potato pancakes to deep-sea cod in sorrel butter and death-by-chocolate cake.

Mathallen Oslo Food Hall €€
(www.mathallenoslo.no; Maridalsveien 17, Vulkan; ⊗8am-1am Tue-Fri, from 9.30am Sat & Sun; ⊞54) Down by the river this former industrial space is now a food court dedicated to showcasing the very best of Norwegian regional cuisine, as well as some excellent internationals. There are dozens of delis, cafes and miniature restaurants, and the place buzzes throughout the day and well into the evening.

🔵 DRINKING & NIGHTLIFE

The locals definitely don't seem to mind the high price of alcohol: Oslo has a ridiculously rich nightlife scene, with a huge range of bars and clubs, and most open until 3am or later on weekends. The compact nature of the city and its interconnecting inner neighbourhoods means bar-crawling is a joy, if expensive.

Tim Wendelboe Cafe
(☏400 04 062; www.timwendelboe.no; Grüners gate 1; ⊗8.30am-6pm Mon-Fri, 11am-5pm Sat & Sun; ⊞Schous plass) Tim Wendelboe is often credited with kickstarting the Scandinavian coffee revolution, and his eponymous cafe and roastery is both a local freelancers' hangout and an international coffee-fiend pilgrimage site. All the beans are, of course, self-sourced and hand-roasted (the roaster is part of the furniture), and yes, all coffees, from an

iced pour over to a regular cappuccino, are world-class.

Torggata Botaniske   Cocktail Bar
(📞980 17 830; Torggata 17b; ⏱5pm-1am Sun-Wed, to 2am Thu, 2pm-3am Fri & Sat; 🚊Brugata) The greenhouse effect done right, with a lush assortment of indoor plants (including a warm herb-growing area) as well as beautiful mid-century light fittings and chairs, chandeliers, and lots of marble and mirrors. If you're not already seduced by the decor, the drinks will do it, with a list that features the bar's own produce, fresh fruit and good-quality spirits.

Territoriet   Wine Bar
(http://territoriet.no/; Markveien 58; ⏱4pm-1am Mon-Fri, from noon Sat & Sun; 🚊Schous plass) A true neighbourhood wine bar that's also the city's most exciting. The grape-loving owners offer up more than 300 wines by the glass and do so without a list – talk to the staff about your preferences and – yes this is Norway – budget and they'll find something you'll adore. Beer and gin and tonic orders won't raise an eyebrow, we promise.

ℹ INFORMATION

Oslo Visitor Centre (📞81 53 05 55; www.visitoslo.com; Jernbanetorget 1; ⏱9am-6pm; 🚊Sentralstasjon) is right beside the main train station. Sells transport tickets as well as the useful Oslo Pass (p203); publishes free guides to the city.

ℹ GETTING THERE & AWAY

AIR

Oslo Gardermoen International Airport
(www.osl.no), the city's main airport, is 50km north of the city. It's used by international carriers, including Norwegian, SAS, Air France and British Airways. It's one of the world's

🏛 Arts & Architecture

Norway is one of Europe's cultural giants, producing world-class writers, composers and painters in numbers far out of proportion to its size. Norwegian artists and performers also excel in the realms of popular culture, from dark and compelling crime fiction to musical strands as diverse as jazz, electronica and heavy metal. And when it comes to architecture, Norway is as known for its stave churches as it is for the zany contemporary creations that are also something of a national speciality.

Akrobaten pedestrian bridge
MIROSLAV110/SHUTTERSTOCK ©

most beautiful airports and has an amazing selection of places to eat and drink as well as Norwegian design shops alongside standard airport shopping.

Some budget flights, including those run by SAS Braathens, Widerøe and Ryanair, operate from Torp International Airport in Sandefjord, some 123km southwest of Oslo. Check carefully which airport your flight is going to. Torp has limited but good restaurants and bars, and extensive parking facilities.

BUS

Long-distance buses arrive and depart from the **Galleri Oslo Bus Terminal** (📞23 00 24 00; Schweigaards gate 8; 🚇Sentralstasjon). The train and bus stations are linked via a convenient overhead walkway for easy connections.

Nor-Way Bussekspress (📞81 54 44 44; www.nor-way.no) provides timetables and bookings. International services also depart from the bus terminal. Destinations include the following:

Bergen (522kr, 11 hours, three daily)

Stavanger (802kr, seven hours, usually one daily) Via Kristiansand.

TRAIN

All trains arrive and depart from **Oslo S** in the city centre. It has **reservation desks** (Jernbanetorget 1; ⏱6.30am-11pm; 🚆Sentralstasjon) and an **information desk** (📞81 50 08 88; Jernbanetorget 1; 🚆Sentralstasjon) that provides details on routes and timetables throughout Norway.

There are frequent train services around Oslofjord (eg Drammen, Skien, Moss, Fredrikstad and Halden). Other major destinations:

Destination	Cost (kr)	Time	Frequency
Bergen via Voss	950	6½ to 7½ hours	four daily

Røros via Hamar	810	five hours	every two hours
Stavanger via Kristiansand	997	40 minutes	six daily
Trondheim via Hamar & Lillehammer	965	6½ to 7½ hours	six daily

ℹ️ GETTING AROUND

All public transport is covered off by the Ruter (https://ruter.no/en/) ticketing system; schedules and route maps are available online or at **Trafikanten** (📞177; www.ruter.no; Jernbanetorget; ⏱7am-8pm Mon-Fri, 8am-6pm Sat & Sun).

○ **Tram** Oslo's tram network is extensive and runs 24 hours.

○ **T-bane** The six-line Tunnelbanen underground system, better known as the T-bane, is faster and extends further from the city centre than most city buses or tram lines.

○ **Train** Suburban trains and services to the Oslofjord where the T-bane doesn't reach.

Astrup Fearnley Museet (p203)

VLADIMIR MUCIBABIC/SHUTTERSTOCK ©

Where to Stay

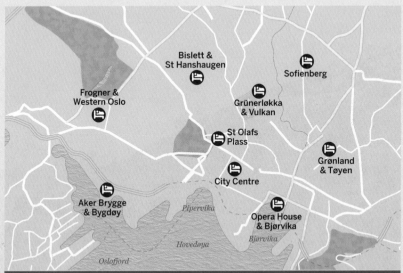

Neighbourhood	For	Against
Aker Brygge & Bygdøy	Scenic, central and close to all the major sites.	Can be a little souless and restaurants are expensive.
City Centre	Close to everything. A wide variety to choose from.	You may not be motivated to explore Oslo's interesting neighbourhoods.
Frogner & Western Oslo	Serene and close to the Slottsparken and city. Very good midrange places.	Restaurants can be expensive and there's little nightlife beyond wine bars.
Grünerløkka & Vulkan	Fantastic choice for experiencing local life, with everything on your doorstep and the city close by.	Not a lot of hotel choice. Can be a little too hipster for some.
Opera House & Bjørvika	Great views, close to everything and increasingly scenic.	Few choices beyond the chains. Not too much neighbourhood life.
Sofienberg, Grønland & Tøyen	Parkland, sights and very down to earth residential neighbourhoods. Close to city and Grünerløkka.	Not a lot of choice beyond private and apartment rentals.
St Olafs Plass, Bislett & St Hanshaugen	Pretty residential areas with an increasing number of places to eat and drink.	Few choices beyond private and apartment rentals. A little further from the main sights.

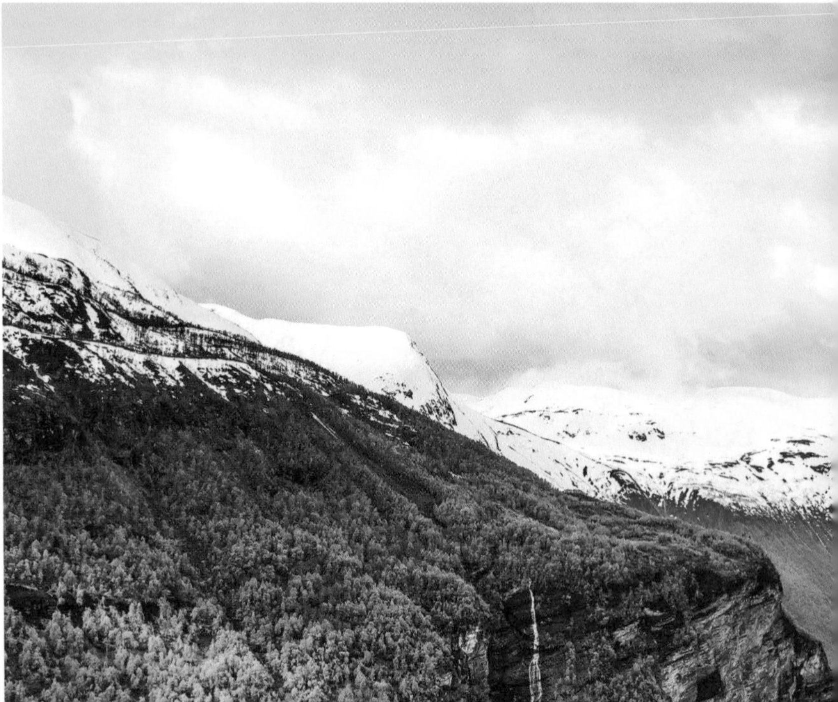

MARCO WONG/GETTY IMAGES ©

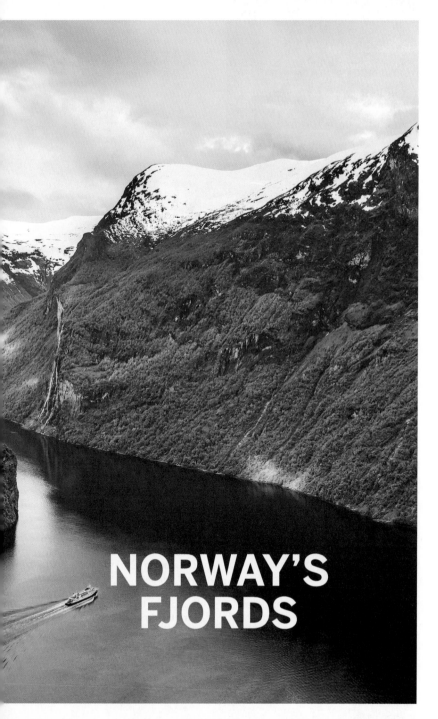

NORWAY'S
FJORDS

Norway's Fjords at a Glance...

If you could visit only one region of Norway and hope to grasp the essence of the country's appeal, this would be our choice. Scoured and gouged by glaciers, western Norway's deep, sea-drowned valleys are covered by steep, rugged terrain. It's a landscape so profoundly beautiful that it's one of the most desirable destinations in the world.

Cool, cultured Bergen is among one of the world's most beautiful cities, with its streets of whitewashed timber cottages climbing steep hillsides from busy Vågen Harbour. It's also the ideal starting point for a journey into splendid Hardangerfjord, or the vast Sognefjorden network.

Two Days in Bergen

Begin with the old port of **Bryggen** (p218) , including **Bryggens Museum** (p222) and the **Torget fish market** (p227). Spend the afternoon exploring stellar art at **KODE** (p219), then dine at **Lysverket** (p227). On day two, take a morning **food tour** (www.bergen foodtours.com), then catch the cable car up **Mt Fløyen** (p223), and hike the trails nearby. For dinner, go traditional at **Pingvinen** (p227).

Four Days in Bergen

With more time, you can extend your sightseeing outside the city centre, with visits to the **Edvard Grieg Museum** (p222) on day three, and a memorable boat trip to the **Ole Bull Museum** (p222) on day four. Restaurants you won't want to miss include the extravagant neo-fjordic cuisine at **Lysverket** (p227), and perhaps for a refined treat, the laid back bistro **Colonialen Litteraturhuset** (p227).

Norway's Fjords Map (p224)

Arriving in Bergen

Bergen is 463km from Oslo via Rv7, and 210km from Stavanger via E39. Bergen Airport is at Flesland, about 18km southwest of the centre.

Where to Stay

Bergen has a reasonably good choice of hotels, but it's very popular and hosts regular conferences and events. It's *always* sensible to book before arriving in town, especially in summer and for festivals.

The tourist office has an accommodation-booking service both online and on-site.

KODE 3

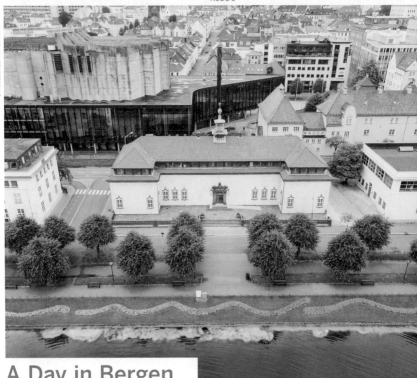

A Day in Bergen

Surrounded by seven hills and seven fjords, Bergen is a beguiling city. Colourful houses creep up hillsides, ferry-boats flit around fjords, and excellent art museums provide a welcome detour.

Great For...

Don't Miss

A tour with Bryggen Guiding (p223) exploring the wharf's colourful history.

Bryggen

Bryggen, Bergen's oldest quarter, runs along the eastern shore of Vågen Harbour (*bryggen* translates as 'wharf') in long, parallel and often leaning rows of gabled buildings. The wooden alleyways of Bryggen have become a haven for artists and craftspeople, and there are bijou shops and boutiques at every turn.

Bryggen

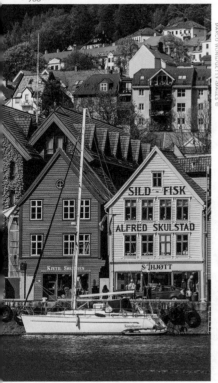

MARCO WONG/GETTY IMAGES ©

Bryggen

Hanseatic Museum

Vågen

Bryggestr...

Nikolaikirkeallm

Øvregaten

Fløibanen Funicular Station

Finnegårdsgaten

Kong Oscars gate

Torget

❶ Need to Know

Early morning is the best time to visit, before the crowds arrive.

✕ Take a Break

Det Lille Kaffekompaniet (p229) makes what could be Bergen's best coffee.

★ Top Tip

Bergen has notoriously fickle weather – always carry an umbrella.

Hanseatic Museum

This interesting **museum** (Hanseatisk Museum & Schøtstuene; Finnegårdsgaten 1a & Øvregaten 50; adult/child 160/60kr; ⊙9am-6pm Jul-Aug, 11am-2pm Tue-Sat, to 4pm Sun Sep-May) provides a window into the world of Hanseatic traders. Housed in a rough-timber building dating to 1704, it starkly reveals the contrast between the austere living and working conditions of the merchant sailors and apprentices, and the comfortable lifestyle of the trade partners.

KODE

A catch-all umbrella for Bergen's art museums, **KODE** (⌨53 00 97 04; www.kodebergen. no; Rasmus Meyers allé; adult/child 100kr/free, includes all 4 museums, valid 2 days) showcases one of the largest art-and-design collections in Scandinavia. Each of the four buildings has its own focus: **KODE 1** (Nordahl Bruns gate 9; ⊙11am-5pm) houses a national silver collection and the renowned Singer art collection; **KODE 2** (Rasmus Meyers allé 3) is for contemporary exhibitions; **KODE 3** (Rasmus Meyers allé 7; ⊙10am-6pm) majors in Edvard Munch; and **KODE 4** (Rasmus Meyers allé 9; ⊙11am-5pm; 👪) focuses on modern art.

Stegastein viewpoint

LUKAS BISCHOFF PHOTOGRAPHY/SHUTTERSTOCK ©

Exploring the Fjords

A trip around Norway's fjord country has all the hallmarks of being Scandinavia's most beautiful journey. If you allow enough time and plan carefully, you'll leave wondering if this truly is God's own country.

Great For...

Don't Miss

The view from Preikestolen, high above Lysefjord.

Hardangerfjord

Running from the Atlantic to the steep wall of central Norway's Hardangervidda Plateau, Hardangerfjord is classic Norwegian fjord country. There are many beautiful corners, although our picks would take in Eidfjord, Ulvik and Utne, while Folgefonna National Park offers glacier walks and top-level hiking. It's also well-known for its many fruit farms, especially apples – Hardanger is sometimes known as the orchard of Norway.

You can easily explore Hardangerfjord from Bergen; www.hardangerfjord.com is a good resource.

Geirangerfjorden

Well, this is the big one: the world-famous, Unesco–listed, oft-photographed fjord

Folgefonna National Park

MARIUS DOBILAS/SHUTTERSTOCK ©

Geirangerfjorden ⊙

Florø ●
Valdresflya

⊙ **Aurlandsfiorden**
Voss ●
●
Fagernes

Bergen ●
Bergen Airport ✈
⊙ **Hardangerfjord**

❶ Need to Know

Norway in a Nutshell (Fjord Tours; ☏81 56 82 22; www.norwaynutshell.com) makes it easy to see the best fjord scenery in a short space of time.

✗ Take a Break

Stalheim Hotel has arguably the best terrace view in Scandinavia.

★ Top Tip

Distances aren't great but travel can be slow due to serpentine roads.

that every visitor to Norway simply has to tick off their bucket list. And in purely scenic terms, it is, quite simply, one of the world's great natural features, a majestic combination of huge cliffs, tumbling waterfalls and deep blue water that's guaranteed to make a lasting imprint on your memory. A ride on the Geiranger–Hellesylt ferry is an essential part of your Norwegian adventure.

Aurlandsfjorden

Branching off the main thrust of Sogneforden, the deep, narrow Aurlandsfjorden runs for about 29km, but is barely 2km across at its widest point – which means it crams an awful lot of scenery into a relatively compact space. The view is best seen from the amazing Stegastein

viewpoint, which juts out from the hillside along the stunning Aurlandsfjellet road.

Aurland and Flåm both sit near the head of the fjord and are the best bases for accommodation and supplies.

Lysefjord

All along the 42km-long Lysefjord (Light Fjord), the granite rock glows with an ethereal light, and even on dull days it's offset by almost-luminous mist. This is the favourite fjord of many visitors, and there's no doubt that it has a captivating beauty. Take a cruise along the fjord, or the four-hour hike to the top of **Preikestolen**, the plunging cliff-face that's graced a million postcards from Norway.

Bergen

Among Scandinavian cities, Bergen has few peers. It's heart-breakingly pretty, dynamic, elegant and cultured, and there's a real buzz that courses through its compact town centre.

◉ SIGHTS

Making time just to wander Bergen's historic neighbourhoods is a must. Beyond Bryggen, the most picturesque are the steep streets climbing the hill behind the Fløibanen funicular station, Nordnes (the peninsula that runs northwest of the centre, including along the southern shore of the main harbour) and Sandviken (the area north of Håkonshallen). It's a maze of winding lanes and clapboard houses, perfect for a quiet wander.

Edvard Grieg Museum   Museum

(Troldhaugen; ☑55 92 29 92; http://griegmuseum.no; Troldhaugvegen 65, Paradis-Bergen; adult/child 100kr/free; ⊙9am-6pm May-Sep, 10am-4pm Oct-Apr) Composer Edvard Grieg and his wife Nina Hagerup spent summers at this charming Swiss–style wooden villa from 1885 until Grieg's death in 1907. Surrounded by fragrant, tumbling gardens and occupying a semi-rural setting – on a peninsula by coastal Nordåsvatnet lake, south of Bergen – it's a truly lovely place to visit.

Ole Bull Museum   Museum

(Museet Lysøen; ☑56 30 90 77; www.lysoen.no; adult/child incl guided tour 60/30kr; ⊙11am-4pm mid-May–Aug, Sun only Sep) This beautiful estate was built in 1873 as the summer residence of Norway's first musical superstar, violinist Ole Bull. Languishing on its own private island, it's a fairy-tale concoction of turrets, onion domes, columns and marble inspired by Moorish architecture. Of particular note is the soaring pine music hall: hard not to imagine Bull practising his concertos in here.

Bryggens Museum   Museum

(☑55 30 80 30; www.bymuseet.no; Dreggsallmenning 3; adult/child 80kr/free; ⊙10am-4pm mid-May–Aug, shorter hours rest of year) This archaeological museum was built on the site of Bergen's first settlement, and the 800-year-old foundations unearthed during its construction have been incorporated into

Edvard Grieg Museum

the exhibits, which include medieval tools, pottery, skulls and runes. The permanent exhibition documenting Bergen circa 1300 is particularly fascinating.

Bergen Kunsthall
Gallery

(📞940 15 050; www.kunsthall.no; Rasmus Meyers allé 5; adult/child 50kr/free, from 5pm Thu free; ⏰11am-5pm Tue-Sun, to 8pm Thu) Bergen's major contemporary-art institution hosts significant exhibitions of international and Norwegian artists, often with a single artist's work utilising the entire space. The cleanly glamorous 1930s architecture is worth a look in itself. The attached venue and bar, Landmark (p228), also hosts video and electronic art, concerts, film, performances and lectures.

ACTIVITIES

Fløibanen Funicular
Cable Car

(📞55 33 68 00; www.floibanen.no; Vetrlidsalmenning 21; adult/child return 90/45kr; ⏰7.30am-11pm Mon-Fri, 8am-11pm Sat & Sun) For an unbeatable view of the city, ride the 26-degree Fløibanen funicular to the top of Mt Fløyen (320m), with departures every 15 minutes. From the top, well-marked hiking tracks lead into the forest; the possibilities are mapped out on the free *Walking Map of Mount Fløyen*, available from the Bergen tourist office (p229).

Ulriken643
Cable Car

(📞53 64 36 43; www.ulriken643.no; adult/child/family return 170/100/460kr; ⏰9am-9pm May-Sep, 9am-5pm Tue-Sun Oct-Apr) Look up to the mountains from the harbour, and you'll spy a radio mast clad in satellite dishes. That's the top of Mt Ulriken (643m) you're spying, and on a clear day it offers a stunning panorama over city, fjords and mountains. Thankfully, you don't have to climb it: a cable car speeds from bottom to top in just seven minutes.

TOURS

Bergen Guide Service (📞55 30 10 60; www.bergenguideservice.no; Holmedalsgården 4; adult/child 130kr/free; ⏰office 9am-3pm Mon-Fri) offers guided walking tours of the city year-round, and in summer, **Bryggen Guiding**

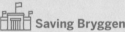 **Saving Bryggen**

So beautiful and popular is Bryggen that it seems inconceivable that conservationists spent much of the 20th century fighting plans to tear it down.

Fire has destroyed Bryggen at least seven times (notably in 1702 and again in 1955, when one-third of the district was destroyed). The tilt of the structures was caused in 1944, when a Dutch munitions ship exploded in the harbour, blowing off the roofs and shifting the pilings. The explosion and a 1955 fire increased the already considerable clamour to tear down Bryggen once and for all; not only was it considered a dangerous fire hazard, but its run-down state was widely seen as an embarrassment. Plans for the redevelopment of the site included modern, eight-storey buildings, a bus station, a shopping centre and a car park.

What saved Bryggen were the archaeological excavations that took 13 years to complete after the 1955 fire, and which unearthed more than one million artefacts. In 1962 the **Bryggen Foundation** (http://stiftelsenbryggen.no) and Friends of Bryggen were formed; the foundation still oversees the area's protection and restoration, although the buildings are privately owned.

One of the greatest challenges is the fact that Bryggen is actually sinking by an estimated 8mm each year. In 1979 Unesco inscribed Bryggen on its World Heritage list. For more information, visit the **Bryggen Visitors Centre** (p229).

Norway's Fjords

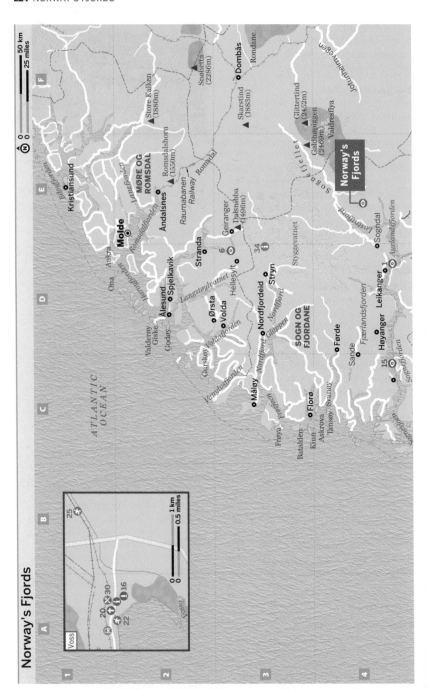

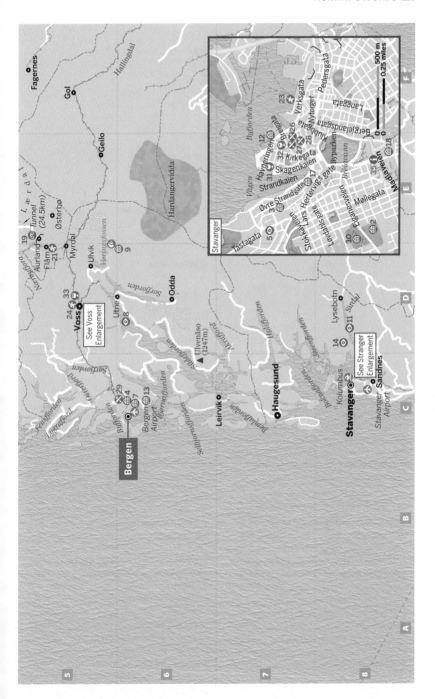

Norway's Fjords

(☑55 30 80 30; www.bymuseet.no; Bryggens Museum, Dreggsallm 3; adult/child 150kr/free) (run by the Bryggen Museum) offers historical walking tours of the Bryggen area.

Fonnafly   Scenic Flights
(☑55 34 60 00; www.fonnafly.no; from 5500kr for 3 passengers) This national group will put together a customised sightseeing trip in a helicopter – the aerial views over the fjords are once-in-a-lifetime stuff, but they don't come cheap.

⊙ Fjord Tours from Bergen

There are dozens of tours of the fjords from Bergen; the tourist office (p229) has a full list, and you can buy tickets there or purchase them online. Most offer discounts if you have a Bergen Card (p229). For a good overview, pick up the *Round Trips – Fjord Tours & Excursions* brochure from the tourist office, which includes tours with private companies.

    Fjord Tours (☑81 56 82 22; www.fjordtours. com) and **Rodne Fjord Cruises** (☑55 25 90 00; www.rodne.no; Torget; adult/child/family 550/350/1250kr; ☺10am & 2.30pm daily Mar-Oct,

10am Wed-Fri, noon Sat & Sun Nov-Feb) are the key operators.

SHOPPING

Aksdal i Muren   Clothing
(☑55 24 24 55; www.aksdalimuren.no; Østre Muralmenning 23; ☺10am-5pm Mon-Fri, 10am-6pm Sat) This enticing shop in a historic landmark building has been ensuring the good people of Bergen are warm and dry since 1883. The city's best selection of rainwear includes cult Swedish labels such as Didriksons, big names like Helle Hansen and Barbour, but also local gems such as Blæst by Lillebøe. We can't think of a better Bergen souvenir.

Colonialen Strandgaten 18   Deli
(☑55 90 16 00; www.colonialen.no; Strandgaten 18; ☺8am-6pm Mon-Fri, 10am-6pm Sat) The latest addition to the Colonialen arsenal, this impeccably cool cafe-deli serves up lavish lunchtime sandwiches, plus an irresistible selection of cold cuts, cheeses, oils, smoked fish and so much more. It's also the best place in town to try baked goodies and breads from Colonialen's own bakery – including their to-die-for cinnamon buns.

ENTERTAINMENT

Bergen has a busy programme of concerts throughout summer, many of them focusing on Bergen's favourite son, composer Edvard Grieg. Most take place at evocative open-air venues such as the Grieg Museum (p222), the **Harald Sæverud Museum** (Siljustøl; ☑55 92 29 92; www.siljustolmuseum.no; Siljustølveien 50, Råda; adult/child 60kr/free; ☺noon-4pm Sun late Jun–mid-Aug), atop Mt Fløyen and in the park adjacent to Håkonshallen. Bergen Cathedral also offers free organ recitals on Sunday and Thursday from mid-June until August.

Garage
Live Music

(☑55 32 19 80; www.garage.no; Christies gate 14; ☺3pm-3am Mon-Sat, 5pm-3am Sun) Garage has taken on an almost mythical quality for music lovers across Norway. They do have the odd jazz and acoustic act, but this is a rock-and-metal venue at heart, with well-known Norwegian and international acts drawn to the cavernous basement. Stop by for their Sunday jam sessions in summer.

Hulen
Live Music

(☑55 32 31 31; www.hulen.no; Olaf Ryes vei 48; ☺9pm-3am Thu-Sat) Another minor legend of the Norwegian music scene, this basement club has hosted top rock and indie bands since opening its doors in 1968. *Hulen* means 'cave' and the venue is indeed underground, in a converted bomb shelter.

USF Vertfet
Live Music

(USF; ☑55 31 00 60; www.usf.no; Georgernes Verft 12; ☺11am-11pm) This huge arts and culture complex in a renovated warehouse space hosts a varied programme of contemporary art exhibitions, theatre, dance, gigs and other cultural events, and also has an excellent cafe, **Kippers** (USF; Georgernes Verft 12; ☺11am-11pm Mon-Thu, noon-midnight Fri & Sat, noon-11pm Sun).

EATING

Torget Fish Market
Seafood €

(Torget; lunches 99-169kr; ☺7am-7pm Jun-Aug, 7am-4pm Mon-Sat Sep-May) For most of its history, Bergen has survived on the fruits of the sea, so there's no better place for lunch than the town's lively fish market, where you'll find everything from salmon to calamari, fish and chips, prawn baguettes and seafood salads.

Pingvinen
Norwegian €€

(☑55 60 46 46; www.pingvinen.no; Vaskerelven 14; daily specials 119kr, mains 159-269kr; ☺noon-3am) Devoted to Norwegian home cooking, Pingvinen is the old favourite of *everyone* in Bergen. They come for meals their mothers and grandparents used to cook, and the menu always features at least one of the following: fish-cake sandwiches, reindeer, fish pie, salmon, lamb shank and *raspeballer* (sometimes called *komle*) – west-coast potato dumplings. Note that whale is served here.

Colonialen Litteraturhuset
Norwegian €€

(☑55 90 16 00; www.colonialen.no/litteraturhuset; Østre skostredet 5-7; lunch 145-245kr, dinner 180-280kr; ☺9-11pm Tue-Fri, 11am-midnight Sat) The more laid-back bistro sister to Colonialen Restaurant, this is a favourite for Bergeners looking for a relaxed but refined lunch. It's a quietly elegant space, with neutral walls and blond-wood tables creating that essential too-cool-for-school Nordic atmosphere, and dishes are full of flavour: leeky fish soup or meat-and-cheese platters for lunch, mountain trout or duck-leg confit for dinner.

Lysverket
Norwegian €€€

(☑55 60 31 00; www.lysverket.no; KODE 4, Rasmus Meyers allé 9; lunch mains 165-195kr, lunch sharing menu with/without dessert 295/395kr, 4-/7-course menu 745/995kr; ☺11am-1am Tue-Sat) If you're going to blow the budget on one meal in Norway, make it here. Chef Christopher Haatuft is pioneering his own brand of Nordic cuisine, which he dubs 'neo-fjordic' – in other words, combining modern techniques with the best fjord-sourced produce. His food is highly seasonal, incredibly creative and full of surprising textures, combinations and flavours. Savour every mouthful.

Colonialen Restaurant
Norwegian €€€

(☑55 90 16 00; www.colonialen.no/restaurant/; Kong Oscars gate 44; 6-/8-course tasting menu 895/1195kr; ☺Mon-Sat 6-11pm) Part of an ever-expanding culinary empire, this flagship fine-diner showcases the cream of Neo–Nordic cuisine. It's playful and pushes boundaries, sure, but the underlying flavours are classic, and employ the very best Norwegian ingredients, especially from the west coast. Presentation is impeccable – expect edible flowers and unexpected ingredients aplenty. Strange it's on the dingy side of town.

DRINKING & NIGHTLIFE

Bergen has a great bar scene, and locals are enthusiastic drinking companions. Most of them favour the places in the centre or southwest of Øvre Ole Bulls plass. Big, multilevel nightclubs cluster around here, too; they are easy to spot, often fabulously trashy, and only admit those aged over 24.

Landmark
Bar, Cafe

(📞940 15 050; Bergen Kunsthalle, Rasmus Meyers allé 5; ⏰cafe 11am-5pm Tue-Sun, bar 7pm-1am Tue-Thu, to 3.30am Fri & Sat) This large, airy room is a beautiful example of 1930s Norwegian design and is named for architect Ole Landmark. It multitasks: day-time cafe, lecture and screening hall; live-performance space, bar and venue for Bergen's best club nights. It's a favourite with the city's large creative scene. The cafe serves yummy lunches, with a choice of open-faced sandwiches and a weekly melt (995-1295kr).

Terminus Bar
Bar

(Zander Kaaesgate 6, Grand Terminus Hotel; ⏰5pm-midnight) Consistently voted one of the word's best whisky bars, this grand old bar in the Grand Hotel Terminus is the perfect place for a quiet dram. It promises more than 500 different tastes, and the oldest whisky dates back to 1960. The 1928 room looks gorgeous both before and after you've sampled a few.

Altona Vinbar
Wine Bar

(📞55 30 40 00; www.augustin.no/en/altona; C Sundts gate 22; ⏰6pm-12.30am Mon-Thu, to 1.30am Fri & Sat) Set in a warren of vaulted underground rooms that date from the 16th century, Altona's huge, carefully selected wine list, soft lighting and murmured conversation make it Bergen's most romantic bar (particularly appealing when the weather's cold and wet). The bar menu tends towards tasty comfort food, such as Norwegian lamb burgers (190kr).

Fløibanen funicular (p223)

Det Lille Kaffekompaniet   Cafe

(Nedre Fjellsmug 2; ⏰10am-8pm Mon-Fri, 10am-6pm Sat & Sun) This was one of Bergen's first third-wave coffee places and retains a superlocal feel. Everyone overflows onto the neighbouring stairs when the sun's out, and you're not sure which table belongs to who.

ℹ INFORMATION

DISCOUNT CARDS

The **Bergen Card** (www.visitbergen.com/bergencard; adult/child 24hr pass 260/100kr, 48hr 340/1130kr, 72hr 410/160kr) gives you free entrance to most of Bergen's main museums, plus discounted entry to the rest. You also get free travel on public transport, free or discounted return trips on the Fløibanen funicular (p223), depending on the time of year; free guided tours of Bergen; and discounts on city- and boat-sightseeing tours, concerts and cultural performances. It's available from the **tourist office**, some hotels, the bus terminal and online.

TOURIST INFORMATION

Bergen Turlag DNT Office (📞55 33 58 10; www.bergen-turlag.no; Tverrgaten 4; ⏰10am-4pm Mon-Wed & Fri, to 6pm Thu, to 3pm Sat) Maps and information on hiking and hut accommodation throughout western Norway.

Bryggen Visitors Centre (Jacobsfjorden, Bryggen; ⏰9am-5pm mid-May–mid-Sep) Maps and activities in the Bryggen neighbourhood.

Tourist Office (📞55 55 20 00; www.visitbergen.com; Strandkaien 3; ⏰8.30am-10pm Jun-Aug, 9am-8pm May & Sep, 9am-4pm Mon-Sat Oct-Apr) One of the best and busiest in the country, Bergen's tourist office distributes the free and worthwhile *Bergen Guide* booklet, as well as a huge stock of information on the entire region. They also sell rail tickets.

ℹ GETTING THERE & AWAY

AIR

Bergen Airport (www.avinor.no/en/airport/bergen-airport) is at Flesland, about 18km southwest of the centre.

Norwegian (www.norwegian.com) Flights to Oslo and Tromsø.

🍽 **Dining Out**

In this rural corner of Norway, you'll find lots of fish from the fjords on menus, as well as local meats, game, cheeses and fruits. In times gone by, many communities would have lived a largely subsistence lifestyle, and local dishes reflect that heritage, with lots of pickles and preserves designed to make the summer bounty last through a long, cold winter – most notably in the classic dish of *klippfisk,* a kind of dried, salted cod similar to *bacalao,* which is usually served with a tomato sauce.

Klippfisk in a tomato sauce
SUGARO607/GETTY IMAGES ©

SAS (www.sas.no) Connects with Oslo and Stavanger.

Widerøe (www.wideroe.no) Flies to Oslo, Haugesund, Stavanger and many coastal destinations as far north as Tromsø.

BOAT

International ferries to/from Bergen dock at **Skoltegrunnskaien**, northwest of the Rosenkrantz tower, while the Hurtigruten coastal ferry leaves from the **Hurtigruteterminalen** (Nøstegaten 30), southwest of the centre.

A number of operators offer express boat services, leaving from the **Strandkaiterminal**.

Norled (📞51 86 87 00; www.norled.no; Kong Christian Frederiks plass 3) offers at least one daily ferry service to Sogndal (1 adult/child 705/353kr, five hours) and Flåm (825/415kr, 5½ hours).

BUS

Flybussen (www.flybussen.no; one way/return adult 90/160kr, child 50/80kr) Runs up to four

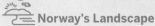

Norway's Landscape

Norway's geographical facts tell quite a story. The Norwegian mainland stretches 2518km from Lindesnes in the south to Nordkapp in the Arctic North, with a narrowest point of 6.3km wide. It also has the highest mountains in northern Europe (Norway's highest is Galdhopiggen) and the fourth-largest land mass in Western Europe (behind France, Spain and Sweden). But these are merely the statistical signposts to the staggering diversity of Norwegian landforms, from glacier-strewn high country and plunging fjords to the tundra-like plains of the Arctic North.

Galdhopiggen, Norway's tallest mountain
MOROZOV67/SHUTTERSTOCK ©

times hourly between the airport, the Radisson Blu Royal Hotel, the main bus terminal and opposite the tourist office on Vågsallmenningen.

Bergen's **bus terminal** (Vestre Strømkaien) is located on Vestre Strømkaien. Various companies run long-distance routes across Norway; **Nor-Way** (www.nor-way.no) provides a useful travel planner.

Destination	Departures (daily)	Cost (kr)	Time (hr)
Lillehammer	1	646	8½
Oslo	4	498-577	10
Stavanger	6	475	5½
Voss	1	190	1½

TRAIN

The spectacular train journey between Bergen and Oslo (349kr to 905kr, 6½ to eight hours, five daily) runs through the heart of Norway. Other destinations include Voss (204kr, one hour, hourly) and Myrdal (299kr to 322kr, 2¼ hours, up to nine daily) for connections to the Flåmsbana railway.

Early bookings can secure you some great discounts.

GETTING AROUND

BICYCLE

Sykkelbutikken (www.sykkelbutikken.no; Kong Oscars gate 81; touring bikes per day/week 250/850kr; ⏲10am-8pm Mon-Fri, 10am-4pm Sat) Bicycle hire near the train station.

Bergen Bike (☎400 04 059; www.norwayactive.no; Bontelabo 2; adult per 2hr/day 200/500kr) Rental bikes near the quay.

BUS & TRAM

Skyss (☎177; www.skyss.no) operates buses and light-rail trams throughout Bergen. Fares are based on a zone system; one-trip tickets cost 37kr to 62kr, and can be bought from the machines at tram stops. Ten-trip tickets are also available, and you get free travel with the **Bergen Card** (p229).

Voss

Voss (also known as Vossevangen) sits on a sparkling lake not far from the fjords, and this position has earned it a world-wide reputation as Norway's adventure capital. The town itself is far from pretty, but everyone is here for white-water rafting, bungee jumping and just about anything you can do from a parasail, most of it out in the fjords.

SIGHTS

Vangskyrkja Church

(Uttrågata; adult/child 20kr/free; ⏲10am-4pm Tue-Sat) Voss' stone church occupies the site of an ancient pagan temple. A Gothic–style stone church was built here in the mid-13th century, and although the original stone altar and unique wooden spire remain, the Lutheran Reformation of 1536 saw the removal of many original features. The 1923 stained-glass window commemorates the 900th anniversary of Christianity in Voss. Miraculously, the building escaped destruction during the intense German bombing of Voss in 1940.

Nearby is the important monument of **St Olav's Cross**.

😊 ACTIVITIES

Voss lives for its outdoor activities, and there are loads to choose from. Bookings can be made direct or through the tourist office (p232).

Although normally done from Oslo or Bergen, the Norway in a Nutshell tour run by Fjord Tours (p226) can also be done from Voss.

Voss Vind   Skydiving
(📞401 05 999; www.vossvind.no; Oberst Bulls veg 28; adult/child 765/565kr; ⊗10am-8pm mid-June–mid-Aug, noon-8pm Wed-Sun rest of year) If you've always wanted to feel what it's like to skydive, but the thought of actually hurling yourself out of a plane fills you with mortal terror, then this amazing place can help. It has a wind tunnel that simulates the experience of freefall only without any danger of turning yourself into a cow-pat. There's a minimum age of five.

Nordic Ventures   Adventure Sports
(📞56 51 00 17; www.nordicventures.com; on the water, near Park Hotel; adult/child 1095/750kr; ⊗Apr–mid-Oct) Take a guided kayak along the fjords from Voss, or book in for a multinight adventure. They have a floating office on the water near the Park Hotel, as they also run tours out of Gudvangen.

Voss Active   Adventure Sports
(📞56 51 05 25; www.vossactive.no; Nedkvitnesvegen 25; ⊗9am-9pm mid-May–Sep) This outdoors company specialises in organising rafting trips on local rivers including the Stranda, Raundalen and Vosso, but more recently it has branched out into lots of other activities, too, from canyoning and abseiling to fishing, guided hikes and – the kids' favourites – a high-wire rope course.

🍽 EATING

Tre Brør   Cafe €
(📞951 03 832; www.trebror.no; Vangsgata 28; sandwiches & light meals 85-185kr; ⊗cafe 11am-8pm Mon-Wed, 11am-2.30am Thu-Sat, 11am-8pm Sun; 🛜) The 'Three Brothers' is the heart of Voss's social scene, and rightly so – it's everything you want from a small-town cafe. There's super coffee from Oslo's Tim Wendelboe and Ålesund's Jacu Roastery, a

Vangskyrkja

CASSINGA/GETTY IMAGES ©

Gamle Stavanger

great range of microbrewed beers from Voss Brewery down the road, and an on-trend menu of salads, soups, wraps, burgers and Asian–tinged dishes. What's not to like?

 DRINKING & NIGHTLIFE

Tre Brør is the centre of the nightlife in Voss.

Voss Bryggeri Microbrewery

(🖉975 40 517; www.vossbryggeri.com; Kytesvegen 396; ⏰by appointment) This much-respected brewery has made a real splash on the beer scene in recent years, with stand-out brews such as their Oregonian pale ale, Natabjødn ('Nut Beer'), an English–style brown beer, and traditional Vossaøl, brewed with juniper tea. It's about 6km north of Voss; guided tours are available by arrangement, otherwise you can taste their beers at Tre Brør.

 INFORMATION

Voss Tourist Office (🖉406 17 700; www. visitvoss.no; Skulegata 14; ⏰9am-6pm Mon-Sat,

10am-5pm Sun mid-June–Aug, 9am-4pm Mon-Fri Sep–mid-June)

ⓘ GETTING THERE & AWAY

Voss is about 100km east of Bergen on the E16, and 45km southwest of Gudvangen.

BUS

Buses stop at the train station, west of the centre. Frequent services:

Bergen (186kr, two hours)

Flåm (121kr, 1¼ hours)

Sogndal (149-229kr, three hours) via Gudvangen and Aurland.

TRAIN

Voss has fast and efficient train links. At Myrdal, you can connect with the **Flamsbåna Railway** (www.visitflam.com/en/flamsbana; adult/child one way 360/180kr, return 480/240kr). Booking ahead can get you some fantastic deals.

Bergen (204kr, one hour, hourly)

Oslo (249kr to 860kr, 5½ to six hours, five daily)

Stavanger

Stavanger's old centre has some of the most beautiful and best-preserved wooden buildings anywhere in Norway, many dating back to the 18th century. It's all very pretty, and in summer the waterfront comes alive in the best port-town style. It's also a perfect launchpad for exploring nearby Lysefjorden, and for tackling the classic hike to Preikestolen (Pulpit Rock).

◉ SIGHTS

Several of Stavanger's museums offer joint admission: one ticket remains valid for the whole day for entry to the **Stavanger Museum** (☑51 84 27 00; www.museumstavanger. no; Muségata 16; adult/child 90/50kr incl other Stavanger museums; ☉10am-4pm daily), the **Stavanger Art Museum**, the Canning Museum, the **Norwegian Children's Museum** (Norsk Barnemuseum; www.stavangermuseum. no/en/samling/samling-norsk-barnemuseum; Muségata 16; adult/child 90/50kr incl other Stavanger museums; ☉10am-4pm; 👫), **Stavanger Maritime Museum** (Sjøfartsmuseet; ☑51 84 27 00; Nedre Strandgate 17-19; adult/child 90/50kr; ☉11am-3pm Tue-Wed & Fri, 11am-7pm Thu, 11am-4pm Sat & Sun), **Breidablikk** (☑51 84 27 00; www.breidablikkmuseum.no; Eiganesveien 40a; adult/child 90/50kr; ☉10am-4pm Sat-Thu) and **Ledaal** (☑51 84 27 00; www.ledaalmuseum. no; Eiganesveien 45; adult/child 90/50kr incl other Stavanger museums; ☉10am-4pm Sat-Thu).

Gamle Stavanger   Area

Gamle (Old) Stavanger, above the western shore of the harbour, is a delight. The Old Town's cobblestone walkways pass between rows of late-18th-century whitewashed wooden houses, all immaculately kept and adorned with cheerful, well-tended flowerboxes. It well rewards an hour or two's ambling.

Canning Museum   Museum

(☑51 84 27 00; www.museumstavanger.no; Øvre Strandgate 88a; adult/child 90/50kr incl other Stavanger museums; ☉11am-5pm Tue-Fri, 11am-4pm Sat & Sun) Don't miss this museum housed in an old cannery: it's one

 Extreme Sports Festival in Voss

The week-long **Extreme Sports Festival** (Veko; www.ekstremsportveko.com; ☉Jun) at the end of June combines all manner of extreme sports (skydiving, paragliding and base jumping) with local and international music acts.

Basejumper near Voss
ANDERS BLOMQVIST/GETTY IMAGES ©

of Stavanger's most entertaining. Before oil, there were sardines, and Stavanger was once home to more than half of Norway's canning factories. By 1922 the city's canneries provided 50% of the town's employment. The exhibits take you through the whole 12-stage process from salting through to threading, smoking, decapitating and packing. Guides are on hand to answer your questions or crank up some of the old machines.

Norsk Oljemuseum   Museum

(Oil Museum; www.norskolje.museum.no; Kjeringholmen; adult/child 120/60kr; ☉10am-7pm daily Jun-Aug, 10am-4pm Mon-Sat, to 6pm Sun Sep-May; 👫) Admittedly, an 'oil museum' doesn't sound like the most promising prospect for an afternoon out. But this state-of-the-art place is well worth visiting – both for its striking, steel-clad architecture, and its high-tech displays explaining the history of North Sea oil exploration. Highlights include the world's largest drill bit, simulated rigs, documentary films, archive testimony and a vast hall of oil-platform models. There are also exhibitions on natural history, energy use and climate change.

Sleeping Over

You'll have no trouble finding a place to sleep in this part of Norway; accommodation is plentiful, encompassing the full spectrum from campsites to boutique hotels. Bergen and Stavanger have the largest choice, and both make good bases for exploring, but prices here tend to be a bit higher than elsewhere. Hostels and campsites are widespread, and are a good way of keeping costs down.

The town of Voss has the best selection of accommodation, and there are some good hotels out in the surrounding countryside, too.

 ACTIVITIES

Stavanger is a great launch-pad for adventures in Lysefjord. Boat cruises and sightseeing trips leave from the town's main Fiskespiren Quay.

 EATING

Stavanger has what we suspect is the most expensive dining scene in Norway.

Renaa Matbaren   International €€
(☑51 55 11 11; www.restaurantrenaa.no; Breitorget 6, enter from Bakkegata; small dishes 59-125kr, mains 165-395kr; ☺4pm-1am Mon-Fri, 11am-1am Sat, 2pm-midnight Sun) Run by top chef Sven Erik Renaa, this smart bistro offers a taste of his food at (reasonably) affordable prices. The menu is classic – mussels in beer, rib-eye with rosemary fries, squid with fennel and shallots, all with a Nordic twist. The glass and wood feels uber–Scandi, and the art collection is stellar (yes, that's an Antony Gormley statue).

Renaa Xpress Sølvberget   Norwegian €€
(Stavanger Kulturhus; ☑51 55 11 11; www.restaurantrenaa.no; Sølvberggata 2; panini 89-98kr, salads 170kr, pizzas 180-199kr; ☺10am-10pm Mon-Thu, to midnight Fri & Sat, noon-10pm Sun) One of three Renaa restaurants in Stavanger, this upmarket cafe pretty much corners the lunchtime market. Go for the daily soup deal, tuck into a huge salad, enjoy a panino topped with *Parmaskinke* (Parma ham) or *røkelaks* (smoked salmon), or order a wood-fired, wild-yeasted pizza (available from 3pm). Needless to say, the cake, pastries and coffee are delicious, too.

Egget   Bistro €€€
(☑984 07 700; Steinkargata 23; dishes from 800kr; ☺6-11pm Tue-Sat) In a clapboard building off Steinkargata, this ramshackle, rough-and-ready eatery is small in size, but strong on ambition: the food is modern, creative, and bang on trend, with an emphasis on freshness, seasonality and Asian–inspired flavours. There's no set menu; dishes are chalked above the bar, from wild trout to kimchi, braised ribs or Asian slaws. The only drawback? It's pricey.

 DRINKING & NIGHTLIFE

Bøker & Børst   Bar
(☑51 86 04 76; www.bokerogborst.webs.com; Øvre Holmegate 32; ☺10am-2am) With all the decorative chic of a well-worn living room – complete with book-lined shelves, retro floor-lamps and old wallpaper – this lovely coffee bar is a fine spot to while away a few hours. There are plenty of beers on tap, plus pub-type snacks and pastries, and a covered courtyard at the back.

Broremann Bar   Bar
(☑406 36 783; www.broremann.no; Skansegata 7; ☺6pm-2am Tue-Thu & Sun, 4pm-2am Fri & Sat, closed Mon) One of Stavanger's best-loved bars, this low-key shopfront place draws a discerning over-30s crowd and, later, local hospitality staff for post-shift drinks

INFORMATION

Tourist Office (☑51 85 92 00; www.regionstavanger.com; Strandkaien 61; ☺9am-8pm Jun-Aug, 9am-4pm Mon-Fri, 9am-2pm Sat Sep-May) Local information and advice on Lysefjord and Preikestolen.

Stavanger Turistforening DNT (☑51 84 02 00; www.stf.no; off Muségata; ☺10am-4pm Mon, Wed, Fri & Sat, 10am-6pm Tue & Thu) Information on hiking and mountain huts.

Norsk Oljemuseum (p233)

❶ GETTING THERE & AWAY

AIR

Stavanger Airport (☑51 65 80 00; https://avinor.no/en/airport/stavanger-airport) is at Sola, 14km south of the city centre. As well as international airlines, there are a number of domestic airline services. Seasonal flights are also available to destinations in the UK and Europe.

Norwegian (www.norwegian.com) Flights to Oslo, Bergen and Trondheim.

SAS (www.sas.no) Services Oslo and Bergen, plus international destinations such as London and Aberdeen.

Widerøe (www.wideroe.no) Flies to Bergen, Kristiansand, Sandefjord, Florø and Aberdeen.

BOAT

International ferries and boat tours of **Lysefjord** (www.norled.no; Lysefjord cruise adult/child/ family 450/280/1100kr, Preikestolen boat-and-bus-ticket 320kr) from Stavanger are available.

Kolumbus (☑81 50 01 82; www.kolumbus.no; Verksgata) also runs an express ferry to Lysebotn (adult/child/car 160/80/567kr, one daily on Monday, Wednesday and Friday), as well as car ferries to several other destinations.

BUS

Destination	Cost (kr)	Time (hr)	Departures
Bergen	475	5½	hourly
Haugesund	241	2	hourly
Kristiansand	406	4½	4 daily
Oslo	742-811	9½	3 daily

TRAIN

Destination	Cost (kr)	Time (hr)	Frequency (daily)
Egersund	177	1¼	hourly
Kristiansand	512	3	5
Oslo	997	8	up to 5

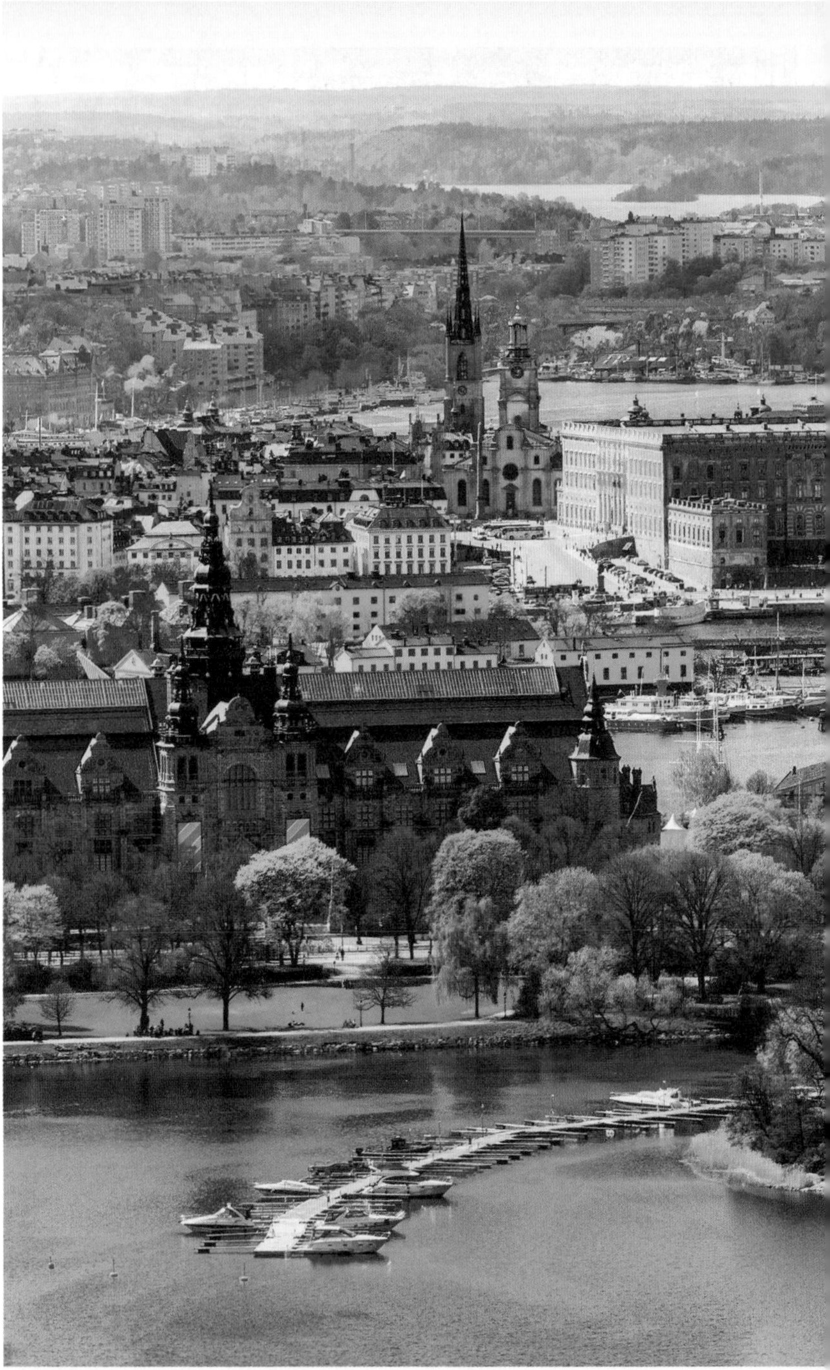

STOCKHOLM, SWEDEN

Stockholm, Sweden at a Glance...

Stockholmers call their city 'beauty on water'. But despite the well-preserved historic core, Stockholm is no museum piece: it's modern, dynamic and ever-changing. Gamla Stan is a saffron-and-spice vision from the storybooks: one of Europe's most arresting historic hubs, with an imposing palace, looming cathedrals and razor-thin cobblestone streets. Stockholm's beauty and fashion sense are also legendary, with good design a given. Travellers also quickly discover that this is a city of food obsessives. If a food trend appears anywhere in the world, Stockholm is on it. The result is one of Europe's most memorable cities.

Two Days in Stockholm

Begin in Gamla Stan. Tour the royal palace, **Kungliga Slottet** (p246) then lunch at **Chokladkoppen** (p251). Walk to Skeppsholmen, where you'll find **Moderna Museet** (p246). Then, dine on traditional Swedish dishes in **Kryp In** (p252).

On day two, head to Djurgården for **Skansen** (p247), then lunch at **Wärdshuset Ulla Winbladh** (p241). Next, head to nearby **Vasamuseet** (p240), then dine at modern Scandinavian restaurant **Gastrologik** (p254).

Four Days in Stockholm

In Södermalm, begin at **Fotografiska** (p247), then climb to the Söder heights for killer city views. Lunch at **Hermann's Trädgårdscafé** (p253), then walk steep cobbled streets to Medborgarplatsen square. Dine at **Meatballs for the People** (p253), then head to Monteliusvägen for amazing sunset views.

On day four, tour **Stadshuset** (p246). Eat at **Östermalms Saluhall** (p254), study Viking lore at **Historiska Museet** (p250), then shop at **Östermalms Saluhall** (p254) and **Svenskt Tenn** (p251). Dine at **Ekstedt** (p254), then it's to **Monks Porter House** (p255) for a beer.

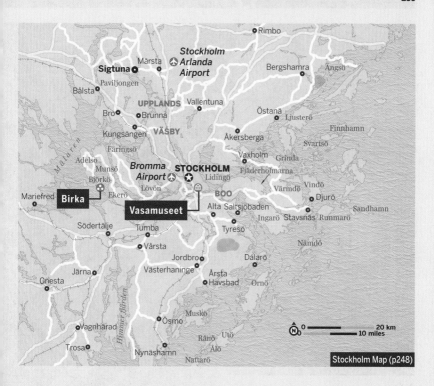

Stockholm Map (p248)

Arriving in Stockholm

Stockholm Arlanda Airport Arlanda Express runs to Centralstationen every 10 to 15 minutes (20 minutes, one-way adult/child 280/150kr, summer two people 350kr).

Cityterminalen Local buses go to Stockholm's neighbourhoods; about 20 minutes to downtown (85kr). Most long distance buses arrive and depart here and it's connected to **Centralstationen.** Trains between the airport and Centralstationen run every 10 to 15 minutes 5am to 12.30am (less frequently after 9pm), taking 20 minutes.

Where to Stay

Expect high-quality accommodation, although it can be expensive. Major hotel chains are cheaper booked online and in advance; rates are also much cheaper in summer and at weekends.

Stockholm's Svenska Turistföreningen (STF) hostels are affiliated with Hostelling International (HI); a membership card yields a 50kr discount. Many have single, double and family rooms. See Where to Stay (p257) to see which Stockholm neighbourhood suits you best.

Vasamuseet

Learn about the short maiden voyage of the massive warship Vasa, which sank within minutes of setting sail. It's one of the most popular museums on Djurgården.

Great For...

Don't Miss

Guided tours, a scale model of the ship, the short film screening, and the upper deck

The Ship

A good-humoured glorification of some dodgy calculations, Vasamuseet is the custom-built home of the massive warship *Vasa*. The ship, a whopping 69m long and 48.8m tall, was the pride of the Swedish crown when it set off on its maiden voyage on 10 August 1628. Within minutes, the top-heavy vessel tipped and sank to the bottom of Saltsjön, along with many of the people on board. The museum details its painstaking retrieval and restoration.

Exhibits

Five levels of exhibits cover artefacts salvaged from *Vasa*, life on board, naval warfare and 17th-century sailing and navigation, plus sculptures and temporary

❶ Need to Know

Vasamuseet (www.vasamuseet.se; Galärvarvsvägen 14; adult/child 130kr/free; ⊙8.30am-6pm Jun-Aug, 10am-5pm Sep-May; P; ⊞44, ⚲Djurgårdsfärjan, ⊞7)

✗ Take a Break

Outside the museum, **Wärdshuset Ulla Winbladh** (www.ullawinbladh.se; Rosendalsvägen 8; mains 175-425kr; ⊙11.30am-10pm Mon, 11.30am-11pm Tue-Fri, 12.30-11pm Sat, 12.30-10pm Sun) has inviting outdoor seating.

★ Top Tip

Guided tours in English depart from the front entrance every 30 minutes in summer.

exhibitions. The bottom-floor exhibition is particularly fascinating, using modern forensic science to re-create the faces and life stories of several of the ill-fated passengers. The ship was painstakingly raised in 1961 and reassembled like a giant 14,000-piece jigsaw. Almost all of what you see today is original.

Meanwhile

Putting the catastrophic fate of *Vasa* in historical context is a permanent multimedia exhibit, *Meanwhile*. With images of events and moments happening simultaneously around the globe – from China to France to 'New Amsterdam', from traders and settlers to royal families to working mothers and put-upon merchants – it establishes a vivid setting for the story at hand.

Scale Model

On the entrance level is a model of the ship at scale 1:10, painted according to a thoroughly researched understanding of how the original would've looked. Once you've studied it, look for the intricately carved decorations adorning the actual *Vasa*. The stern in particular is gorgeous – it was badly damaged but has been slowly and carefully restored.

Upper Deck

A reconstruction of the upper gun deck allows visitors to get a feel for what it might have been like to be on a vessel this size. *Vasa* had two gun decks, which held an atypically large number of cannons – thought to be part of the reason it capsized.

The Monument of Ansgar

Day Trip to Birka

The historic Viking trading centre of Birka, on Björkö in Lake Mälaren, makes a fantastic day trip. Few places in Scandinavia carry quite as many Viking echoes.

Great For...

Don't Miss

Birka Museum, one of Scandinavia's best Viking museums

A History Lesson

A Unesco World Heritage site, Birka was founded around AD 760 to expand and control trade in the region. The village attracted merchants and craft workers, and the population quickly grew to about 700. A large defensive fort with thick dry-stone ramparts was constructed nearby. Birka was abandoned in the late 10th century when Sigtuna took over the role of commercial centre.

The Cemetery & Around

The village site is surrounded by the largest Viking–era cemetery in Scandinavia, with around 3000 graves. Most people were cremated, then mounds of earth were piled over the remains, but some Christian coffins and chambered tombs have been

Model of Viking settlement, Birka Museum

ANDERS BLOMQVIST/GETTY IMAGES ©

STOCKHOLM

Färingsö

Adelsö
Munsö

Björkö

Birka ✪

Ekerö

Lövön **Bromma Airport**

Mälaren

ℹ Need to Know

Birka (www.birkavikingastaden.se/en;
Björkö; adult/child 395/198kr; ⊘May-Sep;
⛴Stromma)

✕ Take a Break

Before setting out from Stockholm,
shop for picnic goodies at Östermalms
Saluhall (p254).

★ Top Tip

Allow the best part of a day for the
excursion.

found. The fort and harbour have also been
excavated.

Many of the finds from the excavations
are in the Birka Museum.

A Lonely Cross

In 830 the Benedictine monk Ansgar was
sent to Birka by the Holy Roman Emperor
to convert the heathen Vikings to Christianity; he hung around for 18 months. A
cross to his memory can be seen on top of
a nearby hill.

Birka Museum

Exhibits at the **Birka Museum** (☎08-56 05
15 40; www.birkavikingastaden.se/en; Björkö;
adult/child 100/50kr; ⊘hours vary, check
schedule online) include finds from the excavations, copies of the most magnificent
objects, and an interesting model of the
village in Viking times.

Ferry to Birka

Strömma Kanalbolaget (☎08-12 00 40
00; www.stromma.se; Svensksundsvägen 17;
200-400kr) runs round-trip cruises to Birka
from Stadshusbron in central Stockholm.
The trip takes two hours each way from
Stockholm; plan on a full day's outing.
Price includes museum admission and a
guided English–language tour of the settlement's burial mounds and fortifications.
No ferries run during the Midsummer
holidays.

Old Town Walking Tour

This exploration of Stockholm's city centre takes you past the best the city has to offer, with a focus on the beguiling old city.

Start Centralstationen
Distance 3km
Duration 2 hours

2 Pop into arts hub **Kulturhuset** (Sergels Torg; www.kulturhuset-stadsteatern.se), with its exhibitions, theatres, cafes and creative spaces.

Classic Photo The statue of 'Saint George and the Dragon at Köpmantorget

Take a Break...
Chokladkoppen (p251) is a long-standing city favourite, right on Stortorget.

6 Källargränd leads southward to **Stortorget**, the cobblestone square where the Stockholm Bloodbath took place (1520).

1 From Centralstationen, head to **Sergels Torg,** a square with frenzied commuters, casual shoppers and the odd demonstration.

Norrmalmstorg 🚇

Hamngatan

Nybroplan

Berzelii Park

Raoul Wallenbergs Torg

3 Next, visit the grand and pretty **Kungsträdgården**, originally the kitchen garden for the Royal Palace.

③ Kungsträdgården

Kungsträdgården 🚇

Nybroviken

Karl XII's Torg

Stallgatan

Gustav Adolfs Torg

Strömgatan

5 Facing the cathedral across the cobblestone square is **Kungliga Slottet** (p246).

Norrbro Norrström

Strömbron

Ladugårdslandsviken

Helgeandsholmen

Slottskajen

Yttre Borggården

Skeppsholmsbron

Riddarhustorget

Mynttorget

⑤

Slottsbacken

Trångsund

④

Köpmantorget

⑥ Köpmangatan

Chokladkoppen

Gamla Stan

4 Head for the city's medieval core, into Storkyrkobrinken and the city's oldest building, **Storkyrkan** (Trångsund 1; www.stockholmsdomkyrkoforsamling.se);

Gamla Stan 🚇

Västerlånggatan

Kornhamnstorg

⑦

Järntorget

Skeppsbron

Munkbroleden

Riddarfjärden

Karl Johanstorg

Strömmen

Sjöbergsplan

7 Explore the old town around **Mårten Trotzigs Gränd**, Stockholm's narrowest lane, on your way back to Centralstationen.

Södermalmstorg

Saltsjöbanans Station 🚇

Hornsgatan

Slussen 🚇

Stadsgårdsleden

Katarinavägen

Ⓝ 0 _____ 400 m
0 _____ 0.2 miles

◉ SIGHTS

◎ Gamla Stan

Kungliga Slottet Palace

(Royal Palace; ☎08-402 61 30; www.theroyalpal
ace.se; Slottsbacken; adult/child 160/80kr, com
bo ticket incl Riddarholmen adult/child 180/90kr;
⊙9am-5pm Jul & Aug, 10am-5pm May-Jun & Sep,
10am-4pm Tue-Sun Oct-Apr; 🚌43, 46, 55, 59
Slottsbacken, 🚇Gamla Stan) Kungliga Slottet
was built on the ruins of Tre Kronor castle,
which burned down in 1697. The north wing
survived and was incorporated into the
new building. Designed by court architect
Nicodemus Tessin the Younger, it took 57
years to complete. Highlights include the
decadent Karl XI Gallery, inspired by Ver-
sailles' Hall of Mirrors, and Queen Kristina's
silver throne in the Hall of State.

◎ Kungsholmen

Stadshuset Notable Building

(City Hall; www.stockholm.se/stadshuset;
Hantverkargatan 1; adult/child 100/50kr, tower
50kr/free; ⊙9am-3.30pm, 🚌3, 62 Stadshuset,
🚇Rådhuset) The mighty Stadshuset dominates Stockholm's architecture. Topping off
its square tower is a golden spire, and the
symbol of Swedish power: the three royal
crowns. Entry is by guided tour only; tours
in English take place every 30 minutes
from 9am until 3.30pm in summer, less
frequently the rest of the year. The tower
is open for visits every 40 minutes from
9.15am to 4pm, or 5pm from May to September; it offers stellar views and a great
thigh workout.

◎ Djurgården & Skeppsholmen

Moderna Museet Museum

(☎08-52 02 35 00; www.modernamuseet.
se; Exercisplan 4; ⊙10am-8pm Tue & Fri, to
6pm Wed-Thu, 11am-6pm Sat & Sun; 🅿; 🚌65,
🚢Djurgårdsfärjan) FREE Moderna Museet
is Stockholm's modern-art maverick,
its permanent collection ranging from
paintings and sculptures to photography,
video art and installations. Highlights
include works by Pablo Picasso, Salvador
Dalí, Andy Warhol, Damien Hirst and Robert
Rauschenberg, plus several key figures in
the Scandinavian and Russian art worlds

Kungliga Slottet

and beyond. There are important pieces by Francis Bacon, Marcel Duchamp and Matisse, as well as their contemporaries, both household names and otherwise.

Skansen
Museum

(www.skansen.se; Djurgårdsvägen; adult/child 180/60kr; ⊙10am-6pm, extended hours in summer; P; 🚌69, 🚢Djurgårdsfärjan, 🚋7) The world's first open-air museum, Skansen was founded in 1891 by Artur Hazelius to provide an insight into how Swedes once lived. You could easily spend a day here and not see it all. Around 150 traditional houses and other exhibits dot the hilltop – it's meant to be 'Sweden in miniature', complete with villages, nature, commerce and industry. Note that prices and opening hours vary seasonally; check the website before you go.

Junibacken
Amusement Park

(www.junibacken.se; Djurgården; adult/child 159/139kr; ⊙10am-6pm Jul-Aug, to 5pm rest of year; 👶; 🚌44, 69, 🚢Djurgårdsfärjan, 🚋7) Junibacken whimsically recreates the fantasy scenes of Astrid Lindgren's books for children. Catch the flying Story Train over Stockholm, shrink to the size of a sugar cube and end up at Villekulla cottage, where kids can shout, squeal and dress up like Pippi Longstocking. The bookshop is a treasure trove of children's books, as well as a great place to pick up anything from cheeky Karlsson dolls to cute little art cards with storybook themes.

ABBA: The Museum
Museum

(📞08-12 13 28 60; www.abbathemuseum. com; Djurgårdsvägen 68; adult/child 250/95kr; ⊙9am-7pm Mon-Fri Jun-Aug, shorter hours rest of year; 🚌67, 🚢Djurgårdsfärjan, Emelie, 🚋7) A sensory-overload experience that might appeal only to devoted ABBA fans, this long-awaited and wildly hyped cathedral to the demigods of Swedish pop is almost aggressively entertaining. It's packed to the gills with memorabilia and interactivity – every square inch has something new to look at, be it a glittering guitar, a vintage photo of Benny, Björn, Frida or Agnetha, a

🏙️ Navigating Stockholm

Stockholm can seem a baffling city to navigate at first, strewn over 14 islands. Although the city centre and other neighbourhoods are easily walkable, the excellent transport system, comprising trams, buses and metro, is the best way to cover the city's more far-flung sights. Most people start their visit at Gamla Stan, a medieval tangle of narrow alleyways and colourful buildings which, although touristy, is extremely picturesque and home to several truly splendid sights.

Note that very few museums in Stockholm are open before 10am – often not until 11am. Plan to *ta det lugnt* ('take it easy').

Gamla Stan
SCANRAIL/GETTY IMAGES ©

classic music video, an outlandish costume or a tour van from the band members' early days.

◉ Södermalm

Fotografiska
Gallery

(www.fotografiska.eu; Stadsgårdshamnen 22; adult/child 135kr/free; ⊙9am-11pm Sun-Wed, to 1am Thu-Sat; 🚇Slussen) A stylish photography museum, Fotografiska is a must for shutterbugs. Its constantly changing exhibitions are huge, interestingly chosen and well presented; examples have included a Robert Mapplethorpe retrospective, portraits by indie film-maker Gus Van Sant and an enormous collection of black-and-white photos by Sebastião Salgado. The attached cafe-bar draws a crowd in summer evenings, with

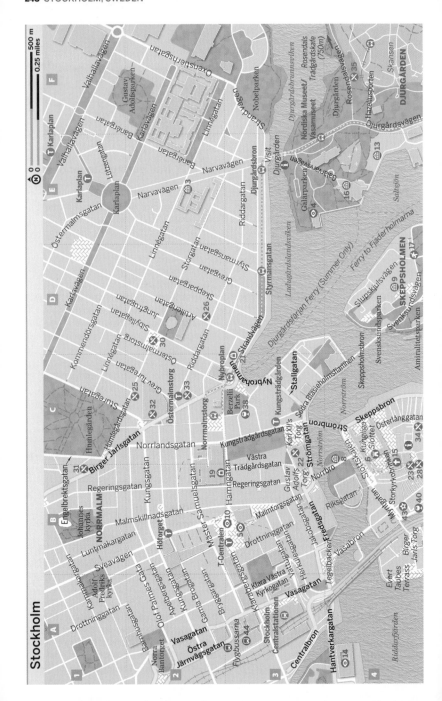

Stockholm

500 m
0.25 miles

Stockholm

DJs, good cocktails and outdoor seating. Follow signs from the Slussen tunnelbana stop to reach the museum.

◎ Östermalm & Ladugårdsgärdet

Historiska Museet   Museum

(📞08-51 95 56 20; www.historiska.se; Narvavägen 13-17; ⊗10am-5pm Jun-Aug, 11am-5pm Tue-Sun, to 8pm Wed Sep-May; 📾44,56, 🚇 Djurgårdsbron, 🚋Karlaplan, Östermalmstorg) **FREE** The national historical collection awaits at this enthralling museum. From Iron Age skates and a Viking boat to medieval textiles and Renaissance triptychs, it spans over 10,000 years of Swedish culture and history. There's an exhibit about the medieval Battle of Gotland (1361), an excellent multimedia display on the Vikings, a room of breathtaking altarpieces from the Middle Ages, a vast textile collection and a section on prehistoric culture.

⊘ TOURS

Millennium Tour   Walking

(www.stadsmuseum.stockholm.se; per person 130kr; ⊗11.30am Sat year-round, 6pm Thu Jul-Sep) Fans of Stieg Larsson's madly popular crime novels (*The Girl with the Dragon Tattoo*) will enjoy this walking tour (in English) pointing out key locations from the books and films. While the Stadsmuseum is closed for renovations, buy tickets online or at the **Medieval Museum** (www.medeltidsmuseet.stockholm. se; Strömparteren; ⊗noon-5pm Tue-Sun, to 8pm Wed; 📾62, 65, Gustav Adolfs torg) **FREE**. Tour meeting points are printed on the tickets.

Far & Flyg Ballooning

(☏070-340 41 07; www.farochflyg.se; 10-person group 25,000kr; ☸late May–mid-Sep) Float over Stockholm in a hot-air balloon for up to an hour and see the city from a rare vantage point. Note that only groups can book trips, so bring your friends, and reserve well ahead.

 SHOPPING

E Torndahl Design

(www.etorndahl.se; Västerlånggatan 63; ☸10am-8pm; ☒Gamla Stan) This spacious design shop, run by the women of the Torndahl family since 1864, is a calm and civilised oasis on busy Västerlånggatan, offering jewellery, textiles and clever Scandinavian household objects.

Studio Lena M Gifts & Souvenirs

(www.studiolenam.wordpress.com; Kindstugan 14; ☸10am-6pm, to 5pm Sat; ☒Gamla Stan) This tiny, dimly lit shop is chock-full of adorable prints and products featuring the distinctive graphic design work of Lena M. It's a great place to find a unique – and uniquely Swedish – gift to bring home, or even just a cute postcard.

Svenskt Tenn Arts, Homewares

(☏08-670 16 00; www.svenskttenn.se; Nybrogatan 15; ☸10am-6pm Mon-Fri, 10am-4pm Sat; ☒Kungsträdgården) As much a museum of design as an actual shop, this iconic store is home to the signature fabrics and furniture of Josef Frank and his contemporaries. Browsing here is a great way to get a quick handle on what people mean by 'classic Swedish design' – and it's owned by a foundation that contributes heavily to arts funding.

NK Department Store

(☏08-762 80 00; www.nk.se; Hamngatan 12-18; ☸10am-8pm Mon-Fri, 10am-6pm Sat, 11am-5pm Sun; ☒T-Centralen) An ultra-classy department store founded in 1902, NK (Nordiska Kompaniet) is a city landmark – you can see its rotating neon sign from most parts

of Stockholm. You'll find top-name brands and several nice cafes, and the basement levels are great for stocking up on souvenirs and gourmet groceries. Around Christmas, check out its inventive window displays.

 ENTERTAINMENT

For an up-to-date events calendar, see www.visitstockholm.com. Another good source, if you can navigate a little Swedish, is the Friday 'På Stan' section of *Dagens Nyheter* newspaper (www.dn.se/pa-stan).

Mosebacke Etablissement Live Music

(http://sodrateatern.com; Mosebacketorg 3; ☸6pm-late; ☒Slussen) Eclectic theatre and club nights aside, this historic culture palace hosts a mixed line-up of live music. Tunes span anything from home-grown pop to Antipodean rock. The outdoor terrace (featured in the opening scene of August Strindberg's novel *The Red Room*) combines dazzling city views with a thumping summertime bar. It adjoins Södra Teatern and a couple of other bars.

Stampen Jazz

(☏08-20 57 93; www.stampen.se; Stora Nygatan 5; cover free-200kr; ☸5pm-1am Tue-Fri & Sun, 2pm-1am Sat; ☒Gamla Stan) Stampen is one of Stockholm's music-club stalwarts, swinging to live jazz and blues six nights a week. The free blues jam (currently on Sundays) pulls everyone from local noodlers to the odd music legend.

EATING

Gamla Stan

Chokladkoppen Cafe €

(www.chokladkoppen.se; Stortorget 18; cakes & coffees from 35kr, mains 85-125kr; ☸9am-11pm Jun-Aug, shorter hours rest of year; 🛜; ☒Gamla Stan) Arguably Stockholm's best-loved

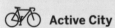 **Active City**

One thing visitors will notice about Stockholm, particularly during the summer months, is how fit and active the majority of locals are. Outdoor activity is a well-integrated part of the city's healthy lifestyle, and there are numerous ways in which a visitor can get in on the action.

Cycling

Stockholm is a very bicycle-friendly city. Cycling is best in the parks and away from the busy central streets and arterial roads, but even busy streets usually have dedicated cycle lanes. There's also a separate network of paved walking and cycling paths that reaches most parts of the city; these paths can be quite beautiful, taking you through green fields and peaceful forested areas. Tourist offices carry maps of cycle routes. Borrow a set of wheels from **City Bikes** (www.citybikes.se; 3-day/season card 165/300kr).

Swimming

Swimming is permitted just about anywhere people can scramble their way to the water. Popular spots include the rocks around Riddarfjärden and the leafy island of Långholmen, the latter also sporting a popular gay beach.

Rock Climbing

Climbers will find around 150 cliffs within 40 minutes' drive of the city, plus a large indoor climbing centre in Nacka.

cafe, hole-in-the-wall Chokladkoppen sits slap bang on the old town's enchanting main square. It's an atmospheric spot with a sprawling terrace and pocket-sized interior with low-beamed ceilings, custard-coloured walls and edgy artwork. The menu includes savoury treats like broccoli-and-blue-cheese pie and scrumptious cakes.

Under Kastanjen   Swedish €€

(☏08-21 50 04; www.underkastanjen.se; Kindstugatan 1, Gamla Stan; mains 182-289kr, dagens lunch 105kr; ⊘8am-11pm Mon-Fri, 9am-11pm Sat, 9am-9pm Sun; ☏; ☒Gamla Stan) This has to be just about the most picturesque corner of Gamla Stan, with tables set on a cobbled square under a beautiful chestnut tree surrounded by ochre and yellow storybook houses. Enjoy classic Swedish dishes like homemade meatballs with mashed potato; the downstairs wine bar has a veritable Spanish bodega feel with its whitewashed brick arches and moody lighting.

Kryp In   Swedish €€€

(☏08-20 88 41; www.restaurangkrypin.nu; Prästgatan 17; lunch mains 135-168kr, dinner mains 198-290kr; ⊘5-11pm Mon-Fri, noon-4pm & 5-11pm Sat & Sun; ☏; ☒Gamla Stan) Small but perfectly formed, this spot wows diners with creative takes on traditional Swedish dishes. Expect the likes of salmon carpaccio, Kalix roe, reindeer roast or gorgeous, spirit-warming saffron aioli shellfish stew. The service is seamless and the atmosphere classy without being stuffy. The three-course set menu (455kr) is superb. Book ahead.

🍴 Djurgården & Skeppsholmen

Rosendals Trädgårdskafe   Cafe €€

(☏08-54 58 12 70; www.rosendalstradgard.se; Rosendalsterrassen 12; mains 99-145kr; ⊘11am-5pm Mon-Fri, to 6pm Sat & Sun May-Sep, closed Mon Feb-Apr & Oct-Dec; Ⓟ◢; ▣44, 69, 76 Djurgårdsbron, ⓐ7) ◢ Set among the greenhouses of a pretty botanical garden, Rosendals is an idyllic spot for heavenly pastries and coffee or a meal and a glass of organic wine. Lunch includes a brief menu of soups, sandwiches (such as ground-lamb burger with chanterelles) and gorgeous salads. Much of the produce is biodynamic and grown on-site.

Södermalm

Hermans Trädgårdscafé   Vegetarian €€

(📞08-643 94 80; www.hermans.se; Fjällgatan 23B; buffet 195kr, desserts from 35kr; ⏰11am-9pm; 🖊; 🚌2, 3, 53, 71, 76 Tjärhovsplan, 🚇Slussen) 🌿 This justifiably popular vegetarian buffet is one of the nicest places to dine in Stockholm, with a glassed-in porch and outdoor seating on a terrace overlooking the city's glittering skyline. Fill up on inventive, flavourful veggie and vegan creations served from a cosy, vaulted room – you might need to muscle your way in, but it's worth the effort.

Meatballs for the People   Swedish €€

(📞08-466 60 99; www.meatballs.se; Nytorgsgatan 30, Södermalm; mains 179-195kr; ⏰11am-10pm Mon-Thu, to midnight Fri & Sat, limited hours Jul & Aug; 🛜; 🚇Medborgarplatsen) The name says it all. This restaurant serves serious meatballs, including moose, deer, wild boar and lamb, served with creamed potatoes and pickled vegetables, washed down with a pint of Sleepy Bulldog craft beer. It's a novel twist on a traditional Swedish dining experience, accentuated by the rustic decor and delightful waiting staff.

Woodstockholm   Swedish €€€

(📞08-36 93 99; www.woodstockholm.com; Mosebacketorg 9, Södermalm; mains 265-285kr; ⏰11.30am-2pm Mon, 11.30am-2pm & 5-11pm Tue-Sat; 🛜🖊; 🚇Slussen) 🌿 This hip dining spot incorporates a wine bar and furniture store showcasing chairs and tables by local designers. The menu changes weekly and is themed, somewhat wackily: think Salvador Dalí or Aphrodisiac, the latter including scallops with oyster mushrooms and sweetbreads with yellow beets and horseradish cream. This is fast becoming one of the city's classic foodie destinations. Reservations essential.

Under Kastanjen

Kvarnen

ADAM GRIMSHAW/LONELY PLANET ©

🟢 Östermalm & Ladugårdsgärdet

Sturekatten   Cafe €

(🖉08-611 16 12; www.sturekatten.se; Riddargatan 4; pastries from 35kr; ⊙9am-7pm Mon-Fri, 9am-6pm Sat, 10am-6pm Sun; 🚊Östermalmstorg) Looking like a life-size doll's house, this vintage cafe is a fetching blend of antique chairs, oil paintings, ladies who lunch and servers in black-and-white garb. Slip into a salon chair, pour some tea and nibble on a piece of apple pie or a *kanelbulle* (cinnamon bun).

Östermalms Saluhall   Market

(www.saluhallen.com; Östermalmstorg; ⊙9.30am-7pm Mon-Fri, to 5pm Sat; 🚊Östermalmstorg) **FREE** Östermalms Saluhall is a gourmet food hall that inhabits a delightful many-spired brick building. It's a sophisticated take on the traditional market, with fresh produce, fish counters, baked goods, butcher shops and tea vendors and some top places to grab a meal. For best results, arrive hungry and curious.

Ekstedt   Swedish €€€

(🖉08-611 12 10; http://ekstedt.nu/en; Humlegårdsgatan 17; 4/6 courses 890/1090kr; ⊙from 6pm till late Tue-Thu, from 5pm Fri, from 4pm Sat; 🚊Östermalmstorg) Dining here is as much an experience as a meal. Chef Niklas Ekstedt's education in French and Italian cooking informs his approach to traditional Scandinavian cuisine – but only slightly. Choose from a four- or six-course set menu built around reindeer and pike-perch. Everything is cooked in a wood-fired oven, over a fire pit or smoked in a chimney.

The Michelin–starred restaurant is frequently named among the best in the world; reservations are essential.

Gastrologik   Swedish €€€

(🖉08-662 30 60; www.gastrologik.se; Artilleriga-tan 14; tasting menu 1595kr; ⊙6-11.30pm Tue-Fri, 5-11.30pm Sat; 🚊Östermalmstorg) Gastrologik is at the forefront of dynamic and modern Scandinavian cooking. Diners choose from a set three- or six-course menu, which changes frequently, as the chefs work closely with suppliers to deliver the freshest and most readily available produce with a nod to sustainability and tradition. Reservations are essential.

🍷 DRINKING & NIGHTLIFE

Akkurat
Bar

(☎08-644 00 15; www.akkurat.se; Hornsgatan 18; ☺3pm-midnight Mon, to 1am Tue-Sat, 6pm-1am Sun; ☒Slussen) Valhalla for beer fiends, Akkurat boasts a huge selection of Belgian ales as well as a good range of Swedish–made microbrews and hard ciders. It's one of only two places in Sweden to be recognised by a Cask Marque for its real ale. Extras include a vast wall of whisky, and live music several nights a week.

Kvarnen
Bar

(☎08-643 03 80; www.kvarnen.com; Tjärhovsgatan 4; ☺11am-1am Mon & Tue, to 3am Wed-Fri, noon-3am Sat, noon-1am Sun; ☒Medborgarplatsen) An old-school Hammarby football fan hang-out, Kvarnen is one of the best bars in Söder. The gorgeous beer hall dates from 1907 and seeps tradition; if you're not the clubbing type, get here early for a nice pint and a meal (mains from 210kr). As the night progresses, the nightclub vibe takes over. Queues are fairly constant but justifiable.

Monks Wine Room
Wine Bar

(☎08-23 12 14; www.monkscafe.se; Lilla Nygatan 2; ☺5pm-midnight Tue-Thu, 4pm-midnight Fri & Sat; ☒Gamla Stan) Set in atmospheric 17th-century surroundings in the heart of the old town, Monks Wine Room has a well-stocked cellar with hundreds of bottles to choose from. Stop by for a quick glass of wine to recharge the batteries, or take some time to sample a cheese and wine pairing.

Monks Porter House
Pub

(☎08-23 12 12; www.monkscafe.se; Munkbron 11; ☺6pm-1am Tue-Sat; ☒Gamla Stan) This cavernous brewpub has an epic beer list, including 56 taps, many of which are made here or at the Monks microbrewery in Vasastan. Everything we tried was delicious, especially the Monks Orange Ale – your

 Tickets & Passes

The same tickets are valid on the tunnelbana, local trains and buses within Stockholm County, and some local ferry routes.

Single tickets are available, but if you're traveling more than once or twice it's better to get a refillable Access card. Keep tickets with you throughout your journey.

A single ticket costs 30-60kr and is valid for 75 minutes; it covers return trips and transfers between bus and metro.

A 24hr/72hr/7-day pass costs 120/240/315kr for an adult, and 80/160/210kr for a child. Add another 20kr for a refillable Access card.

Metro station, Stockholm
LAIMONAS CIŪNYS/500PX ©

best bet is to ask the bartender for a recommendation (or a taste). Check online for beer-tasting events.

ℹ️ INFORMATION

DISCOUNT CARDS

Destination Stockholm (☎08-663 00 80; www.stockholmpass.com; adult 1-/2-/3-/5-day pass 595/795/995/1295kr, children half-price) offers the Stockholm Pass, a discount package that includes free sightseeing tours and admission to 75 attractions.

TOURIST INFORMATION

Tourist Center (☎08-550 882 20; www.guide stockholm.info; Köpmangatan 22; ☺10am-4pm Mon-Fri year-round, 11am-2pm Sat & Sun Jun-Sep;

Gamla Stan) Tiny office in Gamla Stan, with brochures and information.

Visit Djurgården (☑08-667 77 01; www.visit djurgarden.se; Djurgårdsvägen 2; ⊘9am-dusk) With tourist information specific to Djurgården, this office at the edge of the Djurgården bridge is attached to Sjöcaféet cafe (☑08-660 57 57; www.sjocafeet.se; Djurgårdsvägen 2; ⊘9am-8pm Mon-Tue & Sun, 9am-9pm Thu-Sat), so you can grab a bite or a beverage as you plot your day.

ℹ️ GETTING THERE & AWAY

AIR

STOCKHOLM ARLANDA AIRPORT

Stockholm Arlanda Airport ((ARN); ☑10-109 10 00; www.swedavia.se/arlanda) Stockholm's main airport, 45km north of the city centre, is reached from central Stockholm by bus, local train and express train. Terminals two and five are for international flights; three and four are domestic; there is no terminal one.

BROMMA AIRPORT

Bromma Airport ((BMA); ☑010-109 40 00; www.swedavia.se/bromma; Ulvsundavägen; 🚌Brommaplan) Located 8km west of the city centre, Bromma is handy for domestic flights but services only a handful of airlines, primarily British Airways, Brussels Airlines and Finnair.

BUS

Most long-distance buses arrive at and depart from **Cityterminalen** (www.cityterminalen.com; ⊘7am-6pm), which is connected to Centralstationen. The main counter sells tickets for several bus companies, including **Flygbuss** (www.flyg bussarna.se; Cityterminalen; 🚌Centralen) (airport coaches), **Swebus** (www.swebus.se; Cityterminalen) and **Ybuss** (www.ybuss.se; Cityterminalen). You can also buy tickets from Pressbyrå shops and ticket machines. Destinations include:

Malmö from 549kr, 8½ hours, two to four times daily

Gothenburg from 419kr, six hours, eight daily

Uppsala 79kr, one hour, six daily

Jönköping from 269kr, five hours, six daily

Halmstad from 569kr, 12 hours, two daily

Nyköping from 89kr, two hours, eight daily

TRAIN

Stockholm is the hub for national train services run by **Sveriges Järnväg** (SJ; ☑0771-75 75 75; www.sj.se), with a network of services that covers all the major towns and cities, as well as services to the rest of Scandinavia, including the following destinations:

Malmö from 632kr, five hours, frequent

Kiruna from 795kr, 17 hours, one daily

Uppsala from 95kr, 35 to 55 minutes, frequent

Gothenburg from 422kr, three to five hours, hourly

Gällivare from 795kr, 15 hours, one daily

Jönköping from 696kr, 3½ hours, one daily

Lund from 632kr, 4½ hours, four daily

Oslo from 1000kr, five hours, four daily

Central Station has left-luggage lockers on the lower level (small/large locker for 24 hours 70/90kr).

ℹ️ GETTING AROUND

Storstockholms Lokaltrafik (SL; ☑08-600 10 00; www.sl.se; Centralstationen; ⊘SL Center Sergels Torg 7am-6.30pm Mon-Fri, 10am-5pm Sat & Sun, inside Centralstationen 6.30am-11.45pm Mon-Sat, from 7am Sun) runs the tunnelbana (metro), local trains and buses within Stockholm county. You can buy tickets and passes at SL counters, ticket machines at tunnelbana stations, and Pressbyrå kiosks. Refillable SL travel cards (20kr) can be loaded with single-trip or unlimited-travel credit. Fines are steep (1500kr) for travelling without a valid ticket.

○ **Tunnelbana** The city's underground rail system is efficient and extensive.

○ **Bus** Local buses thoroughly cover the city and surrounds.

○ **Tram** Tram lines serve Djurgården from Norrmalm.

○ **Ferry** In summer, ferries are the best way to get to Djurgården, and they serve the archipelago year-round.

Where to Stay

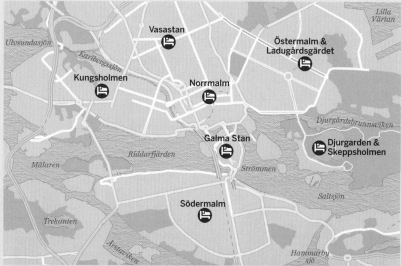

Neighbourhood	For	Against
Gamla Stan	Central and romantic.	Pricier than other neighbourhoods.
Norrmalm	Handy for trains and buses.	Busier, less atmospheric, sometimes noisy.
Södermalm	Fun, budget-friendly part of town, good for nightlife.	Farther from train and bus stations.
Kungsholmen	Great for exploring restaurants.	A bit out of the way.
Östermalm & Ladugårdsgärdet	Ideal for shopping and nightlife.	Can be expensive.
Suburbs	Some excellent hostels and campgrounds.	Up to an hour from the city centre.
Vasastan	Central enough, but with more of a residential neighbourhood feel.	A little farther from the trains, buses and ferries.
Djurgården & Skeppsholmen	Close to several prime attractions.	Busy and less convenient to trains and buses.

TALLINN, ESTONIA

Tallinn, Estonia at a Glance...

Tallinn is a proud European capital with an allure that's all its own. The city is lively yet peaceful, absurdly photogenic and bursting with wonderful sights – ancient churches, medieval streetscapes and noble merchants' houses. Throw in delightful food and vibrant modern culture and it's no wonder Tallinn is so popular.

Despite the boom of 21st-century development, Tallinn safeguards the fairy-tale charms of its Unesco-listed Old Town – one of Europe's most complete walled cities. And the blossoming of first-rate restaurants, atmospheric hotels and a well-oiled tourist machine makes visiting a breeze.

Two Days in Tallinn

Spend your first day exploring **Old Town**, stopping for lunch in **Chocolats de Pierre** (p274). Spend the afternoon exploring the **Town Hall Square** (p268) and the Estonian History Museum at the **Great Guild** (p267). In the evening, dine at posh Russian restaurant **Tchaikovsky** (p274).

The following day, head to the **Estonian Open-Air Museum** (p263) to explore rural Estonia in an urban location. In the evening, hit the **Rotermann Quarter** (p272).

Four Days in Tallinn

Four days is enough to cover the remainder of central Tallinn's highlights. Round out your days with trips to **St Mary's Lutheran Cathedral** (p268), **Kadriorg Art Museum** (p269) and **Kumu** (p269). Allow some time to wander around super-hip **Telliskivi Creative City** (p268).

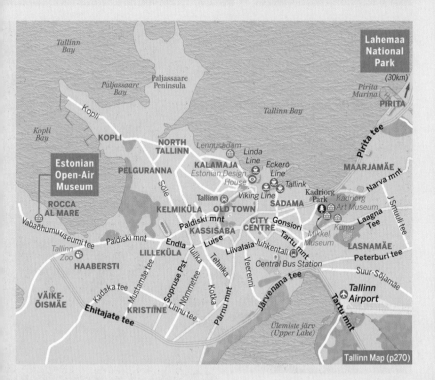

Tallinn Map (p270)

Arriving in Tallinn

From the airport, bus 2 will take you into central Tallinn and then on to the passenger ferry port. A taxi between the airport and the city centre should cost less than €10.

Buses connect the ferry terminals with the city centre. A taxi between the city centre and any of the terminals should cost about €5.

Where to Stay

Tallinn has a good range of accommodation to suit every budget. Most of it is congregated in Old Town and its immediate surrounds, where even backpackers might find themselves waking up in a converted merchant's house. Of course, Tallinn is no secret any more, and it can be extremely difficult to find a bed on the weekend in summer.

Estonian Open-Air Museum

Part folk museum, part architectural showpiece, this fine open-air museum takes rural Estonia and gives it an urban location. As an introduction to the country's traditions, it has few peers.

Great For...

Don't Miss

If you're here on Midsummer's Eve (23 June), come for the traditional celebrations, bonfire and all.

The Museum's Collection

If tourists won't go to the countryside, let's bring the countryside to them. That's the modus operandi of this excellent, sprawling complex, where historic Estonian buildings have been plucked and transplanted among the tall trees. In summer the time-warping effect is highlighted by staff in period costume performing traditional activities among the wooden farmhouses and windmills. There's a chapel dating from 1699 called Kolu Kõrts.

i Need to Know

Estonian Open-Air Museum (Eesti vabaõhumuuseum; ☏654 9101; www.evm. ee; Vabaõhumuuseumi tee 12, Rocca Al Mare; adult/child €9/6 high season, €7/5 low season; ☺10am-8pm 23 Apr-28 Sep, to 5pm 29 Sep-22 Apr)

✖ Take a Break

Kolu Kõrts, an old wooden tavern, serves traditional Estonian cuisine

★ Top Tip

Combined family tickets include **Tallinn Zoo** (Tallinna loomaaed; ☏694 3300; www. tallinnzoo.ee; Paldiski mnt 145, Veskimetsa; adult/child €8/5; ☺9am-8pm May-Aug, to 7pm Mar, Apr, Sep & Oct, to 5pm Nov-Feb), which is a 20-minute walk away.

Traditional Activities

Some of the activities you can try your hand at include weaving, blacksmithing and traditional cooking. Children love the horse-and-carriage rides (adult/child €9/6), and bikes can be hired (€3 per hour).

Getting to the Museum

To get here from the centre, take Paldiski mnt. When the road nears the water, veer right onto Vabaõhumuuseumi tee. Bus 21 (departing from the railway station at least hourly) stops right out front.

Altja

Lahemaa National Park

Estonia's largest rahvuspark (national park), the 'Land of Bays' is 725 sq km of unspoiled rural Estonia, making it the perfect country retreat from the nearby capital.

Great For...

Don't Miss

Kuusekännu Riding Farm (Kuusekännu Ratsatalu; ☎325 2942; www.kuusekannuratsatalu.ee; riding per hr €20) arranges trail rides through Lahemaa.

A microcosm of Estonia's natural charms, the park takes in a stretch of deeply indented coast with several peninsulas and bays, plus 475 sq km of pine-fresh hinterland encompassing forest, lakes, rivers and peat bogs, and areas of historical and cultural interest.

Altja

First mentioned in 1465, this fishing village has many restored or reconstructed traditional buildings, including a wonderfully ancient-looking tavern, which was actually built in 1976. Altja's Swing Hill (Kiitemägi), complete with a traditional Estonian wooden swing, has long been the focus of Midsummer's Eve festivities in Lahemaa. The 3km circular Altja Nature & Culture Trail starts at Swing Hill and takes in net sheds, fishing cottages and the stone field known as the 'open-air museum of stones'.

WESTEND61/GETTY IMAGES ©

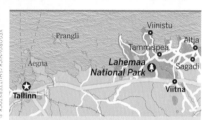

Clock tower and gate of Sagadi Manor

ⓘ Need to Know

Lahemaa is best explored by car or bicycle, with limited buses in the park.

✕ Take a Break

In a thatched, wooden building, uber-rustic Altja Kõrts serves delicious traditional fare.

★ Top Tip

The excellent Lahemaa National Park Visitor Centre has information on hiking, accommodation and guides.

Sagadi Manor & Forest Museum

Completed in 1753, this pretty pink-and-white baroque **mansion** (Sagadi Mõis & Metsamuuseum; ☑676 7888; www.sagadi. ee; adult/child €3/2; ⊗10am-6pm May-Sep, by appointment Oct-Apr) is surrounded by glorious gardens (which are free to visit), encompassing a lake, numerous modern sculptures, an arboretum and an endless view down a grand avenue of trees. The house ticket includes admission to the neighbouring Forest Museum.

Tammispea Boulder

Over the millennia it has split into several pieces, but this gigantic 7.8m-high erratic boulder is still an impressive sight. It's hidden within a lovely stand of forest. To find it, leave the main coastal road and head through Tammispea village, continuing on to the unsealed road.

Viinistu Art Museum

Viinistu (Kunstimuuseum; www.viinistu. ee; adult/child €4/2; ⊗11am-6pm Wed-Sun) houses the remarkable private art collection of Jaan Manitski. It's devoted entirely to Estonian art and pays particularly strong attention to contemporary painting (although you'll also find sculpture, etchings, drawings and more traditional canvasses).

Tallinn's Old Town Walking Tour

Wandering around the medieval streets of Tallinn is one of Scandinavia's most rewarding urban pastimes, and you could spend days in this pleasurable pursuit.

Start Freedom Square
Distance 4km
Duration three hours

3 Castle Square (Lossi plats) is dominated by the pretty, onion-domed **Alexander Nevsky Orthodox Cathedral** (p269).

4 At Danish King's Garden, artists set up their easels in summer to capture the ageless vista over Tallinn's rooftops.

2 From Linda Hill (Falgi tee) you can see the remaining medieval elements of **Toompea Castle** (p274).

Take a Break...
Stop off for down-home Estonian cooking at **Vanaema Juures** (p274).

5 Lower Town Wall (Väike-Kloostri 1) links nine of the 26 remaining towers (there were once 45).

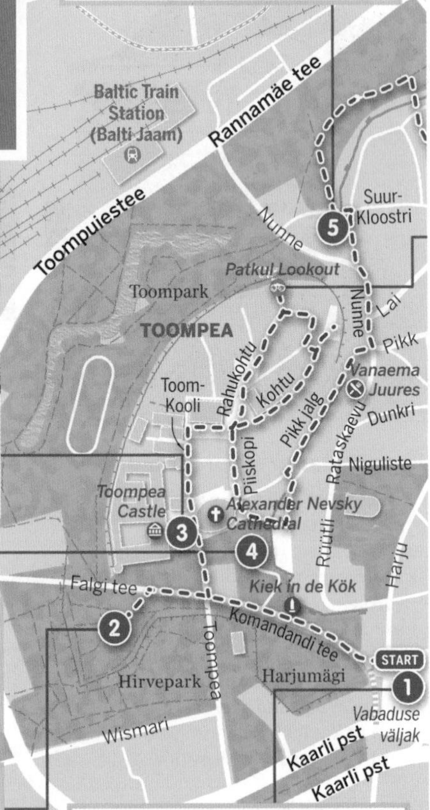

Baltic Train Station (Balti Jaam)

Rannamäe tee

Toompuiestee

Numne

Suur-Kloostri

5

Patkul Lookout

Toompark

Lai

TOOMPEA

Nunne

Pikk

Rahukohtu

Toom-Kooli

Kohtu

Vanaema Juures

Pikk jalg

Dunkri

Piiskopi

Rataskaevu

Niguliste

Toompea Castle

Alexander Nevsky Cathedral

3

4

Rüütli

Harju

Paldiski mnt

Falgi tee

Kiek in de Kök

2

Komandandi tee

Toompea

START

1

Hirvepark

Harjumägi

Vabaduse väljak

Wismari

Kaarli pst

Kaarli pst

Luise

1 Starting at **Freedom Square** (Vabaduse väljak), take the stairs up into Toompea, noting the famous **Kiek in de Kök** (Komandandi tee 2; www.linnamuuseum.ee) tower on your right.

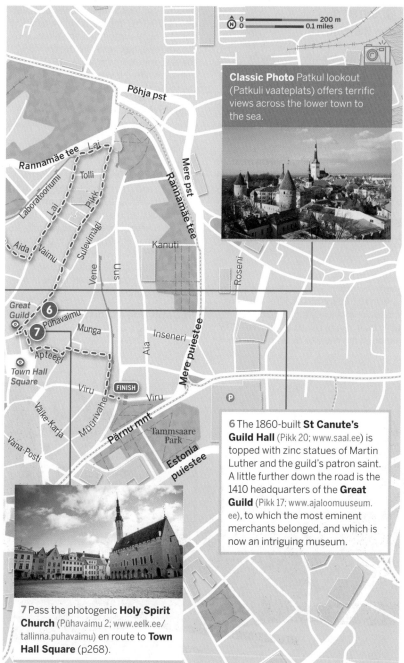

Classic Photo Patkul lookout (Patkuli vaateplats) offers terrific views across the lower town to the sea.

Põhja pst

Rannamäe tee — Lai

Tolli

Laboratooriumi

Lai

Pikk

Aida

Vaimu

Sulevimägi

Vene

Uus

Kanuti

Roseni

Mere pst

Rannamäe tee

Great Guild

6

7

Pühavaimu

Munga

Inseneri

Aia

Mere puiestee

Apteegi

Town Hall Square

Viru

FINISH

Viru

Väike-Karja

Müürivahe

Pärnu mnt

Tammsaare Park

Vana-Posti

Estonia puiestee

6 The 1860-built **St Canute's Guild Hall** (Pikk 20; www.saal.ee) is topped with zinc statues of Martin Luther and the guild's patron saint. A little further down the road is the 1410 headquarters of the **Great Guild** (Pikk 17; www.ajaloomuuseum. ee), to which the most eminent merchants belonged, and which is now an intriguing museum.

7 Pass the photogenic **Holy Spirit Church** (Pühavaimu 2; www.eelk.ee/tallinna.puhavaimu) en route to **Town Hall Square** (p268).

3 TTSTUDIO/SHUTTERSTOCK © 7 SKREIDZELEU/SHUTTERSTOCK © CLASSIC PHOTO TSUGULIEV/SHUTTERSTOCK ©

◎ SIGHTS

Town Hall Square   Square

(Raekoja plats) In Tallinn all roads lead to Raekoja plats, the city's pulsing heart since markets began setting up here in the 11th century. One side is dominated by the Gothic **town hall** (Tallinna raekoda; ✆645 7900; www.raekoda.tallinn.ee; Raekoja plats; adult/student €5/2; ☺10am-4pm Mon-Sat Jul & Aug, shorter hrs rest of year; ♿), while the rest is ringed by pretty pastel-coloured buildings dating from the 15th to 17th centuries. Whether bathed in sunlight or sprinkled with snow, it's always a photogenic spot.

St Mary's
Lutheran Cathedral   Church

(Tallinna Püha Neitsi Maarja Piiskoplik toomkirik; ✆644 4140; www.toomkirik.ee; Toom-Kooli 6; church/tower €2/5; ☺9am-5pm May & Sep, to 6pm Jun-Aug, shorter hrs/days rest of year) Tallinn's cathedral (now Lutheran, originally Catholic) had been initially built by the Danes by at least 1233, although the exterior dates mainly from the 15th century, with the tower completed in 1779. This impressive building was a burial ground for the rich and titled, and the whitewashed walls are decorated with the elaborate coats of arms of Estonia's noble families. Fit view-seekers can climb the tower.

Telliskivi Creative City   Area

(Telliskivi Loomelinnak; www.telliskivi.eu; Telliskivi 60a; ☺shops 10am-6pm Mon-Sat, 11am-5pm Sun; ♿) Once literally on the wrong side of the tracks, this set of abandoned factory buildings is now Tallinn's most alternative shopping and entertainment precinct, with cafes, a bike shop, bars selling craft beer, graffiti walls, artist studios, food trucks and pop-up concept stores. But it's not only hipsters who flock to Telliskivi to peruse the fashion and design stores, drink espressos and riffle through the stalls at the weekly flea market – you're as likely to see families rummaging and sipping.

St Catherine's Cloister   Church

(www.claustrum.eu; Müürivahe 33; adult/child €2/1; ☺11am-5pm mid-May–Sep) Perhaps

Kumu

ANDRII ZHEZHERA/SHUTTERSTOCK ©

Tallinn's oldest building, St Catherine's Monastery was founded by Dominican monks in 1246. In its glory days it had its own brewery and hospital. A mob of angry Lutherans torched the place in 1524 and the monastery languished for the next 400 years until its partial restoration in 1954. Today the ruined complex includes the gloomy shell of the barren church (which makes an atmospheric venue for occasional recitals) and a peaceful cloister lined with carved tombstones.

Kadriorg Art Museum   Museum

(Kardrioru kunstimuuseum; ☑606 6400; www.kadriorumuuseum.ekm.ee; A Weizenbergi 37, Kadriorg Palace; adult/child €6.50/4.50; ☺10am-6pm Tue & Thu-Sun May-Sep, to 5pm Thu-Sun Oct-Apr, to 8pm Wed year-round) Kadriorg Palace, a baroque beauty built by Peter the Great between 1718 and 1736, houses a branch of the Estonian Art Museum devoted to Dutch, German and Italian paintings from the 16th to the 18th centuries, and Russian works from the 18th to early 20th centuries (check out the decorative porcelain with Communist imagery upstairs). The pink building is exactly as frilly and fabulous as a palace ought to be, and there's a handsome French–style formal garden at the rear.

Kumu   Gallery

(☑602 6000; www.kumu.ekm.ee; A Weizenbergi 34, near Kadriorg Park; adult/student €8/6; ☺10am-8pm Thu, to 6pm Wed & Fri-Sun year-round, plus 10am-6pm Tue Apr-Sep) This futuristic, Finnish–designed, seven-storey building is a spectacular structure of limestone, glass and copper, nicely integrated into the landscape. Kumu (the name is short for *kunstimuuseum*, or art museum) contains the country's largest repository of Estonian art as well as constantly changing contemporary exhibits. There's everything from venerable painted altarpieces to the work of contemporary Estonian artists such as Adamson-Eric.

 Sweat It Out

Locals attribute all kinds of health benefits to a good old-fashioned sweat and, truth be told, a trip to Estonia just won't be complete until you've paid a visit to the sauna. You won't have to look far – most hotels have one – but Tallinn also has some good public options.

SPACES IMAGES/GETTY IMAGES ©

Alexander Nevsky Orthodox Cathedral   Cathedral

(☑644 3484; http://tallinnanevskikatedraal.eu; Lossi plats 10; ☺8am-7pm, to 4pm winter) The positioning of this magnificent, onion-domed Russian Orthodox cathedral (completed in 1900) at the heart of the country's main administrative hub was no accident: the church was one of many built in the last part of the 19th century as part of a general wave of Russification in the empire's Baltic provinces. Orthodox believers come here in droves, alongside tourists ogling the interior's striking icons and frescoes. Quiet, respectful, demurely dressed visitors are welcome, but cameras aren't.

✪ ACTIVITIES

Harju Ice Rink   Ice Skating

(Harju tänava uisuplats; ☑56246739; www.uisuplats.ee; Harju; per hr adult/child €5/3; ☺10am-10pm Nov-Mar; ⛄) Wrap up warmly to join the locals at Old Town's outdoor ice rink – very popular in the winter months. You'll have earned a *hõõgvein*

Tallinn

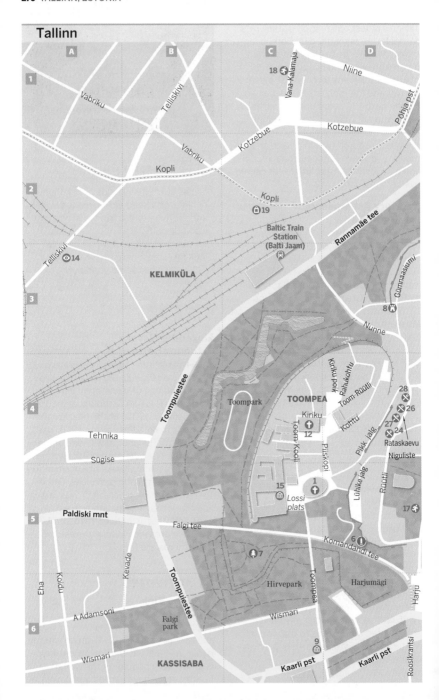

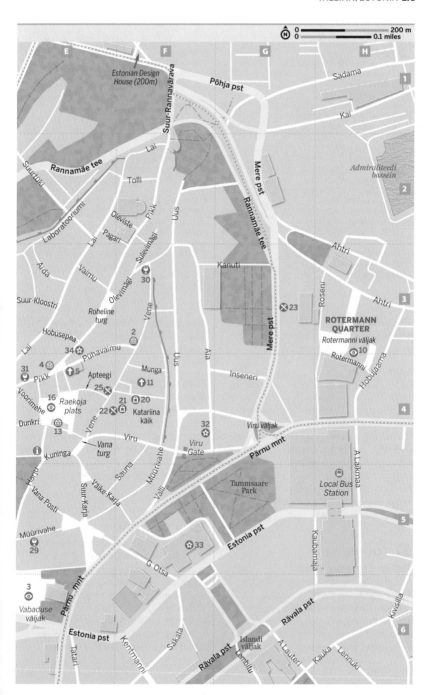

Tallinn

(mulled or 'glowing' wine) in the warm indoor cafe by the end of your skating session. Skate rental costs €3.

Kalma Saun Spa

(☎627 1811; www.kalmasaun.ee; Vana-Kalamaja 9a; €9-10; ⏰11am-10pm Mon-Fri, 10am-11pm Sat & Sun) In a grand 1928 building behind the train station, Tallinn's oldest public sauna still has the aura of an old-fashioned, Russian–style *banya* (bathhouse) – flagellation with a birch branch is definitely on the cards. It has separate men's and women's sections (the women's is slightly cheaper), and private saunas are available (per hour €20; up to six people).

 TOURS

Tallinn Traveller Tours Tours

(☎58374800; www.traveller.ee) This outfit runs entertaining tours – including a two-hour Old Town walk departing from outside the tourist office (p276) (private groups of 1-15 people from €80, or there's a larger free tour, for which you should tip

the engaging guides). There are also ghost tours (€15), bike tours (from €19), pub crawls (€20) and day trips as far afield as Rīga (€55).

Euroaudioguide Walking

(www.euroaudioguide.com; iPod rental €15) Pre-loaded iPods are available from the tourist office (p276), offering excellent commentary on most Old Town sights, with plenty of history thrown in. If you've got your own iPod, iPhone or iPad you can download the tour as an e-book (€10).

 SHOPPING

The city's glitziest shopping precinct is the **Rotermann Quarter** (Rotermanni kvartal; ☎626 4200; www.rotermann.eu; Rotermanni 8), a clutch of former warehouses now sheltering dozens of small stores selling everything from streetwear to Scandinavian–designed furniture, artisanal cheese, good wines, top-notch bread and dry-aged beef. Telliskivi

Creative City (p268) has fewer but more unusual shops, and you'll be tripping over *käsitöö* (handicraft) stores everywhere in Old Town.

Katariina Käik
Arts & Crafts

(St Catherine's Passage; www.katariinagild.eu; off Vene 12; ⊙noon-6pm Mon-Sat) This lovely medieval lane is home to the Katariina Guild, comprising eight artisans' studios where you can happily browse the work of 14 female creators. Look for ceramics, textiles, patchwork quilts, hats, jewellery, stained glass and beautiful leather-bound books. Opening hours can vary amongst the different studios.

Masters' Courtyard
Arts & Crafts

(Meistrite Hoov; www.hoov.ee; Vene 6; ⊙10am-6pm) Archetypal of Tallinn's amber-suspended medieval beauty, this cobbled 13th-century courtyard offers rich pickings – a cosy chocolaterie/cafe, a guesthouse and artisans' stores and workshops selling quality ceramics, glass, jewellery, knitwear, woodwork and candles.

Balti Jaama Turg
Market

(Baltic Station Market; https://astri.ee/bjt; Kopli 1; ⊙9am-7pm Mon-Sat, to 5pm Sun) The gentrification of the train station (p277) precinct is manifest in this sleek new market complex, where niche food vendors trade from tidy huts on the former site of a famed but slightly seedy outdoor market. There's also a supermarket, meat, dairy and seafood halls, greengrocers, fashion retailers, a gym and underground parking.

Estonian Design House
Gifts & Souvenirs

(Eesti Disaini Maja; www.estoniandesignhouse. ee; Kalasadama 8; ⊙11am-7pm Mon-Fri, to 6pm Sat & Sun) This slick little store showcases the work of more than 100 Estonian designers – everything from shoes to lamps, furniture to ceramics. Keep an eye out for the 'slow fashion' of local designer

Reet Aus, who creates great clothes for her label out of offcuts from mass-production processes.

ENTERTAINMENT

Find Tallinn's best English–language listings in the bimonthly *Tallinn In Your Pocket* (€2.50, or free at www.inyourpocket.com). There's also *Tallinn This Week* (actually also bimonthly, and free) www.culture.ee, www. concert.ee, www.draamamaa.ee and the ticketing service Piletilevi (www.piletilevi.ee).

Estonia Concert Hall
Classical Music

(Eesti Kontserdisaal; ☑614 7771; www. concert.ee; Estonia pst 4) The city's biggest classical concerts are held in this double-barrelled venue, built in the early 20th century and reconstructed after WWII bomb damage. It's Tallinn's most prestigious performance venue, housing both the Estonian National Opera and Ballet (www.opera.ee), and the Estonian National Symphony Orchestra (www. erso.ee).

Chicago 1933
Live Music

(☑627 1266; www.chicago.ee; Aia 3; ⊙noon-midnight Mon & Tue, to 1am Wed & Thu, to 3am Fri, 2pm-3am Sat, 2pm-midnight Sun; ☜) With a dim, wood-panelled speakeasy vibe, live blues and jazz played by Estonian and international artists most nights, and seriously comfortable horseshoe banquettes amongst the stylish fittings, Chicago is easy to like. There are also bar snacks (sold in bulk – 15 pieces for €21), a good cigar selection and a smoking room in which to enjoy them.

✖ EATING

Vegan Restoran V
Vegan €

(☑626 9087; www.vonkrahl.ee; Rataskaevu 12; mains €9-11; ⊙noon-11pm Sun-Thu, to midnight Fri & Sat; ✍) Visiting vegans are spoiled for choice in this wonderful restaurant. In summer everyone wants one

 Visit the Toompea Citadel

Lording it over the lower part of Old Town is the ancient hilltop citadel of **Toompea** (Lossi plats). In German times this was the preserve of the feudal nobility, literally looking down on the traders and lesser beings below. It's now almost completely given over to government buildings, churches, embassies and shops selling amber knick-knacks and fridge magnets, and is correspondingly quieter than the teeming streets below.

YEGOROVNICK/SHUTTERSTOCK ©

of the four tables on the street, but the atmospheric interior is just as appealing. The food is excellent – expect the likes of tempeh and veggies on brown rice with tomato-coconut sauce, and kale and lentil pie with creamy hemp-seed sauce.

Chocolats de Pierre Cafe €
(☑641 8061; www.pierre.ee; Vene 6; mains €8-11; ☺8am-11pm) Nestled inside the picturesque Masters' Courtyard (p273) and offering respite from the Old Town hubbub, this snug cafe is renowned for its delectable (but pricey) handmade chocolates, but it also sells pastries, sandwiches and quiches, making it a great choice for a light breakfast or lunch. As the day progresses, pasta finds its way onto the menu.

Von Krahli Aed Modern European €€
(☑58593839; www.vonkrahl.ee; Rataskaevu 8; mains €13-16; ☺noon-midnight Mon-Sat, to 11pm Sun; ☺☑) You'll find plenty of greenery on your plate at this rustic, plant-filled restaurant (*aed* means 'garden'), beneath the rough beams of a medieval merchant's house. Veggies star here (although all dishes can be ordered with some kind of fleshy embellishment) and there's care taken to offer vegan dishes and gluten-, lactose- and egg-free options.

Vanaema Juures Estonian €€
(☑626 9080; www.vonkrahl.ee/vanaemajuures; Rataskaevu 10/12; mains €12-14; ☺noon-10pm) Food just like your grandma used to make, if she was a) Estonian, and b) a really good cook. 'Grandma's Place' was one of Tallinn's most stylish restaurants in the 1930s, and still rates as a top choice for traditional, homestyle Estonian fare such as blood sausages with lingonberry jam. Antiques and photographs lend the dining room a formal air.

Tchaikovsky Russian, French €€€
(☑600 0600; www.telegraafhotel.com; Vene 9; mains €24-25; ☺noon-3pm & 6-11pm Mon-Fri, 1-11pm Sat & Sun; ☺) Located in a glassed-in pavilion within the **Hotel Telegraaf** (☑600 0600; www.telegraafhotel.com; Vene 9; r €225-255; P☀☺☺), Tchaikovsky offers a dazzling tableau of blinged-up chandeliers, gilt frames and greenery. Service is formal and faultless (as is the carefully contemporized menu of Franco–Russian classics) and the experience is capped by live chamber music. The €25 three-course weekday lunch is excellent value and there's terrace seating in summer.

Ö New Nordic €€€
(☑661 6150; www.restoran-o.ee; Mere pst 6e; degustation menus €59-76; ☺6-11pm Mon-Sat, closed Jul) Award-winning Ö (pronounced 'er' and named for Estonia's biggest island, Saaremaa) has carved a unique space in

Tallinn's culinary world, delivering inventive degustation menus showcasing seasonal Estonian produce. There's a distinct New Nordic influence at play, deploying unusual ingredients such as fermented birch sap and spruce shoots, and the understated dining room nicely complements the theatrical but always delicious cuisine.

🍸 DRINKING & NIGHTLIFE

Don't worry about Tallinn's reputation as a stag-party paradise: it's easy to avoid the 'British' and 'Irish' pubs in the southeast corner of Old Town where lager louts congregate (roughly the triangle formed by Viru, Suur-Karja and the city walls).

Levist Väljas   Bar
(☑5077372; Olevimägi 12; ⊙3pm-3am Mon-Thu, to 6am Fri & Sat, to midnight Sun) Inside this much-loved Tallinn cellar bar (usually the last pit stop of the night) you'll find broken furniture, cheap booze and a refreshingly motley crew of friendly punks, grunge kids and anyone else who strays from the well-trodden tourist path.

The discreet entrance is down a flight of stairs.

No Ku Klubi   Bar
(☑631 3929; Pikk 5; ⊙noon-1am Mon-Thu, to 3am Fri, 2pm-3am Sat, 6pm-1am Sun) A nondescript red-and-blue door, a key-code to enter, a clubbable atmosphere of regulars lounging in mismatched armchairs – could this be Tallinn's ultimate 'secret' bar? Once the surreptitious haunt of artists in Soviet times, it's now free for all to enter – just ask one of the smokers outside for the code. Occasional evenings of low-key music and film are arranged.

Gloria Wine Cellar   Wine Bar
(☑640 6804; www.gloria.ee; Müürivahe 2; ⊙noon-11pm Mon-Sat) Set in a cellar beneath the inner face of the town wall, this atmospheric wine bar and shop stocks thousands of bottles across a series of vaulted stone chambers. Credenzas, heavy carpets, antique furniture and walls hung with paintings greet you inside, and the passing life of Tallinn outside, should the weather encourage an alfresco glass.

Chocolats de Pierre

STOCKPHOTOVIDEO/SHUTTERSTOCK ©

Tourist Information Centre

ℹ INFORMATION

DISCOUNT CARDS

With the **Tallinn Card** (www.tallinncard.ee), you'll pay €25/37/45 for a one/two/three-day adult card (children €14/19/23) and get free entry to more than 40 sights and attractions (including most of the big-ticket ones), unlimited use of public transport and plenty of other discounts on shopping, dining and entertainment. You can buy the Tallinn Card online, from the **Tourist Information Centre**, or from many hotels.

TOURIST INFORMATION

Tallinn Tourist Information Centre (☑645 7777; www.visittallinn.ee; Niguliste 2; ⊗9am-7pm Mon-Sat, to 6pm Sun Jun-Aug, shorter hrs rest of year) A very well-stocked and helpful office. Many Old Town walking tours leave from here.

ℹ GETTING THERE & AWAY

AIR

Tallinn Airport (Tallinna Lennujaam; ☑605 8888; www.tallinn-airport.ee; Tartu mnt 101) is conveniently located just 4km southeast of the city centre and offers air connections with 34 other Baltic and European destinations.

BOAT

Ferries fan across the Baltic from Tallinn to Helsinki, St Petersburg, Mariehamn and Stockholm.

Eckerö Line (☑6000 4300; www.eckeroline. fi; Passenger Terminal A, Vanasadam; adult/ child/car from €19/12/19; ⊗ticket office 8.30am-7pm Mon-Fri, to 3pm Sat & Sun) Twice-daily car ferry from Helsinki to Tallinn (2½ hours).

Linda Line (☑699 9331; www.lindaliini.ee; Patarei Sadam, Linnahall Terminal) Operates smaller, faster (and more expensive) hydrofoil connections between Tallinn and Helsinki, from late March to late December.

Tallink (☑631 8320; www.tallink.com; Terminal D, Lootsi 13) Runs multiple daily services between Tallinn and Helsinki, and an overnight ferry to Stockholm, via the Åland islands.

Viking Line (☑666 3966; www.vikingline.com; Terminal A, Varasadam; passenger & vehicle from €42) At least four daily car ferries between Helsinki and Tallinn (2½ hours).

BUS

Regional and international buses depart from Tallinn's **Central Bus Station** (Tallinna bussijaam; ☎12550; www.bussijaam.ee; Lastekodu 46; ⊙ticket office 7am-9pm Mon-Sat, 8am-8pm Sun), about 2km southeast of Old Town; bus 2 or tram 4 will get you there. The national bus network is extensive, linking Tallinn to pretty much everywhere you might care to go. All services are summarised on the extremely handy Tpilet site (www.tpilet.ee).

TRAIN

The **Baltic Train Station** (Balti Jaam; Toompuiestee 35) is on the northwestern edge of Old Town; despite the name, it has no direct services to other Baltic states. **GoRail** (www.gorail.ee) runs a daily service stopping in Narva (€8.10, 2½ hours) en route to St Petersburg and Moscow.

ℹ GETTING AROUND

Tallinn is very compact, with excellent, cheap public transport. If you're staying in or near Old Town, as most visitors do, you may find shoe leather the most efficient means of transport.

Tallinn has an excellent network of buses, trams and trolleybuses running from around 6am to 11pm or midnight. The major **local bus station** is beneath the Viru Keskus shopping centre. All local public transport timetables are online at www.tallinn.ee.

Public transport is free for Tallinn residents, children under seven and adults with children under three. Others need to pay, either buying a paper ticket from the driver (€2 for a single journey, exact change required) or by using the e-ticketing system. Buy a Ühiskaart (a smartcard, requiring a €2 deposit which can't be recouped within six months of validation) at an R-Kiosk, post office or the Tallinn City Government customer service desk, add credit, then validate the card at the start of each journey using the orange card-readers. E-ticket fares are €1.10/3/6 for an hour/day/five days.

👫 Introducing Estonians

Despite (or perhaps because of) centuries of occupation by Danes, Swedes, Germans and Russians, Estonians have tenaciously held onto their national identity and are deeply, emotionally connected to their history, folklore and national song tradition. The Estonian Literary Museum in Tartu holds more than 1.3 million pages of folk songs, the world's second-largest collection (Ireland has the largest), and Estonia produces films for one of the world's smallest audiences (only Iceland produces for a smaller audience).

According to the popular stereotype, Estonians (particularly the men) are reserved and aloof. Some believe it has much to do with the weather – those long, dark nights breeding endless introspection. This reserve also extends to gross displays of public affection, brash behaviour and intoxication – all frowned upon. This is assuming that there isn't a festival under way, such as Jaanipäev, when friends, family and acquaintances gather in the countryside for drinking, dancing and revelry.

Estonians are known for their strong work ethic, but when they're not toiling in the fields, or putting in long hours at the office, they head to the countryside. Ideal weekends are spent at the family cottage, picking berries or mushrooms, walking through the woods, or sitting with friends soaking up the quiet beauty. Owning a country house with a sauna is one of the national aspirations.

Estonian folk dancers, Tallinn
YEGOROVNICK/SHUTTERSTOCK ©

Stadshuset, Stockholm (p246)

In Focus

Wind turbines, Norway

DRIMAFILM/SHUTTERSTOCK ©

Scandinavia Today

The Nordic nations tend to be table-toppers on global measures of equality, development, sustainability and liveability. Despite the impact of the financial crisis, these countries remain at the forefront of all that is forward-thinking and progressive. The world has come knocking at Scandinavia's door, regardless of its history of isolation, in the shape of immigration and climate change.

Immigration

Exacerbated by the financial crisis, the relatively rapid influx of immigrants to formerly homogeneous Nordic societies has raised tensions in recent years, resulting in anti-immigration and far-right political parties gaining substantial portions of the popular vote. Local opinion has polarised, raising the question of whether the region's famed tolerance was just a veneer. Much of the debate has been focused on the 2017 terrorist attack in Stockholm by a failed asylum seeker cited by politicians across the region as evidence of the need for tighter controls. On the other side, Anders Breivik's 2011 massacre of Norwegian teenagers or Finland's troubled history with guns could be seen as powerful evidence that local extremism is a bigger problem.

belief systems
(% of population)

65 Lutheran | 26 unaffiliated | 4 other | 3 Muslim | 2 Catholic

if Scandinavia were 100 people

38 live in Sweden
21 live in Denmark
20 live in Finland
19 live in Norway
1 live in Tallinn
1 live in Iceland

population per sq km

≈ 30 people

Scandinavia | UK | USA

There has always been a divide between Scandinavia's liberal cities and its more conservative countryside, and the settlement of refugees in rural areas has brought global issues to remote doorsteps. For some, particularly older generations, the perception of overwhelming immigration – combined with the sharp decline of churchgoing in recent decades, and plus various technological developments – has led to worries about the loss of traditional values and culture.

Environment

Scandinavia is a model of sustainability, with high – 100% in the cases of Norway and Iceland – renewable electricity output, a firm and long-standing commitment to recycling, stringent environmental certifications and lots of investment in green technology. Firm government commitments have pledged to make most of the Nordic nations carbon neutral within a few years.

Nevertheless, Norway's oil industry is a major contribution to the world's fossil fuels, and dramatically changed weather patterns have already affected the region, with much milder winters and a corresponding decrease in snow cover. The rapid warming of the polar region – some scientists predict that ice-free summers at the North Pole may come as early as 2030 – will have a huge, potentially devastating effect on the Scandinavian ecosystem, impacting everything from fisheries to indigenous rights. Less snow and ice cover means that more heat is absorbed rather than reflected by the earth's surface, exacerbating the rapid warming; the consequent thawing of layers of permafrost will release yet more trapped carbon into the atmosphere. Reindeer herding in the north has already been severely affected.

As members of the Arctic Council (www.arctic-council.org), which strives to protect the northern environment, the Nordic countries are intimately engaged with trying to find solutions. However, questions about the management of resources under the ice cap in Russian and Canadian territories remain unanswered.

The European Union

If the European Union is a house party, then festivities have been badly soured by the economic crisis and immigration issue. Finns grumbled that they were paying for everyone else to have a good time, while Danes and Swedes wanted to tighten up their formerly liberal policies on those some perceived as gate-crashers. Then Britain left in a huff and those remaining have begun to feel that maybe the party isn't so bad after all – it's cold outside and there's a big bear lurking. Meanwhile, friendly neighbour Norway isn't a party person but now wonders if its standing invitation to share the food and beer might be re-evaluated after the commotion of Britain's exit. And Iceland? Still dithering by the doorbell, wondering if the party is worthwhile.

Viking drakkar (Dragon ship)

GORARIO8/SHUTTERSTOCK ©

History

From Vikings to social democrats, through wars, treaties and peace, Scandinavia has had an interesting ride. Innovation has been a constant theme, from longships ploughing furrows across the known world and beyond to wholesale religious change, from struggles for independence to postwar democracies that changed the idea of what it meant to be a citizen of a nation-state. The sparsely populated Nordic lands often punch well above their weight.

12,000–9000 BC	4000 BC	AD 793
In the wake of the receding glaciers of the last Ice Age, the reinhabiting of Scandinavia begins.	Agriculture begins in Denmark and southern Sweden.	The first recorded sacking of an English monastery marks the beginning of the Age of the Vikings.

Petäjävesi Vanha Kirkko (p143)

FEDERICA GENTILE/GETTY IMAGES ©

The Vikings

Our view of the Vikings is often heavily conditioned by accounts written by terrified monks of the plundering of their monasteries by fierce dragonship-borne warriors from across the sea. In fact, though the Norse sagas bear out the fact that they were partial to a bit of sacking and skull-crushing, the portrait of these fascinating Scandinavians is a more complex one.

Developing marvellous seafaring skills, the Vikings, whose era is normally considered to have begun in the late 8th century, became inveterate traders whose influence – and, sometimes, pillaging – eventually extended across much of Europe. Often voyaging on their own account or for local warlords rather than for any ruler, they explored, settled, fought, farmed and mixed with locals right across northern Europe, through the whole Mediterranean, well into modern-day Russia and across the Atlantic, establishing Iceland and reaching America.

As belief in Valhalla's free bar and the end-of-days vision of Ragnarök were superseded by heavenly harps and the Last Judgement, so the Vikings blended gradually into what came afterwards. The best example is the defeat of Harald Hardrada, king of Norway, in England in 1066.

850	**1000–1170**	**1397**
Norse settlers begin to take up residence in Iceland.	Christianity takes over the region, with Finland the last to be evangelised.	The Kalmar Union joins much of Scandinavia together under the direction of a common monarch.

The Secrets of Viking World Domination

The main god who provided strength to the Viking cause was Odin (Oðinn), the 'All-Father' who was married to Frigg. Together they gave birth to a son, Thor (Þór), the God of Thunder. The Vikings believed that if they died on the battlefield, the all-powerful Odin would take them to a paradise by the name of Valhalla, where Viking men could fight all day and then be served by beautiful women.

Not surprisingly, it was considered far better for a Viking to die on the battlefield than in bed of old age, and Vikings brought a reckless abandon to their battles that was extremely difficult for enemies to overcome – to die or to come away with loot, the Vikings seemed to say, was more or less the same. Equally unsurprising was the fact that the essential Viking values that emerged from their unique world view embodied strength, skill in weapons, heroic courage, personal sacrifice and a disregard for death.

But the Vikings were as much the sophisticates of the Middle Ages as they were its fearless warriors. Viking ships were revolutionary, fast, manoeuvrable vessels capable of withstanding torrid and often long ocean journeys. Longboats were over 30m long, had a solid keel, a flexible hull and large, square sails, and could travel up to 12 knots (22km/h); they enabled the Vikings to launch and maintain a conquest that would go largely unchallenged for 200 years.

It's often cited as the end of the Viking Age, yet victorious King Harold's forebears were Viking royalty, and the Norman conquerors who defeated *him* at Hastings shortly thereafter took their name from 'Norsemen' and were descended from Vikings who had settled in northwest France.

Danish & Swedish Dominance

For around 600 years from the early 13th to the early 19th centuries, Scandinavia was dominated by the kingdoms of Sweden and Denmark, who signed treaties, broke them, fought as allies and enemies, conquered territory across northern Europe and lost it again. Finland basically became a Swedish possession and was a frequent venue for Sweden's territorial squabbles with Novgorod (Russia), which ended up taking control of Finland after heavily defeating Sweden in 1809. Norway was a junior partner to Sweden, then Denmark, then Sweden again. Iceland fell under Danish control, with Danish merchants establishing a legal monopoly on Iceland's resources that lasted nearly 200 years.

During the second quarter of the 16th century, the Reformation swept through Scandinavia, and Lutheran Protestantism was adopted by royal decrees and force. Catholicism, which had taken over from the Norse gods some five centuries earlier, almost ceased to exist in the region.

By the end of the 19th century, independence movements in Finland, Norway and Iceland were strong, and by 1920 all three were autonomous. The Nordic nations as we know them today were in place.

1517–50	1905	1939–40
The Reformation sweeps across Scandinavia, establishing Lutheran Protestantism as the totally dominant religion.	Norway finally regains independence, followed by Finland (1917) and Iceland (1918, 1944).	Finland is invaded by the Soviet Union, and Denmark and Norway by Germany.

World War II

The Nordic nations all had a different experience of the Second World War. The first to be attacked was Finland, whose heroic but ultimately unsuccessful harsh winter struggle against Soviet invasion began in November 1939. A few months later, in April 1940, Germany occupied Denmark without a struggle and simultaneously invaded Norway, which finally succumbed after bitter fighting from Norwegian and other Allied troops.

Iceland, in a royal union with Denmark, remained free but army-less and soon accepted British, then American troops to prevent this strategically placed North Atlantic island from falling under German control. Meanwhile, Sweden had declared itself neutral and remained so – more or less – throughout the war.

Finland, forced to cede territory to the Soviets and ignored by the other Allies, now looked to Germany for help and soon was at war with Russia again as the Germans launched their doomed invasion. They reclaimed their lands but Russia bounced back in 1944. Finland had to cede more territory and then drive the Germans out. As the Wehrmacht retreated across northern Finland and Norway, they destroyed everything in their path, leaving large parts of Lapland devastated. When peace came, the Danes and Norwegians – whose resistance throughout the war had cost them many lives – celebrated the end of occupation with gusto, Sweden dusted itself down slightly sheepishly, Iceland grabbed full independence and the luckless Finns were left without a big chunk of territory and forced to pay reparations to the Allies.

The Social Democratic Years

After the war it was time to rebuild, and there was a chance for the Nordic countries to ask themselves what sort of country they wanted to construct. Governments across the region began laying the foundations for social democratic states in which high taxes and a socially responsible citizenry would be recompensed with lifelong medical care, free education, fair working conditions, excellent infrastructure, comfortable pensions and generous welfare payments for parents and the unemployed.

These nations became standard-bearers for equality and tolerance, and overall wealth increased rapidly, leaving the privations of the war years to memory. Women achieved significant representation at all levels of society, and forward-thinking in policy was much in evidence.

Though the political consensus for the social democratic model of government has waned in recent decades – taxes have fallen and some benefits have been sheared away – in general Scandinavians are still very well looked after by the state, and inequality here is low.

1989	**1995**	**2000**
Beer is legalised in Iceland.	Finland and Sweden join what is now the EU. Denmark had already joined in 1973.	The Øresund Bridge is completed, physically linking Sweden (and hence Norway and Finland) to Denmark and the rest of northern Europe.

Skuespilhuset, Copenhagen (p47)

Architecture

Scandinavia's architecture has always been an enduring part of the region's appeal, with Norway, Sweden and Denmark in particular leading the way. The story begins with traditional turf-roofed houses and stave churches in Norway, the round churches of Bornholm in Denmark, and gabled wooden structures across the region and progresses to urban style icons that give expression to Denmark and Sweden's passion for design.

Traditional Architecture

Norway

Timber and stone are the mainstays of traditional Norwegian architecture; nowhere is this more evident than in the former mining village of Røros, where many of the colourful timber houses date back to the 17th and 18th centuries. Bergen's waterfront Brygge district is one of the finest examples of maritime architecture in a region famous for the genre.

Tallinn, Estonia

The medieval jewel of Estonia, Tallinn's Old Town (*vanalinn*) is without a doubt the country's most fascinating locality. Picking your way along the narrow, cobbled streets is like strolling into the 15th century. You'll pass the ornate stone facades of Hanseatic merchants' houses, wander into hidden medieval courtyards, and find footworn stone stairways leading to sweeping views of the red-roofed city. It's staggeringly popular with tourists, but manages to remain largely unspoilt: while most historic buildings have helpful bilingual plaques, pleasingly few have been turned into pizza restaurants.

Contemporary Architecture

Stave Churches

Seemingly conceived by a whimsical child-like imagination, the stave church is an ingenious adaptation to Norway's unique local conditions. Originally dating from the late Viking era, these ornately worked houses of worship are among the oldest surviving wooden buildings on earth, albeit heavily restored. Named for their vertical supporting posts, these churches are also distinguished by detailed carved designs and dragon-headed gables resembling the prows of classic Viking ships. Of the 500 to 600 that were originally built, only about 20 of the 28 that remain retain many of their original components.

Denmark

Functional, humanistic, organic and sympathetic are all adjectives that might be used to describe the defining features of classic postwar Danish architecture, best embodied in the work of architects such as Jørn Utzon and Arne Jacobsen. Their usually restrained take on modernism has been superseded since the 1990s, often by a much bolder, brasher, even aggressive type of building.

Here is a handful of Copenhagen's most iconic modern buildings:

Radisson Blu Royal Hotel (Arne Jacobsen) Not content with merely creating a building, Jacobsen designed every item in the hotel, down to the door handles, cutlery and the famous Egg and Swan chairs. Room 606 remains entirely as it was on opening day in 1960.

The Black Diamond (Schmidt, Hammer & Lassen) Completed in 1999, Copenhagen's monolithic library extension offers sharp contrast to the original red-brick building. While the latter sits firmly and sombrely, the black granite extension floats on a ribbon of raised glass, leaning towards the harbour as if wanting to detach and jump in.

Operaen (Henning Larsen) While its squat exterior has drawn comparisons to a toaster, the maple-wood and Sicilian marble interior is a triumph.

Royal Danish Playhouse (Lundgaard & Tranberg) Completed in 2008 and facing Operaen, the award-winning Skuespilhuset is dark, subdued and elegant. Its glasshouse design includes a projected upper floor of coloured glass, a playful contrast to the building's muted-grey, English clay bricks.

Den Blå Planet (3XN) Denmark's National Aquarium made quite a splash with its spiral, whirlpool-inspired design. Hitting the scene in 2013, its gleaming silver facade is clad in shingles – diamond-shaped aluminium plates designed to adapt to the building's organic form.

Norway

Due to the need to rebuild quickly after WWII, Norway's architecture was primarily governed by functionalist necessity (the style is often called *funkis* in the local vernacular)

Northern Lights Cathedral, Alta, Norway

rather than any coherent sense of style. Nowhere is this exemplified more than in the 1950, red-brick **Oslo Rådhus** (Fridtjof Nansens plass; ⊘9am-6pm, guided tours 10am, noon & 2pm Jun–mid-Jul; 🚇Kontraskjæret) **FREE**. As the style evolved, functionality was wedded to other concerns, such as recognising the importance of aesthetics in urban renewal (for example in Oslo's Grünerløkka district), and ensured that the country's contemporary architectural forms once again sat in harmony with Norway's environment and history.

Tromsø's Arctic Cathedral (p160), designed by Jan Inge Hovig in 1964, mimics Norway's glacial crevasses and auroral curtains. Another beautiful example is the Sami Parliament (p162) in Karasjok, where Arctic building materials (birch, pine and oak) lend the place a sturdy authenticity, while the use of lights to replicate the Arctic night sky and the structure's resemblance to a Sami *lavvu* are extraordinary. Alta's **Northern Lights Cathedral** (http://nordlyskatedral.autoweb.no/index.jsp; Løkkeveien; adult/child 50/25kr, incl Borealis Alta show 150/75kr; ⊘11am-9pm Mon-Sat & 4-9pm Sun mid-Jun–mid-Aug, 11am-3pm Mon-Sat rest of year) is weird and wonderful, and the creative interpretation of historical Norwegian shapes also finds expression at the **Viking Ship Sports Arena** (Vikingskipet; ☎62 51 75 00; www.hoa.no; Åkersvikaveien 1; 50kr; ⊘9am-8pm Mon-Fri, 9.30am-5pm Sat & Sun 1-17 Aug, 9am-3pm Mon-Fri mid-Oct–Mar, closed rest of year) in Hamar, while Oslo's landmark new opera house (p203) powerfully evokes a fjord-side glacier.

Sweden

The post-industrial city of Malmö has become a hotspot of design and innovation. The old docks northwest of Gamla Staden (Old Town) were converted into ecologically focused housing for the new century. Its landmark Turning Torso (2005) – a twisting residential tower designed by Catalan architect Santiago Calatrava – is an arresting sight dominating the skyline.

Close by is the Öresund bridge (Georg KS Rotne; 2000) connecting the metropolitan areas of Malmö and Copenhagen. After it reaches the end of the bridge section, the road and rail lines literally disappear into the water.

Within Stockholm, contemporary design and culture found a robust home in 1974 in Kulturhuset, a large modernist pavilion holding a wide range of cultural activities. Designed by Peter Celsing, it's like a big set of drawers offering their wares onto the large plaza outside, Sergels Torg; the *torg* (town square) is the modern heart of Stockholm, and standing at its centre is *Kristallvertikalaccent* (Crystal Vertical Accent), a wonderful, luminescent monument to modernity and glassmaking traditions. Designed by sculptor Edvin Öhrström, it was the result of a 1962 competition.

More recently, the planned suburb Hammarby Sjöstad, just south of Stockholm's centre, has taken shape as a sustainably built, ecoconscious neighbourhood. Its approach to mindful integration of infrastructure, transportation, public spaces and energy conservation has been widely influential in urban planning.

Tore Bruvoll playing at Traenafestival, Norway

MELANIE LEMAHIEU/SHUTTERSTOCK ©

Music

Despite their relatively low populations, the Nordic nations' influence on global music has been extraordinary. Scandinavia is a bastion of quality classical music and folk traditions; pop acts ABBA, A-ha and Björk have sold tens of millions of albums internationally; and the region's contribution to the metal scene is legendary. There's an excellent range of music festivals, with everything from chamber music to cutting-edge electronica.

Classical & Traditional

Grieg and Sibelius are the big names in Nordic classical music, and both helped – by their music and by their enthusiastic collaboration with other artists and writers – create a romantic nationalism that was an important factor driving eventual Norwegian and Finnish independence. Across the region, classical music is loved and cared for, with state-of-the-art concert halls, festivals and musical education. Finland, in particular, produces an astonishing number of top-grade classical performers and conductors.

Traditional music includes a range of folk styles. Particularly noteworthy are the Icelandic *rímur*, chants from the sagas that have preserved an ancient form of oral storytelling, and Norwegian folk, which incorporates the distinctive Hardanger fiddle.

The Sami of Lapland use a traditional form called the *yoik* (joik). Part chant, part poem, part song, it is an a cappella invocation or description of a person or place that has huge significance in Sami culture. In recent years, Sami artists have incorporated *yoiking* into various styles of modern music with great success. Artists to look out for include Wimme, Mari Boine and Ulla Pirttijärvi.

Norwegian Folk Music

Folk music is a central pillar of Norwegian music, and the Hardanger fiddle – which derives its distinctive sound from four or five sympathetic strings stretched out beneath the usual four strings – is one of Europe's best-loved folk instruments.

Some of the hottest folk acts include Tore Bruvoll and Jon Anders Halvorsen, who perform traditional Telemark songs *(Nattsang);* the live Norwegian performances of Bukkene Bruse (heavy on the Hardanger fiddle; *Spel*); Rusk's impressively wide repertoire of music from southeastern Norway *(Rusk);* Sigrid Moldestad and Liv Merete Kroken, who bring classical training to bear on the traditional fiddle *(Spindel);* and Sinikka Langeland, whose *Runoja* draws on ancient runic music. In 2009 Alexander Rybak, a Norwegian composer, fiddler and pianist of Belorussian descent, won the Eurovision Song Contest.

Traditional Icelandic Music

Until rock and roll arrived in the 20th century, Iceland was a land practically devoid of musical instruments. The Vikings brought the *fiðla* and the *langspil* with them – both a kind of two-stringed box rested on the player's knee and played with a bow. They were never solo instruments but merely served to accompany singers.

Instruments were generally an unheard-of luxury, and singing was the sole form of music. The most famous song styles are *rímur* (poetry or stories from the sagas performed in a low, eerie chant; Sigur Rós have dabbled with the form), and *fimmundasöngur* (sung by two people in harmony). Cut off from other influences, the Icelandic singing style barely changed from the 14th century to the 20th century; it also managed to retain harmonies that were banned by the church across the rest of Europe on the basis of being the work of the devil.

You'll find choirs around Iceland performing traditional music, and various compilation albums, such as *Inspired by Harpa – The Traditional Songs of Iceland* (2013), give a sampling of Icelandic folk songs or *rímur*.

Sami Music

Several Finnish Sami groups and artists have created excellent modern music with the traditional *yoik* (chant; also *joiks* or *juoiggus*) form. The *yoik* is traditionally sung a capella, often invoking a person or place with immense spiritual importance in Sami culture. Wimme is a big name in this sphere, and Angelit produce popular, dance-floor-style Sami music. One of their former members, Ulla Pirttijärvi, releases particularly haunting solo albums, while Vilddas are on the trancey side of Sami music, combining it with other influences. Look out too for rockier offerings from SomBy and Tiina Sanila, Sami hip-hop artist Ailu Valle and electro-acoustic compositions from Niko Valkeapää.

In Norway, recent Sami artists such as Ingor Ánte Áilu Gaup, Sofia Jannock, Mari Boine and Nils Aslak Valkeapää have performed, recorded and popularised traditional and modern versions of the *yoik*. Boine in particular has enjoyed international air-time and her distinctive sound blends folk-rock with *joik* roots.

Classical Estonia

On the international stage, the area in which Estonia has had the greatest artistic impact is classical music. Estonia's most celebrated composer is Arvo Pärt (b 1935), the intense and reclusive master of hauntingly austere music many have misleadingly termed minimalist. Pärt emigrated to Germany during Soviet rule and his *Miserere Litany, Te Deum* and *Tabula Rasa* are among an internationally acclaimed body of work characterised by dramatic bleakness, piercing majesty and nuanced silence. He's now the world's most performed living classical-music composer.

The main Estonian composers of the 20th century remain popular today. Rudolf Tobias (1873–1918) wrote influential symphonic, choral and concerto works as well as fantasies on folk song melodies. Mart Saar (1882–1963) studied under Rimsky-Korsakov in St Petersburg but his music shows none of this influence. His songs and piano suites were among the most performed pieces of music in between-war concerts in Estonia. Eduard Tubin (1905–82) is another great Estonian composer whose body of work includes 10 symphonies. Contemporary composer Erkki-Sven Tüür (b 1959) takes inspiration from nature and the elements as experienced on his native Hiiumaa.

Estonian conductors Tõnu Kaljuste (who won a Grammy in 2014 for a Pärt recording), Anu Tali and Paavo Järvi are hot tickets at concert halls around the world.

Pop & Beyond

Bursting onto the scene in the 1970s, ABBA brought Swedish music bang into the international spotlight. Their phenomenal global success paved the way for spiritual followers like Roxette and Aqua and set the trend for Scandinavian artists to sing in English. Singing about love, dancing and normal suburban life, ABBA won the hearts of a generation and beyond.

With the path to stardom from Scandinavia now an easier one, the region has cranked out pop and rock success story after success story in the decades since. A-ha, Europe, Ace of Base, the Cardigans, the Rasmus, the Hives, Robyn and Mando Diao have made it big worldwide. Björk, who almost deserves a musical category to herself, brought lonely Iceland into the picture and has been followed by bands like Sigur Rós and Of Monsters and Men.

Jazz is strong across the region, particularly in Norway and Denmark, with a thriving local scene backed by international festivals. Electronica has also been a strong suit, with '90s dancefloor legends like Darude backed by more recent arrivals such as Avicii, Eric Prydz, Kygo and Galantis. Reykjavík, in particular, has a brilliant scene. Hip hop has also gained traction across the region, especially in Finland and Iceland.

The Heavy Stuff

Though its influence isn't quite what it once was, with many millennials preferring Norwegian electronica or Finnish hip hop, Scandinavian bands have been immensely influential in the harder rock and metal scenes, with several metal subgenres basically invented here.

Norway started the trend in the 1980s, with a thriving black metal scene and outrageous antics. It has continued to produce quality bands, with famous names on the black and death metal side of things including Emperor, Burzum, Mayhem, Darkthrone and Dimmu Borgir.

Finnish metal bands have achieved notable international success, with HIM's 'love metal' and Nightwish's gloriously symphonic variety the most prominent. The 69 Eyes, Apocalyptica (who are classically trained cellists), Children of Bodom and Finntroll all represent different genres. Lordi memorably brought the scene to Eurovision, winning in 2006 with Hard Rock Hallelujah.

Sweden has produced legends like Bathory, who moved from hard black metal to a more melodic style based on Viking mythology, Sabaton, HammerFall, Dark Tranquillity and Therion. Denmark has a thriving scene but its bands haven't, in the main, had quite the same international profile. They can, however, claim Lars Ulrich, the Metallica drummer. The Faroes chip in with Týr's Viking metal, and Iceland's most famous metallists are Sólstafir.

Arctic fox, Norway

ONDREJ PROSICKY/SHUTTERSTOCK ©

Nature

The real soul of Scandinavia resides in its glorious natural landscapes. Some of Europe's wildest places are here. From soaring fjord walls in Norway to Iceland's volcanic brutality, from autumn's forest palette to charming Baltic islands, from sparkling summer lakes to Arctic snowscapes, there's a feast of distinct beauty spots, populated by a range of intriguing creatures.

Landscapes

Scandinavia's diverse scenery encompasses gentle pastoral landscapes in the south to untamed canvases wrought by nature's forces in the north. Wild, rugged coasts and mountains, hundreds of kilometres of forest broken only by lakes and the odd cottage, and unspoilt Baltic archipelagos make up a varied menu of uplifting visual treats.

Flat Denmark in the south doesn't have the mountainous magnificence of Norway or the volcanoes of Iceland but has a charming coastal landscape across its hundreds of islands. Offshore Bornholm, and the Baltic archipelagos of Sweden and Finland present a fascinating patchwork where charmingly rural farms alternate with low rock polished smooth by the glaciers of the last Ice Age.

Norway's phenomenal coastline is famous for a reason; the fjords here take your breath away, while the northern mountains are heart-achingly beautiful. Inland, much of mainland Scandinavia is taken up with forests. The region has some of the world's highest tree cover, and the woods – largely managed for forestry, some wild – stretch for hundreds of kilometres. Mainly composed of spruce, pine and birch, these forests are responsible for the crisp, clean, aromatic northern air and are dotted with lakes.

Iceland, thrown up in the middle of the Atlantic by violent geothermal activity, offers a very distinct landscape, with bleak and epic scenery that is at once harsh and gloriously uplifting. The juxtaposition of frozen glaciers and boiling geysers make it a wild scenic ride.

Iceland's Volcanoes

Thin crust and grating plates are responsible for a host of exciting volcanic situations in Iceland. The volcanoes are many and varied – some are active, some extinct, and some are dormant and dreaming, no doubt, of future destruction. Fissure eruptions and their associated craters are probably the most common type of eruption in Iceland. The still-volatile Lakagígar crater row around Mt Laki mountain is the country's most extreme example. It produced the largest lava flow in human history in the 18th century, covering an area of 565 sq km to a depth of 12m.

Several of Iceland's liveliest volcanoes are found beneath glaciers, which makes for dramatic eruptions as molten lava and ice interact. The main 2010 Eyjafjallajökull eruption was of this type: it caused a *jökulhlaup* (flooding caused by volcanic eruption beneath an ice cap) that damaged part of the Ring Road, before throwing up the famous ash plume that grounded Europe's aeroplanes. Iceland's most active volcano, Grímsvötn, which lies beneath the Vatnajökull ice cap, behaved in a similar fashion in 2011.

Recent eruptions in Iceland have tended to be fairly harmless – they're often called 'tourist eruptions' because their fountains of magma, electric storms and dramatic ash clouds make perfect photos but cause relatively little damage. This is partly due to the sparsely populated land, and partly because devastating features such as fast-flowing lava, lahars (mudslides) and pyroclastic surges (like the ones that obliterated Pompeii and Herculaneum) are usually absent in this part of the world. As of 2016, the volcanoes to watch are Katla and Hekla, both well overdue for eruption.

Norway's Fjords

Norway's signature landscape, the fjords rank among the most astonishing natural landforms anywhere in the world. The Norwegian coast is cut deeply with these inlets distinguished by plunging cliffs, isolated farms high on forested ledges and an abundance of ice-blue water extending deep into the Norwegian interior.

Norway's fjords are a relatively recent phenomenon in geological terms. Although Norwegian geological history stretches back 1.8 billion years, the fjords were not carved out until much later. During the glacial periods over this time, the elevated highland plateaus that ranged across central Norway subsided at least 700m due to an ice sheet up to 2km thick. The movement of this ice, driven by gravity down former river courses, gouged out the fjords and valleys and created the surrounding mountains by sharpening peaks and exposing high cliffs of bare rock. The fjords took on their present form when sea levels rose as the climate warmed following the last Ice Age (which ended around 10,000 years ago), flooding into the new valleys left behind by melting and retreating glaciers. Sea levels are thought to have risen by as much as 100m, creating fjords whose waters can seem impossibly deep.

In 2005 Unesco inscribed Geirangerfjord and Nærøyfjord on its World Heritage List because they 'are classic, superbly developed fjords', which are 'among the most scenically outstanding fjord areas on the planet'.

Wildlife

Vast tracts of barely populated land away from the bustle of central Europe make Scandinavia an important refuge for numerous species, including several high-profile carnivores, myriad seabirds and lovable marine mammals.

Estonia

Estonia has 64 recorded species of land mammals, and some animals that have disappeared elsewhere have survived within the country's extensive forests. The brown bear faced extinction at the turn of the 20th century but today there are more than 600 in Estonia. The European beaver, which was also hunted to near extinction, was successfully reintroduced in the 1950s, and today the population is around 20,000.

While roe deer and wild boar are present in their tens of thousands, numbers are dwindling, which some chalk up to predators – though these animals are hunted and appear on the menu in more expensive restaurants (along with elk and bear). Estonia still has grey wolves (thought to number around 135) and lynx (more than 750), handsome furry cats with large, impressive feet that act as snowshoes. Lynx, bears, wolves and beavers are just some of the animals that are hunted each year, although a system of quotas aims to keep numbers stable.

Estonia also has abundant birdlife, with 363 recorded species. Owing to the harsh winters, most birds here are migratory. Although it's found throughout much of the world, the barn swallow has an almost regal status in Estonia and is the 'national bird'; it reappears from its winter retreat in April or May. Another bird with pride of place in Estonia is the stork. While their numbers are declining elsewhere in Europe, white storks are on the increase – you'll often see them perched on the top of lamp posts in large round nests. Black storks, on the other hand, are in decline.

Iceland

Apart from birds, sheep and horses, you'll be lucky to have any casual sightings of animals in Iceland. The only indigenous land mammal is the elusive Arctic fox, best spotted in remote Hornstrandir in the Westfjords – wildlife enthusiasts can apply in advance to monitor these creatures while volunteering at the Arctic Fox Center (www.arcticfoxcenter. com). In East Iceland, herds of reindeer can sometimes be spotted from the road. Reindeer were introduced from Norway in the 18th century and now roam the mountains in the east. Polar bears very occasionally drift across from Greenland on ice floes, but armed farmers make sure they don't last long.

In contrast, Iceland has a rich marine life, particularly whales. On whale-watching tours from Húsavík in northern Iceland, you'll have an excellent chance of seeing cetaceans, particularly dolphins, porpoises, minke whales and humpback whales. Sperm, fin, sei, pilot, orca and blue whales also swim in Icelandic waters and have been seen by visitors. Seals can be seen in the Eastfjords, on the Vatnsnes Peninsula in Northwest Iceland, in the Mýrar region on the southeast coast (including at Jökulsárlón), in Breiðafjörður in the west, and in the Westfjords.

Norway

Norway is home to some of Europe's most charismatic fauna, and tracking them down can be a highlight of your trip. While Norway's unique settlement pattern spreads the human population thinly and limits wildlife habitat, the country more than compensates with its variety of iconic northern European species including musk oxen, reindeer, Arctic fox and elk on the mainland and polar bears and walruses on Svalbard. And offshore, whales have survived the best efforts of hunters to drive them to extinction.

Sweden

Sweden's big carnivores – the bear, wolf, wolverine, lynx and golden eagle – are all protected species. Wolf hunting was banned in the 1970s, after the wolf population had been driven nearly to extinction, but in 2010 the Swedish parliament authorised a cull to bring the newly resurgent species' numbers back down. Most of the country's wolf population is in Dalarna and Värmland.

The wolverine, a larger cousin of the weasel, inhabits high forests and alpine areas along the Norwegian border. There are an estimated 680 in Sweden, mostly in Norrbotten and Västerbotten.

Brown bears were persecuted for centuries, but recent conservation measures have seen numbers increase to about 3200. Bears mostly live in forests in the northern half of the country but are spreading south.

Norway's Wild Reindeer

Wild *reinsdyr* (reindeer) exist in large herds across central Norway, usually above the treeline and sometimes as high up as 2000m. The prime viewing areas are on the Hardangervidda Plateau, where you'll find Europe's largest herd (around 7000). Sightings are also possible in most national parks of central Norway, as well as the inland areas of Trøndelag.

The reindeer of Finnmark in Norway's far north are domestic and owned by the Sami, who drive them to the coast at the start of summer, then back to the interior in winter.

Another fascinating forest dweller is the lynx, which belongs to the panther family and is Europe's only large cat. Sweden's 1200 to 1500 lynx are notoriously difficult to spot because of their nocturnal habits.

Not all of Sweden's wild creatures are predatory, of course. The iconic elk is a gentle, knob-by-kneed creature that grows up to 2m tall. Though they won't try to eat you, elk are a serious traffic hazard, particularly at night: they can dart out in front of your car at up to 50km/h.

Around 260,000 domesticated reindeer roam the northern areas under the watchful eyes of Sami herders. Like elk, reindeer can be a major traffic hazard.

Lemmings are famous for their extraordinary reproductive capacity. Every 10 years or so the population explodes, resulting in denuded landscapes and thousands of dead lemmings in rivers and lakes and on roads.

National Parks

It is an indication of how the Nordic nations value their natural environments that the region has well over a hundred national parks, conserving everything from jewel-like Baltic archipelagos to glaciers and snowy wastes. As well as being crucial drivers of conservation, many of these parks also offer the best chance to appreciate Scandinavia's deep nature.

Some of Europe's best hiking can be done on the short- and long-distance trails in the national parks of Finland, Sweden, Norway and Iceland. These trails offer excellent facilities, including reliable waymarking, well-maintained campsites with firewood and shared cabins where you can sleep. Rules are strict so that the impact from visitors is minimised.

Standout parks for trekking include **Jotunheimen** (www.jotunheimen.com; 17km SW of Lom), **Jostedalsbreen** (Jostedalsbreen Nasjonalparksenter; www.jostedalsbre.no; Oppstryn; adult/child 80/40kr; ⊘10am-4pm or 6pm May–mid-Sep), **Hardangervidda** (⊘53 67 40 00; www.hardangerviddanatursenter. no; Øvre Eidfjord; adult/child 130/65kr; ⊘9am-7pm mid-Jun–mid-Aug, 10am-6pm Apr–mid-Jun & mid-Aug–Oct) and Rondane in Norway; Abisko, **Padjelanta** (Badjelánnda National Park), Skuleskogen, **Sarek** in Sweden; Urho Kekkonen in Finland, Pallas-Yllästunturi, **Oulanka** (Oulangan; www.nationalparks. fi) and Lemmenjoki in Finland; **Snæfellsjökull** and Vatnajökull in Iceland (the wonderful hiking around Þórsmörk is perhaps soon to be national-park covered); and **Mols Bjerge** (http://eng. nationalparkmolsbjerge.dk) in Denmark.

Geirangerfjord, Norwa (p220)y

ANDREY ARMYAGOV/SHUTTERSTOCK ©

Survival Guide

Directory A–Z

Accommodation

Scandinavia has a wide range of accommodation, from hostels to boutique hotels and self-catering cottages. Booking ahead in summer is a good idea and is essential year-round in Iceland, where the tourist boom has squeezed accommodation availability.

Hotels Generally bland, chain options. Outside major cities, you can often get discount rates in summer and on weekends.

Camping Grounds Very popular. Most have good-value cabins.

Hostels Great network in Sweden and good options in other countries.

Self-catering From urban apartments to wilderness cottages, this is an excellent option across the region.

B&Bs, Guesthouses & Hotels

● B&Bs, where you get a room and breakfast in a private home, can often be real bargains. Pensions and guesthouses are similar but usually slightly more upmarket.

● Most Scandinavian hotels are geared to business travellers and have prices to match. But excellent hotel discounts are often available at certain times (eg at weekends and in summer in Finland, Norway and Sweden) and for longer stays. Breakfast in hotels is usually included in the price of the room.

● If you think a hotel is too expensive, ask if it has a cheaper room. In non-chain places it can be easy to negotiate a discount in quiet periods.

Camping

● Camping is immensely popular throughout the region. The Camping Key Europe card (www.campingkey.com) offers good benefits and discounts.

● Camping grounds tend to charge per site, with a small extra charge per person. Tent sites are often cheaper than van sites.

● National tourist offices have booklets or brochures listing camping grounds all over their country.

● In most larger towns and cities, camping grounds are some distance from the centre. If you've got no transport, the money you save by camping can quickly be outweighed by the money spent commuting in and out of town.

● Nearly all mainland Scandinavian camping grounds rent simple cabins – a great budget option if you're not carrying a tent. Many also have more upmarket cottages with bedrooms, bathrooms and proper kitchens, perfect for families who want to self-cater.

● Camping other than in designated camping grounds is not always straightforward but in many countries there's a right of common access that applies. Tourist offices usually stock official publications in English explaining your rights and responsibilities.

Hostels

Hostels generally offer the cheapest roof over your head. In Scandinavia hostels are geared for budget travellers of all ages, including families, and most have dorms and private rooms.

Most hostels are part of national Youth Hostel Associations (YHA), known collectively throughout the world as Hostelling International (www.hihostels.com).

You'll have to be a YHA or HI member to use some affiliated hostels (indicated

Book Your Stay Online

For more accommodation reviews by Lonely Planet authors, check out http://hotels.lonelyplanet.com. You'll find independent reviews, as well as recommendations on the best places to stay. Best of all, you can book online.

by a blue triangle symbol) but most are open to anyone. Members get substantial discounts; it's worth joining, which you can do at any hostel, via your local hostelling organisation or online. There's a particularly huge network of HI hostels in Denmark and Sweden.

Comfort levels and facilities vary markedly. Some hostels charge extra if you don't want to sweep your room out when you leave.

Breakfast Many hostels (exceptions include most hostels in Iceland) serve breakfast, and almost all have communal kitchens where you can prepare meals.

Bookings Some hostels accept reservations by phone; they'll often book the next hostel you're headed to for a small fee. The HI website has a booking form you can use to reserve a bed in advance – but not all hostels are on the network. Popular hostels in capital cities can be heavily booked in summer, and limits may be placed on how many nights you can stay.

Linen You must use a sleep-sheet (ie a cotton or silk sleeping bag) or linen in hostels in most Scandinavian countries; regular sleeping bags are not permitted. It's worth carrying your own sleep-sheet or linen, as hiring these at hostels is comparatively expensive.

Travellers with disabilities Specially adapted rooms for visitors with disabilities are common, but check with the hostel first.

Self-Catering

○ There's a huge network (especially in Norway, Sweden, Denmark and Finland) of rental cottages that make excellent, peaceful places to stay and offer a chance to experience a traditional aspect of Scandinavian life.

○ Many Scandinavians traditionally spend their summers in such places. Renting a cottage for a few days as part of a visit to the region is highly recommended.

Customs Regulations

From non-EU to EU countries For EU countries (ie Denmark, Sweden, Finland and Estonia), travellers arriving from outside the EU can bring duty-free goods up to the value of €430 without declaration. You can also bring in up to 16L of beer, 4L of wine, 2L of liquors not exceeding 22% vol or 1L of spirits, 200 cigarettes or 250g of tobacco.

Within the EU If you're coming from another EU country, there is no restriction on the value of purchases for your own use.

Åland islands Arriving on or from the Åland islands (although technically part of the EU) carries the same import restrictions as arriving from a non-EU country.

Other Nordic countries Norway, Iceland and the Faroe Islands have lower limits.

Discount Cards

Seniors Cards Discounts for retirees, pensioners and those over 60 (sometimes slightly younger for women; over 65 in Sweden) at museums and other sights, public swimming pools, spas and with transport companies. Make sure you carry proof of age around with you.

Student Cards If you are studying in Scandinavia, a local student card will get you megadiscounts on transport and more.

Camping Key Europe (www.campingkeyeurope.com) Discounts at many camping grounds and attractions, with built-in third-party insurance. In Denmark and at some Swedish camping grounds, it's obligatory to have this or a similar card. Order through regional camping websites, or buy from camping grounds throughout the region (this is sometimes cheaper). It costs around €16 depending on where you get it.

Camping Card International (www.campingcardinternational.com) Widely accepted in the region, this camping card can be obtained from your local camping association or club.

European Youth Card (www.eyca.org) If you're under 30, you can pick up this card in almost any European country (some specify a maximum age of 26 though). It offers significant discounts on a wide range of things throughout the region. It's available for a small charge to anyone, not just European residents, through student unions, hostelling organisations or youth-oriented travel agencies.

Hostelling International (www.hihostels.com) The HI membership card gives significant discounts on accommodation, as well as some transport and attractions.

International Student Identity Card (www.isic.org) Discounts on many forms of transport, reduced or free admission to museums and sights, and numerous other offers – a worthwhile way of cutting costs. Check the website for a list of discounts by country. Because of the proliferation of fakes, carry your home student ID as back up. The same organisation also issues an International Youth Travel Card for under-30s, and the International Teacher Identity Card.

Oslo Pass (www.visitoslo.com/en/activities-and-attractions/oslo-pass; 1/2/3days adult 395/595/745kr, child 210/295/370kr), sold at the tourist office, is a good way of cutting transport and ticket costs around the city. The majority of the city's museums are free with the pass, as is public transport within the city limits (barring late-night buses). Other perks include restaurant and tour discounts. If you're planning to visit just the city-centre museums and galleries, it's worth checking which on your list are free before buying a pass.

Electricity

Type C
220V/50Hz

Type F
230V/50Hz

Etiquette

Greetings Shake hands with men, women and children when meeting them for the first time.

Shoes Take them off when entering someone's home.

Saunas Naked is normally the way to go.

Gifts Bring flowers, pastries, wine or chocolate when invited to someone's house.

LGBT Travellers

Denmark, Finland, Iceland, Norway and Sweden are very tolerant nations, although public displays of affection are less common in rural areas, particularly Lapland.

Health

Travel in Scandinavia presents very few health problems. The level of hygiene is high and there are no endemic diseases.

The extreme winter climate poses a risk; you must be aware of hypothermia and frostbite. In summer, biting insects, such as mosquitoes, are more of an annoyance than a real health risk. Always dress warmly when temperatures are low, and heed weather local warnings.

Before You Go

Health Insurance

Citizens of the European Economic Area (EEA) are covered for emergency medical treatment in other EEA countries (including Denmark, Finland, Iceland, Norway and Sweden) on presentation of a European Health Insurance Card (EHIC), though they may be liable to pay a daily or per-appointment fee as a local would. Enquire about EHICs at your health centre, travel agency or (in some countries) post office well in advance of travel.

Citizens from countries outside the EEA should find out if there is a reciprocal arrangement for free medical care between their country and the country visited. If not, travel health insurance is recommended.

Availability & Cost of Health Care

The standard of health care is extremely high and English is widely spoken by doctors and medical-clinic staff. Even if you are covered for health care here, you may be required to pay a per-visit fee as a local would. This is likely to be around €30 to €100 for a doctor or hospital visit.

Internet Access

● Wireless (wi-fi) hotspots are rife. Numerous cafes and bars, and nearly all hostels and hotels offer the service for free. A number of towns and cities in the region have free public wi-fi across the centre.

● Data is cheap. Buy a local SIM card, pop it in an unlocked phone, laptop or USB modem, and away you go. Deals may mean you pay as little as €15 to €20 for a month's unlimited access.

● Internet cafes are increasingly uncommon, but libraries provide free or very cheap internet service.

Money

ATMs Widespread, even in small places. This is the best way to access cash in Scandinavia. Find out what your home bank will charge you per withdrawal before you go as you may be better off taking out larger sums.

Cash cards Much like debit or credit cards but are loaded with a set amount of money. They also have the advantage of lower withdrawal fees than your bank might otherwise charge you.

Changing money All Scandinavian currencies are fully convertible.

Charge cards These include cards like American Express and Diners Club. Less widely accepted than credit cards because they charge merchants high commissions.

Debit and credit cards Scandinavians love using plastic, even for small transactions, and you'll find that debit and credit cards are the way to go here.

Foreign currencies Easily exchanged, with rates usually

Government Travel Advice

The following government websites offer travel advisories and information for travellers.

Australian Department of Foreign Affairs & Trade (www.smartraveller.gov.au)

Canadian Department of Foreign Affairs & International Trade (www.voyage.gc.ca)

French Ministère des Affaires Étrangères et Européennes (www.diplomatie.gouv.fr/fr/conseils-aux-voyageurs)

Italian Ministero degli Affari Esteri (www.viaggiaresicuri.mae.aci.it)

New Zealand Ministry of Foreign Affairs & Trade (www.safetravel.govt.nz)

UK Foreign & Commonwealth Office (www.gov.uk/foreign-travel-advice)

US Department of State (www.travel.state.gov)

Exchange Rates

		Denmark (DKK)	Finland (€)	Iceland (ISK)	Norway (NOK)	Sweden (SEK)
Australia	A$1	4.99	0.67	85.10	6.28	6.37
Canada	C$1	5.11	0.69	87.19	6.44	6.53
Eurozone	€1	7.45	–	126.98	6.37	6.51
Japan	¥100	5.63	0.76	95.94	7.08	7.19
New Zealand	NZ$1	4.55	0.61	77.53	5.72	5.81
UK	£1	8.47	1.14	144.46	10.67	10.82
US	US$1	6.24	0.84	106.30	7.85	7.96

For current exchange rates, see www.xe.com.

slightly better at exchange offices rather than banks. Avoid exchanging at airports if possible; you'll get better rates downtown. Always ask about the rate and commission before handing over your cash.

Tax A value-added tax (VAT) applies to most goods and services throughout Scandinavia. International visitors from outside the European Economic Area can claim back the VAT above a set minimum amount on purchases that are being taken out of the country. The procedure for making the claim is usually pretty straightforward.

Travellers cheques Rapidly disappearing but still accepted in big hotels and exchange offices.

Tipping

Tipping isn't very usual or required in Scandinavia. Rounding up a bill or cab fare is about as far as most locals go. Tips will be gratefully received, however.

Safe Travel

Scandinavia is a very safe place to travel, with very low crime rates.

○ Extreme winter temperatures must be taken seriously: wear proper protective clothing when outdoors.

○ In northern Scandinavia, biting insects can be a major annoyance in summer.

Telephone

To call abroad dial 🖉00 (the IAC, or international access code from Scandinavia), the country code (CC) for the country you are calling, the local area code (usually dropping the leading zero if there is one) and then the number.

Emergencies The emergency number is the same throughout Scandinavia: 🖉112.

Internet Calling via the internet is a practical and cheap solution for making international calls, whether from a laptop, tablet or smartphone.

Mobile phones Bring a mobile that's not tied to a specific network (unlocked) and buy local SIM cards.

Phone boxes Almost nonexistent in most of Scandinavia.

Phonecards Easily bought for cheaper international calls.

Reverse-charge (collect) calls Usually possible, and communicating with the local operator in English should not be much of a problem.

Roaming Roaming charges for EU phones within the EU have been abolished and are low for other European Economic Area (EEA) countries.

Mobile Phones

○ Local SIM cards are cheap and widely available. You need an unlocked phone.

○ Data packages are cheap and easy.

○ Normal tariff for EU SIM cards in EU countries.

○ Otherwise roaming rates.

Telephone Codes

Country	Country Code (CC)
Denmark	45
Finland	358
Iceland	354
Norway	47
Sweden	46
Estonia (Tallinn)	372

All countries use 00 as an International Access Code (IAC). Use the country code to call into that country. Use the international access code to call abroad from that country.

Time

Scandinavia sprawls across several time zones. The 24-hour clock is widely used. Note that Europe and the US move clocks forward and back at slightly different times. The following table is a seasonal guide only.

City	Time in Winter	Time in Summer
New York	11am (UTC -5)	noon (UTC -4)
Reykjavík	4pm (UTC)	4pm (UTC; no summer time)
London	4pm (UTC)	5pm (UTC +1)
Oslo	5pm (UTC +1)	6pm (UTC +2)
Copenhagen	5pm (UTC +1)	6pm (UTC +2)
Stockholm	5pm (UTC +1)	6pm (UTC +2)
Helsinki, Tallinn	6pm (UTC +2)	7pm (UTC +3)

Toilets

Public toilets are usually good, but often expensive; they can cost €1 or €2 or equivalent to enter.

Tourist Information

Facilities Generally excellent, with piles of regional and national brochures, helpful free maps and friendly employees. Staff are often multilingual, speaking English and perhaps other major European languages.

Locations Offices are at train stations or centrally located (often in the town hall or central square) in most towns.

Opening hours Longer office hours over summer, reduced hours over winter; smaller offices may open only during peak summer months.

Services Will book hotel and transport reservations and tours; a small charge may apply.

Websites Most towns have a tourist information portal, with good information about sights, accommodation options and more.

Travellers with Disabilities

○ Scandinavia leads the world as the best-equipped region for travellers with disabilities. By law, most institutions must provide ramps, lifts and special toilets for people with disabilities; all new hotels and restaurants must install disabled facilities. Most trains and city buses are also accessible by wheelchair.

○ Some national parks offer accessible nature trails, and cities have ongoing projects in place designed to maximise disabled access in all aspects of urban life.

○ Iceland is a little further behind the rest of the region – check access issues before you travel. Scandinavian tourist office websites generally contain good information on disabled access.

○ Before leaving home, get in touch with your national support organisation – preferably the 'travel officer' if there is one. They often have complete libraries devoted to travel and can put you in touch with agencies that specialise in tours for the disabled. One such agency in the UK is Can Be Done (www.canbedone.co.uk).

● Download Lonely Planet's free Accessible Travel guide from http://lptravel.to/AccessibleTravel.

Visas

● Denmark, Estonia, Finland, Iceland, Norway and Sweden are all part of the Schengen area. A valid passport or EU identity card is required to enter the region.

● Most Western nationals don't need a tourist visa for stays of less than three months. South Africans, Indians and Chinese, however, are among those who need a Schengen visa.

● A Schengen visa can be obtained by applying to an embassy or consulate of any country in the Schengen area.

Transport

Getting There & Away

Scandinavia is easily accessed from the rest of Europe and beyond. There are direct flights from numerous destinations into Sweden, Norway, Denmark and Finland. There

---

Climate Change & Travel

Every form of transport that relies on carbon-based fuel generates CO_2, the main cause of human-induced climate change. Modern travel is dependent on aeroplanes, which might use less fuel per kilometre per person than most cars but travel much greater distances. The altitude at which aircraft emit gases (including CO_2) and particles also contributes to their climate change impact. Many websites offer 'carbon calculators' that allow people to estimate the carbon emissions generated by their journey and, for those who wish to do so, to offset the impact of the greenhouse gases emitted with contributions to portfolios of climate-friendly initiatives throughout the world. Lonely Planet offsets the carbon footprint of all staff and author travel.

---

is less choice to Iceland. Estonia is serviced by 11 European airlines to Tallinn year-round, with additional routes added in summer.

Denmark, Sweden and Norway can be accessed by train from Western Europe, while Baltic and North Sea ferries are another good option for accessing these Nordic countries.

Flights, cars and tours can be booked online at lonelyplanet.com/bookings.

Air

As well as the many national carriers that fly directly into Scandinavia's airports, there are several budget options. These routes change frequently and are best investigated online.

Airports & Airlines

The following are major hubs in Scandinavia:

Stockholm Arlanda Airport (www.swedavia.com/arlanda) Sweden

Helsinki Vantaa Airport (www.helsinki-vantaa.fi) Finland

Copenhagen Kastrup Airport (www.cph.dk) Denmark

Reykjavík Keflavík Airport (www.kefairport.is) Iceland

Oslo Gardermoen Airport (www.osl.no) Norway

Tallinn Airport (www.tallinn-airport.ee) Estonia

SAS (www.flysas.com) is the national carrier for Sweden, Norway and Denmark, **Finnair** (www.finnair.com) for Finland and **Icelandair** (www.icelandair.com) for Iceland. Other important regional airlines include **Norwegian** (www.norwegian.com). Estonian Air (www.estonian-air.ee) flies between Tallinn and Vilnius four times per week, while **airBaltic** (www.airbaltic.com) runs multiple daily flights between Tallinn and Rīga.

Land

Bus

Without a rail pass, the cheapest overland transport from Europe to Scandinavia

Departure Tax

Departure tax is included in the price of a ticket.

is the bus, though a cheap flight deal will often beat it on price. Eurolines (www.euro lines.com), a conglomeration of coach companies, is the biggest and best-established express-bus network, and connects Scandinavia with the rest of Europe. Advance ticket purchases are usually necessary and sometimes cheaper.

Car & Motorcycle

Driving to Scandinavia means either driving into Denmark from Germany (and on to Sweden via the bridge-tunnel), going through Russia or taking a car ferry.

Train

○ Apart from trains into Finland from Russia, the rail route into Scandinavia goes from Germany into Denmark, then on to Sweden and then Norway via the Copenhagen–Malmö bridge-tunnel connection. Hamburg and Cologne are the main gateways in Germany for this route.

○ See the exceptional Man in Seat 61 website (www. seat61.com) for details of all train routes.

○ Contact **Deutsche Bahn** (www.bahn.com) for details of frequent special offers and for reservations and tickets.

○ For more information on international rail travel (including Eurostar services), check out www. voyages-sncf.com.

Sea

Services are year-round between major cities: book ahead in summer, at weekends and if travelling with a vehicle. Many boats are amazingly cheap if you travel deck class (without a cabin). Many ferry lines offer 50% discounts for holders of Eurail, Scanrail and InterRail passes. Some offer discounts for seniors, and for ISIC and youth-card holders; enquire when purchasing your ticket. There are usually discounts for families and small groups travelling together. Ferry companies have detailed timetables and fares on their websites. Fares vary according to season.

Ferry Companies

The following is a list of the main ferry companies operating to and around Scandinavia, with their websites and major routes. See websites for contact telephone numbers, times, durations and sample fares.

BornholmerFærgen (www. faergen.com) Denmark (Bornholm)–Sweden, Denmark (Bornholm)–Germany.

Color Line (www.colorline.com) Norway–Denmark, Norway–Germany, Norway–Sweden.

DFDS Seaways (www. dfdsseaways.com) Denmark–Norway, Sweden–Lithuania, Sweden–Estonia.

Eckerö Line (www.eckeroline. fi for Finland–Estonia, www. eckerolinjen.se for Finland–Sweden) Finland (Åland)–Sweden, Finland–Estonia.

Finnlines (www.finnlines.com) Germany–Sweden, Sweden–Finland, Germany–Finland.

Fjord Line (www.fjordline. com) Denmark–Norway, Norway–Sweden.

Linda Line (www.lindaline.fi) Finland–Estonia.

Polferries (www.polferries.pl) Sweden–Poland.

St Peter Line (www.stpeterline. com) Sweden–Russia, Finland–Russia, Estonia–Russia.

Scandlines (www.scandlines. com) Denmark–Germany.

Smyril Line (www.smyrill-ine.com) Denmark–Faroe Islands–Iceland.

Stena Line (www.stenaline. com) Denmark–Norway, Denmark–Sweden, Sweden–Germany, Sweden–Poland, Sweden–Latvia.

Syltfähre (www.syltfaehre.de) Denmark–Germany (Sylt).

Tallink/Silja Line (www. tallinksilja.com) Finland–Sweden, Finland–Estonia, Sweden–Estonia, Sweden–Latvia.

TT-Line (www.ttline.com) Sweden–Germany, Sweden–Poland, Denmark (Bornholm)–Poland.

Unity Line (www.unityline.eu) Sweden–Poland.

Viking Line (www.vikingline. com) Sweden–Finland, Finland–Estonia.

Wasaline (www.wasaline.com) Finland–Sweden.

Baltic Countries

There are numerous sailings between Tallinn, Estonia and

Helsinki, Finland, operated by Eckerö Line, Linda Line (fast boats), Tallink/Silja Line and Viking Line. Tallink/Silja also sails from Tallinn to Stockholm via Mariehamn, and DFDS Seaways runs from Paldiski (Estonia) to Kapellskär (Sweden).

Stena Line runs from Nynäshamn, Sweden to Ventspils, Latvia. Tallink/Silja does a Stockholm to Riga run.

DFDS operates between Karlshamn (Sweden) and Klaipėda (Lithuania).

Germany

Denmark BornholmerFærgen runs between the island of Bornholm and Sassnitz, in eastern Germany. Scandlines runs from Rødby to Puttgarden, and between Gedser and Rostock. There's also a service from Havneby, at the southern tip of the Danish island of Rømø, to List on the German island of Sylt; this is run by Syltfähre.

Finland Finnlines runs from Helsinki to Travemünde.

Norway Color Line runs daily from Oslo to Kiel.

Sweden Stena Line runs Trelleborg to Rostock, Trelleborg to Sassnitz and Gothenburg to Kiel. TT-Line runs Trelleborg to Travemünde and Trelleborg to Rostock. Finnlines runs Malmö to Travemünde.

Poland

Denmark TT Line runs between the island of Bornholm and Świnoujście.

Sweden Polferries runs Ystad to Świnoujście, as does Unity Line, while TT-Line runs

Trelleborg to Świnoujście. Polferries also links Nynäshamn with Gdańsk. Stena Line runs between Karlskrona and Gdynia.

Russia

St Peter Line runs from St Petersburg, Russia to Helsinki, Tallinn, and Stockholm, Sweden.

Getting Around

Getting around Scandinavia's populated areas is generally a breeze, with efficient public transport and snappy connections. Remote regions usually have trustworthy but infrequent services.

Bus Comprehensive network throughout region; only choice in many areas.

Train Efficient services in the continental nations, none in Iceland.

Car Drive on the right. Hire is easy but not cheap. Few motorways, so travel times can be long. Compulsory winter tyres.

Ferry Great-value network around the Baltic; spectacular Norwegian coastal ferry, and service to Iceland via the Faroe Islands.

Bike Very bike-friendly cities and many options for longer cycling routes. Most transport carries bikes for little or no charge. Hire widely available.

Planes Decent network of budget flights connecting major centres. Full-fare flights comparatively expensive.

Air

Flights are safe and reliable. Can be expensive, but often cheaper than land-based alternatives for longer journeys, and can save days of travelling time.

There are reduced rates for internet bookings on internal airline routes. The main budget operators in the region are Ryanair and Norwegian.

Good bus and train networks between airports and city centres.

Bicycle

Scandinavia is exceptionally bike-friendly, with loads of cycle paths, courteous motorists, easy public transport options and lots of flattish, picturesque terrain.

Bike shops Widespread in towns and cities.

Hire Often from train station bike-rental counters, tourist offices, camping grounds; in some cases it's possible to return hire bikes to another outlet so you don't have to double back. Several cities have bike-sharing schemes accessible for a small fee.

No-nos Cycling across the Øresund bridge between Denmark and Sweden is prohibited. A new summer-only bike ferry opened in 2017 as an alternative.

On public transport Bikes can be transported as luggage, either free or for a small fee, on slower trains and local buses in Scandinavia.

Theft Not uncommon in big cities; take a decent lock and use it when you leave your bike unattended.

Boat

Ferries are a major part of Scandinavian travel, connecting islands and countries on both the Baltic and North Sea sides.

Ferry

You can't really get around Scandinavia without using ferries extensively. The shortest routes from Denmark (Jutland) to Norway and from southern Sweden to Finland are ferry routes. Denmark is now well connected to mainland Europe and Sweden by bridges.

Ferry tickets are cheap on competitive routes, although transporting cars can be costly. Bicycles are usually carried free. On some routes, train-pass holders are entitled to free or discounted travel.

Weekend ferries, especially on Friday night, are significantly more expensive. Teenagers are banned from travelling on some Friday-night ferries due to problems with drunkenness.

Denmark–Faroe Islands–Iceland Smyril Line runs the popular *Nörrona* ferry from Hirtshals, Denmark to Seyðisfjörður, Iceland via Tórshavn on the Faroe Islands.

Denmark–Norway There are several connections. From Hirtshals, Fjord Line sails to Bergen, Kristiansand, Langesund and Stavanger. Color Line goes to Kristiansand and Larvik. From Frederikshavn, Stena Line goes to Oslo. From Copenhagen, DFDS Seaways goes to Oslo.

Denmark–Sweden Stena Line runs the connections from Grenaa to Varberg and Frederikshavn to Gothenburg. The short Helsingør to Helsingborg crossing is covered by Scandlines, while BornholmerFærgen goes from Rønne on Bornholm to Ystad.

Norway–Sweden Fjord Line and Color Line connect Strömstad, Sweden, with Sandefjord, Norway.

Sweden–Finland Connections from Stockholm to Helsinki or Turku via Åland are operated by Tallink/Silja and Viking Line. Eckerö Line runs from Grisslehamn to Eckerö on Åland, Finnlines runs Kapellskär to Naantali, while further north, Wasaline connects Umeå with Vaasa.

Steamer

o Scandinavia's main lakes and rivers are served by boats during summer, including some historic steamers. Treat these as relaxing, scenic cruises; if you view them merely as a way to get from A to B, they can seem quite expensive.

o Sweden has numerous routes. Most leave from Stockholm and sail east to the Stockholm archipelago and west to historic Lake Mälaren. You can also cruise the Göta Canal, the longest water route in Sweden.

o The legendary *Hurtigruten* ferry provides a link between Norway's coastal fishing villages.

o In Finland, steamships ply the eastern lakes, connecting the towns on their shores.

Bus

Buses provide a viable alternative to the rail network in Scandinavian countries, and are the only option in Iceland and parts of northern Sweden, Finland and Norway.

Cost Compared to trains, they're usually cheaper and slightly slower. Connections with train services (where they exist) are good.

Advance reservation Rarely necessary. But you do need to pre-purchase your ticket before you board many city buses, and then validate your ticket on board.

International routes There are regular bus services between Denmark and Sweden, and Sweden and Norway. Services between Finland and Norway run in Lapland, and you can change between Swedish and Finnish buses at the shared bus station of the border towns of Tornio/Haparanda.

Car & Motorcycle

Travelling with a vehicle is the best way to get to remote places and gives you independence and flexibility.

Bringing Your Own Vehicle

Documentation Proof of ownership of a private vehicle should always be carried (this is the Vehicle Registration Document for British–registered cars). You'll also need an insurance document valid in the countries you are planning to visit. Contact your local automobile association for further information.

Border crossings Vehicles crossing an international border should display a sticker showing their country of registration. The exception is cars with Euro-plates.

Safety It's compulsory to carry a warning triangle in most places, to be used in the event of breakdown, and several countries require a reflective jacket. You must also use headlamp beam reflectors/converters on right-hand-drive cars.

Driving Licences

An EU driving licence is acceptable for driving throughout Scandinavia, as are North American and Australian licences, for example. If you have any other type of licence, you should check to see if you need to obtain an International Driving Permit (IDP) from your motoring organisation before you leave home.

If you're thinking of going snowmobiling, you'll need to bring your driving licence with you.

Fuel

Fuel is heavily taxed and very expensive in Scandinavia. Most types of petrol, including unleaded 95 and 98 octane, are widely available; leaded petrol is no longer sold. Diesel is significantly cheaper than petrol in most countries. Usually pumps with green markings deliver unleaded fuel, and black pumps supply diesel.

Car Hire

Cost Renting a car is more expensive in Scandinavia than in other European countries. Be sure you understand what's included in the price (unlimited or paid kilometres, injury insurance, tax, collision damage waiver etc) and what your liabilities are. Norway is the most expensive so it may pay to rent a car in neighbouring Sweden and take it across.

Insurance Decide whether to take the collision damage waiver. You may be covered for this and injury insurance if you have a travel-insurance policy: check.

Companies The big international firms – Hertz, Avis, Budget and Europcar – are all present. Sixt often has the most competitive prices. Using local firms can mean a better deal. Big firms give you the option of returning the car to a different outlet when you've finished with it, but this is often heavily charged.

Booking Pre-booking always works out cheaper. Online brokers often offer substantially cheaper rates than the company websites themselves.

Fly/drive combination SAS and Icelandair often offer cheaper car rentals to their international passengers. Check their websites for deals.

Border crossings Ask in advance if you can drive a rented car across borders. In Scandinavia it's usually no problem.

Age The minimum rental age is usually 21, sometimes even 23, and you'll need a credit card for the deposit.

Practicalities

Smoking Widely forbidden in public spaces, but some countries have dedicated smoking rooms in hotels and smoking areas in bars. Vaping laws depend on the country.

Weights & Measures The metric system is used across the region, though old local miles are still sometimes referred to.

Motorcycle and moped rental Not particularly common in Scandinavian countries, but possible in major cities.

Insurance

Third-party motor insurance A minimum requirement in most of Europe. Most UK car-insurance policies automatically provide third-party cover for EU and some other countries. Ask your insurer for a Green Card – an internationally recognised proof of insurance (there may be a charge) – and check that it lists all the countries you intend to visit.

Breakdown assistance Check whether your insurance policy offers breakdown assistance overseas. If it doesn't, a European breakdown-assistance policy, such as those provided by the AA or the RAC, is a good investment. Your motoring organisation may also offer reciprocal coverage with affiliated motoring organisations.

Road Conditions & Hazards

Conditions and types of roads vary widely across Scandinavia, but it's possible to make some generalisations.

Iceland Specific challenges include unsealed gravel roads, long, claustrophobic single-lane tunnels, frequent mist and the wild, lonely, 4WD-only F-roads. See the videos at www.drive.is for more info.

Main roads Primary routes, with the exception of some roads in Iceland, are universally in good condition. There are comparatively few motorways.

Minor roads Road surfaces on minor routes are not so reliable, although normally adequate.

Norway Has some particularly hair-raising roads; serpentine examples climb from sea level to 1000m in what seems no distance at all on a map. Driving a campervan on this kind of route is not recommended.

Tolls In Norway, there are tolls for some tunnels, bridges, roads and entry into larger towns, and for practically all ferries crossing fjords. Roads, tunnels, bridges and car ferries in Finland and Sweden are usually free, although there's a hefty toll of €56 per car on the Øresund bridge (www.oresundsbron.com) between Denmark and Sweden.

Winter Snow tyres are compulsory in winter, except in Denmark. Chains are allowed in most countries but almost never used.

Livestock on roads Animals is motion, including sheep, elk, horses and reindeer, are a potential hazard. If you are involved in an animal incident, by law you must report it to the police.

Road Rules

- Drive on the right-hand side of the road in all Scandinavian countries.

- Seatbelts are compulsory for driver and all passengers.

- Headlights must be switched on at all times.

- In the absence of give-way or stop signs, priority is given to traffic approaching from the right.

- It's compulsory for motorcyclists and their passengers to wear helmets.

- Take care with speed limits, which vary from country to country.

- Many driving infringements are subject to on-the-spot fines in Scandinavian countries. In Norway these are stratospheric. Drink-driving regulations are strict.

Train

There are no trains in Iceland nor in far-north Finland and Norway.

Costs Full-price tickets can be expensive; book ahead for discounts. Rail passes are worth buying if you plan to do a reasonable amount of travelling. Seniors and travellers under 26 years of age are eligible for discounted tickets in some countries, which can cut fares by between 15% and 40%.

Reservations It's a good idea (sometimes obligatory) to make reservations at peak times and on certain train lines, especially long-distance trains. In some countries it can be a lot cheaper to book in advance and online.

Express trains There are various names for fast trains throughout Scandinavia. Supplements usually apply on fast trains and it's wise (sometimes obligatory) to make reservations at peak times and on certain lines.

Overnight Trains

These trains usually offer couchettes or sleepers. Reservations are advisable, particularly as sleeping options are generally allocated on a first-come, first-served basis.

Couchettes Basic bunk beds numbering four (1st class) or six (2nd class) per compartment are comfortable enough, if lacking a little privacy. In Scandinavia, a bunk costs around €25 to €50 (on top of the train fare) for most trains, irrespective of the length of the journey.

Sleepers The most comfortable option, offering beds for one or two passengers in 1st class and two or three passengers in 2nd class.

Food Most long-distance trains have a dining car or snack trolley – bring your own nibbles to keep costs down.

Car Some long-distance trains have car-carrying facilities.

Train Passes

There is a variety of passes available for rail travel within

Scandinavia, or in various European countries including Scandinavia. There are cheaper passes for students, people under 26 and seniors. Supplements (eg for high-speed services) and reservation costs are not covered by passes, and terms and conditions change – check carefully before buying. Pass-holders must always carry their passport on the train for identification purposes.

Eurail Passes

Eurail (www.eurail.com) Offers a good selection of different passes available to residents of non-European countries; should be purchased before arriving in Europe.

Eurail Scandinavia Pass Gives a number of days of travel in a two-month period, and is valid for travel in Denmark, Sweden, Norway and Finland. It costs €215 for three days in 2nd class, up to €353 for eight days. There are also single-country passes.

Eurail Global Pass Offers travel in 28 European countries – five or seven days in a month, 10 or 15 days in a two-month period or unlimited travel from 15 days up to three months. It's much better value for under 28s, as those older have to buy a 1st-class pass.

Select Pass Gives a number of days of travel in a two-month period; you can choose up to four adjoining countries.

Discounts Most passes offer discounts of around 25% for under 28s, or 15% for two people travelling together. On most Eurail passes, children aged between four and 11 get a 50% discount on the full adult fare. Eurail passes give a 30% to 50% discount on several ferry lines in the region; check the website for details.

InterRail Passes

If you've lived in Europe for more than six months, you're eligible for an InterRail (www.interrail.eu) pass. InterRail offers two passes valid for train travel in Scandinavia.

InterRail One Country Pass Offers travel in one country of your choice for three/four/six/eight days in a one-month period, costing €119/150/201/241 in 2nd class for Denmark or Finland, and €175/199/259/300 for Sweden or Norway.

Global Pass Offers travel in 30 European countries and costs from €267 for five days' travel in any 15, to €632 for a month's unlimited train travel.

Discounts On both the above passes, there's a discount of around 20% for under 28s. InterRail passes give a 30% to 50% discount on several ferry lines in the region; check the website for details.

Behind the Scenes

Acknowledgements

Climate map data adapted from Peel MC, Finlayson BL & McMahon TA (2007) 'Updated World Map of the Köppen-Geiger Climate Classification', Hydrology and Earth System Sciences, 11, 163344.

This Book

This guidebook was researched and written by Anthony Ham, Alexis Averbuck, Belinda Dixon, Carolyn Bain, Oliver Berry, Cristian Bonetto, Peter Dragicevich, Catherine Le Nevez, Virginia Maxwell, Hugh McNaughtan, Becky Ohlsen, Andy Symington and Donna Wheeler.

This guidebook was produced by the following:

Destination Editors Gemma Graham, James Smart

Product Editor Genna Patterson

Senior Cartographer Valentina Kremenchutskaya

Book Designer Gwen Cotter

Assisting Editors Michelle Bennett, Jennifer Hattam, Charlotte Orr, Susan Paterson, Sam Wheeler

Cover Researcher Naomi Parker

Thanks to Egill Bjarnason, Mark Elliott, Shona Gray, Sandie Kestell, Kate Kiely, Craig McLachlan, Doug Rimington, Angela Tinson, Mara Vorhees

Send Us Your Feedback

We love to hear from travellers – your comments keep us on our toes and help make our books better. Our well-travelled team reads every word on what you loved or loathed about this book. Although we cannot reply individually to postal submissions, we always guarantee that your feedback goes straight to the appropriate authors, in time for the next edition. Each person who sends us information is thanked in the next edition, the most useful submissions are rewarded with a selection of digital PDF chapters.

Visit lonelyplanet.com/contact to submit your updates and suggestions or to ask for help. Our award-winning website also features inspirational travel stories, news and discussions.

Note: We may edit, reproduce and incorporate your comments in Lonely Planet products such as guidebooks, websites and digital products, so let us know if you don't want your comments reproduced or your name acknowledged. For a copy of our privacy policy visit lonelyplanet.com/privacy.

Index

Symbols & Map Key

Look for these symbols to quickly identify listings:

- ◉ Sights
- ✪ Activities
- ✪ Courses
- ✪ Tours
- ✪ Festivals & Events
- ✪ Eating
- ✪ Drinking
- ✪ Entertainment
- ✪ Shopping
- ✪ Information & Transport

These symbols and abbreviations give vital information for each listing:

- 🍃 Sustainable or green recommendation
- **FREE** No payment required

- 📞 Telephone number
- ⊙ Opening hours
- P Parking
- ⊖ Nonsmoking
- ❄ Air-conditioning
- @ Internet access
- 📶 Wi-fi access
- 🏊 Swimming pool

- 🚌 Bus
- ⛴ Ferry
- 🚊 Tram
- 🚆 Train
- 📖 English-language menu
- 🥗 Vegetarian selection
- 👪 Family-friendly

Find your best experiences with these Great For... icons.

 Art & Culture

🏖 Beaches

💳 Budget

☕ Cafe/Coffee

🚲 Cycling

 Detour

🍷 Drinking

 Entertainment

🎆 Events

 Family Travel

🍽 Food & Drink

 History

💬 Local Life

🐦 Nature & Wildlife

📷 Photo Op

🔭 Scenery

🛍 Shopping

 Short Trip

🏀 Sport

🚶 Walking

❄ Winter Travel

Sights

- 🏖 Beach
- 🐦 Bird Sanctuary
- ☸ Buddhist
- 🏰 Castle/Palace
- ✝ Christian
- ☯ Confucian
- 🕉 Hindu
- ☪ Islamic
- 卐 Jain
- ✡ Jewish
- 🗽 Monument
- 🏛 Museum/Gallery/ Historic Building
- 🏚 Ruin
- ⛩ Shinto
- ☬ Sikh
- ☯ Taoist
- 🍷 Winery/Vineyard
- 🦁 Zoo/Wildlife Sanctuary
- ◉ Other Sight

Points of Interest

- 🏄 Bodysurfing
- ⛺ Camping
- ☕ Cafe
- 🛶 Canoeing/Kayaking
- • Course/Tour
- 🤿 Diving
- 🍸 Drinking & Nightlife
- 🍴 Eating
- 🎭 Entertainment
- ♨ Sento Hot Baths/ Onsen
- 🛍 Shopping
- ⛷ Skiing
- 🛏 Sleeping
- 🤿 Snorkelling
- 🏄 Surfing
- 🏊 Swimming/Pool
- 🚶 Walking
- 🏄 Windsurfing
- ✪ Other Activity

Information

- 💲 Bank
- 🏛 Embassy/Consulate
- ➕ Hospital/Medical
- @ Internet
- 👮 Police
- 📮 Post Office
- 📞 Telephone
- 🚻 Toilet
- ℹ Tourist Information
- • Other Information

Geographic

- 🏖 Beach
- ⊱ Gate
- ⛺ Hut/Shelter
- 🗼 Lighthouse
- 🔭 Lookout
- ▲ Mountain/Volcano
- 🌴 Oasis
- 🌳 Park
-)(Pass
- 🧺 Picnic Area
- 💧 Waterfall

Transport

- ✈ Airport
- Ⓑ BART station
- ⊗ Border crossing
- Ⓣ Boston T station
- 🚌 Bus
- 🚡 Cable car/Funicular
- 🚲 Cycling
- ⛴ Ferry
- Ⓜ Metro/MRT station
- 🚝 Monorail
- P Parking
- ⛽ Petrol station
- Ⓢ Subway/S-Bahn/ Skytrain station
- 🚕 Taxi
- 🚉 Train station/Railway
- 🚊 Tram
- ⊙ Tube Station
- Ⓤ Underground/ U-Bahn station
- • Other Transport

Telegraph (UK) and *Corriere del Mezzogiorno* (Italy). Instagram: rexcat75.

Belinda Dixon

Belinda has been (gleefully) travelling, researching and writing for Lonely Planet since 2006. Belinda is also an adventure writer and a trained radio journalist. See her VideoBlog posts at belindadixon.com

Peter Dragicevich

With a background in newspaper and magazine publishing, Peter turned to travel writing. Over the last decade he has written literally dozens of guidebooks for Lonely Planet on an oddly disparate collection of countries, all of which he's come to love. He calls Auckland, New Zealand his home – although his current nomadic existence means he's often elsewhere.

Catherine Le Nevez

With a Doctorate of Creative Arts in Writing, Masters in Professional Writing, and postgrad qualifications in Editing and Publishing, Catherine has written scores of Lonely Planet guides and articles covering Paris, France, Europe and far beyond. Her work has also appeared in numerous online and print publications. Topping Catherine's list of travel tips is to travel without any expectations.

Virginia Maxwell

Although based in Australia, Virginia spends at least half of her year updating Lonely Planet destination coverage in Europe and the Middle East. Though the Mediterranean is her major area of interest – she has covered Spain, Italy, Turkey, Syria, Lebanon, Israel, Egypt and Morocco for LP guidebooks – Virginia also writes LP guides to Finland, Armenia, Iran and Australia. Follow her @maxwellvirginia on Instagram and Twitter.

Hugh McNaughtan

A former English lecturer, Hugh swapped grant applications for visa applications, and turned his love of travel intro a full-time thing. Having done a bit of restaurant-reviewing in his home town (Melbourne) he's now eaten his way across four continents. He's never happier than when on the road with his two daughters. Except perhaps on the cricket field.

Becky Ohlsen

Becky is a freelance writer, editor and critic based in Portland, Oregon. She writes guidebooks and travel stories about Scandinavia, Portland and elsewhere for Lonely Planet. She has a master's degree in journalism from NYU's Cultural Reporting and Criticism program.

Andy Symington

Andy has written or worked on over a hundred books and other updates for Lonely Planet (especially in Europe and Latin America) and other publishing companies, and has published articles on numerous subjects for a variety of newspapers, magazines, and websites.

Donna Wheeler

Donna has written guidebooks for Lonely Planet for over ten years, including the Italy, Norway, Belgium, Africa, Tunisia, Algeria, France, Austria and Australia titles. She became a travel writer after various careers as a commissioning editor, creative director, digital producer and content strategist. Born and bred in Sydney, Australia, Donna travels widely (and deeply) in Europe, North Africa, the US and Asia. She loves cities, mountains and the sea.

Our Story

A beat-up old car, a few dollars in the pocket and a sense of adventure. In 1972 that's all Tony and Maureen Wheeler needed for the trip of a lifetime – across Europe and Asia overland to Australia. It took several months, and at the end – broke but inspired – they sat at their kitchen table writing and stapling together their first travel guide, *Across Asia on the Cheap*. Within a week they'd sold 1500 copies. Lonely Planet was born.

Today, Lonely Planet has offices in Franklin, London, Melbourne, Oakland, Dublin, Beijing, and Delhi, with more than 600 staff and writers. We share Tony's belief that 'a great guidebook should do three things: inform, educate and amuse'.

Our Writers

Anthony Ham

Anthony is a freelance writer and photographer who specialises in Spain, East and Southern Africa, the Arctic and the Middle East. When he's not writing for Lonely Planet, Anthony writes about and photographs Spain, Africa and the Middle East for newspapers and magazines in Australia, the UK and US.

Alexis Averbuck

A travel writer for over two decades, Alexis has lived in Antarctica for a year, crossed the Pacific by sailboat and written books on her journeys through Asia, Europe and the Americas. She's also a painter – visit www.alexisaverbuck.com – and promotes travel and adventure on video and television.

Carolyn Bain

A travel writer and editor for more than 20 years, Carolyn has lived, worked and studied in various corners of the globe, including Denmark, London, St Petersburg and Nantucket. She moved from Melbourne to Reykjavík recently and writes about travel and food for a range of publishers; see carolynbain.com.au for more.

Oliver Berry

Oliver Berry is a writer and photographer from Cornwall. He has worked for Lonely Planet for more than a decade on more than 30 guidebooks. He is also a regular contributor to many newspapers and magazines, including *Lonely Planet Traveller*. His latest work is published at www.oliverberry.com.

Cristian Bonetto

Cristian has contributed to over 30 Lonely Planet guides to date, including New York City, Italy, Venice & the Veneto, Naples & the Amalfi Coast, Denmark, Copenhagen, Sweden and Singapore. Lonely Planet work aside, his musings on travel, food, culture and design appear in numerous publications around the world, including *The*

More Writers

STAY IN TOUCH LONELYPLANET.COM/CONTACT

AUSTRALIA The Malt Store, Level 3, 551 Swanston St, Carlton, Victoria 3053 ☎03 8379 8000, fax 03 8379 8111

IRELAND Digital Depot, Roe Lane (off Thomas St), Digital Hub, Dublin 8, D08 TCV4, Ireland

USA 124 Linden Street, Oakland, CA 94607 ☎510 250 6400, toll free 800 275 8555, fax 510 893 8572

UK 240 Blackfriars Road, London SE1 8NW ☎020 3771 5100, fax 020 3771 5101

 twitter.com/lonelyplanet
 facebook.com/lonelyplanet
 instagram.com/lonelyplanet
 youtube.com/lonelyplanet
 lonelyplanet.com/newsletter